Happy Birthday Jane

July 16, 09

Love from Auntie Sheila

Happy Birthday Jane

Food
for your
Body

Food
for your

How to look
and feel your best

Body

PUBLISHED BY THE READER'S DIGEST ASSOCIATION LIMITED

LONDON • NEW YORK • SYDNEY • MONTREAL

Food for your body

was created and produced by
Carroll & Brown Limited,
20 Lonsdale Road,
London NW6 6RD
for The Reader's Digest Association Limited, London

First English Edition Copyright © 2001
The Reader's Digest Association Limited,
11 Westferry Circus, Canary Wharf,
London E14 4HE.
www.readersdigest.co.uk

If you have any comments or suggestions about
this book, e-mail us at:
gbeditorial@readersdigest.co.uk

Copyright © 2001 Reader's Digest Association Far
East Limited.
Philippines Copyright © 2001 Reader's Digest
Association Far East Limited.

Printed in Belgium
ISBN 0 276 42480 8

The information in this book is for reference only; it
is not intended as a substitute for a doctor's
diagnosis and care. The editors urge anyone with
continuing medical problems or symptoms to
consult a doctor.

Managing Editor
Yvonne Deutch
Managing Art Editor
Adelle Morris
Assistant Editor
Janice Anderson
Designer
Evie Loizides

CONSULTANT EDITOR
Jane Thomas
Lecturer in Nutrition and Dietetics
King's College, University of London

CONTRIBUTORS
Fiona Hunter
Azmina Govindji
Nicola Graimes
Janette Marshall
Judy More
Fiona Wilcock

FOR THE READER'S DIGEST
Editor Jonathan Bastable
Art Editor Joanna Walker
Editorial Assistant Jenny Rathbone

READER'S DIGEST GENERAL BOOKS
Editorial Director Cortina Butler
Art Director Nick Clark
Executive Editor Julian Browne
Development Editor Ruth Binney
Publishing Projects Manager Alastair Holmes
Picture Research Editor Martin Smith
Style Editor Ron Pankhurst

FOREWORD

Food is one of life's great pleasures. We all feel the same peckish tingle of anticipation when warm aromas are wafting from the oven, and we know the deep contentment that can descend at the end of a good meal.

But eating well is not just a joy, it is also a skill. You will get more out of your food if you understand what food is, what good (and bad) things different foods contain, how much nourishment you need, and how to be sure you are getting it.

It also pays to know how food affects every aspect of your physical and mental health. Some people have found that a very minor change in their eating habits can transform for the better their whole sense of well-being. That old saying – you are what you eat – is barely an exaggeration.

And let's not forget that food can be a big adventure: cooking and tasting new things, sharing dinner with friends, all the alchemy of the kitchen and the dining table – these are things that few of us would like to be without. 'It's good food,' said the French playwright Molière, 'and not fine words, that keeps me alive.'

CONTENTS

INTRODUCTION

Food provides the great majority of the nutrients which the human body needs to stay healthy. So understanding food is the key to keeping you and your family in good shape. *Food For Your Body* gives you this knowledge in an immediate, accessible way.

The book is divided into four sections. The first, *Bodyworks,* describes how food affects your body and its functions; *Journey Through the Years* explains how and why nutritional needs vary at different stages of your life; *Mind and Body* explores our attitudes to eating, and the complex relationship between food and mood; and *Ways of Living* describes how to tailor what you eat to suit your own lifestyle.

But *Food For Your Body* is above all a practical book. In its pages you will find many inspirational menu ideas and delicious recipes, all of which apply the best principles of good nutrition, taking into account your age and lifestyle. There are also panels focusing on healthy cooking methods, on ways to beat specific health problems, and on 'superfoods' – common or exotic ingredients which have especially valuable health-giving properties.

Eating (it goes without saying) is something we do every day, but we often pay little or no attention to our diets and eating habits. *Food For Your Body* will help you to think more closely about what you eat, to make the most of your food, and so get the very best out of life.

Using the recipes Ingredients are given in both metric and Imperial measures. These are not exact equivalents: use either metric or Imperial measures when cooking, and do not mix the two.
• All spoon measures are level, unless otherwise stated; a 5 ml spoon equals 1 level teaspoon and a 15 ml spoon equals 1 level tablespoon.
• All eggs are large unless otherwise specified.
• Many recipes specify black pepper; for the best flavour this should be freshly ground. Parmesan cheese should also be freshly grated, if possible.

• Use fresh herbs if you can. If you have to use dry herbs, use 1-1½ teaspoons for 1 tablespoon of fresh.

Nutritional analyses The figures given for each recipe are averages. They do not include optional accompaniments, such as bread with soup. For main course dishes, the figures include vegetables or accompaniments only when they are part of the dish, such as in Grilled Chicken with Celeriac and Coriander Mash (page 87).

A balanced diet

Your body needs a regular, well-balanced supply of nutrients to be healthy. Many nutrients can only be supplied by the food you eat. Getting the balance right has enormous benefits: a healthy diet reduces the risk of problems such as heart disease, certain cancers, obesity, maturity-onset diabetes, high blood pressure and osteoporosis.

Two kinds of nutrients, called macro-nutrients and micronutrients, are obtained from food. Macronutrients include carbohy-drates, fats and proteins. Carbohydrates and fats supply the body with energy, some of which may be stored as body fat. Fats also supply essential fatty acids the body cannot make for itself and carry the fat-soluble vitamins A, D, E and K. Protein provides amino acids, the building blocks needed for muscle growth, lean tissue and cell repair.

Micronutrients include the minerals and vitamins known to be essential for good health. Minerals are used by the body for growth and repair and to regulate body processes. There are two kinds of vitamin – water-soluble (the B vitamins and vitamin C) and fat-soluble (vitamins A, D, E and K). Water-soluble vitamins are not stored in the body and so must be eaten daily to prevent deficiency. Fat-soluble vitamins can be stored in the body, but some – notably vitamins A and D – are toxic if taken in excess. Take them in small, regular amounts.

Many people benefit from taking vitamins and other nutrients in supplement form. Unless advised by your doctor, stay within the recommended dosages for all supplements because taking them in excessive amounts can cause health problems.

6–11 SERVINGS DAILY

THE FIVE FOOD GROUPS

Nutritionists have devised a simple way to help you make the right food choices. They divide foods into five groups, depending on their nutrient content, and suggest the size of a serving and the proportion each one should make in a daily well-balanced diet.

Bread, potatoes and other cereals

Typical servings are: 1 slice bread or toast; 3 tablespoons breakfast cereal; 3 crispbreads or crackers; 1 medium potato; 2 heaped tablespoons boiled rice or pasta.

The 'other cereals' in this group are pasta and noodles, breakfast cereals, rice, oats, maize, millet and cornmeal. Beans and pulses are also included in the group. These foods are rich in energy-giving carbohydrates, B vitamins and selenium, and contain some calcium and iron. They are also important sources of fibre.

Their valuable carbohydrate and fibre content means that you should eat a lot of these foods every day – enough to add up to 33 per cent of a well-balanced daily diet. They give bulk to your diet and so fill you up without adding many calories (provided that they are not fried or served with rich, cream-laden sauces or a lot of butter).

The fibre in the foods in this group is essential for digestion and can protect your health. Insoluble fibre, which is found mostly in cereals and grains, as well as in fibrous vegetables and nuts, helps to prevent constipation and bowel disorders by speeding up the passage of food through the large intestine. Soluble fibre, found mainly in pulses and oats, has been shown to help reduce blood cholesterol and to even out the peaks in blood sugar levels. Wholemeal bread, brown rice and wholegrain cereals contain the most fibre but all cereal foods contribute some.

Adults should aim to eat at least 18 grams (¼ ounce) of fibre a day: one slice of wholemeal bread has 2 grams; an apple 2.7 grams. Fibre-rich cereal foods are less suitable for young children, who may become full before they have eaten the variety of foods needed for a balanced diet.

fruit and veg

AT LEAST 5 SERVINGS DAILY

Fruit and vegetables

Typical servings are: 1 medium piece of fresh fruit; 1 medium-size portion of vegetables or salad; 6 tablespoons stewed or canned fruit; 1 small glass (100 ml/3½ fl oz) fruit juice. Foods from this group (which can also include beans and pulses) should make up 33 per cent of a daily well-balanced diet.

Fruit and vegetables are highly nutritious, being rich in vitamins, especially A, C and E, in minerals such as calcium, magnesium and potassium and iron, and in antioxidants which may offer protection against certain cancers and heart disease. Many also contain valuable phytochemicals, which protect against disease and also give colour and flavour to foods.

Fruit and vegetables contain virtually no fat, are low in calories, and are good sources of both soluble and insoluble fibre. You should aim to eat about 400 g (14 oz) a day. This is easily achieved as fruit and vegetables come in so many forms: raw or cooked, fresh or frozen, canned, dried and as juice.

Meat, fish and alternatives

Typical servings are: 3 slices 70 g (2½ oz) each of beef, pork, ham, lamb, liver, kidney, chicken or oily fish; 115–140 g (4–5 oz) white fish;
2 eggs (but no more than 4 in a week); 5 tablespoons baked beans or other pulses or lentils; 2 tablespoons nuts, peanut butter. Foods in this group are our main source of protein, which is essential for most of the body's vital functions, including the growth, maintenance and repair of cells. The proteins in meat, fish, dairy foods and eggs supply eight essential amino acids which the body cannot synthesise itself.

The body requires protein in quite small amounts, so foods from this group should make up only 12 per cent of your daily diet. Men require 55 g (2 oz) of protein-rich foods a day, women 45 g (1½ oz). Children aged between seven and ten years need less – 28 grams, or just over an ounce, each day.

Meat, poultry and fish are rich in minerals such as iron, zinc and magnesium, and important B vitamins. They also contain fat (see below). Modern breeding produces very lean meat, but processed meat products such as sausages, pies and pasties can be very high in fat. Although the white meat of poultry is low in fat, the dark meat contains more and the skin is extremely high in fat.

Oily fish contains omega-3 fatty acids which protect against heart disease and strokes, and can help those with arthritis or

naturally occurring monounsaturates or polyunsaturates.

Sugary foods include soft drinks, chocolate and other confectionery, jams, baked goods such as biscuits, cakes and desserts. Eat them sparingly, and ideally at mealtimes to reduce the risk of tooth decay.

VEGETARIANS AND VEGANS

For meat eaters, the proteins in meat, fish, and dairy foods supply all the essential amino acids. But getting sufficient protein to provide these amino acids can be a problem for vegetarians and vegans. Proteins from plant sources do not contain all the essential amino acids, and as vegans do not eat cheese eggs and milk, they need to combine plant proteins to get them.

The ideal way to do this is to combine pulses with plant foods and wholegrains such as rice or bread (beans on toast are a good example); or to eat nuts and seeds with bread, grains and pulses.

Vegetarians and vegans also need to find other sources of nutrients commonly obtained from meat. These include:

Vitamin B$_{12}$ Vegetarians who eat dairy foods will probably get enough B$_{12}$. Vegans may need to take supplements as well as eating foods fortified with B$_{12}$, including yeast extract, some vegetable stocks, foods made with fortified textured vegetable protein (TVP), soya drinks and breakfast cereals.

Iron Dark green leafy vegetables, pulses, tofu, eggs, dried fruit, wholemeal bread and fortified breakfast cereal are good sources. Iron from plant foods is less easily absorbed than iron in meat, so eat plenty of foods rich in vitamin C to enhance your take-up.

Zinc Pulses, brown rice, wholemeal and rye bread, eggs, carrots, peanuts and cheese supply adequate zinc.

Calcium is available from wholegrain cereals, fortified white bread, muesli, oatmeal, pulses, nuts and seeds, dark green vegetables and dried fruit.

Food, energy and your weight

The energy you get from food can be measured in two ways: Calories (kcal) or joules (kJ). One kcal equals about 4kJ.

Calories are a measure of the amount of energy contained in food. You use most of the calories you consume just to stay alive – to maintain your organs, and keep your muscles working. What makes you fat is not calories, but consuming more calories in food than you need. As the balloons here show, the number of calories you use depends on your size, how long you exercise and the intensity of the activity.

Many of the calories from food are quickly used. Food energy that is not required for immediate activity is transformed into chemicals that are stored in the muscles or converted to fat. This is why you use up fat – and lose weight – if you take in fewer calories than you use. From about the age of 30, your metabolism begins to slow down. One reason for this is that as the body

ages, the muscle mass – the percentage of the body's weight that is made of lean tissue – slowly decreases. You lose about 10 per cent of this muscle tissue between the ages of 20 and 50. It is gradually replaced with body fat (unless you exercise regularly and eat fewer calories).

The major sources of energy in our diets are carbohydrates and fats. Digesting food uses energy. However, fats, weight for weight, require less energy to

INACTIVE ADULTS
Men: about 2400 Calories a day
Women: about 2000 Calories a day

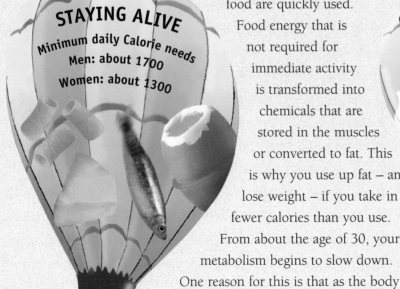

STAYING ALIVE
Minimum daily Calorie needs
Men: about 1700
Women: about 1300

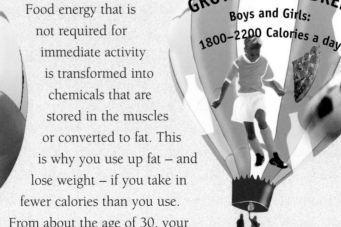

GROWING CHILDREN
Boys and Girls:
1800–2200 Calories a day

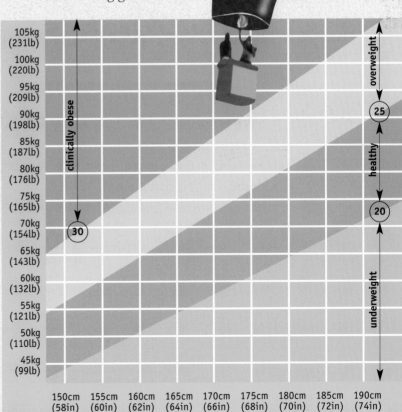

ACTIVE ADULTS
Men: about 2850 Calories a day
Women: about 2150 Calories a day

LATER IN LIFE
Men: about 2200 Calories a day
Women: about 1850 Calories a day

digest than proteins or complex carbohydrates. They are also the highest source of calories. To help keep your weight in balance, aim to get at least 50 per cent of your daily energy needs from carbohydrate and no more than 35 per cent from fat. Your Body Mass Index (or BMI: see the chart, below) is a good check on your weight. Calculate it by lining your weight up with your height. A BMI over 25 indicates that you are overweight.

QUENCHING YOUR THIRST

Water makes up two-thirds of the body's weight. The amount of liquid you need in the short term depends on such factors as your size, how active you are and how hot the weather is. But in general everyone should drink at least 6–8 glasses of fluid, or about 1.5 litres (2¾ pints), a day.

Water is the best drink for rehydrating the body. Tea and coffee are fine in moderation but they contain stimulants such as caffeine, theobromine and tannin which hinders absorption of iron and zinc. For this reason, it is best to leave a 30-minute gap after a meal before drinking tea. Coffee and tea are diuretic, and accelerate the loss of water-

soluble C and B vitamins in urine.

Fruit juice, drunk straight or diluted, is more nutritious than tea, coffee, cola or fizzy drinks.

While some alcohol does have certain health benefits, it should not be viewed as part of your daily liquid intake (see page 97 for safe drinking guidelines).

**BMI readings: under 20 = underweight, 20-25 = healthy,
over 25 = overweight, over 30 = clinically obese**

choosing
SEASONAL FARE

winter

Game, such as pheasant, partridge and other birds, venison and wild rabbit, are good sources of protein, iron, zinc, magnesium and potassium, vitamin B12 and folates. Game contains a higher proportion of unsaturated fat than farmed meat.

Oranges and other citrus fruit contain vitamin C to boost immunity, and bioflavonoids to strengthen blood capillaries.

Purple sprouting broccoli and Brussels sprouts are rich in folate, iron, antioxidants for protection against heart disease and certain cancers, plus protective phytonutrients.

Cranberries contain the same nutrients as other berry fruits (Summer) but also help to prevent urinary tract infections by discouraging the adhesion of bacteria to the walls of the tract.

Asparagus is a good source of folate.

Rhubarb is rich in potassium, which helps to regulate nerve and muscle functions.

Gooseberries contain vitamin C and fibre.

Globe artichoke extracts are used medicinally to help reduce cholesterol levels.

Mackerel and herring (traditional season April–July) are good sources of omega-3 fatty acids which reduce inflammation, are protective against heart disease and helpful in the treatment of psoriasis and arthritis.

spring

There was a time, not so long ago, when everybody's diet was ruled by the slow carousel of the seasons. The idea of pears in winter, or blackberries in the spring, would have as seemed bizarre and unnatural as Christmas in July.

Modern growing methods and foreign imports mean that most fresh produce is available most of the year round. This adds welcome variety, but one consequence is that many people are now completely unaware of seasonal foods and how to go about buying them. In 1999, a survey for the National Farmers Union showed that nearly half of Britons were unaware that homegrown apples are picked in September and October, and more than two thirds had no idea at all when broccoli is in season.

Forgotten pleasures In some ways this lack of awareness is a shame. Part of the skill of shopping is knowing when to buy things at their peak. With the best will in the world, a fresh tomato salad is not going to taste all that good in February.

Seasonal food is also bound up with the annual rituals that help to give our lives

MANY FOODS, GROWN AND STORED UNDER CONTROLLED CONDITIONS, CAN BE BOUGHT ALL YEAR ROUND. SEASONAL PRODUCE – LOCAL ASPARAGUS, STRAWBERRIES AND GARDEN PEAS – OFTEN TASTES BETTER AND MAY BE MORE NUTRITIOUS. USE THIS GUIDE TO CHOOSE FRUIT, VEGETABLES AND OTHER FOODS IN SEASON.

summer

Salmon is a good source of omega-3 fatty acids.
Berry fruits such as raspberries, strawberries and blackcurrants are a rich source of vitamin C and other antioxidants, and also of protective phytonutrients.
Peas contain vitamin C, soluble fibre, and B vitamins.
Shellfish are high in zinc, needed for healing and reproductive health.
Tomatoes are rich in lycopene, an antioxidant protective against certain cancers, particularly prostate cancer.
Melon is a good source of beta carotene and lycopene.

autumn

Walnuts contain omega-3 fatty acids.
Carrots are rich in beta carotene for valuable cancer protection.
Onions contain quercetin, an antioxidant that may lower the risk of heart disease and cancer.
Apples contain quercetin and pectin, a soluble fibre.
Pumpkin is a rich source of carotenes.
Sweetcorn contains carotenoids, lutein and zeaxanthin to protect against cataracts and other degenerative eye diseases.
Root vegetables, such as swede and turnip, contain phytochemicals that may help protect against cancer. They are also good sources of vitamin C.

meaning. It is not just about fruit and veg: hot cross buns are surely less of a treat when they can be had on any day of the year.

Worth preserving In many parts of Europe it is still common to salt or pickle all kinds of seasonal food: the Germans make big jars of sauerkraut for the cold months; the Scandinavians love their herring and salt cod; and the Russians are a nation of obsessive mushroom-picklers.

These are fine culinary arts, and there is nothing to stop British cooks, in the depths of a British winter, trying their hand at making marmalade with the knobbly Seville oranges that appear in February.

The time is ripe But you do not have to be a cook or have specialised knowledge to get the best food in season. All it takes is a moment's thought in the supermarket. If it's springtime, have lamb for Sunday dinner; eat lots of green salad through the summer when it is at its best.

And if strawberries are out of season, give them a rest for a while. You will appreciate them all the more when – come Wimbledon fortnight – it is their turn again.

Shopping wisely

Buying food to ensure healthily-balanced eating for up to a week at a time is an essential task. Supermarkets and their huge range of foods will work best for you if you are well-informed about all aspects of food and eating, from understanding food labels to knowing when foods are at their best.

READING FOOD LABELS

All processed and prepared foods must by law carry a label containing ingredient and nutrition information. One panel lists all the ingredients in the food, in order of quantity, while the nutrition panel lists the amount of energy, protein, carbohydrate (sometimes broken down into total carbohydrate and sugars), fat, fibre and sodium in the product. It is expressed both as grams per 100 grams and as grams in a typical serving.

For example, if the label is on a ready-prepared meal for two, then the typical serving will be half the contents. If the food is for one person, such as a small pot of yoghurt or an individually wrapped health food bar or flapjack, the typical serving will be the entire pack. Some labels also state how much of certain vitamins and minerals the food contains.

You should check the label for any additives; some are used to preserve food; others add flavour and colour. There is some evidence that additives cause allergic reactions in some people. They may suffer reactions such as asthma attacks, eczema and hyperactive behaviour. The most common triggers are the 'E numbers' – particularly tartrazine (E102), Sunset yellow (E110), Erythrosine (E127) and Benzoic acid (E219). Also, monosodium glutamate may cause reactions such as headaches.

EXERCISING CHOICE

Knowing about the nutrients in food is one aspect of informed shopping; another is being aware of how food is produced. As organic and wholefood ranges become more popular, foods that have been commercially processed (canned or frozen, for example) may be dismissed as nutritionally inferior. This is not always so: modern methods of freeze-drying fruit, for instance, ensure that minimal amounts of vitamin C are lost. The nutritional values of frozen foods are often very close to – or better than – their fresh equivalents. In general, as long as you avoid too much highly refined, over-processed food, you can eat healthily.

Organic food Many proponents of organic food say that it tastes better; there is also some evidence to show it contains more vitamins and minerals than conventionally grown food. Organic fruit and vegetables are produced without artificial chemicals such as fertilisers, pesticides, herbicides, or fungicides. And organically raised animals are not routinely treated with antibiotics and growth-promoting hormones.

On the other hand, food produced by organic methods is more expensive. It is up to you to decide if you think the extra cost is worth it.

Wholefoods When grains such as rice and wheat are milled to make polished rice or white flour, there is a significant loss of both nutrients and fibre. For example, there are 2.7 grams of fibre in 28 grams (1 ounce) of wholemeal flour compared with one gram in white flour. But this does not mean that a loaf of bought white bread is low in nutrients. Although it contains less fibre, it is fortified by manufacturers and contains twice as much calcium as wholemeal bread as well as added niacin, iron and thiamin.

Wholemeal bread may be made entirely from wholegrain flour, or white flour with bran and wheatgerm added. It has 40 per cent more iron and three times more zinc than white bread and higher levels of magnesium, manganese, and B vitamins. Brown rice, pasta and bread do contain more nutrients and fibre than white; but their white equivalents also have a useful role to play in a balanced diet. A mixture of both

provides variety of texture and flavour. Brown rice retains its outer layer of bran and contains more vitamins, minerals and fibre than white rice. But the bran inhibits the absorption of calcium and iron. Eating too much can result in mineral deficiencies.

Genetically modified foods Genetic modification (GM) is the process of transferring genes from one species to another. For example, a tendency to ripen early or grow tall can be implanted in a crop that would not naturally have that characteristic.

Only three GM foods (soya, maize and tomato purée) are currently approved in the United Kingdom. Soya and maize are widely used in processed food such as crisps, ready-made meals and vegetarian products.

Debate about GM foods is passionate on both sides. More research is needed to know whether GM foods can really deliver their potential or whether the costs to humans and the environment outweigh any benefit.

PREPARING FOOD

There are simple ways to avoid potential problems such as food poisoning.

• Wash your hands before handling food, and after using the lavatory, coughing or sneezing. Do not cough or sneeze near food.

• Use separate clean chopping boards and utensils for raw and cooked foods.

• Clean up frequently during preparation and wash surfaces when you have finished.

• Keep all bins covered.

The right temperature To destroy bacteria that may be in raw ingredients, food needs to reach a temperature of 70°C (158°F) for at least two minutes during cooking. Always cook it thoroughly and serve it piping hot.

Do not leave cooked food at room temperature for more than two hours, as bacteria will multiply rapidly, and do not reheat it more than once. Cool cooked food quickly; once it is cold, cover and refrigerate immediately. Do not re-freeze thawed food.

High-risk foods

Eggs and poultry are particularly susceptible to the dangerous bacteria, salmonella, which can only be destroyed at relatively high temperatures.

• To ensure salmonella bacteria in eggs is destroyed, they should be cooked to 71°C (160°F), the temperature at which the yolk is hard-cooked.

• Poultry should never be undercooked. Test the thickest part of the meat with a skewer: the juices will run clear when it is cooked.

• Pâté, soft-ripened cheeses such as Brie and Camembert and ready-prepared cook-chill meals may contain *listeria* bacteria which can cause listeriosis. Pregnant women in particular, and other vulnerable people are susceptible to this. Cooking or re-heating cook-chill meals to piping hot in the centre should destroy listeria, but pâté and soft cheeses are best avoided altogether if you are in one of the vulnerable groups. Babies and infants under two years, pregnant women, the elderly, and anyone who is ill or has an impaired immune system – should not eat raw or lightly cooked eggs. They should also avoid mayonnaise, custard, hollandaise sauce, meringues, ice cream, sorbets, soufflés, mousses and royal icing, unless they have been made with pasteurised eggs.

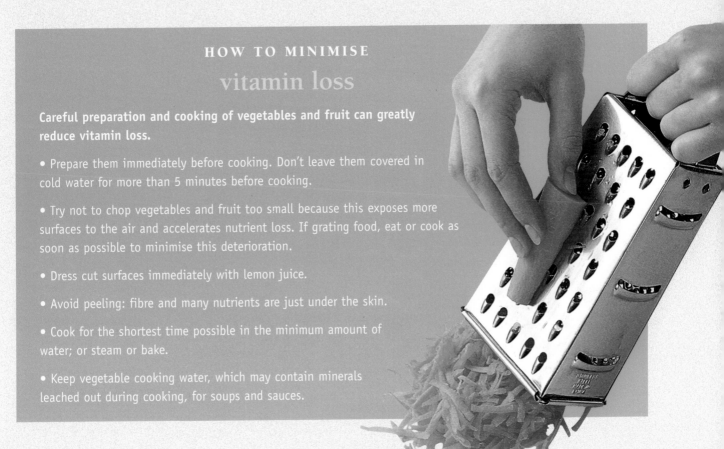

HOW TO MINIMISE
vitamin loss

Careful preparation and cooking of vegetables and fruit can greatly reduce vitamin loss.

• Prepare them immediately before cooking. Don't leave them covered in cold water for more than 5 minutes before cooking.

• Try not to chop vegetables and fruit too small because this exposes more surfaces to the air and accelerates nutrient loss. If grating food, eat or cook as soon as possible to minimise this deterioration.

• Dress cut surfaces immediately with lemon juice.

• Avoid peeling: fibre and many nutrients are just under the skin.

• Cook for the shortest time possible in the minimum amount of water; or steam or bake.

• Keep vegetable cooking water, which may contain minerals leached out during cooking, for soups and sauces.

PART ONE

Bodyworks

The food you eat affects every part of your body: healthy skin and shining hair are the most immediate signs that you are getting the right nutrients. But food works subtly and in depth. It can make all the difference to your energy levels, your resistance to infection, alertness, strength and endurance. By enjoying a richly varied, well-balanced range of foods, you can build solid foundations for your long-term well-being.

Shining with health

Clear skin and glossy hair are the direct result of what you eat, and are also an accurate reflection of your state of health. If you want to look good and feel well, invest in the long-term benefits of food that makes a real difference, from top to toe.

The skin is your body's largest organ and performs a vital protective role. It acts as a barrier between your internal organs and the outside world, protecting them from injury, harmful sunlight, and invasion by bacteria. It is also highly sensitive, due to nerve cells that respond to touch, temperature and pressure.

Skin is waterproof: it stops water entering the body and prevents the loss of vital fluid. It also plays a key role in temperature control. When the body gets cold, tiny blood vessels in the skin narrow to conserve heat. When it is hot, sweat glands produce perspiration which evaporates and cools the skin, while the blood vessels widen, drawing heat away from the body's surface.

UNDER THE SKIN

The skin is made up of three main components. There is a thin outer layer called the epidermis, and a thicker inner layer, called the dermis. Beneath these is fatty subcutaneous tissue that plumps up the skin.

The surface of the epidermis has a tough protective covering of dead cells. These constantly flake off or are worn away, and are quickly replaced by new cells produced in the lower layers of the epidermis. A regular supply of oxygen and the right nutrients from your food are essential for this renewal process.

Some epidermal cells make keratin, a hard protein comprising most of the tough, outer layer of the epidermis; it is the main component of hair and nails. Other cells produce melanin, the pigment which gives skin its colour and forms a protective tan in response to the sun's rays.

Ageing skin The dermis is made up of connective tissue containing collagen and sebaceous glands. Collagen is a tough fibrous protein which gives skin its strength and elasticity. It breaks down with age, causing the skin to wrinkle. This begins around 30 years of age, or earlier with excessive exposure to sunlight or cigarette smoke. You can help to prevent wrinkles by reducing the effect of free radicals. These naturally occurring substances damage all cells in your body, including the skin; if you eat foods rich in the antioxidants beta carotene, vitamins C and E and selenium, however, you can limit the damage. Turn to page 118 to read more about antioxidants.

A healthy turnover Your skin and hair need essential nutrients for regular growth and renewal. Fresh vegetables, oil-rich walnuts and avocados (above and right) are the perfect foods for the task. Try the recipe for Avocado and Walnut Salad on page 35.

Your skin is also kept supple by sebaceous glands that produce an oily substance called sebum. These either open into hair follicles or discharge their sebum directly on to the skin's surface. The scalp and face contain the most sebaceous glands.

Self healing As long as you follow the balanced, healthy diet outlined in the Five Food Groups (see pages 11-15), your food will provide all the nutrients your skin needs to repair and maintain itself. When you cut or graze your skin, blood forms a clot in the area of damage and fibrous tissue is laid down to support the growth of new skin cells. The undamaged cells around the wound proliferate and eventually cover it.

Hair and nails There are tiny pits in your skin called hair follicles. These contain the roots of each hair, which grows upward, nourished by blood vessels inside the follicle. Hair colour is determined by the amount and shade of melanin produced by cells in the follicle, and curliness is determined by the follicle's shape.

The hair on your scalp grows about one centimetre (half an inch) a month. Each of the 300,000 or so hairs on your scalp grows for about three years, then falls out. A new hair grows from the same hair follicle. It takes six months for a fingernail to grow from base to tip, and about a year for a toenail.

FOODS FOR HAIR AND SKIN

If you want your skin, hair and nails to be healthy, you need a wide range of nutrients. These include protein, essential fatty acids, vitamin A, beta

Hard working skin Each layer of skin performs different tasks, all vital to your survival. Eating the right foods will help your skin to work at peak efficiency.

IF COLD, CAPILLARIES NARROW

CELLS FLAKE OFF

SWEAT COOLS

CAPILLARIES OPEN WHEN HOT

THE PROTECTIVE OUTER LAYER OF THE SKIN, IS TOUGH, WATERPROOF AND SUNPROOF

CONNECTIVE TISSUE PROVIDES STRENGTH AND ELASTICITY

KERATIN IS NEEDED FOR HAIR, SKIN AND NAILS

SEBACEOUS GLANDS OIL HAIR AND SKIN

THE INNER LAYER KEEPS SKIN STRONG, MOISTURISED AND SUPPLE

FATTY TISSUE PROVIDES A SUPPORTIVE, PROTECTIVE CUSHION FOR YOUR SKIN

carotene, vitamin C, vitamin E, the B vitamins, especially B_{12}, zinc and water. Protein is vital for growth and repair of hair and skin. Meat, fish, poultry, cereals such as oats, rice and bread, eggs, cheese, pulses and nuts are good sources. The protein is broken down into amino acids, used to make collagen and keratin.

Fish as skin food

A rich source of protein (one small portion supplies between a third and a half of the protein needed each day), fish also provides other important skin nutrients. White fish such as cod, haddock and plaice are low in fat, and rich in vitamin B_{12}. For healthy eating, they should be grilled or baked rather than fried.

Oily fish such as sardines and mackerel supply omega-3 fatty acids, vitamins A and D, and zinc. Sardines also contain iron. Eating these oily fish in canned form is inexpensive and accessible. The bones are edible, and provide calcium, fluoride and phosphorus as an added bonus.

Essential fatty acids These are part of the make-up of all cells, including skin cells. Your body cannot make essential fatty acids, so it must get them from food. For more about essential fatty acids, turn to page 56.

Omega-6 fatty acids are mainly derived from the linoleic acid in safflower, sunflower, wheat germ and corn oils. In the body, linoleic acid is turned into gamma linoleic acid (GLA), essential for the production of keratin and collagen, and for maintaining hormonal balance.

Omega-3 fatty acids mostly come from the linolenic acid in oily fish, however, canola oil and soya bean oil contain a mixture of both omega-3 and omega-6 fatty acids.

To help unsightly broken veins on the skin, boost your intake of citrus fruits, peppers and buckwheat. These foods contain rutin, a bioflavonoid which helps to strengthen small blood vessels.

BUCKWHEAT *(left) is a rich source of rutin. Available in health stores, it is mostly used as a flour to make pancakes.*

EAT TO BEAT **broken veins**

NECESSARY NUTRIENTS

Healthy skin and hair depend on the growth and renewal of cells.

Vitamin A, a powerful antioxidant is a vital part of this process – it is plentiful in offal, such as liver and kidneys, oily fish, full-fat milk, egg yolk, cheese, margarine and butter. Beta carotene in orange, red, yellow and dark green fruit and vegetables such as melon, carrots, pumpkin, broccoli, apricots and mangoes is turned into vitamin A in the body. An effective antioxidant, it protects against skin (and other) cancers.

Vitamin C, another antioxidant, is crucial to the production of collagen. It combines with nutrients such as rutin in citrus fruits, peppers and buckwheat, to strengthen the tiny blood vessels in the surface of the skin. It also plays an important role in the healing process. Citrus fruit, strawberries, blackcurrants, guavas, kiwi fruit and peppers are all good sources, but as vitamin C is easily destroyed in cooking, it is wise to eat fruit and vegetables raw.

Vitamin E works in tandem with essential fatty acids. It prevents fats

being oxidised, thereby producing harmful free radicals (see page 118). You will find plentiful amounts in seeds and seed oils, margarine, avocados, nuts, wheatgerm, wholemeal bread, egg yolks and wholegrain cereals.

The B vitamins, especially B_{12}, are vital for growth and division of cells; they enable the hair to grow and the skin to constantly replace dead cells with new ones. Any protein from an animal source will supply plenty of B_{12} (a serving of white fish or one egg provides an adult's entire daily need). Other B vitamins are found in wholegrains, yeast extract, dairy food, lentils and other pulses, liver, green vegetables, seafood, lean meat, eggs, nuts, seeds and dried fruit.

Zinc is mainly found in shellfish, particularly oysters, and also in pulses, pumpkin seeds, wholemeal bread and other wholegrain cereals. Eat foods rich in zinc to help your skin heal quickly and also to prevent skin infections.

Water your skin When the water level falls in the epidermis your skin becomes dry and cracked. Drink at

MENUPLAN
hair and skin boosters

Nourish your skin and hair with these simple, vitamin-rich treats

SALAD FEASTS Enjoy griddled peppers drizzled with olive oil; raw vegetables dipped in guacamole; baby leaves drizzled with lime juice and walnut oil, sprinkled with walnuts; grated carrot with lemon juice

GOLDEN FRUIT Make a salad of yellow-fleshed fruits such as apricots, oranges, peaches, melons, mangoes and grapefruit.

SEAFOOD Choose zinc-rich shellfish such as oysters and crabs; or buy pots of shrimps and prawns.

SKIN DRINKS Drink at least 8 glasses of water daily; intersperse these with fruit juices, including citrus, apple, apricot and pineapple; also vegetable juices, especially carrot, tomato and celery.

SNACKS An avocado, pitted and drizzled with olive oil; and the occasional handful of mixed nuts such as walnuts and almonds.

Kippers and poached egg – a simple recipe for healthy skin

least eight glasses of water daily – keep a bottle at your desk and sip it regularly, especially if you work in a centrally-heated environment.

SOLVING SKIN PROBLEMS

Common skin problems such as spots often respond to quite simple adjustments in lifestyle. Plenty of sleep, exercise, water to drink and some healing sunshine usually do the trick. And it certainly helps if you keep your skin clean – use warm water and a mild cleanser rather than harsh scrubbing. More severe, chronic skin conditions need professional attention, but many of these can be relieved and even solved by eating a well-balanced diet.

Hormones and acne The production of sebum is partly controlled by androgens, male sex hormones present in both men and women. When hormone levels are high, for example during adolescence or before menstruation, too much sebum can be produced, resulting in greasy hair and skin and acne.

Acne spots develop when hair follicles become blocked with sebum, and bacteria multiply, resulting in inflammation and redness. Acne is triggered by hormonal changes at puberty. It is more common in males, and there may be a genetic factor. Blackheads occur when the sebaceous gland is blocked with a greasy material made up of sebum and keratin.

It was long believed that eating too much chocolate and greasy foods caused acne. But iodine-containing chemicals in salt may be the real aggravating factor.

Ways to prevent acne Many processed foods such as burgers and crisps contain large amounts of salt, and chips are often heavily salted. If you suffer from acne, you should cut down on processed and refined foods and also avoid adding salt to your meals.

Acne is also caused by what you don't eat. Many teenagers have a diet based on sweets, snacks, fast foods and fizzy drinks or alcohol; this deprives them of key vitamins and minerals needed for a healthy skin. A diet based on wholegrains, fresh fruit and vegetables, lean meat and some polyunsaturated oils would considerably reduce their acne.

Vitamin A is highly effective against acne, and is contained in synthetic form in several anti-acne drugs. It should never be taken in large doses, and should be avoided by pregnant women (see page 163).

To increase your vitamin A intake it is perfectly safe to eat foods rich in beta carotene. Try munching carrot sticks or dried apricots as a snack and replace sugar-filled cakes and puddings with a fruit salad made with mango, melon and peaches.

Because zinc helps to prevent infection, it is useful against acne; and acidophilus, the bacteria in live yoghurt, also help to prevent spots. Eating vitamin E-rich foods may assist healing and reduce scarring.

Eczema

Eczema is one of the commonest skin problems. It is characterised by an extremely itchy, scaly red rash which often appears in creases in the skin or on the face but can affect the whole body. If the rash is scratched, the skin may weep and bleed, and may become infected.

Like hay fever and asthma, eczema is an allergic reaction. A food allergy (as opposed to things such as washing powder, fabrics and animal hair) is thought to be responsible for up to half of all cases.

The main allergy-causing foods are milk, eggs and dairy products, although fish, shellfish, tomatoes, nuts, wheat, yeast and some food colourings, particularly the yellow and orange tartrazine colourings, can all trigger allergic reactions. If you think your eczema is caused by a food allergy, there are several ways of dealing with this, but you will need expert help. For information on food allergies turn to pages 124-126.

Some food supplements are also believed to help eczema. Evening primrose oil and fish-oil capsules may give relief and there is some evidence, but no scientific proof, that zinc supplements may be helpful.

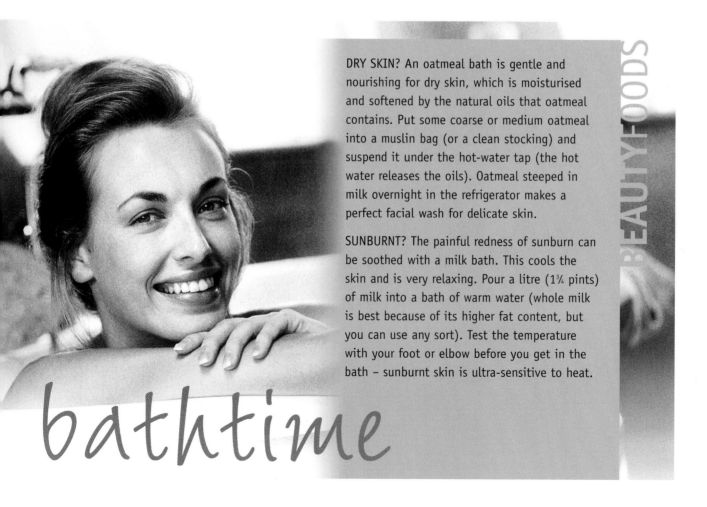

BEAUTYFOODS

DRY SKIN? An oatmeal bath is gentle and nourishing for dry skin, which is moisturised and softened by the natural oils that oatmeal contains. Put some coarse or medium oatmeal into a muslin bag (or a clean stocking) and suspend it under the hot-water tap (the hot water releases the oils). Oatmeal steeped in milk overnight in the refrigerator makes a perfect facial wash for delicate skin.

SUNBURNT? The painful redness of sunburn can be soothed with a milk bath. This cools the skin and is very relaxing. Pour a litre (1¾ pints) of milk into a bath of warm water (whole milk is best because of its higher fat content, but you can use any sort). Test the temperature with your foot or elbow before you get in the bath – sunburnt skin is ultra-sensitive to heat.

bathtime

Healing oils *The omega-3 fatty acids in oily fish such as anchovies (left) help to calm skin inflammation. Eating oily fish is particularly helpful for psoriasis.*

Psoriasis

The symptoms of psoriasis are inflamed, thickened patches of skin, most commonly on the knees, elbows, trunk, back and scalp. Psoriasis may also affect the nails, causing pitting and the separation of the nail from its bed. About two per cent of the population are affected; and the condition tends to run in families, so there may be a genetic factor. The problem is caused by new skin cells proliferating about ten times faster than normal and accumulating in scaly pink patches. It is not clear why this happens.

Although psoriasis is not an allergic disorder, it has been found to respond well to changes in diet. A low-fat diet may help to relieve symptoms. Omega-3 fatty acids help to control the inflammatory reaction believed to bring on psoriasis. Eating more oily fish or taking a fish oil supplement may help. Oily fish also contains vitamin D which is now used to treat severe psoriasis.

Some people have found that cutting certain foods out of their diet has helped to alleviate their psoriasis symptoms. Excluding foods such as dairy products, animal fats, meat and spices from your diet may help. Do not attempt this without consulting a doctor: you may become deficient in key nutrients.

Many sufferers find that sunlight relieves psoriasis. To enhance the effect of the sun, eat plenty of foods that contain psoralens, compounds which make skin more sensitive to

sunlight. These include fruit, vegetables and herbs, particularly celery, parsley, lettuce, and citrus fruits such as limes and lemons. Vitamin E, onions and garlic may also help, as they are known to help reduce inflammation.

Burns and cuts

Healing makes extra demands on the body's nutrient reserves. After a burn, for instance, fluids, minerals and essential fatty acids can be lost from the body and must be replaced. Collagen, the tough protein found in the dermis, is particularly important for quick, effective healing of wounds and burns. To accelerate the process, eat plenty of foods high in vitamins C, E and A and zinc (see page 29 for good sources). Potassium and calcium also help with healing.

Bananas, grapes and mixed vegetable soups and stews are good sources of potassium, while calcium can be obtained from milk and dairy products, tofu and tahini.

To maintain fluid levels, avoid diuretics such as tea and coffee. Avoid alcohol, too, as it dries out the skin. People with burns, including those with sunburn, should drink plenty of water at regular intervals to combat dehydration.

HAIR AND NAIL REPAIR

Old hair is constantly being replaced by new and it is normal to lose 100–150 scalp hairs a day. Excessive hair loss can be caused by several factors. Certain illnesses and drugs, stress, pregnancy and some skin complaints may all be responsible. Hair loss by men with 'male pattern baldness' is impossible to treat; the condition is inherited, so efforts to find a cure have had no success.

It is now thought that there is a link between excessive hair loss and low iron levels. This may be a sign of anaemia (see page 60) which is also indicated by brittle, or ridged nails. If you think your hair loss or poor nail condition is due to anaemia, ask your doctor for a blood test.

You may need to boost your intake of iron-rich foods such as lean red meat, game and offal, egg yolks, pulses and dark green vegetables such as spinach. To help you to absorb iron from your food, be sure to consume plenty of vitamin C from citrus fruits and other foods.

Protein-rich foods will help too, because hair follicles and nails have extremely high requirements for the essential amino acids they contain. It has also been found that low protein levels hinder the body's ability to build good stores of iron.

Biotin deficiency Hair loss can be caused by a lack of biotin in the body. Biotin is a nutrient mainly produced by bacteria in the gut, but it is also found in foods such as cooked eggs, peanut butter, wholegrain foods and liver.

A common pattern of hair loss results in bald patches which may re-grow only to be replaced by new bald patches. This is called alopecia areata and the condition can also cause pitting of the nails. In around half of all cases the main cause is stress. People suffering from stress are short of B vitamins, so if you suffer from alopecia increasing your intake of B vitamins may help. Eat plenty of wholegrains, yeast extract, dairy food, lentils and other pulses, liver, green vegetables, seafood, lean meat, nuts, seeds and dried fruit.

Dry scalp and dandruff Flaky particles shed from your scalp affect

the look of your hair. Dandruff is caused by the skin of the scalp shedding its dead cells at a faster rate than normal. As with other skin problems, this is a sign that the body is not in peak health.

Too much junk food, and a lack of vitamins and polyunsaturated oils can contribute to the problem. A dry scalp and dandruff may also be a sign of zinc deficiency, so include more foods rich in this mineral in your diet (see above). Essential fatty acids also help prevent dry skin and a flaky scalp. These are found in vegetable oils, nuts and oily fish.

Occasionally, a flaky scalp can be a sign of an underlying disorder; if the problem persists after changing your diet and using antidandruff shampoos, consult your doctor.

A healthy scalp *Dandruff flakes on your clothes may be a signal to eat more zinc-rich foods. You should also avoid harsh shampoos and be sure you rinse the hair clean of all soap.*

hot **duck breast** salad

Enjoy the succulent texture and rich flavours of Barbary duck on a bed of crispy salad and orange dressing. The fat on the duck breast can be easily removed, leaving a lean red meat. Grill for 5 minutes to serve it lightly cooked, longer if you prefer it well done.

preparation time: **25 minutes**

cooking time: **5–7 minutes**

serves **4**

NUTRIENTS PER SERVING	
calories	275
carbohydrate	10 g
(sugars)	9 g
protein	31 g
fat	13 g
(saturated)	3 g
fibre	2 g

4 Barbary duck breast fillets, each about 140 g (5 oz)
3 tablespoons dark soya sauce
Juice of 1 orange
2 red or green chillies, deseeded and sliced
5 cm (2 in) piece root ginger, peeled and grated
125 g (4½ oz) watercress sprigs
1 medium head lettuce such as Romaine, leaves washed and dried
2 oranges, peeled and cut into segments
Zest of ½ orange, cut into fine strips
FOR THE DRESSING
Juice of 1 orange
2 tablespoons extra virgin olive oil
Salt and black pepper (optional)

1 Heat the grill to hot. Remove the skin and thick layer of fat from the duck fillets. Slice each breast into about 6 pieces. Place in a shallow gratin dish.

2 Mix together the soya sauce, orange juice, chillies and ginger and pour over the duck, turning the slices to coat them well. Lay the duck slices on the grill rack and grill for 5–7 minutes, turning once or twice, until cooked to your liking. Baste with the soya sauce mixture during cooking. Remove the cooked duck slices from under the grill.

3 Arrange the watercress, lettuce leaves and orange segments in a serving dish and toss in the duck pieces. Scatter over the strips of orange zest. Put the dressing ingredients in a clean screw-top jar and shake to combine. Serve the dressing separately.

roasted red **pepper** and **lentil** soup

The flavour of red peppers and the nutty textures of lentils combine beautifully. Choose your colour – the soup is red with the tomato purée and split red lentil combination and browner with the continental lentil and red pesto. Both are equally delicious.

preparation time: **20 minutes**

cooking time: **30 minutes**

serves **6** as a starter

3 red peppers, deseeded and quartered
2 tablespoons olive oil
1 tablespoon tomato purée or red pesto
    (reduce olive oil by 1 tablespoon
    if using pesto)
1 medium onion, diced
1 clove garlic, crushed
2 large carrots, quartered
115 g (4 oz) split red lentils or continental
    (brown/green) lentils, washed
1.2 litres (2 pints) vegetable stock (recipe
    page 338)

1 Place the peppers under a hot grill for about 15 minutes, or until the skin is black. Cover with a clean wet cloth, or place in a plastic bag, and allow to cool for 10 minutes. Peel the skin from the peppers and blot them dry with some kitchen paper.

2 Heat the oil and tomato purée or pesto in a heavy-based pan. Add the onion and garlic and fry gently for about 5 minutes, until softened but not browned. Stir in the pepper pieces, cover and continue to cook for another 5 minutes, stirring occasionally.

3 Put the carrots and lentils in a large saucepan with the stock and bring to the boil. Reduce the heat and simmer for 15 minutes. Add the onion and red pepper mixture, cover and simmer for 10–15 minutes, until the vegetables and lentils are completely soft.

4 Remove the pan from the heat and pour the contents into a food processor. Blend to a purée. Return the soup to the pan to reheat before serving.

NUTRIENTS PER SERVING	
calories	150
carbohydrate	22 g
(sugars)	11 g
protein	7 g
fat	4.5 g
(saturated)	1 g
fibre	4 g

avocado and **walnut** salad

This salad combines the rich flavour of avocados, walnuts and walnut oil. It's not only delicious but is full of nutrients that help to give you glossy hair and lovely skin, including Vitamin E (in the avocados) and essential fatty acids (in the nuts).

preparation time: **10 minutes**

serves **4**

2 ripe avocados, peeled, halved and pitted
1 teaspoon lemon juice (optional)
50 g (1¾ oz) rocket
2 Little Gem lettuce hearts
100 g (3½ oz) walnut pieces
FOR THE DRESSING
2 tablespoons walnut oil
Juice of 1 orange
2 teaspoons white wine vinegar
Sea salt and black pepper (optional)

1 Cut the avocados into thin slices. Rub lightly with lemon juice or a little walnut oil to prevent browning.

2 Toss the rocket and lettuce leaves in a serving dish. Arrange the avocado slices on top of the salad greens and sprinkle over the walnuts.

3 Put the dressing ingredients in a clean screw-top jar and shake to combine. Serve the dressing separately.

NUTRIENTS PER SERVING	
calories	370
carbohydrate	4 g
(sugars)	2.5 g
protein	5 g
fat	37 g
(saturated)	5 g
fibre	2 g

Alert and responsive

The brain is your body's control centre, enabling you to think, see, speak, hear and touch. It also allows you to smell, taste and enjoy your food. If you choose foods that are rich in B vitamins, antioxidants and minerals, your brain and nervous system will function at their best.

Your nervous system is a miracle of organisation. Every moment of your life your brain is receiving, sorting, interpreting and storing a wealth of information arriving from the network of nerves extending to every part of your body.

There are two parts to your body's nervous system: central and peripheral. The brain and spinal cord comprise the central nervous system. Made up of millions of nerve cells (neurons), this controls the entire system. The peripheral nervous system is the linking network that connects the central nervous system to 'input' sites (such as sense organs and receptors) and to 'output' sites

(such as the muscles and glands). The brain houses regulatory glands: including the hypothalamus which controls the hormonal system, appetite, thirst, temperature, sleep, emotion and sexual behaviour and the pituitary which controls the thyroid and adrenal glands.

Much of the information that is processed by the brain comes from your five senses, allowing you to see, hear, smell, taste and feel. Although the senses are separate they work closely together, coordinated by the brain. For example, your sense of smell and taste are intricately connected – they compensate for, and enhance, each other. Your

tongue can only differentiate sweet, sour, bitter and salty flavours while your nose is able to detect thousands of different scents. The aromas from food enter your nose and pass over the back of your throat, so smell determines how food and drink tastes. This is why you cannot taste food properly when you have a cold and your nose is blocked.

PLANNING PREGNANCY

The brain is one of the first organs to develop in an embryo. About three weeks after conception, three basic layers of cells are formed from which organs and tissues develop.

The B vitamin called folic acid (folate) works in conjunction with vitamin B_{12} to produce the genetic materials DNA and RNA. Folic acid is so crucial to the development of the brain and spinal cord at this stage that a supplement of 400 micrograms a day (double the normal adult requirement) is advised for women planning a pregnancy (see pages 164-165). It is best to start taking folic acid

Taste and smell Information from these senses is so closely coordinated you can identify food even when blindfolded.

BROWN RICE *Because it is rich in vitamin B$_1$, unprocessed rice protects the health of your nervous system. The vitamin is preserved in the bran (outer layer of the rice), which is removed when making white rice.*

1 *Vitamin B$_1$ (thiamin): eat brown rice, peas, beans, breakfast cereals, wholemeal breads, pork, bacon and liver.*

2 *Vitamin B$_2$ (riboflavin): you can find this in liver, kidneys, meat, milk, breakfast cereals, eggs, cheese, yeast extract.*

3 *Niacin (nicotinic acid): eat meat, oily fish, poultry, bread, potatoes and breakfast cereals.*

4 *Biotin: the richest sources are brown rice, wholemeal bread, liver, kidneys, nuts, cauliflower, peas, beans and eggs.*

5 *Pantothenic acid: eat plenty of breakfast cereals, wholegrain bread, nuts, dairy products, dried fruits, kidneys and liver.*

CAUTION: Liver should be avoided during pregnancy because of its very high vitamin A content.

FIVE WAYS TO boost B vitamins

three months before the planned conception and through to the 12th week of pregnancy to reduce the risk of spina bifida (a malformation of the baby's spine) and other nervous system defects.

Foods naturally rich in folic acid (see the folates chart on page 39) should be eaten regularly – they supply other nutrients both for the mother and for the developing baby. Vegetables should be lightly cooked as prolonged boiling destroys most of their folate content.

One helping of Brussels sprouts or of fortified breakfast cereal contains 100 micrograms of folates; a large glass of fresh orange juice provides 40 micrograms and a slice of wholemeal bread has 15 micrograms. **Avoid liver during pregnancy** Even though liver is rich in folic acid it should be avoided by pregnant women because of its very high vitamin A content which can damage the developing foetus. An excess can build up if the vitamin A in liver is added to the amount in a balanced diet, as it cannot be excreted in urine.

What's best for your brain?

The foods that are most beneficial to your brain and the rest of your nervous system contain nutrients that tend to accumulate in the brain. These nutrients include the B vitamin group, vitamin E and zinc.

For the body to function at all, energy needs to be released from your food: this is the main role of the B vitamins. With the exception of B$_{12}$, they cannot be stored in the body and should be replenished every day from a wide range of foods (see the panel above).

The B vitamins work as a group, but some are particularly active within the nervous system. Thiamin (vitamin B$_1$) is found in brown rice, peas, beans and other vegetables, fortified breakfast cereals, wholemeal

A feast for brain and body Fresh fish and vegetables supply the vitamins, minerals and other nutrients needed to boost your brain power in spicy Creole Fish Soup. The recipe is on page 42.

breads and cereals, pork, bacon and liver. Without it, toxic substances that can damage your nervous system can build-up. The combined action of folic acid and vitamin B_{12} (found only in foods of animal origin) keeps your nerve cells healthy on a day-to-day basis and plays a key role in the first stages of the growth of the nervous system. They help the metabolism of the fatty acids which maintain the myelin sheath (the layer of insulation around the nerves) and the healthy structure of nerve cells.

You would get definite warning signs if you became deficient in vitamin B_{12}, including numbness and tingling, clumsiness and difficulty with walking. Elderly people are particularly vulnerable if they are deficient in B_{12} – they may become confused and deteriorate mentally. High intakes of B vitamins are usually safe, but B_6 (pyridoxine), a popular over-the-counter treatment for premenstrual syndrome (see pages 223-225), has caused concern. Some women have taken extremely high amounts over a long period of time, resulting in a loss of sensation in the hands and feet. Turn to page 225 for the recommended dose.

Brain power and antioxidants

The role of antioxidants (see page 118) in helping to promote mental alertness, improved memory capacity and the overall health of the nervous system is now widely recognised. They prevent damage to nerve cells or neurons, probably by preventing free radicals from breaking down the cells' structure.

Polyunsaturated fats are essential for healthy nerves and brain activity – vitamin E prevents these from being oxidised and producing harmful free radicals. Foods such as seed oils (sunflower, safflower, olive) muesli, wheatgerm, avocados, nuts, leafy green vegetables, wholemeal bread, cereals and egg yolks have abundant supplies.

Vitamin C also has an active antioxidant function. You'll find plentiful amounts in most fresh fruit (especially citrus fruit), fresh vegetables and fruit juices. Eat foods rich in vitamin C every day, as it cannot be stored in the body.

Food and memory In countries where people eat a lot of olive oil, such as Italy, Spain, Greece, southern France and other regions in the Mediterranean, older people have been shown to have better memory and cognitive function (thinking, problem solving and recall) than in countries where olive oil is not abundant in the diet.

FOLATES IN FOODS

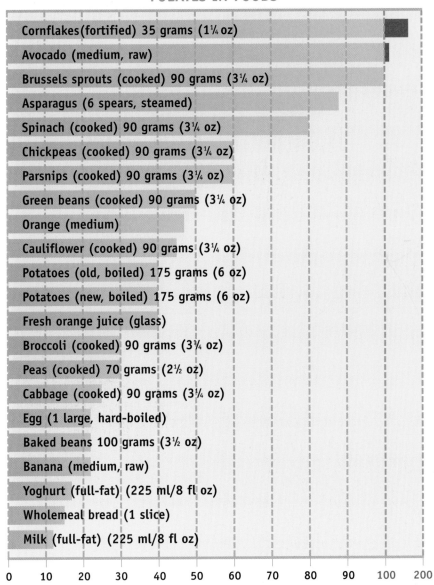

Cornflakes (fortified) 35 grams (1¼ oz)	
Avocado (medium, raw)	
Brussels sprouts (cooked) 90 grams (3¼ oz)	
Asparagus (6 spears, steamed)	
Spinach (cooked) 90 grams (3¼ oz)	
Chickpeas (cooked) 90 grams (3¼ oz)	
Parsnips (cooked) 90 grams (3¼ oz)	
Green beans (cooked) 90 grams (3¼ oz)	
Orange (medium)	
Cauliflower (cooked) 90 grams (3¼ oz)	
Potatoes (old, boiled) 175 grams (6 oz)	
Potatoes (new, boiled) 175 grams (6 oz)	
Fresh orange juice (glass)	
Broccoli (cooked) 90 grams (3¼ oz)	
Peas (cooked) 70 grams (2½ oz)	
Cabbage (cooked) 90 grams (3¼ oz)	
Egg (1 large, hard-boiled)	
Baked beans 100 grams (3½ oz)	
Banana (medium, raw)	
Yoghurt (full-fat) (225 ml/8 fl oz)	
Wholemeal bread (1 slice)	
Milk (full-fat) (225 ml/8 fl oz)	

0   10   20   30   40   50   60   70   80   90   100   200

Micrograms of folic acid in average servings (recommended daily intake is 200 micrograms)

MENUPLAN
for the brain

Choose foods that keep you sharp. Here's how to keep your brain and nervous system alert and responsive.

KEEP IN MIND Drink at least 8 glasses of fluid throughout the day, including fruit juice and herbal teas, and make sure that you eat at least five portions of vegetables and fruit every day.

WAKE-UPS Marmite 'soldiers' with boiled egg; peanut butter on wholemeal toast; muesli rich in nuts and dried fruit; breakfast cereal with skimmed milk; kippers poached in milk.

STAY-ALERT SNACKS Banana sandwiches on wholemeal bread; egg sandwiches on wholemeal bread; handfuls of dried fruits and nuts; crudités made with red, orange and green vegetables such as carrots and pepper accompanied by a guacamole or hummous dip.

MAIN MEALS Stir-fries with seafood and crispy fresh vegetables; fresh vegetable soup; griddled fish; griddled Mediterranean vegetables; baked potato with baked beans; cauliflower cheese; liver and onions; pasta dishes made with wholemeal pasta.

DESSERTS Fresh fruit topped with low-fat crème fraîche or low-fat yoghurt; grilled fruit — a Charred Fruit Platter (recipe page 301).

Research into fatty acids is also promising: omega-3 fatty acids, found mainly in oily fish and walnuts, are essential for the health of nerves and brain function. Lack of these may play a role in causing the abnormal cell formation that characterises Alzheimer's disease. Although omega-3 fatty acids have not been proved to prevent Alzheimer's, it makes good sense to eat omega-3-rich foods regularly.

Fruit and vegetables Memory tests (see pages 264-265) have provided positive results about the benefits of eating fruit and vegetables. People with the highest scores were those who consumed the highest amounts. By eating the recommended five servings a day (see page 12), you will maintain consistently high blood levels of vitamin C and beta carotene which help to enhance your memory.

A steady nerve

Minerals such as calcium and magnesium, iron and potassium are all required for healthy nerves. There is a known link between lack of iron and problems with attention, memory and learning in small children, and adolescents who have low levels may have mood swings and be unable to concentrate.

Zinc has a special function. It is needed by the pituitary gland, and if you don't have enough, you may experience deficiency symptoms such as mood swings, irritability depression and loss of appetite (see pages 228-231).

Zinc also helps in the production of hormones and a deficiency can disrupt neurotransmitters in the brain. These chemical messengers released from nerve endings relay messages from nerve cell to nerve cell throughout the body.

Zinc is plentiful in red meat, liver, shellfish (especially oysters), egg yolks, wholegrain cereals and pulses. It is most easily absorbed from foods of animal origin.

Fuel for your brain

Your brain needs a constant supply of glucose to supply the energy it needs to function properly. You may be tempted to grab a chocolate bar or gulp down a sugary drink to obtain an instant glucose boost, but this is not a good idea, as these foods are nutritionally empty.

Complex carbohydrate foods such as pulses, beans, bread, rice, pasta, potatoes, breakfast cereals and snacks such as muesli bars are a much better choice. They are broken down into simple sugars such as glucose to give energy – and also supply valuable nutrients.

Food for your mood

All activities in the brain involve neurotransmitters, and certain nutrients in your food can influence their activity. Foods that are high in

carbohydrates raise the levels of tryptophan (an essential amino acid) in your brain. The tryptophan then helps to boost the production of serotonin, a brain chemical which improves your mood (see page 218). Carbohydrate-craving is often a symptom of premenstrual syndrome and may be a sign that you need extra serotonin (see page 223).

If your diet is meat-free

Vegetarians need to make special efforts to ensure they get a supply of vitamin B_{12} because the richest sources are in foods from animals. Deficiency of B_{12} can result in damage to nerves and degeneration of the spinal cord. A high intake of folates can mask a B_{12} deficiency so you may not spot the symptoms until damage has already occurred.

If you eat dairy products and eggs you will obtain B_{12} from these. Otherwise, you must eat foods that are fortified with vitamin B_{12} – these include bread, yeast extracts, soya drinks and other soya foods and breakfast cereals. Always check labels to ensure the vitamin is present. The alternative is vitamin B_{12} supplements.

Zinc and iron Low zinc and B_{12} levels are common in vegetarian diets because these minerals are most abundant in animal foods.

If you don't eat meat, good sources of zinc include egg yolks, shellfish, wholegrain cereals and pumpkin seeds. Iron can also be obtained from canned tomatoes, carrots, roasted peanuts, peas and sweetcorn.

It is important that you absorb zinc properly: if you eat excess phytates in bran-enriched foods, tea, wholegrain foods and legumes, your absorption can be diminished.

alcohol

FOODS TO WATCH

- **Even a small amount of alcohol** will have some effect on the brain.

- **While alcohol is a stimulant** for your heart it has the opposite effect on the brain and nervous system.

- **Alcohol depresses** the parts of your brain that control behaviour, impairs your senses and interferes with coordination. Regular, heavy intake of alcohol can kill nerve cells and cause the brain to shrink, causing permanent damage to the brain (as well as to your heart and liver).

- **Heavy drinking** may also lead to psychological problems such as insomnia, depression, anxiety and forgetfulness (for recommended safe levels of alcohol intake see page 97).

caffeine

FOODS TO WATCH

- **Caffeine has a direct stimulatory effect** on the brain, which is why people consume coffee, tea and cola drinks to keep alert.

- **Coffee contains** about 40 per cent more caffeine than tea and chocolate; amounts in cola drinks vary (always check the label).

- **People differ in their response,** some find coffee so stimulating they are unable to sleep if they drink it in the evening; others are unaffected.

- **Between eight and ten cups** of coffee a day can result in irregular heartbeat, shaking, confusion, stomach upsets and even convulsions. You may even get withdrawal symptoms such as trembling – a sign that you may have become addicted. Check with your doctor for advice.

Zinc from the sea Enjoy the exquisite flavours of fresh clams and at the same time know that you are getting vital zinc.

A satisfying meal If you avoid meat but eat eggs, the yolks provide you with iron, other minerals, vitamins and protein.

salmon **kulebyaka**

The enticing aromas of this traditional Russian salmon and rice pie stimulate the appetite. It makes a nourishing, satisfying meal – but if you are watching your weight, ready-made filo pastry is an excellent lower-fat alternative to the puff pastry.

preparation time: **30 minutes**

cooking time: **30 minutes**

serves **6**

NUTRIENTS PER SERVING	
calories	410
carbohydrate	33 g
(sugars)	1 g
protein	18 g
fat	23 g
(saturated)	2 g
fibre	0

350 g (12 oz) ready-made puff pastry, defrosted if frozen

250 g (9 oz) cooked brown rice (85 g/3 oz raw weight)

2 hard-boiled eggs, chopped

2 tablespoons chopped fresh parsley

Salt and black pepper

300 g (10½ oz) salmon fillet, cooked and flaked

Beaten egg for glazing

1 Heat the oven to 200°C (400°F, gas mark 6). Roll the pastry out on a floured surface to a rectangle 35 x 25 cm (14 x 10 in) and transfer to an oiled baking tray.

2 Mix the rice, eggs, parsley and seasoning in a bowl. Spread half the rice mixture in a strip along the pastry, lengthways. Put the flaked fish on top, then add the remaining rice in a layer.

3 Brush the edges of the pastry with beaten egg and fold over, sealing the edge. Trim off any excess pastry, roll it out again and cut into thin strips to decorate the top. Brush all over with beaten egg and bake for 30 minutes, until the pastry is golden.

4 Serve with a large green or mixed salad for a complete meal. There's no need for potatoes or bread.

creole **fish** soup

This spicy soup is an excellent way of cooking mackerel, an inexpensive, delicious fish. Tomatoes, spinach and lime provide a sharp, fresh contrast to the richness of mackerel flesh, and a home-made fish stock adds to the health benefits.

preparation time: **25 minutes**

cooking time: **30 minutes**

serves **4**

NUTRIENTS PER SERVING	
calories	400
carbohydrate	8 g
(sugars)	7 g
protein	32 g
fat	28 g
(saturated)	5 g
fibre	2 g

1 tablespoon olive oil

2.5 cm (1 in) piece of root ginger, peeled and grated

1 onion, chopped

1 red pepper, deseeded and chopped

400 g (14 oz) canned chopped tomatoes

125 g (4½ oz) spinach leaves, washed and roughly sliced

Juice of 1 lime

300 ml (½ pint) fish stock (recipe page 339)

4 mackerel fillets, cut into strips

Salt and black pepper

1 Heat the oil in a heavy-based pan, add the ginger, onion and red pepper and fry for 12 minutes until softened.

2 Add the tomatoes, spinach, lime juice and stock and simmer for a further 5 minutes, stirring occasionally

3 Lay the fish on top and cover the pan. Cook gently for a further 10 minutes, or until the fish is cooked through. Stir the fish into the other ingredients and serve in warmed bowls. Serve with chunks of crusty fresh bread.

brilliant black-eye bean curry

The beans in this dish melt in the mouth. They absorb a tremendous amount of flavour and yet hold their shape. This recipe conjures up the flavours of India and, despite its comprehensive list of spices, it is very simple to make.

preparation time: **20 minutes plus overnight soaking**

cooking time: **30 minutes**

serves **4**

225 g (8 oz) black-eye beans, soaked overnight and drained

2 onions, chopped

1 green or red chilli, deseeded and diced

2.5 cm (1 in) piece of root ginger, peeled and grated

2 green cardamom pods

6 black peppercorns

2.5 cm (1 in) piece of cinnamon stick

6 cloves

1 tablespoon olive oil

2 cloves garlic, crushed

1 teaspoon turmeric

1 teaspoon ground cumin

1 teaspoon ground coriander

¼ teaspoon chilli powder

3 tablespoons fresh coriander, plus extra to garnish (optional)

1 teaspoon garam masala

3 tablespoons lemon juice

1 Put the beans in a saucepan with half the onion, the chilli, ginger, cardamom pods, peppercorns, cinnamon stick and cloves. Cover with cold water and bring to the boil. Reduce the heat and simmer for about 50 minutes, until the beans are tender. Drain, reserving the stock.

2 Heat the oil in a heavy-based pan. Add the remaining onion and garlic and fry for 2 minutes. Add the turmeric, cumin, coriander and chilli powder and stir well. Add the drained beans and stir gently. Mix the fresh coriander, garam masala and lemon juice into the beans and pour in enough reserved stock to make a sauce. Heat through and serve.

NUTRIENTS PER SERVING	
calories	250
carbohydrate	36 g
(sugars)	6 g
protein	14 g
fat	6.5 g
(saturated)	1 g
fibre	5 g

alert and responsive

Building a solid frame

We think of bones as being hard, rigid and static. In fact, they are active, living tissue, made up of a rich mix of protein and minerals. What you eat has a massive influence on your bones' strength: the right food can help you to walk well and stand tall throughout your life.

The supportive framework for your body, the skeleton, is made of bones. Working in harmony with your muscles and aided by your joints, bones enable you to move around and also help to protect your internal organs. Building and maintaining healthy bones plays a major role in keeping you mobile and flexible.

Bone tissue is made up of a network of fibres, packed with bone crystals. These crystals contain calcium and various other minerals. About 700 milligrams of calcium enter the bones every day, deposited by the osteoblast cells, one of the two types of constituent cells involved in bone growth. The other type, osteoclasts, remove minerals from the bones.

DYNAMIC BONES

Bone tissue is replaced and built all the time, depending on what your body needs and what stresses it incurs. In a healthy body, there is a constant turnover of calcium and the body's supplies are kept in balance.

However, in conditions such as osteoporosis or brittle bone disease (see below) or during periods of

Busy stockrooms The mineral salts of calcium, phosphorus and magnesium in bones are constantly being broken down and built up again. This process is called remodelling, and is vital for bone growth and repair. Calcium can be released from the bones and used all over the body.

Food to build strong bones *A perfect choice for lunch or a light supper, the watercress, olives and grapefruit in Griddled Goat's Cheese with Coriander Salad provide a refreshing contrast of flavours. And the high levels of calcium help to keep your bones and teeth strong and healthy. The recipe is on page 52.*

prolonged immobility, this balance is upset: the rate of calcium withdrawn then exceeds the rate of calcium deposited.

Throughout childhood and early adulthood, bones not only grow in length and width, but also in density, as they accumulate bone minerals (see pages 145-146). It is this density which provides them with their strength. The stronger they are, the less likely they are to fracture.

The process of accumulating minerals in the bones continues for 25–30 years, when the density of the bone reaches its height. This point is often referred to as peak bone mass. In young, active people, a healthy equilibrium is maintained: supplies of calcium enter and leave the bones in equal measure.

Brittle bones With advancing age, more calcium is removed from the bones than is replaced. Your bones then become less dense, or 'lighter', making them weak and more prone to fractures. This is true for both men and women, but for women, the risk of developing osteoporosis in later life increases during

menopause (see page 181). This is because oestrogen plays a crucial role in maintaining bone density in women. Consequently, declining levels of the hormone during menopause leads to calcium loss.

The best approach to maintaining strong bones throughout life is to follow a healthy lifestyle, with a balanced diet and regular exercise. This was the conclusion of a 1998 United Kingdom Government report on diet and bone health. The report emphasised the value of eating foods rich in calcium and vitamin D.

CALCIUM – DAILY NEEDS

Many nutritionists recommend more calcium than the Reference Nutrient Intake (see page 341):

Both sexes, aged 4-10	*c.*550 mg
Both sexes, aged 11–24	1000 mg
Breastfeeding mothers	*c.*1200 mg
Both sexes, over 50 years	*c.*1500 mg

Good food sources of calcium include:

225 ml (8 fl oz) full-fat milk	290 mg
225 ml (8 fl oz) skimmed milk	302 mg
150 g (6 oz) low-fat yoghurt	285 mg
115 g (4 oz) fromage frais	89 mg
50 g (2 oz) Cheddar cheese	89 mg
100 g (3½ oz) roast chicken, **dark meat, without skin**	179 mg
100 g (3½ oz) roast chicken, **light meat, without skin**	216 mg
1 large egg	90 mg
1 medium baked potato in its skin	115 mg

Calcium – the main factor

Bones and teeth store about 99 per cent of total body calcium. The rest circulates in the blood. It is vital for cell function, transmission of nerve impulses to muscle fibre, muscle contraction and blood clotting.

It is sensible to obtain calcium from as wide a range of foods as possible, in order to benefit from their other nutrients. This is most important for lactose-intolerant people who cannot eat dairy foods, the major source of calcium.

Milk, cheese, fromage frais and yoghurt have high levels. Lower-fat dairy products such as skimmed and semi-skimmed milks and low-fat hard cheeses contain similar amounts of calcium to full-fat versions, but have less vitamin D. Canned sardines, salmon and mackerel are other good sources of calcium. The small soft bones of these fish contain particularly high levels. Calcium is also found in bread, breakfast cereals, pulses, sesame seeds and green leafy vegetables.

The sunshine vitamin

Vitamin D has a pivotal role in the absorption and utilisation of calcium. Although you can obtain it from food, most of the vitamin D the body needs comes from sunshine. The action of sunlight on the skin converts a chemical naturally present in the body into active vitamin D – which is why vitamin D is known as 'the sunshine vitamin'.

Once made, the active vitamin is stored in the liver for use during the winter, when less is generated because days are shorter and hours of sunshine are fewer. Most people make enough vitamin D from sunlight, but there are some groups who may not get sufficient amounts from this source.

Vulnerable people include children under four years old, people over 65 (especially if housebound) and people who rarely go out of doors or, when they do, wear clothes that cover their skin. If the food they eat does not supply enough vitamin D, a supplement may be required.

Lack of vitamin D can lead to rickets in children, a disorder with

symptoms which include bow legs, knock-knees and pigeon chests. In adults, vitamin D deficiency can lead to osteomalacia, a condition typified by aching bones, muscle spasms and curvature of the spine.

The richest food sources of vitamin D are oily fish such as mackerel, herrings and sardines. It is also found in butter, margarine, most low-fat spreads, full-cream milk, fortified milks, some fortified breakfast cereals and eggs.

Bran – a complicating factor

If you have low vitamin D levels and are also consuming very large amounts of extra fibre, such as unprocessed natural bran, your body's ability to absorb calcium may be reduced. This is because raw bran contains high levels of phytic acid, which combines with calcium and some other minerals in the gut preventing them from being absorbed into the body.

The role of magnesium Around 60 per cent of the magnesium in the body is found inside your bones and teeth; the rest is needed for transmitting nerve impulses, for muscle contraction and for enzyme activity in the body. Magnesium

deficiency is very rare because the mineral is widespread in foods. Wholegrain cereals, nuts, peanut butter, meat, fish and dairy products all contain good amounts.

Phosphorus for strong bones

Eighty-five per cent of the body's phosphorus is found inside bones and teeth in the form of a complex mixture with the body's calcium. Phosphorus gives strength and resilience to your bones because, in partnership with calcium, it plays a major part in laying down bone tissue. So, although this process is known as calcification, it could more accurately be called mineralisation. Phosphorus also releases energy from cells and aids the absorption of nutrients, including proteins.

Foods high in protein and calcium are generally high in phosphorus; this is true of milk, cheese, yoghurt, meat, chicken, fish and nuts. So, if you eat a varied diet and include foods containing calcium, you will get sufficient phosphorus.

Watch the salt It is now believed that your salt intake may have an effect on the health of your bones. Controlled studies have shown that when salt intake is increased in women after the menopause, there is an increase in calcium lost in the urine. There is also an apparent increase in the hormones involved in moving calcium from bone tissue.

The reverse has also been shown: when salt intake is decreased, there is a reduction in the amount of calcium lost in the urine and there are lower levels of the bone-loss hormones. Anyone vulnerable to calcium loss would be wise to avoid foods high in salt and to reduce their salt intake (see page 59).

continued on page 50

Catch the sun It is particularly important to get outside in the sun during the winter months. And walking is a great way of building strong bones and muscles at any season of the year. Sunlight can work its magic on your skin, making vitamin D for your body.

steps to prevent
OSTEOPOROSIS

About one in four women over the age of 50 are at risk of bone fractures from osteoporosis, and one in twelve men are vulnerable after the age of 70. Women are more prone to the condition because they tend to have smaller, less dense bones than men and because their loss of bone mass speeds up after the menopause. The risk of osteoporosis is lower in Afro-Caribbeans than in white or Asian people, because their bone structure is more dense.

The impact of osteoporosis

In the United Kingdom it is estimated that osteoporosis is a contributing factor to 150,000 fractures every year. About 60,000 of these are hip fractures – they are most likely to result in a seriously impaired quality of life, or even death. Some degree of osteoporosis is an inevitable consequence of ageing and may be accompanied by pain

and disability. There are several factors which influence the extent and rate of the loss of bone density.

Eating sufficient levels of calcium and vitamin D will slow the onset of osteoporosis (see pages 44-46). But watch your salt intake. Anyone vulnerable to osteoporosis should cut down on salt in cooking and seasoning as it is linked with increased calcium loss. You should also moderate the amount of alcohol you drink – a high intake may reduce calcium absorption, accelerating bone loss.

Physical activity is very important. Regular weight-bearing exercise, undertaken two or three times a week, will strengthen bones and maintain their solidity.

The hormone oestrogen helps to protect against osteoporosis. While both men and women suffer bone loss simply because of ageing, hormonal changes at the

Osteoporosis is a progressive loss of bone tissue, causing a weakened bone structure and an increased risk of fractures, particularly of the hip, wrist and vertebrae. As decreased bone density is a natural part of getting older, everyone is at risk of osteoporosis, but it effects can be minimised.

PREVENTING OSTEOPOROSIS *Healthy bone tissue is dense. Take regular weight-bearing exercise and follow a diet rich in calcium to prevent progressive loss of bone tissue – this is particularly important for white and Asian people, and women after the menopause.*

menopause increase the rate for women. Hormone replacement therapy can slow this down in women. Cigarette smoking is linked with lower bone density and a greater loss of bone mass with age, so either cut down or, better still, stop smoking completely.

Bone-strengthening food

Milk and dairy products such as cheese, yoghurt and fromage frais are excellent sources of calcium, the nutrient essential for strong bones. Low-fat varieties contain about the same amount as full-fat and will help to keep your

weight in check. This, combined with regular exercise, will help you to maintain a healthy heart and a pain-free back. Soya products are also good sources of calcium (see pages 184-185).

• At every meal include one of these foods: bread, breakfast cereals, potatoes, yams, plantain, rice or pasta.

• Every day, in addition to potatoes, eat five portions of any kind of fruit and vegetables.

• Eat 2-3 portions from the following types of food every day: lean meat, poultry, fish, eggs, beans, peas, lentils or other pulses. These provide protein and essential vitamins and minerals for building bone tissues.

• Foods containing a high proportion of fat and sugar, such as crisps, biscuits, confectionery and soft drinks, offer little nutritional benefit; eat these very sparingly.

MENUPLAN
best for your bones

To make sure that your bones are solid and your muscles strong and supple, include these simple dishes in your diet. They are all rich in calcium and vitamin D.

TOAST TOPPERS *Sardines; poached or boiled eggs; smoked mackerel or trout pâté; grilled chicken livers; lamb's kidneys (thinly sliced).*

SNACKS *Baked potato filled with low-fat cottage cheese; an omelette filled with low-fat Cheddar cheese, asparagus or courgettes; a poached egg on a bed of spinach, sprinkled with Parmesan.*

DRINKS *Chilled semi-skimmed milk; Smoothies (see index for recipes); milkshakes made with low-fat ice cream.*

GARNISHES *Sesame seeds sprinkled over green salads or added to low-fat yoghurt; poppy seeds scattered over steamed pak choi or broccoli.*

FORTIFYING FISH *Grilled or griddled fish – try salmon, mackerel, tuna, or fresh sardines; or stir-fried shrimp, drizzled with lemon juice.*

Grilled mushrooms
Remove the stalks from 2 large, open-cap mushrooms, rinse, pat dry on kitchen paper, drizzle with olive oil, sprinkle with seasoned breadcrumbs, and place under a hot grill for 2–3 minutes. Serve on wholemeal toast. Serves 2

NUTRIENTS PER SERVING: Calories **140** Carbohydrate **22 g** (sugars **1 g**) Protein **5 g** Fat **4 g** (saturated **1 g**) Fibre **3 g**

For a quick snack, grill mushrooms with breadcrumbs

Shake those bones
However assiduously you try to build the strength of your bones by eating the right foods, there is another crucial element in the formula for success: regular exercise. Physical activity ensures that the nutrients you take from your food are then converted into bone. When you place your bones under stress during exercise, they become bulkier and stronger, and their overall mass and density also increases.

Exercise should be a life-long habit. Regular exercise before you are 30, when peak bone density is achieved, means stronger bones. After this, when bone density is lessened by the natural process of ageing, continuing to get plenty of exercise helps the bones stay strong.

Weight-bearing exercises such as walking or jogging are best because they put high levels of stress on your bones. But any extra physical activity is beneficial to your bones and these can easily be integrated into your normal daily routine (see page 99).

JOINTS AND MUSCLES
Bones give your body rigidity and support, while the skeletal muscles and joints that are attached to them enable you to move about.

There are approximately 600 skeletal muscles in the human body. When a nerve impulse is relayed to a muscle, a change in the electrical properties of the cell surface spreads this electrical signal to the whole muscle fibre. Calcium is released, and causes the muscle to contract.
Stay flexible You use muscles every minute of the day, even just to sit in a chair or stand upright. As with bones, exercise is the best way to maintain healthy muscles. Without exercise your muscles will atrophy (decrease in size) and you will lose strength, suppleness and flexibility.

Muscles are mainly made up of protein. Most adults need only 55 grams of this nutrient a day: this can easily be achieved by eating a varied, balanced diet, including foods such as lean meat, poultry, fish, cereals, dairy foods, nuts and potatoes.

Every time a muscle contracts it uses energy. The preferred source of energy for movement and exercise is glucose, which the muscle gets from the glycogen (a carbohydrate) and fat stored in the body (see page 278). A low-fat, high-carbohydrate diet with moderate amounts of protein, as recommended in the Five Food Groups (see pages 11-15), supplies the healthiest energy sources.

Back problems Backache has several causes, including inflamed joints, damaged vertebrae (the bones of the spinal column) or damaged back muscles. There is no magic food 'cure' for a bad back, but those foods that help maintain strong bones and muscles are good for the back, too.

Bad backs are often caused by poor posture, arising from sitting wrongly, and lifting heavy loads, such as shopping bags. Make sure you sit properly and that you learn how to lift objects without damaging your back.

HEALTHY TEETH

Teeth are made of the same material as bones, but they are more exposed to damage. The outer, protective layer of the tooth is made up of enamel. This is very hard, but can be dissolved over time by the action of acids in the mouth.

Bacteria living naturally in the mouth ferment sugars from food and drink and turn them into acids that can erode tooth enamel. This erosion can start from our earliest years, which is why it is so important to protect children's teeth from harmful foods and drinks as early as possible.

The best drinks for babies and young children are water or breast or formula milk. Up to five years, full-fat milk is best. The fruit acids in fruit juice, fruit squash, fizzy drinks and cola drinks can directly damage teeth. If you offer children fruit juice or squashes make sure that they are well-diluted, and avoid fizzy drinks and colas. Sugars eaten as part of a

meal, rather than between meals, do less damage, especially if children brush their teeth after they have eaten. Chewing sugar-free gum is good for young teeth. The sweetener, xylitol, stimulates saliva, which helps clear food particles, and also reduces bacteria in the mouth.

In the United Kingdom, current figures show that 15-year-olds have an average of 2.5 teeth filled or extracted through preventable decay. Everyone should avoid foods high in sucrose (common white sugar) which is quickly converted into acid. The sugars found in fruit (fructose) and milk (lactose) are less harmful.

Good oral hygiene For healthy teeth and gums, try to brush your teeth twice a day (toothpaste with fluoride helps to prevent decay) and visit a dentist and hygienist regularly. If you have sore gums, try a herbal mouthwash. An infusion of sage, cloves or rosemary is soothing and also freshens the breath.

FISH OILS, *such as cod liver oil and halibut oil, are important sources of omega-3 fatty acids, and of vitamins A and D, all of which are essential for healthy joints, but you need only small daily amounts. Current advice is that eating oily fish at least once a week is the best way to obtain enough omega-3 fatty acids.*

EVENING PRIMROSE OIL *contains gammalinolenic acid (GLA), an effective anti-inflammatory agent. This makes it helpful for people with arthritis. It is often combined with fish oil in capsules. Starflower oil has similar properties and contains even higher levels of GLA.*

SOYA BEAN OIL *(left) contains a mix of omega-6 and omega-3 fatty acids. Both fatty acids have anti-inflammatory properties, and may help to alleviate the symptoms of rheumatoid arthritis, an inflammatory disorder of the joints. Safflower, sunflower, corn and wheatgerm oils are other rich sources of omega-6; and the oil in nuts and peanuts is also beneficial.*

EAT TO BEAT painful joints

griddled **goat's cheese** with coriander **salad**

Velvety goat's cheese is griddled gently and served on a bed of coriander-flavoured salad leaves. The sharp flavours of grapefruit and olives complete this simple but attractive salad.

preparation time: **10 minutes**

cooking time: **10 minutes**

serves **2**

NUTRIENTS PER SERVING	
calories	320
carbohydrate	9 g
(sugars)	9 g
protein	9 g
fat	27 g
(saturated)	8 g
fibre	3 g

100 g (3½ oz) round goat's cheese, halved
    horizontally
75 g (2¾ oz) watercress
1 pink grapefruit, flesh only, segmented
15 pitted black olives
FOR THE DRESSING
3 tablespoons extra virgin olive oil
2 tablespoons lime juice
2 tablespoons fresh coriander, chopped
Black pepper
Pinch of sugar

1 Warm a griddle pan, lay the halves of goat's cheese on it and cook gently for 2-3 minutes, turning once, so that both sides are lightly hatch-marked.

2 Arrange the watercress in a shallow dish. Top the leaves with the cheese, grapefruit segments, and olives.

3 Mix the dressing ingredients together. Pour over the salad. Serve immediately, garnished with lime zest, if liked.

iced berry fruit **sorbet**

A refreshing ending for a rich meal, this iced dessert is made from strawberries, but you could use any other summer berries. If fresh fruit is unavailable, frozen will work almost as well.

preparation time: **10–15 minutes**

freezing time: **3–4 hours**

serves **6**

NUTRIENTS PER SERVING	
calories	285
carbohydrate	23 g
(sugars)	23 g
protein	4 g
fat	20 g
(saturated)	12.5 g
fibre	1 g

450 g (1 lb) strawberries, hulled
100 g (3½ oz) caster sugar
1 tablespoon lemon juice
225 g (8 oz) mascarpone cheese
175 g (6 oz) Greek yoghurt
2 egg whites
TO SERVE
Fresh strawberries and/or other summer
    berries

1 Put the strawberries, sugar and lemon juice into a food processor or blender, and purée until smooth.

2 Beat the cheese and yoghurt together, then mix in the strawberry purée.

3 Whisk the egg whites until they form soft peaks. Using a metal spoon, fold them gently into the fruit mixture.

4 Spoon the mixture into a shallow non-reactive metal or glass serving dish. Cover with foil and freeze for about 1 hour, until crystals start to form around the edges.

5 Whisk the partly-frozen mixture briskly or put it through the food processor again. Return to the freezer. After about 1 hour, repeat the whisking process. Repeat once or twice more, or until the dessert is smooth and frozen.

6 Scoop into long-stemmed glasses and serve garnished with summer berries.

tofu stir-fry **with satay** sauce and **wild rice**

This dish has an exotic Eastern flavour. Tofu, a good source of calcium, is perfect for stir-frying. It is used here with an aromatic satay sauce. Serve it on a bed of mixed basmati and wild rice, and serve the sauce separately.

preparation time: **40 minutes, plus 25–30 minutes marinating**

cooking time: **40 minutes**

serves **4**

FOR THE MARINADE

1 tablespoon light soya sauce
1 tablespoon Thai fish sauce
2 teaspoons sesame oil

FOR THE SAUCE

1 teaspoon sunflower or corn oil
1 small onion, finely chopped
½ teaspoon crushed garlic
125 g (4½ oz) crunchy peanut butter
1 teaspoon paprika
Pinch chilli powder
300 ml (½ pint) unflavoured soya drink

FOR THE STIR-FRY

150 g (5½ oz) firm tofu, cut into cubes
2 tablespoons groundnut or corn oil
1 clove garlic, crushed
175 g (6 oz) shiitake mushrooms, halved
1 tablespoon chopped fresh basil
½ teaspoon crushed ginger
1 red pepper, deseeded and cut into strips
1 green pepper, deseeded and cut into strips
450 g (1 lb) fresh or frozen Chinese mixed vegetables, defrosted if frozen
Few drops hot chilli sauce
55 g (2 oz) roasted unsalted cashew nuts, chopped, to garnish

1 Mix the marinade ingredients well, add the tofu and marinate for 25–30 minutes.

2 For the sauce, heat the oil and fry the onion and garlic until softened. Add the remaining sauce ingredients and heat through, stirring continuously. Remove from the heat and allow to cool.

3 For the stir-fry, heat a wok and pour in 1 tablespoon of the groundnut or corn oil. Add the garlic, stir-fry for a few seconds, then put in the mushrooms and basil. Sauté for 2 minutes, until the mushrooms are just cooked.

4 Remove the mushroom mixture with a slotted spoon. Put the remaining oil in the wok, add the ginger and stir-fry briefly. Spoon in the tofu and juices and stir-fry for 3-5 minutes, until golden.

5 Add the red and green peppers and stir-fry for a further 2 minutes. Then put in the Chinese vegetables and cook until they are just tender. Stir in the mushrooms, flavour with chilli sauce to taste and heat through. Serve on a bed of rice garnished with cashew nuts.

NUTRIENTS PER SERVING	
calories	485
carbohydrate	20 g
(sugars)	14 g
protein	21 g
fat	36 g
(saturated)	7 g
fibre	7 g

Every **beat** of your **heart**

If you want to keep your heart and circulation strong and resilient, there are certain foods that can help you to achieve this. Eating for a healthy heart makes sense at every stage of your life – and the good news is that this can be a pleasure for your tastebuds too.

The key to looking after your heart and circulation is simple. You do not have to cut out your favourite food – simply moderate your intake of the foods that are less good for you and fill up on the many delicious foods that protect your heart. Add to that a little extra regular physical activity, and you will see your health improve dramatically.

The heart is the strongest muscle in the body. It pumps tirelessly, moving blood around the entire body via the network of arteries and capillaries, and receiving blood back through the veins. Blood carries life-giving oxygen and nutrients around the muscular, elastic blood vessels to every cell in the body and takes away waste products such as carbon dioxide.

Durable though your heart and circulatory system are, they are not invincible: abuse them and they will eventually let you know by sending out distress signals. It is therefore absolutely essential to protect them from damage. Your diet can help you to do this, so now is the time to take a fresh look at your overall eating and shopping habits.

Healthy extra A drizzle of virgin olive oil adds a mouth-watering flavour to almost any dish; it is also great for your heart as it helps to keep cholesterol levels low.

A healthy heart and circulation pumps more blood around the arteries and veins with optimum efficiency. But a narrowing in one of the vessels impedes this movement of the blood. And in someone with high blood pressure, the heart has to pump against too strong a resistance.

Consequently, heart and circulatory (cardiovascular) disease may develop. You can use your diet to help to prevent this from happening. This means moderating your intake of fats, reducing your blood cholesterol levels, maintaining a sensible weight, and limiting how much salt you eat in order to help you to avoid high blood pressure.

The way in which you prepare foods will also affect your cardiovascular health, so it is worth experimenting with heart-friendly cooking methods.

BE CHOLESTEROL AWARE

Knowing about cholesterol makes it much easier to look after your heart. A type of fat, or lipid, cholesterol has several functions in your body. There are two kinds: the cholesterol in food and the cholesterol in the blood. Blood (or serum) cholesterol is manufactured in the liver and has little relationship to the cholesterol in food. It is essential for the creation of certain types of hormones, in the production of bile (needed for the digestion of fats), and in the

A healthy cuisine The Mediterranean diet is thought to account for the low rate of heart disease in the region. Olive oil, fish, fruit and vegetables and extensive use of rice, bread, pasta and cereals are typical of the cuisine, and far less meat is eaten than in the United Kingdom.

construction of cell membranes. The bad news is that cholesterol can also build up in the blood, where it may start to cause problems.

Excess blood cholesterol poses a risk to your heart. Oxygen-rich blood is delivered to the heart in the coronary arteries but, as you get older, deposits of cholesterol, fatty acids and other materials (atheroma) are laid down in the artery walls and form plaque. This hardens and causes narrowing of the arteries, a process called atherosclerosis.

The hardened plaque is easily damaged, so the blood cells form a protective clot around it. A large clot can block the artery completely, and if this occurs in a coronary artery a heart attack will result.

Lipoproteins In common with other fats, cholesterol does not dissolve in the blood, but is attached to a protein which carries it around the body. There are two major types of these cholesterol-carrying packages: low-density lipoproteins (LDLs) and high-density lipoproteins (HDLs). LDLs latch onto receptor sites produced by the cells when they need cholesterol; after they have absorbed enough they stop producing receptor sites. The surplus

LDLs stay in the blood and can irritate the lining of blood vessels. This causes plaque to form, a major factor in atherosclerosis, heart disease and stroke.

'Good' cholesterol HDLs are often referred to as 'good' cholesterol because they react with the excess LDL cholesterol in the tissues and arteries and take it to the liver for excretion. So, while excessive LDLs are harmful to your heart, HDLs fight to protect it.

Your doctor can measure your blood cholesterol levels by taking a small blood sample (home-testing kits are available from pharmacies, but these are less accurate). Blood cholesterol is measured in millimoles/litre (mmol/l). An overall cholesterol level of less than 5.2 mmol/l is desirable for adult men and women. Other, more accurate tests, can measure different types of cholesterol in the blood. Your doctor will help you to interpret the results and may also

Banishing the bad High density lipoproteins (HDLs) are widely known as 'good' cholesterol because they efficiently clean up and dispose of the excess cholesterol left on the artery walls by low density lipoproteins (LDLs).

advise you on changes to your diet. Other measures will help you to lower high cholesterol levels – such as stopping smoking, losing weight, if necessary, and getting more exercise.

BEST FOR YOUR HEART

A major aim of a heart-healthy diet is to lower the levels of harmful LDLs in the blood and to raise the levels of protective HDLs. If you have high blood cholesterol levels, you can decrease them by 25 per cent just by choosing a healthy diet. Although 75 per cent of blood cholesterol is made in the body whatever food you eat, this 25 per cent reduction makes all the difference in lessening your risk of developing heart disease.

Avoid saturated fat Some people believe that foods such as eggs, shrimps, prawns, offal (particularly liver and brains) and butter should be completely avoided because they are high in cholesterol. But these have much less influence over the level of cholesterol in your blood than the amount of saturated fats you eat. So, while foods that are high in cholesterol should be eaten in moderation, you needn't cut them out of your diet altogether: the cholesterol they contain is broken down in your body relatively easily.

Defining the fat

The basic building blocks of fats are called fatty acids. There are two main types – saturated and unsaturated. Foods are classified according to the type of fatty acid that predominates. Saturated fats are present in large amounts in foods such as butter, cream, lard, many processed foods, fatty meat, the skin on poultry, and also in coconut and palm oil.

Saturated fats stimulate the liver to produce LDLs, and eating foods with high levels will raise the LDLs in your blood. As this is potentially harmful to your heart, these foods should be kept to a minimum. Ideally, they should supply no more than ten per cent of your total calorie intake. Simple changes such as choosing the leanest cuts of meat, removing any visible fat and grilling or griddling make a great difference.

The healthier fats From the point of view of controlling your weight, you should limit your intake of all fats. But where possible, you should try to choose foods high in unsaturated fats. Unsaturated fats can be subdivided into monounsaturated and polyunsaturated fats. Oils rich in

monounsaturates, such as olive, rapeseed and groundnut oil, and foods such as avocados, nuts and seeds, will effectively reduce the amount of cholesterol in your blood.

Fatty acids

Polyunsaturated fats come in two main groups. Omega-3 fatty acids, which are contained mainly in fish oils, reduce LDLs and may be eaten freely (see opposite). Omega-6 fatty acids are mostly found in grain and seed oils. They are healthier than saturated fats, but are best eaten in moderation. Safflower and sunflower oils and spreads are rich sources. Soya oil contains both kinds: 51% omega-6 fatty acid and 7% omega-3.

There is yet another kind of unsaturated fat known as trans fatty acid. This results from the deliberate saturating of unsaturated fats to harden them for manufacturing processed foods such as margarines, spreads, biscuits and cakes. This process is known as hydrogenation. These fats not only raise the level of LDLs in the same way as saturates, they are also thought to lower the level of the good HDLs and may lead to blood clotting. Current advice is to keep these to a minimum.

WEIGHT WATCHING

Every extra pound on your body places a strain on your heart. This is why it is a good idea to watch your calorie intake. When you consume more calories in your diet than you burn, the extra energy is stored as body fat (see page 91). This may increase your risk of health problems such as diabetes, high blood pressure and high cholesterol levels. And these conditions can contribute to cardiovascular disease.

Apples and pears You can check whether you are a desirable weight for your height by referring to the Body Mass Index (BMI) chart on page 17. You can use this to assess the distribution of your weight. Measure the circumference of your waist in relation to your height, then look at how and where you are carrying any excess fat.

It is now thought that the shape and location of this extra weight may be more important than how overweight you are. This is the 'apple and pear' hypothesis: adding excess weight around the abdomen in an apple shape (the classic potbelly), is a known risk factor in coronary heart disease. Conversely, being pear-shaped – with extra weight on your hips and thighs – is less dangerous.

Men are more likely to become apple-shaped than women; this may help to explain why they are at greater risk of heart disease. But, as hormones appear to control the pattern of fat distribution, when the production of the female sex hormone oestrogen declines during the menopause, women then tend to accumulate apple-shaped abdominal fat. This increases the risk of heart disease, so women should pay close attention to diet and exercise at this time. For more on weight and shape changes during the menopause, turn to page 181.

Lean and healthy

One of the best things you can do for your heart is to shed any excess weight. Do this by eating a healthy, balanced, low-fat diet, and by taking regular exercise. To find out more on how to control your weight safely, turn to pages 97-99.

Physical activities – such as a brisk 20-minute walk each day – are doubly beneficial. They help you to shed unwanted weight, and also protect you from heart disease by improving the efficiency of your heart and lungs.

The balloons on pages 16-17 provide guidelines on how many calories you should aim to consume each day. If you need to cut down, avoid fatty foods (they are usually very high in calories) and choose those highest in unsaturated fats. Try to eat at regular intervals: this will help you to resist the temptation to snack on unhealthy, high-fat, high-

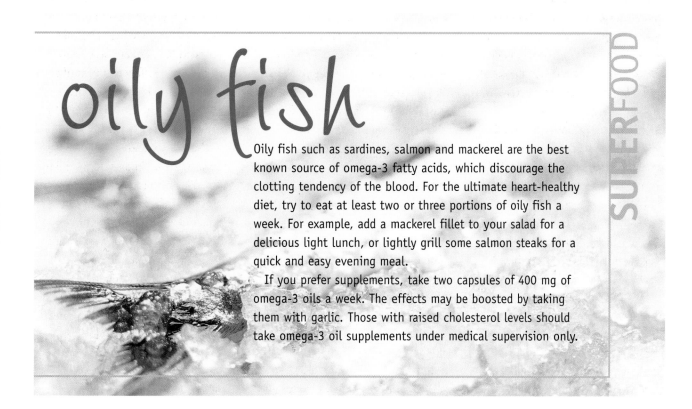

oily fish

SUPERFOOD

Oily fish such as sardines, salmon and mackerel are the best known source of omega-3 fatty acids, which discourage the clotting tendency of the blood. For the ultimate heart-healthy diet, try to eat at least two or three portions of oily fish a week. For example, add a mackerel fillet to your salad for a delicious light lunch, or lightly grill some salmon steaks for a quick and easy evening meal.

If you prefer supplements, take two capsules of 400 mg of omega-3 oils a week. The effects may be boosted by taking them with garlic. Those with raised cholesterol levels should take omega-3 oil supplements under medical supervision only.

calorie foods. Instead, fill up on bulkier carbohydrates, and choose fruit-based desserts rather than sugary sweets and cakes.

You should also be sensible about how much you drink: alcohol is high in calories and can, in excess, damage the heart. On the other hand, some studies suggest that small amounts of alcohol may protect the heart (see below).

Crash dieting and constant fluctuations in your weight can be just as harmful to the heart as being overweight, so it is better to take a long-term approach to weight control than losing too much too quickly.

DRINK TO GOOD HEALTH?

Evidence first began to emerge decades ago that people who drink alcohol in moderation tend to live longer than those who are teetotal. Now, after years of controversy, experts are telling us that a little alcohol is good for your heart. Indeed, recent studies have shown that one or two drinks a day can reduce the risk of heart disease by up to 30 per cent.

Alcohol is believed to help increase the levels of HDL cholesterol in the blood, thereby protecting the artery walls from the build-up of fatty plaques. It is also thought to reduce the level of fibrinogen in circulation. Fibrinogen is a protein that causes the blood to clot, so alcohol may help to lower the risk of heart attack.

While alcohol in moderation can be good for your heart, drinking to excess can lead to cardiovascular problems, such as abnormal heart rhythms and high blood pressure, as well as other serious diseases such as

cirrhosis of the liver and liver cancer. Remember that it is much better to pace your drinking and enjoy a glass or two a day – binge drinking is not good for you, and is not the way to protect your heart.

THE PRESSURE'S ON

One of the best ways to improve the health of your heart is to keep your blood pressure within healthy limits – it may be a good idea to have it checked annually. Contributing factors to high blood pressure or hypertension include poor fitness, being overweight, eating too much salt and drinking too much alcohol.

The higher your blood pressure, the harder your heart has to pump. High blood pressure is the most common risk factor in heart and circulatory disease. This is because it makes the heart work harder, as well as making the arteries increasingly susceptible to atherosclerosis.

HEALTH OR HYPE?
drink red wine for your heart

The alleged benefits of red wine are based on the relatively low rate of coronary heart disease in France. It is claimed that, as the average French diet is high in fat, it must be their high intake of red wine that reduces heart disease.

However, although fat consumption in France is similar to the USA, the high level in France is relatively recent. Since it takes decades of eating a high-fat, high-cholesterol diet for the arteries to firm up, this means a time-lag effect is taking place, and in years to come the level of heart disease may be as high in France as America.

What studies do show, however, is that red wine confers no special advantage in itself. What does make a difference is your drinking pattern. The blood-thinning effects of alcohol are thought to last less than 24 hours, so having a small amount of wine each day is better than drinking a lot of it at once.

Just a drop *Balsamic vinegar (above left) has a rich, aromatic taste. Use it on food and you won't need to add salt. Lime juice (above right) is a perfect way to add zest and piquancy – just sprinkle a few drops onto your food – you'll find that this greatly reduces the need for salt.*

Deliciously seasoned *The broccoli in this dish (left) has been flavoured with nuts and soya sauce instead of salt. Soya sauce is lower in sodium than table salt, but even so, individuals with high blood pressure should halve the amount of soya sauce in the recipe for Nutty Broccoli on page 64.*

The role of salt According to some experts, salt raises blood pressure only in certain susceptible people. But it is difficult to judge whether or not you are one of these. It is best to favour caution and restrict the amount of salt you use. The chemical name for salt is sodium chloride, and it is the sodium which is harmful if taken in excess.

It is estimated that people in the United Kingdom consume at least ten grams (two teaspoons) of salt each day. Most of the salt you eat comes from manufactured foods. If you rely heavily on processed meals and snacks it is likely that you are consuming far more than this. To protect your health, keep your total daily salt intake (including manufactured foods) to six grams (just over a teaspoon). The following tips can help you to avoid eating too much salt.

• Measure the amount of salt you add in cooking and gradually cut down until a recipe that serves four people uses around half a teaspoon.
• Avoid adding salt at the table.
• Experiment with other flavourings such as freshly ground spices, dried and fresh herbs, paprika and freshly milled black pepper.
• If you find it hard to become accustomed to less salt, you can try a salt substitute. Some leading brands of salt substitute contain two-thirds less sodium than ordinary salt, making them a practical and convenient way of reducing your salt intake. But you should avoid salt substitutes if you have a kidney problem: they contain large amounts of potassium which can damage diseased kidneys.

• Use low-salt products such as vegetables canned in water or unsalted bread and butter. These are widely available in supermarkets.
• For varied flavours try lime juice, balsamic vinegar, and chilli sauce.
• Read food labels carefully: salt may be disguised as sodium, or as sodium chloride, mono-sodium glutamate or bicarbonate of soda.
• Cut down on salty foods such as salted crisps, nuts and savoury biscuits. Choose fresh fruit, unsalted nuts and unsalted popcorn instead.
• Salted and smoked foods such as cheese, bacon, sausages, smoked fish, some canned fish such as anchovies and other processed

convenience foods are often very high in salt. Whenever possible, use fresh foods such as fish, lean meat, fruit and fresh vegetables, which contain only a small amount.

PROTECTIVE FOODS

Although there are some foods you should limit or avoid in your diet, there are many more delicious and nutritious foods that are positively beneficial for the heart.

The heart's bodyguards

Free radicals (by-products of body metabolism) can be over-produced by the body, and may attack cholesterol in the blood. Fatty deposits then start building up in the arteries, allowing cardiovascular disease to develop. Antioxidants neutralise the effects of these free radicals, and are essential allies in the fight against heart disease. Boost your intake of antioxidants by eating foods rich in beta carotene, such as spinach, carrots, watercress, and broccoli; citrus and berry fruits for vitamin C; and seeds, seed oils, margarine, avocados, nuts, wheatgerm, wholemeal bread and wholegrain cereals for vitamin E. To read more about free radicals and antioxidants, turn to page 118.

The protective nutrients

Some vitamins, minerals and other micronutrients offer specific protection for your heart.

Iron One of the main functions of the blood is to carry oxygen around the body. Haemoglobin, the red pigment in blood, transports oxygen. But it can only do this adequately if there is sufficient iron in the diet. Most adult women need between 12 and 15 milligrams a day (men slightly less). Pregnant women need extra iron (see page 167) because the foetus gets its iron from the mother.

Deficiency of iron is the most common cause of anaemia, a condition in which the number of red blood cells falls below normal levels. This is most prevalent in adolescent girls and women in their reproductive years – usually because of menstrual blood loss. Men can lose blood too – from haemorrhoids and ulcers, for example, and this may place them at risk of anaemia.

You can obtain iron from a range of foods – although the iron in vegetables is harder to absorb. Your body will take up iron more efficiently if you consume vitamin C at the same time. For example, if you drink a glass of orange juice with spaghetti bolognese and a spinach salad, this will help you to make better use of the iron in the meat sauce and green vegetables.

On the other hand, tea inhibits your absorption of iron, so avoid drinking it with an iron-rich meal.

griddle

COOKFORHEALTH

Heart-friendly advantages of griddling

LOW FAT you hardly need to use any oil or fat, particularly with the many non-stick griddle pans on the market.

VARIETY there are many foods that can be griddled, including vegetables, fish, poultry and game, and various kinds of meat.

The method The basic method is simple – you sear food quickly in the hot pan on both sides to form a crust and seal in the juices. Buy a good quality pan to withstand high temperatures.

Flavourings Griddling food keeps in all the natural flavours, and you can add fresh herbs, spices, lemon or lime juice and balsamic vinegars for variety.

Red meat and liver are particularly rich sources of iron, but you can also obtain it from dark green leafy vegetables such as spinach and from lentils. Cooking food in cast-iron utensils such as a balti dish (see page 64) increases its iron content.

Vitamin B$_{12}$ Found only in foods of animal origin, B$_{12}$ helps to form red blood cells, and prolonged deficiency can lead to anaemia. You only need tiny amounts (1.5 micrograms) of the vitamin each day, and a varied diet will usually provide enough. Meat, poultry, fish, eggs and dairy products are good sources. But vegans should take a supplement, or choose cereals fortified with B$_{12}$.

Soluble fibre You can use fibre to reduce your blood cholesterol levels. It prevents the absorption into the blood of some fats and bile acids in the small intestine. Soluble fibre ensures that these fats are carried to the large intestine to be excreted. Lentils, baked beans, sweetcorn, peas, chick peas, black-eye beans, kidney beans, oats and citrus fruits are all rich sources of fibre.

Find ways of incorporating extra soluble fibre in your diet: for example, use beans and lentils to extend meat dishes, as in chilli con carne, or base meals on pulses, as in Red Lentil Dhal (see recipe page 64). Oat-based cereals such as muesli and porridge oats are excellent choices for breakfast.

Plant pigments Most fruit and vegetables contain pigments known as flavonoids (or bioflavonoids). There are over 4000 kinds and their protective power is thought to be due to their antioxidant action – they have been positively linked to a lower risk of heart disease and

stroke. The highest levels are found in vividly coloured fruit and vegetables. A single fruit such as an apricot contains a wide range of flavonoids, and 40 different kinds have been isolated in lemons and other citrus fruits. Carrots, spinach broccoli, red grapes and green tea also contain abundant amounts.

Lycopene The red pigment present in tomatoes and red peppers is called lycopene, and this is now regarded

as a supremely powerful antioxidant. It has been shown to be even more potent in preventing heart disease than beta carotene. More research is needed in order to see exactly how lycopene functions. It is released from food during cooking, so ketchup, purée, foods canned in tomato sauce and tomato topping on pizzas may all significantly reduce the risk of heart disease. For more on lycopene turn to page 111.

MENUPLAN
for a healthy heart

Eat to your heart's content and stay in tip-top health by eating foods that are both delicious and good for you.

A GOOD START Make a fresh fruit cocktail; or whip berry fruits into porridge oats and top with low-fat fromage frais. Slice fresh fruit into muesli which has no added sugar or salt; eat wholemeal toast with reduced-fat olive oil spread; and enjoy an occasional kipper or poached egg.

SNACKS Munch on a muesli bar or a handful of unsalted popcorn.

POSITIVE CHOICES Fish is very good for the heart — try Mediterranean Salmon (recipe page 65). Cook chicken without the skin, and serve with salads and fresh vegetables. Flavour vegetables such as roasted peppers, broccoli and green beans with a sprinkling of sesame seeds.

DESSERTS Top fresh fruit salad with reduced-fat ice cream.

Sweet new potatoes are delicious eaten in their skin

Folates are also good for your heart. Population studies in the USA show that people who consume high levels of folic acid are less likely to suffer from heart disease (particularly heart attacks). Green leafy vegetables, pulses, fortified cereals and liver are all rich sources of folic acid.

The power of potassium Middle-aged men following a diet rich in potassium are less likely to die of heart disease. A major survey in Boston, USA, studied 40,000 men for eight years. In total, they suffered 328 strokes. The men with the lowest intakes of potassium were almost twice as likely to have a stroke compared to those with the

Foods that help your heart Griddled fresh vegetables are a pleasure to eat and full of flavour. This method uses hardly any oil and the results are delicious. The peppers all contain heart-protective flavonoids, and the red ones also contain lycopene, a highly effective antioxidant.

The choice is yours Think of versatile ways to serve foods. For example, this spicy Red Lentil Dhal (right). Here it is folded inside a light wholemeal wrap; but it can also be served on Indian naan bread, or with rice. All these alternatives are beneficial for your heart. The recipe is on page 64.

highest intakes. These protective effects were greatest amongst men with high blood pressure. Foods high in potassium include bananas, oranges, potatoes, leafy green vegetables, pulses and avocados.

Protection from soya The plant oestrogens (called isoflavones) present in soya beans seem to act as antioxidants (see page 118). The cholesterol-lowering properties of soya have been known for over 80 years, but their heart-protective powers have only recently been discovered. The rates of heart disease are far lower in countries where soya is eaten regularly. Read more on the benefits of soya on pages 184-187.

PLANNING YOUR MEALS

A wide range of foods are good for your heart, so you have plenty of scope to cook meals that the whole family will enjoy. As a general guide to planning a healthy, balanced diet, read about the Five Food Groups (see pages 11-15).

Base your meals around complex carbohydrate foods such as wholegrain bread, pasta, rice, cereals and potatoes (look at the recipe index on pages 342-343 for inspiration). These foods will ensure that even the hungriest members of the family feel satisfied, and have less need for high-calorie, fatty dishes.

Eat generous amounts of fruit and vegetables – at least three portions of fruit and two of vegetables each day. You can happily graze on fruit between meals without feeling guilty. Packed with antioxidants and fibre, fruit positively protects your heart.

Alternatively, accompany meals with a platter of fresh crudités (raw, chopped vegetables such as cauliflower, tomatoes and strips of peppers, carrots and cucumber).

Watch the fat Choose olive oil and other monounsaturated fats for cooking and salad dressings. And be very sparing with your use of butter, margarine, full-fat mayonnaise, and other spreadable or pourable fats. Try switching over to low-fat dairy products such as semi-skimmed or skimmed milk and low-fat yoghurts. However, make sure that children under five have full-fat milk and dairy foods (see pages 143-144).

Cut down on meat You may be accustomed to eating red meat every day, but you will benefit your heart and circulation immensely if you choose fish, skinless poultry or vegetarian dishes instead.

This does not mean that you have to avoid meat entirely. Modern selective breeding methods are producing animals with much leaner meat.

Beef and pork are particularly low in fat, but you should still choose the leanest cuts and, if necessary, tenderise the meat by marinating it before cooking. Lemon juice, wine, and wine vinegar are good bases for marinades. You can also make your own mince from high quality lean meat, or ask your butcher to do it.

Healthy cooking methods The way you cook and prepare meat or fish can reduce its fat content. Trim any excess fat from meat, and remove the skin from chicken joints. Also, try healthy cooking techniques such as griddling, grilling, poaching and steaming (see the index for details) instead of high-fat methods such as sautéing and deep-frying.

Use non-stick pans for cooking and avoid frying vegetables, or serving them drenched in butter. Cook them in a steamer or microwave to retain their vitamins and minerals, season with a twist of pepper, and garnish them with a sprinkling of herbs.

Keeping a check To maintain a healthy weight, try to reduce the amount of sugar you add to tea, coffee and desserts. And choose unsweetened fruit juices and reduced-sugar foods. Always check the labels on packaged or processed foods to make sure they are not too high in salt, sugar or fat.

Drink alcohol in moderation, and avoid drinking binges. Have a glass of mineral water, soda water or unsweetened fruit juice as your first drink of the evening. This will slake your thirst before you go on to wine, beer or spirits.

nutty broccoli

Fresh and full of flavour, the broccoli in this recipe is only just cooked, to preserve all its natural goodness. The enticing aroma of sesame oil and the crunch of the peanuts add a medley of unusual flavours and textures.

preparation time: **5 minutes**

cooking time: **15 minutes**

serves **4**

NUTRIENTS PER SERVING	
calories	330
carbohydrate	11 g
(sugars)	7 g
protein	17 g
fat	24 g
(saturated)	4 g
fibre	6 g

175 g (6 oz) unsalted peanuts
2 teaspoons sesame oil
1 teaspoon rapeseed or corn oil
450 g (1 lb) fresh or frozen broccoli florets
1 sweet yellow pepper, diced
1 tablespoon soya sauce
Coarsely ground black pepper
A few fresh basil leaves, to garnish
Black pepper

1 Dry-roast the peanuts in a pan for about 5 minutes over a medium heat until brown.

2 Heat a wok or large frying pan. Swirl in the oils and then add the vegetables.

3 Flavour with the soya sauce and black pepper.

4 Stir in the peanuts and serve, garnished with whole basil leaves.

red lentil dhal

This beautifully spiced dhal is versatile and delicious – you can serve it with hot Indian bread such as naan, or with rice. Vegetarian meals may be low in iron, so this recipe uses garam masala and a balti dish, both of which provide extra iron.

preparation time: **20 minutes**

cooking time: **30 minutes**

serves **4**

NUTRIENTS PER SERVING	
calories	230
carbohydrate	36 g
(sugars)	5 g
protein	14 g
fat	3.5 g
(saturated)	0.5 g
fibre	4 g

1 tablespoon rapeseed oil
1 onion, finely chopped
2 cloves garlic, crushed
1 cm (½ inch) piece of root ginger, crushed
250 g (9 oz) can chopped tomatoes
¼ teaspoon turmeric
½ teaspoon red chilli powder
1 teaspoon ground garam masala
1 teaspoon ground coriander
225 g (8 oz) dried red lentils
425 ml (¾ pint) hot water
Salt and ground black pepper
Juice of 1 lemon
55 g (2 oz) coriander leaves, roughly chopped

1 Heat an iron balti dish with a lid, or alternatively use a non-stick pan. Swirl in the oil and add the onions, garlic and ginger. Stir-fry for 5 minutes.

2 Add the tomatoes, turmeric, chilli, garam masala and ground coriander. Lower the heat and cook through for 5 minutes, stirring occasionally.

3 Add the lentils and hot water. Cover and simmer for about 20 minutes until the dahl is cooked but not mushy. Add a little more water if necessary.

4 Gently stir in the seasoning, lemon juice and coriander leaves.

mediterranean salmon

You'll enjoy the sunny flavours of the Mediterranean in this fragrant salmon recipe, cooked with an array of vegetables and pure olive oil. Serve it with new potatoes in their skins, or a crisp green salad and a chunk of French bread.

preparation time: **10 minutes**

cooking time: **25 minutes**

serves **4**

1 tablespoon olive oil, plus oil for greasing
1 small onion, finely chopped
1 green pepper, sliced
1 red pepper, sliced
600 g (1 lb 5 oz) salmon fillets, cut into
   4 pieces
3 tomatoes, sliced
2 cloves garlic, crushed
2 tablespoons balsamic vinegar
1 bay leaf
1 heaped tablespoon fresh dill, chopped
6 large basil leaves, shredded
A little salt and pepper

1 Preheat the oven to 190°C (375°F, gas mark 5). Lightly grease a shallow ovenproof dish.

2 Heat the oil in a frying pan and sauté the onions and peppers to soften.

3 Place the fish in the dish and layer with the other ingredients, including the onion and pepper mixture and season.

4 Drizzle a little more olive oil on top and cover the dish with foil. Bake in the centre of the oven for about 20 minutes until the fish is cooked.

NUTRIENTS PER SERVING	
calories	340
carbohydrate	7 g
(sugars)	6 g
protein	29 g
fat	22 g
(saturated)	4 g
fibre	3 g

every beat of your heart

The **breath** of life

Day after day, without your thinking about it, the respiratory system delivers life-giving oxygen to your body. Fruit and vegetables are your best allies in fighting respiratory infection and maintaining healthy lungs. Include them in your diet, and you won't run out of puff so easily.

Your respiratory system is a sophisticated machine designed to extract the oxygen from air and deliver it to your bloodstream. Air is breathed in through your nose and mouth and reaches your lungs via your windpipe (trachea) and the airways branching off it (bronchi). It then passes to tiny air sacs (alveoli) in the lungs. Blood vessels on the surface of these take up oxygen and release carbon dioxide, a waste product from the working of your body's cells.

Your respiratory system is self-cleansing – it protects itself from dirt particles in the atmosphere by filtering it through tiny hairs in your nose which trap foreign bodies and dust. The windpipe is also covered in mucus to trap any particles breathed in.

FOOD FOR HEALTHY LUNGS

People who eat at least five servings of vegetables and fruit every day have the healthiest lungs. This is no coincidence – the same nutrients from these foods ensure a healthy immune system (see page 117).

How do these nutrients benefit your respiratory system? It is thought that the high levels of antioxidant

HEALTHY BLENDS *Liquidised vegetables (left) will give you extra protection from cold and flu viruses. The immunity-boost is from tomatoes rich in lycopene and carrots high in beta carotene (vitamin A), a key antioxidant for keeping your lungs healthy.*

CITRUS FRUIT JUICES *are rich in vitamin C, which actively fights bacteria, while apricot nectar contains zinc which can help to shorten the duration of your cold.*

EAT TO BEAT a cold

vitamins C and E and beta carotene provided by vegetables and fruit protect your airways from infection by boosting your immunity. They also mop up free radicals, the by-products of oxidation and pollution and prevent them from irritating your airways. (For more on free radicals, turn to page 118.)

How antioxidants work Vitamin C helps to fight the bacteria that cause some respiratory illnesses and encourages the production of a natural airway-widening substance (called a bronchodilator) that makes breathing easier. Although this action of vitamin C is known, taking extra-large doses to prevent or treat colds is not a proven strategy; it is now thought that much of the extra vitamin may not even be absorbed. And there is no reliable evidence that it works to discourage colds.

Vitamin E is another powerful antioxidant and has a major role in the health of your lungs. Premature

Breathe easier Crisp, fresh crunchy vegetables make a colourful mixed salad super-rich in antioxidants that combat infections such as colds and flu. This is fine food for respiratory health – peppers contain beta carotene and aromatic oils which combat nasal congestion.

babies whose lungs have not fully developed are often treated with oxygen. They are also given vitamin E to prevent them from contracting a chronic lung disease.

Professional athletes are familiar with the virtues of vitamin E. Their intake of oxygen is greater than normal, so they run the risk of more oxidative (free-radical) damage to their cells. Vitamin E supplements have been shown to halve the risk.

Susceptibility to lung damage from air pollution and smoking can also be reduced by vitamin E; it is a powerful free-radical scavenger and is effective in preventing free radicals from damaging your membranes, enzymes, proteins and DNA.

Another antioxidant, vitamin A, is vital for the repair of cells, especially those forming the protective mucus lining of the lungs.

Beneficial mineral Magnesium has a direct action on respiratory health – it helps to relax the muscles of the airways. People who lack magnesium are more likely to have difficulty with their breathing than those who have high levels.

Zinc shortens the length of time that a cold lasts, and is therefore very useful. It is not known whether it helps to prevent colds, but many people claim that it is effective for this purpose too.

Finding the best nutrients

Some foods are richer than others in important nutrients that help to protect your respiratory system. You can get them from the following sources:

Vitamin C Fresh fruit (especially citrus fruits) and vegetables, and fruit juices are rich in vitamin C.

Vitamin A Fish oils, dairy foods, spinach, liver, carrots, apricots and margarine are good sources.

Vitamin E Seed oils such as corn, sunflower, safflower; the outer germ of cereals, olive oil, avocados, pears, muesli, nuts, leafy green vegetables, wholemeal bread, cereals and egg yolks are abundant in vitamin E.

Beta carotene Orange, red, yellow and dark green fruit and vegetables such as carrots, red peppers, spinach, mangoes, peaches and

apricots are rich food sources.
Magnesium is naturally present in refined cereals and vegetables, peanuts and wholemeal bread.
Zinc Lean red meat, liver, shellfish (especially oysters), egg yolks, wholegrain cereals and pulses provide plenty of zinc.

RESPIRATORY INFECTIONS

A throat or chest infection makes you cough. This is because any inflammation of the membranes of the windpipe and the airways branching off it irritates the nerves that trigger the coughing reflex. Usually this is an automatic action and is effective in unblocking dust particles from your airways. But the frequency is increased when you have an infection.

Coughing allows you to clear mucus and phlegm from your bronchi and windpipe and also helps to unblock your airways so that you can breathe more easily.

Virus transmission Sneezing is an involuntary way of clearing your nose of anything irritating the lining whether this is simply dust or a virus. It is also the means of spreading the common cold. And once it has left your body, it is free to replicate itself in someone else's.

Colds, flu and upper respiratory tract infections such as sore throats, tonsillitis, laryngitis, croup or sinusitis, are all caused by viral and bacterial infections. Viruses and bacteria also cause lower respiratory tract infections which affect the trachea, bronchi and lungs. These conditions include bronchitis, bronchiolitis and pneumonia.

A virus is an infectious particle that can reproduce itself only by invading and taking over a living cell. The invaded cell produces a protein called interferon, which stops the virus from spreading. Antibiotics have no effect on viral infections, only on those of bacterial origin.

Bacteria are tiny micro-organisms found all around us – in air, soil, food, water and inside the body. Some, like the 'friendly' bacteria inside your gut, help to fight infections, but other bacteria cause illness. Examples range from pneumonia, which affects the lungs, to tonsillitis (inflamed tonsils).

Most colds are confined to your nose and throat. The symptoms are a runny nose and perhaps watery eyes, a slight fever, sore throat, a cough and various aches and pains. The lining of the respiratory tract becomes inflamed, and coughing may produce mucus. This can become phlegm if your cold turns into a bacterial infection, and your doctor may then prescribe an antibiotic to kill the bacteria.

Foods for respiratory health

Phytochemicals (plant chemicals) interact with the chemistry of your body to protect your immune

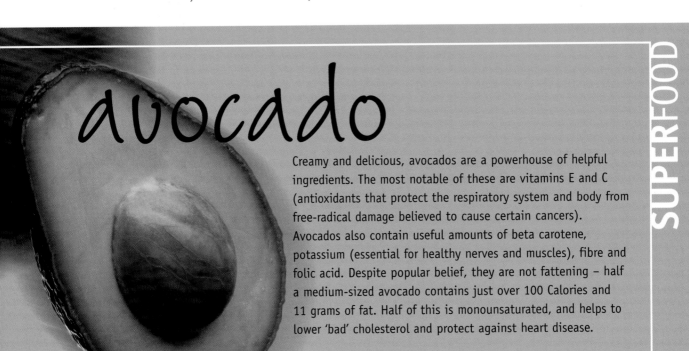

avocado

Creamy and delicious, avocados are a powerhouse of helpful ingredients. The most notable of these are vitamins E and C (antioxidants that protect the respiratory system and body from free-radical damage believed to cause certain cancers). Avocados also contain useful amounts of beta carotene, potassium (essential for healthy nerves and muscles), fibre and folic acid. Despite popular belief, they are not fattening – half a medium-sized avocado contains just over 100 Calories and 11 grams of fat. Half of this is monounsaturated, and helps to lower 'bad' cholesterol and protect against heart disease.

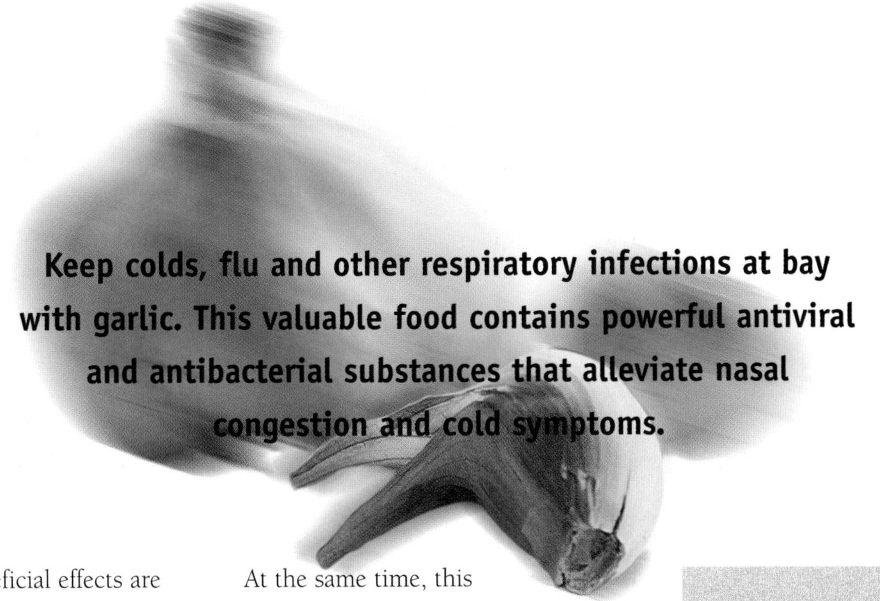

Keep colds, flu and other respiratory infections at bay with garlic. This valuable food contains powerful antiviral and antibacterial substances that alleviate nasal congestion and cold symptoms.

system. Their beneficial effects are impressive, whether they work in addition to, or in conjunction with, other vitamins and minerals.

Traditional remedies Garlic, onions and other members of the allium family are especially rich in antiviral substances. They have been used to treat respiratory complaints for centuries. Garlic and onions contain chemicals that act on the airways, either by helping to prevent constriction, or dilating them.

Ginger is a traditional stimulant used to 'loosen' phlegm so that it can be expelled by coughing, thereby relieving congested airways. Natural blackcurrant juice helps to ease a sore throat; this is because the blackcurrants are rich in flavonoids which have highly effective anti-inflammatory properties.

Marshmallow and comfrey teas both help to clear dry coughs. And a drink made with honey, a mild sedative that improves saliva production, and vitamin C-rich lemon, provides welcome relief for a sore throat.

Eating sizzling hot chillies will make your eyes and nose water. The combination of their dilating effect on blood vessels and the increase in mucus flow clears the congested airways caused by coughs and colds.

At the same time, this can also help to relieve a blocked nose.

A boost in immunity Live yoghurt is very helpful because it creates beneficial bacteria in the gut and these promote the production of interferon in your immune system. Interferon inhibits viruses from multiplying and increases the activity of lymphocytes, the body's natural killer cells. These help to fight off respiratory and other infections.

Cancer protection The role of soya and soya products in preventing cancer, including cancers of the throat and lungs, is a promising area of nutritional research. Soya's efficacy varies with different types of cancer, but you may like to look at ways to boost your intake of soya in order to benefit from its cancer-preventing properties (see pages 184-185).

Smoke damage

Cigarette smoking is very destructive to your lungs and immune system – the damage is done whether the smoke is inhaled directly, or through passive smoking. It has a suppressant effect on your immune system by increasing the production of free radicals (see page 118), and also by depleting the body's levels of protective antioxidants.

stop smoking

Giving up smoking is one of the best things you can do to protect your health. There are various ways to help yourself:

Restore your immune system Boost your antioxidants every day by eating five servings of foods such as carrots and red peppers (for beta carotene); oranges and broccoli (for vitamin C); sunflower oil and peanuts (for vitamin E); wholegrains and vegetables (for selenium); bread, nuts and seeds (for zinc) and liver for vitamin A and copper.

Satisfy your oral craving Need a cigarette? Reach for a glass of orange juice, or indeed any fruit or vegetable juice. Chew sugar-free gum; nibble on crudités; keep the fruit bowl full for snack attacks.

Avoid weight gain Don't replace one craving with another: avoid high-sugar, high-fat snacks; drink eight glasses of water during the day – and get more exercise.

Smoking causes or contributes to serious long-term damage, leading to cancer, heart disease, strokes and rheumatoid arthritis. Smokers need more vitamin C as well as massive amounts of antioxidant and B vitamins to combat the toxic effects. The best sources of these are foods that contain them. Supplements do not contain their naturally occurring antioxidant phytochemicals.

Air pollution from vehicle emissions, gas fumes and chemical pollutants produce free-radicals which may inflame your airways and make breathing more difficult.

Hot stuff to help you breathe freely
Foods such as fresh ginger root (above) and chillies (left) contain volatile aromatic substances that stimulate your body to clear congested airways.

Cut down on salt

Many people are surprised to learn that too much salt will make the airways more liable to contract, thereby restricting the flow of oxygen to the lungs. This contraction response is more common in males. However, both men and women suffering from respiratory problems have shown marked improvements when they cut their consumption of salt by half.

Alcohol and caffeine may also cause the airways to constrict. But individuals react differently and in many cases these substances can actively dilate the airways.

Improving lung capacity

It is well established that the efficiency and health of your lungs are directly affected by what food you eat. People who consume at least five servings of vegetables and fruit daily have better lung function than those eating lower amounts.

Your lung power or how much dynamic 'puff' you have in your lungs can be accurately measured with specialist equipment. Researchers used this to assess the lung capacity of 3000 middle-aged men from Finland, the Netherlands and Italy.

The results were clear: those with the highest scores had above-average intakes of antioxidant vitamins. These came from a varied range of fruit and vegetables in the diet.

In Finland, vitamin E intake was above average; the main source was from vegetable oils, and wild berries such as blueberries provided vitamin C. In Italy the antioxidant link was with the vitamin C in fruit. In the Netherlands the key antioxidant vitamin was beta carotene contained

MENUPLAN
take a deep breath

For a healthy respiratory system and increased lung power, eat foods which contain powerful nutrients that protect your immune system. Follow the general tips below, and look at the index for more recipes.

ESSENTIAL GUIDELINES Drink plenty of fluid (at least eight glasses throughout the day) — more if you have a cold; make sure that you eat at least five portions of vegetables and fruit a day.

FOODS FOR COLDS AND FLU Add chilli, garlic and ginger to vegetable stir-fries and seafood soups; compose salad platters from vitamin-rich vegetables such as peppers, carrots, broccoli florets, watercress and spring onions; and create mixed fruit platters. Fill half an avocado with prawns, drizzle with olive oil and a squeeze of lime.

IMMUNITY BOOSTING DRINKS Blend combinations of vegetables or fruits for protection against colds; drink hot blackcurrant and honey cordials; or drink freshly squeezed lemon and honey.

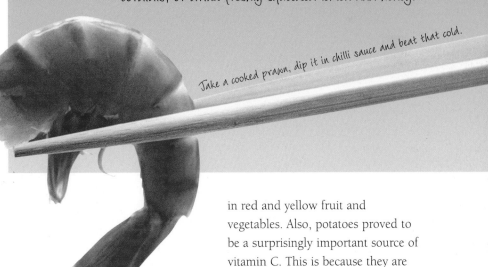

Take a cooked prawn, dip it in chilli sauce and beat that cold.

in red and yellow fruit and vegetables. Also, potatoes proved to be a surprisingly important source of vitamin C. This is because they are eaten in large quantities in the Netherlands (as they are in the United Kingdom), and so contribute a significant amount of the vitamin to the diet. This is even more pronounced if potatoes are eaten in their skins, which contain more vitamin C than the flesh.

roast poussins with shallots and garlic

Infused with the aromatic essences of garlic and shallots, these miniature chickens smell and taste delicious. Allow one bird for each person and serve with steamed mixed vegetables as well as the roasted shallots and a piece of crispy Parma ham.

preparation time: **10 minutes**

cooking time: **45 minutes**

serves **4**

NUTRIENTS PER SERVING	
calories	450
carbohydrate	8 g
(sugars)	5 g
protein	37 g
fat	30 g
(saturated)	9 g
fibre	1.5 g

12 cloves garlic
4 oven-ready poussins, each about
*   400 g (14 oz)*
1 lemon, cut in half
2 tablespoons olive oil
Salt and black pepper
16 sage leaves
16 shallots, peeled
4 slices of Parma ham

1 Heat the oven to 220ºC (425ºF, gas mark 7). Put the garlic cloves in the bottom of a non-corrosive roasting tin, and arrange the poussins on top, breast sides up. Squeeze some lemon juice over the poussins, then rub them all over with the lemon halves. Coat each bird with olive oil and season with salt and pepper to taste. Arrange four sage leaves on each poussin breast, and surround with the shallots.

2 Roast in the centre of the oven for 30 minutes, until golden brown. Baste with the pan juices. Roast for a further 10 minutes, then place 1 slice of ham on each poussin. Roast for 5 minutes, or until the juices run clear when the thickest part of the thigh is pierced.

3 Remove from the oven. Discard the garlic cloves, and leave the poussins, shallots and ham in a warm place for 5 minutes before serving. Meanwhile, skim off any excess fat from the pan juices, and transfer the aromatic gravy to a jug to serve separately.

melon with berry fruit coulis

You can use fresh or frozen berries for this colourful dessert – the nutrient content is the same. But, for the widest range of vitamins, try to include lots of different varieties such as blackberries, blackcurrants, redcurrants, raspberries and strawberries.

preparation time: **15 minutes**

cooking time: **5 minutes**

serves **4**

450 g (1 lb) fresh or frozen berries such as blackberries, blackcurrants, raspberries, strawberries, defrosted if frozen; reserve a few whole fruits to decorate

1 generous sprig of fresh mint

2 tablespoons blackcurrant jam or redcurrant jelly

½ Cantaloupe or similar orange-fleshed melon, deseeded, sliced and peeled

½ Galia melon, prepared as for Cantaloupe

1 Put the berries and mint in a pan with 2 tablespoons of water and bring gently to simmering point. Allow the juices to run for a few minutes then transfer the fruit to a sieve or food processor with the jam or jelly. Sieve or process the fruit to make a coulis (fruit sauce).

2 Arrange the melon slices on a serving dish, decorate with the reserved fruit and offer the sauce separately.

3 Serve with natural yoghurt or vanilla ice cream. It is also good with a thin slice of almond or polenta cake or *langue du chat* or biscotti biscuits.

NUTRIENTS PER SERVING	
calories	100
carbohydrate	24 g
(sugars)	24 g
protein	2 g
fat	0
(saturated)	0
fibre	2 g

chinese chilli prawns

This recipe is positively warming but there is plenty of scope for increasing the chilli content, if you like it really hot. Small chillies are fiercer than larger ones. For extra heat, add a dash or two of Tabasco sauce to the dish with the prawns.

preparation time: **15 minutes**

cooking time: **25 minutes**

serves **4**

1 tablespoon olive oil

1 onion, chopped

1 clove garlic, crushed

2 red chillies, deseeded and sliced

1 green pepper, deseeded and chopped

1 red pepper, deseeded and chopped

¼ teaspoon chilli powder or cayenne pepper

1 tablespoon white wine vinegar

400 g (14 oz) canned chopped tomatoes

250 g (9 oz) cooked and peeled prawns, defrosted if frozen

2 heads of pak choi or Swiss chard, washed and shredded, or 125 g (4½ oz) spinach leaves

1 Heat the oil in a heavy-based pan. Add the onion, garlic, chillies, peppers and chilli powder and sauté over medium-high heat for 12 minutes, or until the onion and peppers are softened.

2 Stir in the vinegar and tomatoes and cook for 15 minutes, uncovered. Add the prawns and pak choi and cook for a further 5 minutes.

3 Serve with cellophane rice noodles dressed with a little rice vinegar.

NUTRIENTS PER SERVING	
calories	140
carbohydrate	12 g
(sugars)	11 g
protein	14 g
fat	4 g
(saturated)	0.5 g
fibre	3 g

The **inside** story

A good digestive system is the cornerstone of your health and sense of well-being, so it's important to look after it. Choosing the right foods is the best way of ensuring that your digestion functions at its best and that you get the maximum benefit from what you eat.

The process of digestion turns the food you eat into the energy you need to live your life, keep your body working efficiently, and help you to fight disease. Your digestive health also affects how thoroughly you are able to absorb nutrients from food.

In 400 BC, Hippocrates wrote that 'a bad digestion is the root of all evil'. Most people take their digestive system for granted and are only aware of it when it goes wrong. Over half the United Kingdom population suffer from digestive problems at some stage. This needn't be the case, as there are simple ways to keep the digestive tract in good order.

GOOD DIGESTION

Our supply of nutrients depends not only on the foods we eat, but also on how well we digest and absorb them. To ensure a good supply of nutrients, the digestive system has to break down food into molecules that can be easily utilised.

Think of fibre first

Despite the fact that fibre passes through the digestive tract largely undigested, it plays a decisive role in helping you to stay fit and healthy. Fibre adds bulk to faeces and speeds their passage through the bowel.

In the early 1970s, doctors discovered that people living in rural African villages rarely suffered from digestive problems common in the Western world. Constipation, haemorrhoids, colon cancer and diverticulitis (a condition in which the intestinal wall becomes distended as a result of straining to move small stools along) were almost unknown.

They reported that the typical African diet, which was based mainly on unprocessed foods, contained around four times as much fibre as the typical British diet. As a result, the average time taken for food to pass through the gut was much quicker, and the faeces produced were larger, softer and easier to pass. They concluded that this was the

main reason for the different incidence of disease between the two groups. Since then, health researchers have confirmed that people who eat plenty of fibre are at less risk of cancer of the colon.

The rough and the smooth The term fibre describes a number of compounds that are found in the cell walls of plants. There are two kinds of fibre – insoluble and soluble. Most plant foods contain both types, but their proportions vary.

Insoluble fibre speeds up the rate at which waste material is passed through the body. This is believed to play an important role in preventing bowel cancer – mainly by reducing the length of time that substances known to cause cancer stay within the digestive system.

Wholegrain cereals, wheat, bran, wholemeal bread, pasta, flour, brown rice, nuts and seeds, and vegetables such as artichokes, beans, parsnips, broccoli and pulses are all good sources of insoluble fibre.

***Deliciously different** Use your imagination when it comes to varying the ways of including fibre in your meals. For example, try these Banana Muffins – they are made with wholemeal flour and fresh fruit and topped with whole sunflower seeds to provide a healthy, nutritious start to the day. The recipe is on page 86.*

bodyworks

Soluble fibre plays an active role in helping to lower high levels of blood cholesterol (see page 61). When fats are digested, soluble fibre binds to cholesterol and enables it to be eliminated in the faeces rather than being reabsorbed into the blood. Oats, oat bran, beans, pulses, apples, pears, cauliflower, carrots, citrus fruits, sweetcorn, pears, potatoes, sweet potatoes, barley and rye are high in soluble fibre.

Protective nutrients There is now good evidence that people who regularly eat plenty of fruit and vegetables are much less likely to develop cancer of the colon. The protective effect of these foods is powerful. It is due not only to their abundant fibre content, but also to a group of compounds they contain (called phytochemicals). So, by eating fruit and vegetables you gain multiple health benefits.

How your digestion works

It takes between 2 and 72 hours to complete the digestive process, depending on what you have eaten (particularly the fibre content) and how much. Lifestyle factors such as the amount of exercise you take and how much sleep you have can also exert an influence, as can genetic tendencies and your overall health.

Digestion begins even before food enters the mouth – the very sight, smell or thought of food is enough to stimulate your digestive juices. Each morsel is broken down by the

The digestive machine Your food's digestive journey starts in your mouth. Your teeth grind and break it down, helped by your saliva which contains specialised enzymes. This is the first stage of converting starchy substances in the food into absorbable nutrients.

teeth and mixed with saliva. This contains enzymes which begin the breakdown of starch into nutrients that can eventually be absorbed across the gut and into the bloodstream

Most of the digestion and the absorption of nutrients takes place in the first part of the small intestine. Digestive juices from the pancreas and gall bladder continue the process. Proteins, fats and carbohydrates are broken down into smaller units, such as amino acids, fatty acids, simple sugars, vitamins and minerals. These are passed into the

1 Add beans and pulses to soups or casseroles.

2 Eat wholemeal bread, pasta, fibre-rich breakfast cereal, and brown rice.

3 Use wholemeal flour for baking.

4 Snack on ready-to-eat dried fruits or add them to your breakfast cereal.

5 Aim to eat at least five servings of fruit and vegetables daily – and eat the skins as well.

WHOLEMEAL BREAD *Eating wholemeal bread every day is one of the simplest ways of increasing your fibre intake. Don't buy brown bread by mistake though – it is not made from wholegrains, and neither is white bread.*

FIVE WAYS TO increase your fibre intake

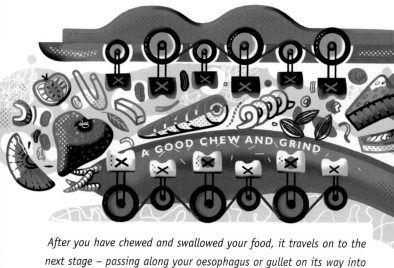

A GOOD CHEW AND GRIND

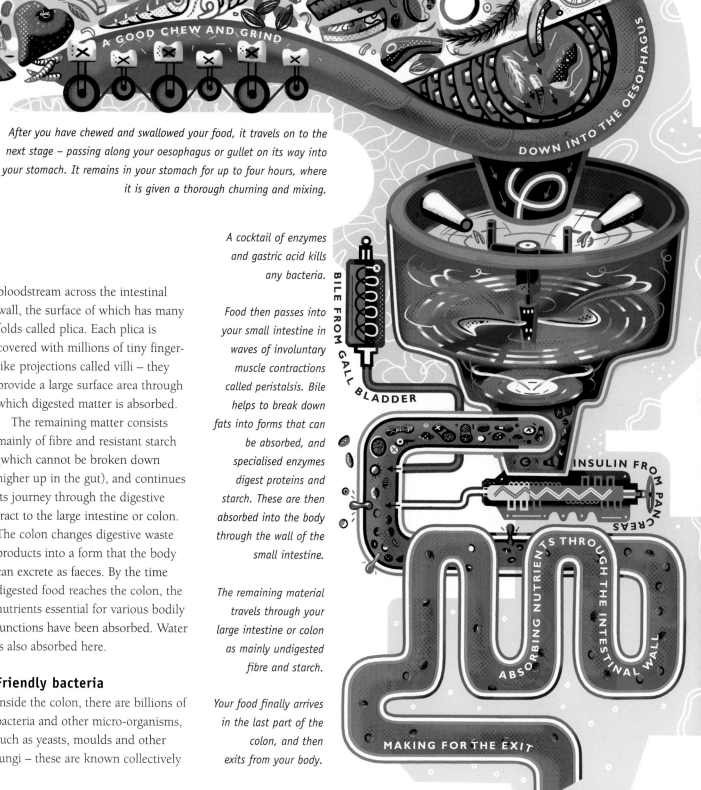

DOWN INTO THE OESOPHAGUS

BILE FROM GALL BLADDER

INSULIN FROM PANCREAS

ABSORBING NUTRIENTS THROUGH THE INTESTINAL WALL

MAKING FOR THE EXIT

After you have chewed and swallowed your food, it travels on to the next stage – passing along your oesophagus or gullet on its way into your stomach. It remains in your stomach for up to four hours, where it is given a thorough churning and mixing.

A cocktail of enzymes and gastric acid kills any bacteria.

Food then passes into your small intestine in waves of involuntary muscle contractions called peristalsis. Bile helps to break down fats into forms that can be absorbed, and specialised enzymes digest proteins and starch. These are then absorbed into the body through the wall of the small intestine.

The remaining material travels through your large intestine or colon as mainly undigested fibre and starch.

Your food finally arrives in the last part of the colon, and then exits from your body.

bloodstream across the intestinal wall, the surface of which has many folds called plica. Each plica is covered with millions of tiny finger-like projections called villi – they provide a large surface area through which digested matter is absorbed.

The remaining matter consists mainly of fibre and resistant starch (which cannot be broken down higher up in the gut), and continues its journey through the digestive tract to the large intestine or colon. The colon changes digestive waste products into a form that the body can excrete as faeces. By the time digested food reaches the colon, the nutrients essential for various bodily functions have been absorbed. Water is also absorbed here.

Friendly bacteria

Inside the colon, there are billions of bacteria and other micro-organisms, such as yeasts, moulds and other fungi – these are known collectively

as the gut flora. In a healthy gut, the largest groups of micro-organisms are lactobacilli and bifidobacteria. These are 'good' bacteria: they help to break down some of the remaining undigested food, and also synthesise vitamin K and small amounts of the B vitamins, B_{12} and biotin.

There is increasing evidence that specific by-products of this bacterial fermentation may help to protect the colon against cancer, and may also help to strengthen the immune system. But the natural ecosystem of flora in the gut is very easily upset by factors such as poor diet, stress and certain drugs such as antibiotics.

Any imbalance may allow yeasts, such as *Candida albicans,* and other potentially harmful organisms to grow, resulting in problems such as thrush, food intolerance and other digestive disorders such as diarrhoea.

The treatment of yeast infection is usually straightforward – your doctor will prescribe medication to deal with this. But many alternative practitioners advise a strict sugar and yeast-free diet.

Acidophilus supplements can be used to reinstate friendly bacteria and help to restore a healthy balance. They are available from pharmacies and health food stores. Follow the instructions on the label for advice on how to use acidophilus – and once you have opened the container, keep it in the refrigerator.

Encouraging helpful bacteria Foods and supplements that contain friendly bacteria are called probiotics. Probiotic foods include live yoghurt as well as fermented foods such as sauerkraut, buttermilk and miso (a soya product). Certain foods, such as artichokes,

asparagus, onions, chicory, leeks, onions, garlic, wheat, rye, barley, bananas and tomatoes, contain a type of dietary fibre that stimulates growth of the friendly bifidobacteria and lactobacillus in the gut, while inhibiting the growth of bad bacteria. Foods and supplements containing this fibre are called prebiotics.

A steady supply of energy

Some foods enable you to feel full for longer, as well as keeping your levels of blood sugar constant (see pages 103-104). This is because they are digested and absorbed by your body at a slower rate than others. For example, carbohydrate foods are digested, converted into simple sugars and absorbed into the blood at different rates. This rate is measured according to a system known as the Glycaemic Index (GI).

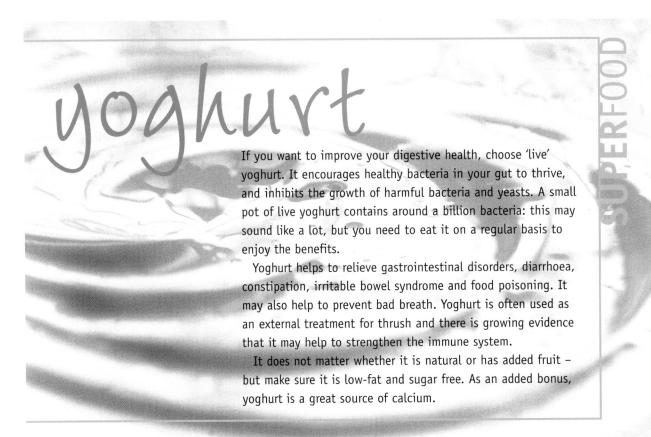

yoghurt

SUPERFOOD

If you want to improve your digestive health, choose 'live' yoghurt. It encourages healthy bacteria in your gut to thrive, and inhibits the growth of harmful bacteria and yeasts. A small pot of live yoghurt contains around a billion bacteria: this may sound like a lot, but you need to eat it on a regular basis to enjoy the benefits.

Yoghurt helps to relieve gastrointestinal disorders, diarrhoea, constipation, irritable bowel syndrome and food poisoning. It may also help to prevent bad breath. Yoghurt is often used as an external treatment for thrush and there is growing evidence that it may help to strengthen the immune system.

It does not matter whether it is natural or has added fruit – but make sure it is low-fat and sugar free. As an added bonus, yoghurt is a great source of calcium.

The food that is absorbed fastest into the bloodstream is pure glucose and this is given a high GI rating of 100. But foods such as kidney beans, chickpeas, lentils, butter beans, baked beans, apples, dried apricots, peaches, pasta and oats, yoghurt, peanuts, avocado, spinach and courgettes all have a low GI rating, which means that they are broken down a lot more slowly than other carbohydrate foods. Again, by choosing these foods, many of which are high in fibre, you have the extra advantage of the fibre while enjoying stable levels of energy.

Water – the benefits

Most people in the United Kingdom do not drink nearly enough water. But it is crucial for your well-being: ideally, you should drink around eight glasses of water a day. But this is only an average amount – people who are overweight, exercise regularly or work in air-conditioned offices need to drink even more.

Most people rely on thirst to tell them when to drink. This is a fairly good indicator of your need for fluid (apart from the elderly, who may have special problems – see page 194). But by the time you feel thirsty your body will already be slightly dehydrated, which is why you should drink at regular intervals. If you work in an office, for example, keep a bottle of water at your desk and take sips throughout the day.

Water is vital for many functions within the body – it is necessary for the digestion and absorption of food, and helps the elimination of waste products by the kidneys. Even mild dehydration can cause symptoms such as headaches, lethargy, dizziness and dry skin, and increase the risk of

MENUPLAN
focus on fruit

Say fibre and most people immediately think of lentils and kidney beans. But think also of fruit, which is a valuable source and also increases your intake of many important vitamins and minerals.

WHY FRUIT? It has fibre in every part of its structure — in its skin and its seeds — and is a much lighter source of fibre than pulses and beans. It can be eaten at any time of day — during meals or between, raw or cooked. Fruit stimulates the digestive juices, and is therefore a particularly good choice at the beginning of a meal. Start with something refreshing like melon or grapefruit.

BREAKFAST TREAT Dried fruits are particularly rich in soluble fibre, so for a fruity, wholesome start to the day, try the Spiced Fruit Compôte shown right (recipe below).

FRESH DESSERTS These can be sensational, especially when you indulge in an exotic fruit platter laden with such tropical delights as mango, pineapple and kiwi fruit.

Spiced Fruit Compôte
Place 250 g (9 oz) mixed dried fruits of your choice, such as apples, apricots, prunes, 1 stick of cinnamon and 3 lightly crushed cardamom pods, in a large bowl. Pour over 300 ml (10 fl oz) apple juice and 300 ml (10 fl oz) of boiling water. Allow to cool, cover, and leave overnight in the fridge. Remove the spices and serve with no-fat Greek yoghurt. Serves 4

Enjoy a mouthwatering fruity compôte any time of day

NUTRIENTS PER SERVING Calories **145** Carbohydrate **36 g** (sugars **36 g**) Protein **6 g** Fat **6 g** (saturate **4 g**) Fibre **3 g**

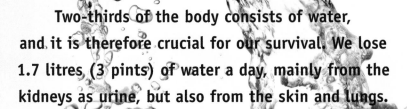

Two-thirds of the body consists of water, and it is therefore crucial for our survival. We lose 1.7 litres (3 pints) of water a day, mainly from the kidneys as urine, but also from the skin and lungs.

Drink copiously Water is a direct, simple and effective way of caring for your body. Try drinking one glass for every cup of coffee you consume to counteract the effects of caffeine on your system.

urinary tract infections, kidney stones and constipation. Although it is possible for humans to survive for around six to nine weeks without food, we can survive for only about three days without water.

Cleansing your system Some complementary practitioners and naturopaths believe that it is possible for toxins and poisons to build up and become trapped in the body, largely as a result of poor eating habits, pesticide residues, pollution,

alcohol and cigarette smoke. They also believe that this build-up of toxins can be responsible for various health problems, ranging from fatigue and migraine to irritable bowel syndrome (see page 84).

These practitioners often recommend special detoxification regimens which they claim will rid the body of accumulated toxins. The theory behind this is that they cleanse the system and allow it to excrete toxins from the body.

Many dietitians and doctors are sceptical about detox diets, as there is little clinical evidence to support their use. They are particularly doubtful about those involving extreme measures, such as fasting. They regard these diets as at best unnecessary, and at worst potentially harmful. But there are simple things that you can do to help your body's natural detox mechanisms:
• Drink plenty of fluids – between 1.7-2.25 litres (3-4 pints) a day.
• Take frequent sips rather than gulping down fluid – you may swallow extra air, causing bloating.
• Step up your intake of organically grown fresh fruit and vegetables.
• Base your meals around high-fibre, carbohydrate-rich foods, which speed up the rate at which waste

material is passed out of the system.
• Take plenty of exercise – waste matter is also excreted as sweat.
• Cut down on fatty foods, caffeine and alcohol.

AVOIDING PROBLEMS

There are many digestive disorders which can upset your good relationship with food and, as a result, take the pleasure out of mealtimes: constipation, peptic ulcer, indigestion, heartburn, stomach cramps, gallstones, hiatus hernia, irritable bowel syndrome and bad breath can be caused by poor eating habits. You may need medical advice for some of these conditions, but you can also do a lot to help yourself.

Don't become constipated

Constipation is a serious problem for many people. But while millions of prescriptions for laxatives are written every year, only two out of ten people in the United Kingdom eat enough fibre to meet the widely recommended target of 18 grams a day. You are liable to become constipated if you don't eat enough foods that are rich in fibre and drink insufficient fluid. Lack of physical activity is another major cause, especially in older people.

Constipation attributed to this combination of factors (called atonic constipation) is due to the loss of tone in the muscles of the colon. It can be remedied by increasing your intake of fibre-rich foods, drinking more fluids and by regular exercise. Compounds contained in foods such as rhubarb, coffee and prunes have a directly stimulant effect on the colon muscles, which is why they are often

PEPPERMINT TEA *contains substances that can ease spasm in the gut walls. Mint or peppermint tea made from fresh mint leaves is said to help improve your digestion and to relieve indigestion after a large meal. It can also help to control nausea.*

CARDAMOM *helps protect against digestive problems such as indigestion, flatulence, stomach cramps and can prevent acid regurgitation and belching. Cardamom has a delicate, spicy flavour and can be added to a variety of sweet or savoury dishes, such as curries, rice puddings, cakes and biscuits. But the* simplest way to use it to improve your digestion is to drink an infusion of the seeds after meals.

FENNEL *can also help to improve digestion and relieve stomach cramps. Fennel tea relieves nausea, flatulence and bloating. In India, toasted fennel seeds are chewed after meals to prevent bad breath. However, fennel seeds are also believed to encourage menstruation and should therefore be avoided by pregnant women.*

MANUKA HONEY (*above*) *is made from the flower of the Manuka, or New Zealand Tea Tree, and possesses strong antibacterial qualities. A dessertspoon of cold-pressed Manuka honey after each meal, and another at bedtime, can help heal stomach ulcers and kill bacteria.*

GINGER (*left*) *can be very helpful in relieving various kinds of nausea, such as morning and travel sickness. Some people find that sucking a piece of crystallised ginger or drinking ginger ale or ginger tea does the trick. To make ginger tea, simply grate a 1 cm (½ inch) piece of fresh root ginger into a mug of boiling water and leave to stand for 10 minutes before drinking.*

EAT TO BEAT indigestion

HOW TO MANAGE
peptic ulcer

A peptic ulcer is a sensitive raw patch in the lining of the stomach or duodenum (the first part of the small intestine). Around 1 in 10 men and 1 in 15 women in the United Kingdom suffer from a peptic ulcer at some point.

Symptoms range from mild discomfort to burning pain in the upper abdomen and, in severe cases, vomiting and weight loss. Always seek medical advice.

Excess salt, spicy foods and alcohol may increase your risk. Eat lots of fruit and vegetables to promote healing and to prevent further damage to the gut wall.

Nutrients that help to heal an ulcer include beta carotene, and vitamin C. Foods rich in zinc such as seafood and wholegrains help with healing.

any undigested carbohydrate and proteins. Mostly, this is not a serious problem – it is part of your digestive process, but if it becomes so uncomfortable that you feel bloated, there are various solutions.

If you have suddenly increased the amount of high-fibre foods in your diet, slow down a little – introduce these gradually and give your system time to adapt. Avoid eating too much food at a time and sip your drinks slowly – don't gulp them down all at once, as this makes you swallow extra air and may cause trapped wind.

Coping with indigestion

Also known as dyspepsia, indigestion causes discomfort in the upper abdomen, and almost everyone suffers from it from time to time. It is triggered by inflammation of the stomach lining, and can occur as a result of the over-production of stomach acid, over-indulgence in alcohol, or it can be caused by an infection. Pregnant women are particularly prone to indigestion because the uterus presses on the digestive tract as the baby grows (see page 167). Some drugs, such as aspirin, can also irritate the stomach.

Some foods are known to be less easy to digest than others and may provoke bouts of indigestion among susceptible individuals. The better-known culprits include hot, spicy foods, raw salad vegetables such as cucumber, radishes and onions, fatty foods, strong tea and coffee, and full-fat cheese.

How to avoid heartburn A burning sensation or pain behind the breastbone, commonly known as heartburn, is believed to affect at least 40 per cent of people at some

Avoiding heartburn If you enjoy oriental foods, give spicy dishes a miss and opt for milder variations – they are just as delicious. Ask for noodles, or boiled or steamed rice rather than fried. Using chopsticks also encourages you to eat a little at a time.

used to help relieve constipation.

Spastic constipation, in which the bowel movements are very irregular, may be caused by stress, nervous disorders, excessive smoking, some irritating foods and an obstruction of the large bowel. It is best to see your doctor if you have these symptoms.
Trapped wind One of the results of eating a very high-fibre diet may be that you suffer from excessive wind (flatulence). This is usually caused by the bacteria in your gut acting on

time in their lives. It is caused by acid stomach contents refluxing up into the oesophagus, which is the tube that connects the mouth and the stomach. Unlike the stomach, the oesophagus does not have a protective lining, so when it is exposed to acid, it becomes inflamed and painful. A ring-like muscle at the base of the oesophagus usually prevents acid from passing into it from the stomach, but if this muscle fails to work, acid reflux occurs.

heartburn

TO HELP PREVENT

Eat little and often and avoid large meals.

Have meals early in the evening to allow plenty of time for your food to digest before going to bed.

Raise the head of the bed six or eight inches. This will help prevent the acid from being regurgitated up into your oesophagus.

Avoid too much caffeine or alcohol and foods that you know from personal experience make the problem worse. These may include acidic fruit drinks, drinks with are too hot, spirits, fatty or spicy meals.

Avoid wearing tight belts or clothing.

Avoid bending down or lying flat after meals.

Don't smoke – smoking relaxes the muscles around the oesophagus making acid regurgitation more likely.

indigestion

Eat several small meals a day but don't miss any.

Take your time over eating and chew your food well.

Avoid fried and fatty foods and any other foods which you know cause you problems (many people find cucumber difficult to digest, for example).

Take paracetamol rather than aspirin for pain relief.

Control stress and avoid tense situations

Pregnancy, smoking, large meals late at night, obesity and wearing tight, restrictive clothing all increase the chances of heartburn.

Hiatus hernia Another common cause of heartburn occurs when a small portion of the stomach, which usually lies in the abdominal cavity, slips up into the opening where the oesophagus passes though the diaphragm. This is known as hiatus hernia, and if you suffer from this, your doctor will advise you. The condition is sometimes present from birth, but it is more common in overweight people, during pregnancy and among those who smoke.

If you have a hiatus hernia, avoid large heavy meals and try to eat four or five small meals a day. Avoid foods that may cause indigestion – fried or fatty foods, or acidic foods such as pickles and vinegar. Some herbs (rosemary, sage, tarragon, fennel, dill and mint) help the digestion, so use these generously in your cooking.

Try drinking teas made with them also – you can either make your own or buy them at health food shops or supermarkets.

Banish bad breath Unless it is a consequence of illness, bad breath (or halitosis) is usually caused by strong-smelling substances such as curry, garlic, alcohol or cigarettes. It can be eliminated by sensible eating habits and good dental hygiene. Constipation, ulcers and indigestion may all provoke bad breath, in

Sage is thought to be of particular benefit in aiding the digestion of rich, heavy food. It also helps to calm indigestion. Make a herb tea with it when you are suffering from indigestion.

which case it is advisable to increase your fibre and fluid consumption. Eat plenty of raw vegetables and apples to protect your teeth and gums, and nibble a few dill or caraway seeds after a meal. Chewing a sprig of fresh parsley is claimed to rid the breath of garlic and alcohol odours. If you cannot get rid of bad breath yourself, seek medical or dental advice.

Irritable bowel syndrome

Around one in three people in the United Kingdom suffers from irritable bowel syndrome (IBS). It is one of the most common medical conditions seen by doctors, and rivals the common cold as a cause of lost working days. Symptoms can vary from one person to another but usually include chronic intermittent abdominal pain and cramping, a bloated sensation, and a disturbance in bowel habit. This may take the form of constipation or diarrhoea, or an alternating pattern of both.

Although some doctors have dismissed IBS as being 'all in the mind', there is now evidence to show that it is accompanied by increased sensitivity of the gut, causing spasm of the bowel muscle. The reason for this hypersensitivity is still unknown but conditions such as stress, anxiety and depression may trigger attacks.

Although it can occur at any age, IBS is more common between the ages of 15 and 40 years. It affects twice as many women as men. Symptoms can vary widely, so what works for one person will not necessarily help another. Many people find that a high fibre diet is particularly helpful, although others discover that too much fibre can make their symptoms worse. Foods that are high in fat often trigger symptoms, as do very rich or spicy foods. Changing meal patterns may be effective (eating little and often, rather than having large infrequent meals).

Although some people feel their problem may be caused by a food allergy or intolerance, doctors believe this is rarely the case. Many people do find, however, that certain foods can make symptoms worse. Milk, bread, meat, coffee, sweetcorn, peas and beans are most commonly reported as trigger foods.

Alternative approaches Taking steps to deal with stress can be an important step towards preventing IBS. Relaxation techniques and various complementary therapies, such as acupuncture, meditation, yoga, and hypnotherapy, can all help to alleviate the symptoms. Massage and aromatherapy have been found to be very beneficial for IBS – mix five drops of peppermint oil with

four teaspoons of a neutral 'carrier' oil, such as almond or sunflower oil, which makes the essential oil safe to use. Massage it into the abdomen, using gentle circular movements. The rubbing action, combined with the effect of the peppermint oil, relaxes the colon muscles and eases the pain. You can also use massage to help to relieve constipation.

Aloe vera, slippery elm and evening primrose are other highly recommended massage oils. Many IBS sufferers claim that peppermint tea is helpful, while others find that antispasmodic drugs and laxatives relieve symptoms. Ask your doctor or pharmacist for advice.

LOOK AFTER YOUR LIVER

Your liver performs a wide range of functions: it processes and eliminates waste products and toxins; stores glucose as glycogen; regulates blood sugar levels; stores fat soluble vitamins; and produces and excretes bile acids and cholesterol.

Certain foods are particularly active in helping to keep your liver healthy. These include carrots, parsnips, beetroot, globe artichokes and foods rich in vitamin C such as citrus fruits and strawberries. Vitamin B_{12} found in liver, fish and dairy products, is also needed for good liver function.

Alternative remedies *A soothing cup of herbal tea such as peppermint tea (above) helps with the symptoms of bloating and also with digestive problems and flatulence.*

Gentle pressure *An aromatherapy massage (left) can work wonders if you have problems with irritable bowel syndrome (IBS).*

Painful gallstones Crystals of bile cholesterol or calcium sometimes form in the gall bladder. They are most common among people who eat foods high in saturated fat. About one in every ten people develops them in the United Kingdom. The chances of developing gallstones are increased by factors such as being overweight, a sedentary lifestyle, high blood cholesterol levels and repeated pregnancies.

The condition should always be managed by your doctor, and you should never try to diagnose it yourself. Gallstones may cause indigestion, particularly after very rich or fatty meals. They also cause inflammation of the gall bladder, which results in intense pain below the right ribs, bloating, wind, fever, nausea and eventually jaundice and liver damage.

A diet that is low in fat and rich in soluble fibre can help to relieve the pain associated with gallstones. It is also effective at reducing high blood cholesterol levels: and this reduces the risk of gallstones developing. Vegetarians are 50 per cent less likely to suffer from gallstones than those who eat meat.

Helpful herbs Many naturopaths and herbalists claim that cynarin, a compound in globe artichokes protects the liver and improves its performance by stimulating the production of bile. It may also help to prevent gallstones and reduce raised blood cholesterol levels. Cynarin is widely available in capsule form from most pharmacies and health food stores.

Silymarin, the active ingredient of the herb milk thistle, is believed to protect the liver by promoting the growth of its regenerative cells.

banana **muffins**

Luxuriously moist and fruity, these banana muffins are simple to make and are a real treat. Serve them for breakfast – they're a good, high-fibre alternative to the usual croissants or Danish pastries, and are lower in fat as well.

125 g (4½ oz) wholemeal flour
25 g (1 oz) wheatgerm
3 level tablespoons caster sugar
2 level teaspoons baking powder
1 egg, beaten
50 ml (2 fl oz) milk
50 ml (2 fl oz) sunflower oil
75 g (3 oz) sunflower seeds
2 ripe bananas, about 225 g (8 oz)
  when peeled
Apricot jam, to glaze
Toasted sunflower seeds, to decorate

NUTRIENTS PER MUFFIN	
calories	295
carbohydrate	13 g
(sugars)	18 g
protein	8 g
fat	14 g
(saturated)	2 g
fibre	4 g

preparation time: **15 minutes**

cooking time: **25–30 minutes**

makes **6**

1 Line 6 muffin tins with paper muffin cases, or grease the tins well. In a large bowl mix the flour, wheatgerm, sugar, baking powder and sunflower seeds. In a separate bowl, whisk together the egg, sunflower oil and milk. Pour into the flour mixture. Stir until blended.

2 Roughly mash the bananas, and stir well into the flour mixture. Do not over-mix.

3 Fill each muffin case two-thirds full. Bake at 200°C (400°F, gas mark 6) for 25–30 minutes or until a skewer inserted into the centre comes out clean. Transfer the muffins to a wire rack to cool slightly. Brush the tops with warm apricot jam, sprinkle over toasted sunflower seeds. Serve warm.

red **pepper** hummous

Open up a can of chickpeas and make them the basis of this creamy hummous, spiced with garlic and flavoured with rich tahini and garlic. Canned beans and pulses are a handy, healthy ingredient – always keep some in your store cupboard.

NUTRIENTS PER SERVING	
calories	217
carbohydrate	16 g
(sugars)	7 g
protein	7 g
fat	14 g
(saturated)	2 g
fibre	5 g

2 red peppers, deseeded and quartered
400 g (14 oz) canned chickpeas, drained
2 level tablespoons tahini
2 tablespoons olive oil
2 cloves garlic, crushed
Juice of 1 large lemon
Wholemeal pitta bread, to serve

1 Place the pepper quarters under a hot grill for about 15 minutes, or until the

preparation time: **15 minutes**

cooking time: **20 minutes**

serves **4**

skin is black. Cover with a clean wet cloth, or place in a plastic bag, and allow to cool for 10 minutes. Remove the skin from the peppers and blot dry with absorbent kitchen paper.

2 Place the peppers in a food processor or blender with the remaining ingredients, and process until smooth. Check taste and consistency, and serve with pitta.

grilled **chicken** with **celeriac** and **coriander mash**

The aromas of herbs and crushed spices sprinkled over grilled chicken make an elegant combination of flavours. Served with sugar snap peas, this is a modern, healthy dish, with plenty of fibre. You can also cook the chicken in a griddle pan.

preparation time: **20 minutes**

cooking time: **30 minutes**

serves **4**

550 g (1 lb 4 oz) potatoes, peeled and cut
  into even-sized pieces
550 g (1 lb 4 oz) celeriac, peeled and cut
  into even-sized pieces
4 skinned, boned chicken breasts
1 tablespoon olive oil
2 tablespoons chopped fresh herbs (rosemary,
  thyme, marjoram, coriander)
1 tablespoon crushed coriander seeds
1 tablespoon lemon juice
Salt and black pepper
100 ml (3½ fl oz) hot milk
15 g (½ oz) butter
2 tablespoons chopped fresh herbs (rosemary,
  thyme, marjoram, coriander)
4 tablespoons chopped fresh coriander

1 Place the potatoes and celeriac in a pan of salted water, bring to the boil and cook for 20 minutes or until soft.

2 Heat the grill to medium. Place the chicken breasts between two sheets of cling film and beat them with a rolling pin to an even thickness. Brush them with the olive oil, sprinkle over the herbs and crushed coriander seeds and drizzle over the lemon juice.

3 Grill the chicken breasts for 5-6 minutes until golden. Turn the breasts over, baste with the pan juices and continue grilling for 5-6 minutes until the chicken juices run clear when pierced with a knife. Set aside and keep warm.

4 Drain the potatoes and celeriac thoroughly. Add the milk, butter and seasoning to taste and mash until smooth. Stir in the chopped coriander.

5 Serve each portion of chicken on a bed of the mash.

NUTRIENTS PER SERVING	
calories	353
carbohydrate	30 g
(sugars)	9.6 g
protein	18 g
fat	9.5 g
(saturated)	4 g
fibre	7 g

the inside story

Food, energy and your weight

The food you eat is your body's fuel, supplying the energy you need for everything you do, every minute of your life. Energy supplies which are not used immediately are stored in your body for future use and accumulate as fat. The only way to lose this weight is to eat fewer calories than you burn.

However unusual or delicious a particular food may be, as far as your body is concerned it is simply a source of fuel that enables you to survive. Whatever you eat, be it the finest caviar or a humble potato – your body uses it in the same way, by breaking the food down into nutrients and converting these into energy.

The energy in food is found in three main forms: proteins, carbohydrates and fats. This energy is measured in kilocalories, also known simply as Calories, and also in kilojoules. In every kilocalorie there are 4.2 kilojoules.

WHAT IS METABOLISM?

If you find it a struggle to keep your weight on an even keel, you may find it helpful to understand what happens to food once it is inside your body. Metabolism is the term used to cover the wide range of constant chemical and physical changes that take place within your body in order to keep it alive and functioning.

The process of metabolism is divided into two major categories: the breakdown of complex chemicals into simple forms so that energy can be released (catabolism); and the building up of complex substances in your organs and tissues to store energy or support your body's growth and repair (anabolism).

Rating your energy

The rate at which your body's metabolism operates, converting the food into accessible energy, is known as its metabolic rate. The smallest amount of energy your body needs just to keep it 'ticking over' is your basal metabolic rate or BMR.

This includes the calories you need for breathing, circulation, digestion and other body functions. The energy you use during sleep is equivalent to your BMR, whereas the

__Get your body moving__ Water provides support while you exercise so you won't strain any part of your body. This is particularly helpful if you are overweight. Thirty minutes sustained swimming a day will increase your stamina, suppleness and strength.

From couch potato to action man *There's no escaping the mathematical logic of the energy equation – if you eat lots of high-calorie food and slouch in front of the television, the result is weight-gain. Conversely, eat foods that are low-fat, high-fibre while increasing your physical activity and you'll be lean, slim and trim.*

energy you use doing something strenuous such as cycling might be around seven times this amount.

Variables in energy Activities vary in their calorie (energy) demands and on your weight. For example, walking for 30 minutes, a 59 kg (9 st 4 lb) woman uses 140 Calories, whereas a 68 kg (10 st 10 lb) man would use 160 Calories.

Your body make-up will also influence the rate of energy that you expend. Maintaining muscles uses more energy than keeping fat stores going. And everyone is different: some people will use up calories more quickly than others. Women tend to burn calories more slowly than men, and genetic make-up

plays a small role. Conditions such as thyroid disorders (see page 104) can also affect metabolic rate.

The energy in food What you eat is significant too. Digesting any food uses energy; but some, especially those high in fat, need less energy to digest than proteins or carbohydrates such as grains and pulses.

All food provides some calories, but some are more concentrated in the amount they contain. Weight for weight, fats are the highest source. For example, an apple, which is mostly water, is low in fat and high in fibre. It contains around 50 Calories whereas an equivalent weight of Cheddar cheese provides around eight times that amount.

Each gram of pure fat provides nine Calories, while a gram of protein or carbohydrate provides about four. Consequently, the way you cook food (frying it, for example) can dramatically raise its total calorie value. And if you overuse a saturated fat such as butter or lard, you may be risking the health of your heart. To read more about looking after your heart, turn to pages 54-65.

The energy equation If the amount of calories from your food is the same as you use in your daily activities, your weight will be stable. But if you consume more calories than your age, size and lifestyle require, the excess is stored as body fat, and you will gain weight.

Conversely, if you eat less than normal, but maintain or increase your levels of physical activity, your fat stores will have to be used up to provide the extra energy. As a result, you will lose weight.

Energy intake and expenditure are not evenly balanced on a daily or even a weekly basis. But if your weight is stable over an extended period of time, then the energy you take in as food will be about the same as the energy you use up.

Raising your metabolic rate

When you exercise, your muscles convert the stored energy from your body into compounds that enable you to move and produce body heat. The main fuels for this process are carbohydrate and fat. Your body stores carbohydrate as glycogen in your muscles and liver.

The point at which you feel fatigued during exercise often coincides with a depletion of your carbohydrate stores. Once these are used up, your body calls upon your reserves of fat, and starts to metabolise fatty acids (the main chemical 'units' of fat) in order to release energy. Your fat reserves are larger than your stored carbohydrate, and this raises your metabolic rate.

Carrying a baby During the last three months of pregnancy the mother's basal metabolic rate is raised. This is due to the baby's nutritional needs and the energy used to carry the extra weight. An expectant mother needs to consume about 200 extra Calories daily to provide extra energy for herself and her baby (see page 165). This is the equivalent of three slices of bread.

But eating a little extra doesn't mean abandoning a healthy eating routine: the varieties and proportions of foods chosen should still follow the guidelines of the Five Food Groups (see pages 11-15).

What decreases the rate? Factors that lower the metabolic rate include extreme dieting regimes (see pages 97-98), ageing and the menopause (see pages 180-187), as well as lack of physical activity. It can also be slowed by an underactive thyroid gland (see page 104).

A STEADY BALANCE

There have been many discoveries about the chemical action of foods inside the body. But one of the most significant is that carbohydrate foods

are not fattening as previously believed; on the contrary, they are positively good for you.

The latest health recommendation is that you should make starchy carbohydrate foods such as bread, rice, pasta, cereals, chapattis and potatoes the main part of your meal. Look at the panel on page 93 for some low-fat ways to cook potatoes.

Balancing pleasure and health *Although you may have to cut down the calories in your food to control your weight, you can still enjoy tasty desserts. This feather-light Exotic Fruit Cheesecake is low in calories and high in the health-boosting benefits of fresh fruit. The recipe is on page 101.*

bodyworks

HEALTHY SWAP LIST

To help you to enjoy your food and not feel deprived even when you're trying to lose weight use this 'swap list' of healthier options. Make small yet important modifications that are practical and realistic for you, and, gradually incorporate other healthy food swaps.

USUAL FOOD	HEALTHIER OPTION
Fatty meat	Eat lean meat, poultry (no skin) or fish
Flaky pastry	Use ready-made filo pastry
Sugar-coated breakfast cereal	Muesli, porridge, high-fibre unsweetened cereals
Mayonnaise	Make your own low-fat yoghurt dressing (see page 97)
Sugared fizzy drink	Unsweetened fruit juice, diet drink, water
Rich iced cakes or doughnut	Fruit loaf, plain biscuits or low-fat cakes
Dairy products such as full-fat milk, cheese, butter	Use low-fat foods such as semi-skimmed milk, half-fat cheese, reduced or low fat spread
Bottled oil for stir-frying vegetables or shallow-frying meat or fish	Add a little stock or soy sauce and lemon juice to vegetables and dry-fry meat and fish in a very hot, heavy-based frying pan or griddle pan
Rich desserts such as mousse, syllabub or trifle	Choose low-fat fruit yoghurt, low-fat ice cream, fresh fruit or in natural juice; low-fat desserts such as Tropical Delight (recipe page 107)

Choose fruit canned in juice, not syrup.

There are many ways to boost your supplies of these valuable carbohydrates. You may like to serve extra bread with main meals, for example (but don't smother it with butter). This helps to promote a slow, steady rise in blood glucose throughout the day; consequently your blood sugar stays on an even keel, and you are not tempted to over eat.

Starchy foods are filling too, and if cooked in the minimum of fat, they can be healthily low in calories. Cutting down on meat and cheese portions and filling up on starchy foods instead can be most helpful if you are trying to lose weight.

More fruit and vegetables

People in the United Kingdom eat only about a third of the amount of fruit and vegetables that are currently recommended (see the Five Food Groups pages 11-15). The ideal aim is to eat five or more portions daily (and this does not include potatoes). If you know that you need to boost your intake, choose at least three pieces of fruit and two helpings of salad or vegetables a day.

Generous helpings of fruit and vegetables provide your body with extra fibre and antioxidant vitamins (see page 118). All these – beta carotene (which is converted to vitamin A in the body), and vitamins E and C – have been linked to a lower incidence of heart disease, and of some cancers and gut problems.

Fruity top-up A glass of pure unsweetened fruit juice counts as one serving of fruit; but be aware that it lacks the fibre of a whole piece of fruit. Make sure you buy pure juice and avoid products called 'drink' or 'nectar' or 'cocktail'. They are mainly sugar and water.

HEALTHY OVEN CHIPS *You can indulge your passion for French fries (right) without risking your health and putting on weight. You needn't deep-fry them in oil or lard. With a little ingenuity and a judicious use of low-fat ingredients, you can achieve gratifying results.*

1 Make your own oven chips: Heat oven to 200°C (400°F, gas mark 6). Cook potatoes in boiling water for 5 minutes. Drain, dry and cut into thick chips. Brush a non-stick baking tray with a little oil. Toss chips in beaten white of 1 egg. Shake off the excess and spread chips out on tray. Bake for 35 minutes, turning half way through.

2 Mash potatoes with skimmed milk and low-fat spread instead of butter.

3 Low-fat roast potatoes: Parboil the potatoes. Heat oven to 200°C (400°F, gas

mark 6). Mix ½ teaspoon salt with 1 tablespoon olive oil in a bowl. Coat the potatoes in the oil, then place on a baking tray and roast for 50–55 minutes, until crispy.

4 Serve jacket potatoes with low-fat natural yoghurt or add lemon juice and black pepper.

5 Make boulangère potatoes with stock instead of cream and cheese. Thinly slice potatoes and an onion. Soak the slices in cold water for 15 minutes. Heat oven to 180°C

(350°F, gas mark 4). Drain and dry potatoes and onions. Layer with salt, pepper and grated nutmeg in a shallow ovenproof dish. Pour over

600 ml (1 pint) vegetable stock mixed with a crushed clove of garlic. Dot with low-fat spread and bake in the oven for 1 hour 30 minutes.

FIVE LOW-FAT WAYS TO cook potatoes

Choosing your protein

Meat, fish, nuts, pulses and eggs are rich in protein and some are good sources of vitamins and minerals. However, some protein foods may be high in fat, and you'll need to find ways to minimise this:
• Choose the leanest cuts of meat and trim off any visible fat.
• Add beans or vegetables to minced meat in a recipe. This adds fibre, makes the meal go further and ensures that it has fewer calories.
• Limit the amount of meat you eat and use low-fat cooking methods.

You can grill, griddle, dry-roast or braise. Always grill sausages, bacon and burgers and drain off the fat.
• Separate the juices from the fat after roasting meat and use them to make gravy.
• Remove the skin from poultry: it contains about 60 per cent of the calories. The thigh and leg pieces are highest in fat.
• Put fish on your weekly menu, and try to eat an oily fish such as salmon, herring or mackerel at least once a week for its heart-protective qualities (see page 56). Choose canned tuna

in spring water or brine; tuna in oil has twice the fat.
• Cheese is rich in protein – eat it judiciously or choose low-fat varieties. Low-fat strong Cheddar has a good flavour.
• Nuts are a major source of protein if you are vegetarian. But they are high in fat and are best eaten as an ingredient in a main meal (such as a nut roast) rather than as a snack.
• Eggs can be poached, boiled or scrambled with low-fat spread and skimmed milk instead of fried.

continued on page 96

steps to successful SLIMMING

Before attempting to change your lifestyle and eating habits in order to reach a more desirable weight for your height and age, you need to get into the right frame of mind. The most successful approach is to set yourself realistic targets – so sit down and make a list of what you feel you can achieve. Your list may include: being able to fit into your favourite clothes, being able to run for the bus (and catch it), looking and feeling more attractive, feeling less breathless, or lowering your blood cholesterol.

The right attitude

If you are practical and clear-sighted about why you want to lose weight, you will improve your chances of success. This means abandoning any illusions that losing weight is the answer to all your problems. You may not end up looking like a fashion model, but the changeover to a

healthier weight may help your confidence, your work, your social life and your belief in yourself. It may also affect the way that you interact with your family, friends, and colleagues.

Making a food diary

It can be very helpful to keep a daily record of exactly what you eat during the early stages: this enables you to follow your progress over a period of time. Include detailed notes about how you were feeling when you deviated from your eating plan. You may then start to make connections between the times you felt like indulging and the mood you were in. Your food diary will equip you to make lasting changes, by making you more conscious of your habits and eating patterns. Follow the healthy eating guidelines on pages 11–15 to help you to

THERE IS NO SUCH THING AS A MIRACLE DIET. LOSING WEIGHT THE HEALTHY WAY TAKES TIME AND PATIENCE. SO ONCE YOU HAVE DECIDED TO SLIM, BE REALISTIC. SET YOURSELF GOALS THAT ARE WITHIN YOUR CAPACITY, BECAUSE THAT WAY YOU ARE MORE LIKELY TO SUCCEED IN THE END.

THINK SLIM *To lose weight successfully, you need to combine a variety of approaches. It's important that you exercise regularly, but don't get obsessed with jumping on the scales every day. When you go shopping, stick to your list, and take the time to make yourself healthy, good tasting meals.*

achieve a balanced intake of the right type of foods. Check the BMI (Body Mass Index) Chart (page 17), then set yourself short-term weight-loss targets and work on these until you are within the ideal range recommended for your age and height.

Tips to help you succeed

Be patient – it took time to put on weight, so getting it off will also take time. The following tips may be useful:
• Weigh yourself once a week only. Your weight fluctuates from day to day and this can be misleading.

• Eat regularly – don't skip meals and snacks.
• Never shop when you are hungry – otherwise you may be tempted by quick-fix fatty, sugary snacks.
• Take a list of the ingredients you need with you to the supermarket and stick to it.
• Avoid night-time snacking and TV dinners. Eat at the table and be conscious of what you're eating.
• Serve meals on a small plate to make them look bigger.
• Distract yourself when you feel like over-indulging – go for a stroll, take a bath or read a magazine.
• Set specific goals such as losing a couple of kilos a month. When you hit a target, reward yourself with a trip to the theatre, or a new book.
• Make sure you get lots of exercise (see page 99 for tips).
• Keep to recommended limits of alcohol (see page 97).

MENUPLAN
stay healthy and slim

The guidelines in this menu will help you to structure a sustainable weight-loss diet that suits your needs.

Daily milk allowance: 1 pint skimmed milk, ³/₄ pint semi-skimmed or ¹/₂ pint whole milk.

BREAKFAST Have a glass of unsweetened fruit juice, or half a grapefruit, 35 g (1¹/₄ oz) of unsweetened high fibre cereal such as branflakes, porridge or 2 wheat biscuits using milk from your daily allowance. And eat 1 slice toast or bread with low-fat spread and reduced-sugar jam. Alternatively, choose 1 boiled or poached egg or 1 rasher of lean back bacon, grilled and served with wholemeal toast.

MID-MORNING Coffee or tea with milk from your daily allowance, fruit or herbal tea, water or freshly squeezed fruit juice. A piece of fruit or a plain biscuit.

LUNCH Choose from the following: a wholemeal sandwich made with 115g (4 oz) portion chicken, lean beef or ham, tuna in spring water, 55 g (2 oz) reduced-fat cheese or 40 g (1¹/₂ oz) low-fat Cheddar cheese; or, 2 grilled vegetable and lean meat or chicken burgers in a bun; or, a small jacket potato with 1 chopped boiled egg; or, 115g (4oz) tuna in spring water, dressed with 1 teaspoon of low-calorie mayonnaise. Fresh fruit or diet yoghurt to follow.

MID-AFTERNOON Same as mid-morning.

DINNER Choose: 85 g (3 oz) cooked rice or pasta or 2 small potatoes with 175 g (6 oz) fish, 115 g (4 oz) chicken, turkey or lean meat, cooked without added fat. Serve 2 large portions of steamed vegetables, such as broccoli and carrots. Follow with a platter of fresh fruit or an 85 g (3 oz) portion of a light, fruit-based dessert.

A taste for fruit When hunger pangs strike and you're longing for something delicious to eat, reach for fruit. It's refreshing, satisfying and there are so many different kinds to enjoy.

• Use low-fat convenience foods.
• To stir-fry foods, use spray oil on a non-stick pan, or use a small pastry brush to add a little oil.

Eat more pulses Beans and lentils are a good source of protein and fibre, especially if you are vegetarian. Eaten with rice and pasta, they make satisfying, nutritious meals. Avoid frying foods such as nut rissoles, as this raises their calorie content.

Low-fat products

Instead of using butter or margarine, choose an alternative spread based on unsaturated vegetable oils such as olive or sunflower. Your supermarket can offer a wide choice of low-fat products. They are often labelled as 'lite' or 'light'. At the dairy counter, buy semi-skimmed or skimmed milk, half-fat Cheddar cheese and low-fat yoghurt, and use them in

your cooking. But don't let the low-fat label lull you into a state of false security – these products will only help you to cut down on calories if you eat moderate amounts. This is particularly true of foods such as taramasalata and hummous.

Lightly dressed Ready-made salad dressings can add unnecessary fat and calories to an otherwise healthy dish. Buy low-fat or fat-free dressings or make your own from low-fat ingredients: stir two teaspoons of lemon juice into a small tub of low-fat natural yoghurt and season with black pepper. Avoid adding butter or margarine to cooked vegetables.

Treat yourself Choose low-fat desserts such as Melon with Berry Fruit Coulis (see recipe on page 73) – but use reduced-sugar jam and serve it with diet yoghurt.

Alcohol – safe limits Health experts say that, without significant risk to health, women can drink between 2-3 units of alcohol a day, men 3-4 units. But remember that alcohol contains a significant amount of calories: if you are trying to lose weight, you should restrict yourself to seven units a week. One unit is equivalent to half a pint of beer or lager, a glass of wine or sherry or a single measure of spirits. If you drink spirits, choose a low-calorie mixer, and make one or two days of your week alcohol-free, especially after a period of heavy drinking.

THE DIET DEBATE

Obesity is an ever-increasing problem in affluent countries. But if you plan to lose weight and stay slim, there is only one answer. You need to find a healthy way of eating that becomes part of your life for ever, not just as a temporary diet.

Along with building extra physical activity into your daily routine, this tried and tested approach is the one that works best.

Quick-fix diets

The main conclusions of research into the success or failure of diet products and weight-loss plans are sobering. They show that, after people stop dieting, most of them regain all the weight they may have lost, while some gain even more.

Glamorous brochures and promises of instant weight loss are undeniably seductive. But miracles do not happen in the real world: fast track diets are impractical and short-sighted. Many take the form of milk shakes, designed to replace one or more meals. The drinks contain a wide range of nutrients. But they have serious drawbacks:
• They offer little or no education about making the gradual changes in eating and exercise routines that are necessary for successful long-term weight control.

CALORIES AND FAT

This checklist supplies the calories and fat in each 100 g of familiar foods.

FOOD	CALORIES	FAT(G)
Plain omelette	191	16.4
Boiled egg	147	10.8
Whole milk	66	3.9
Semi-skimmed milk	46	1.6
Skimmed milk	33	0.1
Cheddar cheese	412	34.4
Brie	319	26.9
Edam	333	25.4
Reduced-fat Cheddar	261	15
French fries	280	15.5
Oven chips	162	4.2
Fried cod in batter	247	15.4
Grilled cod	95	1.3
Roast chicken (breast with skin)	216	14
Roast chicken (breast without skin)	148	5
Medium-fat soft cheese (Light brands)	179	14.5

A hot spice such as cayenne pepper will temporarily raise your metabolic rate as it increases your body temperature. Cayenne is very pungent – you need just a pinch to enliven a dish.

• They frequently encourage rapid weight loss, even though there is no healthy way to achieve this.

• They produce a typical 'dieting mentality': using the products means that you are 'going on a diet' rather than choosing a regular, healthy eating pattern. This attitude to food has its own psychological pitfalls and can be highly demotivating.

• They may be misused by people who are obsessed with being thin and who do not need to lose weight.

Yo-Yo dieting Some diets do promote gradual, steady weight-loss. But others promise results within an unrealistically short time. This creates an endless cycle: sudden weight-loss followed by equally fast weight-gain. This 'on-again, off-again' approach can be harmful: fluctuating changes in weight put a strain on the heart. One study has shown that changes such as these

during adulthood increase the risk of heart disease and cancer. Extreme dieting may also lead to irregular menstruation: this is especially the case in young girls, some of whom take dieting to such excess, they stop menstruating completely.

Joining a club Reputable slimming groups provide support and advice while you lose weight. The aim of most clubs is to help you to change your eating behaviour.

Portion-control Ready-made calorie-counted meals are popular choices. They are often labelled as 'diet' or 'low-calorie'. But the portion sizes tend to be small: this is usually why they are so low in calories. But you can always give a positive boost to the health values of these meals by accompanying them with the recommended servings of fruit and vegetables from the Five Food Groups (see pages 11-15).

SIMPLY THE BEST

A healthy diet, tailored to your needs may not sound all that exciting. But all the evidence shows that it is the safest and best way of losing weight. If you are seriously overweight and need help, your doctor may put you in touch with a qualified dietitian who will help you to review your current eating habits and lifestyle and encourage you to lose weight slowly but steadily.

Helping yourself Once you know more about the food you eat, and its effect on your body, you have the means to control your weight. But counting calories is only part of the picture: setting realistic goals is equally essential.

The chart on page 17 will help you to assess whether you are within a desirable weight range. It is also useful to have some idea of how many calories you need to consume.

poaching

The health benefits of poaching

LOW FAT Poaching requires no extra fat.
VARIETY Eggs and fish such as salmon are popular foods for poaching but you can also poach light meats such as poultry.

The method Poaching is simple – place the food in a container (such as a fish or egg poacher), add the poaching liquid, cover with foil or a close-fitting lid and cook in the oven or on the stove.

Liquids for poaching These include acidulated water (add lemon juice or vinegar when poaching eggs in a pan of water); milk, or a light aromatic stock for fish and poultry.

COOKFORHEALTH

Dance yourself slim Line dancing is a great way of getting extra exercise and has the added bonus of helping you to keep your weight down. It improves your health and fitness, and is a fun, sociable activity, suitable for people of all ages.

The balloon chart on pages 16-17 give the current recommendations on desirable energy (calorie) intakes for men and women. The chart gives the number of Calories you need to maintain a healthy weight. But these amounts vary according to activity levels: sedentary types need fewer calories than active individuals.

For those wishing to lose weight, the guidelines are that men should consume about 1500-1700 Calories a day, and women should aim for 1200 Calories.

Getting physical

The most effective way to maintain a balanced weight and healthy metabolism is to increase your levels of physical activity. This triggers the release of endorphins, the body's natural painkillers: these combat stress and also help to energise you.

Try to incorporate simple activities into your routine and work up to 30 minutes of daily sustained exercise.
• Walk as much as possible; walk the dog, take the children out or simply park the car farther away from the house.
• Always walk at a pace that leaves you slightly out of breath.
• Use the stairs instead of the lift, or run up and down the steps at home.
• If you have an exercise bike, set it up in front of your television and cycle through your favourite soap.
• Take up a fun sport: go swimming or line-dancing with friends.

Measurable targets Here are a few examples of the energy expenditure derived from various activities. They are all measured in Calories-per-hour units: you should check the time you spend on the activity and work out the sum from that:

Light to moderate exercise These use 50-300 Calories per hour: ironing; making beds; sweeping floors; hand-washing clothes; light gardening; washing your car; walking at 2–3 mph on a level surface; cycling at 5½ mph on a level surface; bowling.

Moderate exercise To use up 300–400 Calories per hour try: digging; mowing the lawn; pulling weeds; badminton; canoeing (at 4 mph); dancing; playing golf (no cart); walking at 3½–4 mph on a level surface; ping-pong; volleyball.

Heavy exercise These will burn up around 420–600 Calories per hour: chopping wood; digging holes; climbing; waterskiing; jogging at 6–7 mph; walking at 5 mph on a level surface, walking upstairs, walking up-hill; cycling at 5–6 mph up and down-hill.

spicy cocktail nibbles

Serve these at parties or as a delicious low-calorie meal. You can use minced chicken, or lean minced lamb instead of turkey. Serve hot or cold with chilli tomato dip and raita (see page 305), or in mini-pitta bread with shredded lettuce.

preparation time: **20 minutes**

cooking time: **6-8 minutes**

makes **20 patties**

NUTRIENTS PER PATTIE	
calories	20
carbohydrate	1 g
(sugars)	0.5 g
protein	3 g
fat	0.3 g
(saturated)	0
fibre	0

FOR THE PATTIES

300 g (10½ oz) minced turkey
1 garlic clove, crushed
1 teaspoon paprika
1 teaspoon cumin seeds
4 tablespoons chopped fresh coriander
1 teaspoon garam masala
2 tablespoons low-fat natural yoghurt
Salt and black pepper

FOR THE SAUCE

3 tablespoons tomato ketchup
1 teaspoon lemon juice
1 teaspoon chilli powder
1 teaspoon mint sauce
2 tablespoons cold water

1 Heat the grill to medium and line the grill pan with foil.

2 To make the patties, mix the ingredients together in a bowl. Take a level dessertspoon of the mixture and shape it into a small pattie. Repeat until you have 20 patties.

3 Put the patties under the grill and cook for about 3–4 minutes on each side, turning once during cooking.

4 Mix the sauce ingredients together in a small bowl and serve with the patties.

Exotic fruit cheesecake

An instant classic with a touch of glamour, this cheesecake uses reduced-fat digestive biscuits and cheese to make a crunchy base with a creamy filling. Use one fruit (star fruit, raspberries or strawberries, for example) or a mixture (see photograph page 90).

preparation time: **30 minutes, plus about 2 hours setting and chilling**

serves **6**

NUTRIENTS PER SLICE	
calories	360
carbohydrate	44 g
(sugars)	24 g
protein	6 g
fat	18 g
(saturated)	3 g
fibre	1.5 g

75 g (2¾ oz) reduced-fat spread
225 g (8 oz) reduced-fat digestive biscuits, crushed
125 g (4½ oz) low-fat soft cheese
100 g (3½ oz) fat-free fromage frais
75 g (2¾ oz) icing sugar, sifted
15 g (½ oz) powdered gelatine dissolved in 3 tablespoons orange juice
350 g (12 oz) exotic fruit, such as star fruit, strawberries, kumquats and cherries

1 Line an 18 cm (7 in) loose-bottomed cake tin with greaseproof paper.

2 Melt the spread and add the crushed biscuits. Mix well and press into the base of the cake tin. Chill in the refrigerator for about 15 minutes, or until firm.

3 Beat together the cheese, fromage frais and icing sugar until creamy. Stir in the dissolved gelatine. Spread evenly over the biscuit base and chill for 1 hour, or until set.

4 Arrange the fruit over the cheesecake. Chill for at least another 30 minutes before serving.

goan seafood stew

This spicy seafood dish from Western India is a hybrid of soup and stew and is healthily low in calories and fat. As an economical alternative, use a 900 g (2 lb) bag of frozen seafood cocktail and add 225 g (8 oz) fresh seafood in the shell.

preparation time: **1 hour**

cooking time: **15 minutes**

serves **4**

600 ml (1 pint) skimmed milk
225 g (8 oz) potatoes, diced
Salt and black pepper
1 large clove garlic, finely chopped
1 red chilli, deseeded and chopped
1 medium courgette, sliced
1 kg (2 lb 4 oz) assorted raw, cleaned and rinsed seafood, such as mussels, clams, cockles (in the shell), and tiger prawns (shelled)
600 ml (1 pint) fish stock (recipe page 339)
1 tablespoon chopped fresh coriander
3 tablespoons half-fat crème fraîche
TO GARNISH
4 large prawns in the shell, cooked
4 sprigs fresh coriander

1 Put the skimmed milk into a pan with the potatoes, seasoning, garlic and chilli. Bring to the boil. Lower the heat and simmer for 3 minutes.

2 Add the courgette, seafood, fish stock and coriander.

3 Bring to the boil, lower the heat and simmer for 10 minutes or until the clams and mussels have opened. (Discard any that have not opened.) Stir in the crème fraîche, and re-heat for a further 2 minutes.

4 Ladle into warm plates or bowls and serve each garnished with a cooked whole prawn, still in its shell, and a sprig of fresh coriander.

NUTRIENTS PER SERVING	
calories	350
carbohydrate	28 g
(sugars)	9 g
protein	48 g
fat	5 g
(saturated)	2 g
fibre	2 g

food, energy and your weight

The body's messengers

Hormones are chemicals that serve as the body's messengers, stimulating organs into action. Because they are made from components of food, what you eat has a direct effect on your hormonal system. But the opposite is also true: hormones help to regulate your appetite and reaction to food.

Hormones are chemicals produced by specialised glands in the body. They act on various cells in the body, giving them direct instructions to work in a certain way. They are carried to their destinations in the blood.

The hormones are chemically formulated to influence a wide range of functions. Insulin tells the cells to take up glucose from the blood and is thus able to regulate sugar levels; gastrin stimulates the cells that release hydrochloric acid, thereby facilitating digestion; adrenalin is secreted when you are under stress; endorphins are released as natural painkillers; thyroxine plays a vital role in metabolism and serotonin helps control both your mood and appetite.

If your hormonal system is already in good working order, a healthy, balanced diet, outlined in the Five Food groups (pages 11-15), is usually sufficient to maintain it. But you also need to keep your weight under control, as obesity can lead to hormonal imbalances. For those with hormonal problems

such as diabetes, medical treatment may be necessary. However, a judicious approach to food can often go a long way towards helping to keep the symptoms under control.

Apart from diabetes, there are other conditions in which the hormonal system plays a significant role. For example, many women experience pre-menstrual syndrome,

Directing the traffic *The concentration of hormones in your body is finely controlled, so when imbalances occur, the body readjusts its levels. Eating the right foods helps to stabilise your hormones.*

a range of distressing physical and emotional symptoms caused by fluctuating levels of the hormone oestrogen (see pages 223-225). They may also experience problems with hormonal imbalances during and after the menopause (see page 180).

DIABETES AND DIET

When you digest food, glucose is produced and enters your bloodstream. In most people, the amount of glucose in the blood is controlled by insulin, a hormone secreted by the pancreas. Insulin helps the cells to take up and use glucose. But a person with diabetes, does not produce enough insulin, or is unable to use it effectively. As a result, too much sugar circulates in the blood, while at the same time, the body tissues are starved of glucose. Diabetes is serious: it can lead to heart disease, nerve damage, kidney disease, vision impairment and other complications. There are two main types:

Insulin-dependent This kind of diabetes occurs when the pancreas is unable to produce any insulin. It is the least common form and usually

***The perfect balance** Eat Pasta Shells with Olives and Basil to maintain steady blood glucose levels. The carbohydrate in the pasta is slowly absorbed, the kidney beans provide soluble fibre for gradual energy release, and the peppers add vitamin C. The recipe is on page 107.*

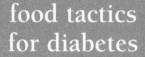

food tactics for diabetes

• Eat regularly and often – 5-6 small meals spaced out through the day are better than 3 eaten at long intervals.

• Maintain a healthy weight.

• Choose foods with a low glycaemic index (see page 79).

• Fill up on starchy foods such as bread, potatoes and rice.

• Cut down on fatty foods such as butter, full-fat cheese, fatty meats, crisps and pastries.

• Eat 3 fruits and 2 large helpings of vegetables a day.

• Swap high-sugar foods, such as canned fruit in syrup, for low-sugar alternatives, such as canned fruit in natural juice.

• Avoid too much salt, to prevent high blood pressure.

• Eat more fish and have oily fish once a week.

develops before the age of 30. Treatment involves daily insulin injections combined with a low-fat, low-sugar diet.

Non insulin-dependent In this type, the pancreas produces some insulin, but in insufficient quantities; it accounts for around 75 per cent of diabetes cases, and is often called late-onset diabetes because it usually occurs after the age of 40. Mild forms can be controlled by diet, but in severe cases medication is needed.

Making adjustments

Being diabetic doesn't mean that you are unable to eat delicious foods. It simply means keeping a watchful eye on what – and when – you eat, so that you can stay in control of your blood glucose levels. One factor is crucial, however. Diabetics have an increased risk of heart disease and circulation disorders, so you must eat as little fat as possible. To read more about heart disease, turn to pages 54-63.

In general, though, the key to good health is to enjoy a wide variety of foods. This will not only ensure a better balance of your blood glucose, but will also help you to obtain a healthy range of nutrients.

Controlling blood sugar The faster a food is broken down during digestion, the quicker the rise in blood glucose. Since one of the main aims in managing diabetes is to keep blood glucose steady throughout the day, foods that cause a sharp rise in blood levels are best kept to a minimum. These foods have a high glycaemic index (GI). For further details about foods and their

glycaemic index, turn to pages 78-79. The surest way to keep your blood sugar stable is to base your diet around foods with a low GI. Wholegrains, and foods high in soluble fibre such as beans and lentils, are good examples. These foods take longer to be broken down by the body and cause a slower rise in your blood glucose levels.

Weight control Filling up on these high-fibre carbohydrates will also mean that you have less room (and less appetite) for fatty foods. This is particularly helpful if you are watching your weight, and will certainly make it easier for you to stay slim and healthy.

A dietitian can help you to work out how to use foods to keep your blood glucose levels on an even keel. You may need to monitor your levels from time to time – ask your doctor for advice about this.

The sugar debate It is a widely held view that diabetics should avoid sugar completely. But this is not entirely accurate. If you unwisely consume sugary foods or drinks – such as chocolate, sweets, biscuits, cakes, canned drinks – on an empty stomach, your blood glucose will rise sharply. But when you eat sugar in conjunction with a high-fibre meal, your blood glucose level will rise more slowly, because the fibre helps to slow down the rate of release. So, unless your doctor or dietitian advises you otherwise, you can have the occasional sweet or biscuit after a high-fibre meal – especially if you keep to small quantities.

Cook's tips

The following ideas and cooking tips are appropriate for the whole family.
• Low-fat cooking methods are best: grill, griddle, boil, dry-roast (without

added fat) and poach or steam foods rather than fry.
• Base your meals and snacks on carbohydrates such as pasta, rice, potatoes and wholegrains.
• Have several small meals during the day, without long gaps between.
• Use unsaturated fat spreads made from olive, sunflower or safflower oil, rather than butter. They lower blood cholesterol (see page 54) and are a good choice for diabetics, who are vulnerable to heart conditions.
• Trim all the fat from your meat.
• Use thick slices of wholemeal bread for sandwiches, and put less filling inside – this fills you up and keeps the calorie content low.
• Use peas, beans, lentils and chickpeas to extend meat dishes, and always use lean meat. For example, mixing cooked lentils into a bolognese sauce will make it go further, and helps to slow down the rise in blood glucose.
• Think of vegetables as the main part of the meal, rather than an accompaniment.
• Base desserts on fresh fruit, fruit canned in natural juice, low-fat natural yoghurt or fromage frais.
• Enjoy crunchy raw vegetables as snacks. You could keep 'hunger boxes' in the fridge, filled with a variety of chopped fresh fruit and vegetables.

DIET AND YOUR THYROID

The thyroid gland, which is situated at the base of the throat, produces thyroxine, a hormone which controls the metabolic rate of the tissues in your body. If the thyroid produces too little thyroxine, the metabolism becomes sluggish, and can cause a condition known as hypothyroidism. But if the gland releases too much

foods to help your thyroid

For an over-active thyroid, eat foods rich in B-vitamins, such as popcorn, wholegrains, fish, Brazil nuts, seeds, beans and brown rice.

For an under-active thyroid, eat foods rich in zinc, such as liver, oysters and other kinds of shellfish, red meat and nuts.

thyroxine, the body uses energy too quickly. This problem, called hyperthyroidism, will usually lead to some degree of weight loss.

Thyroid conditions are thought to be auto-immune disorders, in which the immune system attacks the thyroid gland. To keep your thyroid healthy, include some seafood in your diet – it is a rich source of iodine and zinc, both of which boost thyroid function. Vitamin C and the B vitamins also help to improve the functioning of the immune system and the thyroid gland.

HORMONE REGULATORS

Oestrogen has a pivotal role in regulating menstruation and pregnancy. It also protects against the bone disease osteoporosis before and during menopause (see pages 45-49) and against heart disease. But women with high levels of oestrogen in their blood are thought to be at greater risk of cancer.

Phytoestrogens These are powerful chemicals that resemble oestrogen, and are found in various plant foods, including soya beans, pulses (such as lentils and chickpeas), nuts, seeds and berries. Their active ingredients are called isoflavones: they act like oestrogen and are thought to help balance levels in the body. A diet rich in phytoestrogens may be helpful for women with high blood levels of oestrogen.

The benefits of soya Soya beans have a high concentration of isoflavones. Chinese and Japanese populations with a traditional diet based on soya have very low rates of hormone-dependent diseases such as cancer of the breast and prostate, or heart disease. For more information on soya, turn to pages 184-185.

Hormones and calcium

Most of the body's calcium is stored in the bones and teeth, where it provides strength and structure. The parathyroid glands secrete two vital hormones, parathormone and calcitonin, which are involved in calcium metabolism. If problems occur with this metabolism, a range of problems may develop, ranging from cramps to brittle bones and an increased risk of fractures.

The metabolism of calcium depends upon an adequate supply of vitamin D. Most of the body's vitamin D is produced when the skin is exposed to ultraviolet rays from sunlight. But you should also eat foods which contain the vitamin. Good sources include oily fish, full-fat milk and dairy products, margarine and other fortified foods, such as skimmed milk powder and some breakfast cereals.

Mixed beans and spring onions — simple, but good.

turkey **fricassée**

Too fatty

Creamy and delicate, yet healthily low in fat, this fricassée features diced turkey and vegetables, gently simmered in ~~Greek yoghurt~~ and fresh chicken stock. Served on a bed of fluffy rice, it makes a light but satisfying supper dish.

preparation time: **40 minutes**

cooking times: **40 minutes**

serves **4**

NUTRIENTS PER SERVING	
calories	**360**
carbohydrate	**25 g**
(sugars)	**13 g**
protein	**47 g**
fat	**8 g**
(saturated)	**2 g**
fibre	**7 g**

1 tablespoon plain flour
Salt and black pepper
4 skinless turkey breasts (weighing around
175 g (6 oz) each), cut into
bite-sized pieces
1 tablespoon rapeseed or sunflower oil
1 medium-size onion, finely chopped
2 cloves garlic, crushed
250 ml (9 fl oz) home-made chicken or
vegetable stock (recipe page 338)
4 carrots, diced
280 g (10 oz) frozen peas
1 green pepper, diced
115 g (4 oz) low-fat Greek yoghurt
4 tablespoons chopped fresh parsley

1 Mix the flour with the seasoning and use this to coat the turkey pieces.

2 Heat the oil in a non-stick pan. Add the onion and garlic and fry for 3–4 minutes to soften them.

3 Add the turkey to the pan and brown over a medium heat for 20–25 minutes. Spoon in a little of the stock if the meat sticks to the pan.

4 Stir in the carrots, peas and remaining stock. Cover and simmer for 5 minutes.

5 Add the peppers and allow to cook, covered, for a further 5 minutes.

6 Stir in the yoghurt and parsley. Warm through and adjust the seasoning. Serve with boiled rice.

tropical delight

Exotic fruits smothered in low-fat fromage frais and topped with flaked chocolate make a luxury dessert. Fromage frais is an excellent substitute for cream, and you can use any fruits you like – canned fruit in natural juice is fine.

preparation time: **20 minutes**

serves **4**

300 g (10 oz) low-fat fromage frais
4 tablespoons granulated artificial
  sweetener
1 mango, peeled, pitted and cut into small
  pieces
1 papaya, peeled, pitted, cut into chunks
2 kiwi fruits, sliced
1 bar Chocolate Flake, broken into strips
Seeds of 2 passion fruits

1 Beat the fromage frais with the sweetener until smooth.

2 Fold in the mango and papaya, and divide the mixture into 4 long-stemmed dessert dishes

3 Decorate with the kiwi fruit, flaked chocolate and sprinkle with the passion fruit seeds. Serve immediately.

NUTRIENTS PER SERVING	
calories	180
carbohydrate	31 g
(sugars)	25 g
protein	8 g
fat	3 g
(saturated)	1.5 g
fibre	4.5 g

pasta shells with olives and basil

Warm the cockles of your heart with the sunny flavours of this classic Italian pasta dish. It looks almost as good as it tastes – serve it with a simple rocket salad, drizzled with olive oil and a squeeze of lemon juice.

preparation time: **20 minutes**

cooking time: **20 minutes**

serves **4**

350 g (12 oz) pasta shells
1 tablespoon olive oil
2 cloves garlic, crushed
1 large onion, finely chopped
1 green pepper, diced
425 g (15 oz) can of red kidney beans
  (with no added sugar or salt), drained
2 teaspoons dried oregano
15 g (½ oz) basil leaves, torn
100 g (3½ oz) pitted black olives
Salt and black pepper
100 g (3½ oz) cherry tomatoes, halved, to
  garnish
Whole basil leaves, to garnish

1 Cook the pasta in lightly salted water, following the instructions on the packet.

2 Meanwhile, heat the oil in a large non-stick pan. Add the garlic, onion and green pepper and fry until the onions are light brown and the peppers are just cooked (about 5–7 minutes).

3 Stir in the kidney beans, oregano, basil leaves and olives, and allow the flavours to develop for a few minutes.

4 Add the cooked pasta, stir gently and season.

5 Serve hot, garnished with cherry tomatoes and whole basil leaves

NUTRIENTS PER SERVING	
calories	480
carbohydrate	89 g
(sugars)	12 g
protein	18 g
fat	8 g
(saturated)	1 g
fibre	10 g

Sex and **sexuality**

A healthy diet is essential for an active and fulfilling sex life, just as it is for a healthy reproductive system. It is now known, too, that there are certain nutrients that you can target both to boost your sex life and to influence the hormones that regulate your reproductive system.

A good sex life doesn't just happen – it requires a little help, which means a balanced and nutritious diet combined with regular moderate exercise and a positive attitude. These are all key elements in helping to keep your sex drive high and your reproductive system in good working order.

In general, a healthy diet which contains a wide range of foods will supply all the vitamins and minerals that you need to enjoy a satisfying love life, as well as ensuring the health of your reproductive organs.

More specifically, several vitamins and minerals are believed to play an important role in maintaining the sex drive and in the production of both ova and sperm. Certain nutrients also have the power to regulate the levels of sex hormones in your body, and some can even help to protect your reproductive system from the potentially damaging effects of infection or disease.

As good nutrition is so influential, it is hardly surprising that poor eating habits can have a dramatically disruptive effect on your love life. For example, a lack of zinc can cause infertility and impotence, and while moderate amounts of alcohol can

help people to feel relaxed, heavy drinking often inhibits sexual performance in men and women. Furthermore, excessive alcohol is known to inhibit ovulation and to interfere with the movement of sperm up the Fallopian tube. Strong drink can actually depress the sex drive of both men and women. And caffeine in coffee, tea and cola drinks can reduce libido.

Watch your weight How much you eat can also have an effect on your sex life. It is well documented that being either over or underweight can reduce the libido and impair fertility.

From a psychological point of view, a negative attitude to your weight or body shape can dent your confidence in sex and relationships. For more information on diet and weight issues for men and women considering starting a family, see pages 160–169.

Amenorrhoea (loss of periods) is a common symptom of anorexia in women and often occurs in ballet dancers and athletes who have particularly low stores of body fat. A certain level of body fat is necessary to regulate the hormones that control ovulation and menstruation, and when fat drops below a certain

critical point, ovulation and menstruation both cease (see page 162). At the other extreme, obesity can impair ovulation in women as well as reducing sperm production in men.

IMPORTANT NUTRIENTS

There are certain foods that are not only delicious but also contain the necessary nutrients to maintain your reproductive health and your libido. These will contribute to your sexual health by maintaining your system in good condition, helping you to regulate your hormonal cycles and boosting your fertility.

Vitamin A This maintains the health of the epithelial tissue which lines all the external and internal surfaces of the body, including the linings of the vagina and the uterus in women. Liver, egg yolk, cheese, butter and carrots are good sources.

B vitamins Deficiencies of both vitamin B_6 and folic acid have been linked with infertility, and women planning a pregnancy should ensure that they eat plenty of foods rich in folic acid well before conception (see pages 164-165). Oral contraceptives increase the requirement for these vitamins.

Sharing the joys of food This is one of the nicest parts of a close, loving relationship. Food is intimately connected with your sex life – both nutritionally and in terms of its sensuous appeal.

Minerals for fertility Zinc is an important nutrient in promoting a man's fertility and there are abundant levels in this delicious, seafood-stuffed artichoke. Lovers will also take great delight in the pleasure of eating the artichoke, leaf by luscious leaf. The recipe is on page 115.

Lean meat, chicken, fish, wheatgerm, brewer's yeast, beans and pulses, peanuts and bananas provide B$_6$. These foods are all rich in folic acid: dark green leafy vegetables such as spinach, watercress and cabbage, liver, oranges, avocado, beetroot and broccoli are all rich in folic acid.

Vitamin C Increasing vitamin C intake may be helpful in boosting fertility, particularly for men; tests have shown that taking 500-1000 milligrams a day can increase the number and quality of sperm produced and reduce abnormalities. This vitamin may also help to prevent the condition known as 'agglutination', in which the sperm become stuck together and are unable to reach the egg. All fruit and vegetables – particularly kiwi fruit, peppers, blackcurrants, strawberries and citrus fruits – contain abundant quantities of vitamin C.

Foods to boost your sex life

The fast pace of modern life leads to stress, tiredness and sometimes a lack of sexual energy. Certain foods can help to combat this.

Vitamin E A powerful antioxidant, vitamin E helps to protect the sperm from damage. Sunflower, safflower oils and some vegetable oils, nuts and seeds, margarine, wheatgerm and avocados contain high levels.

Zinc There is probably more than a grain of truth in the theory that oysters are good for your sex life, as they are the richest food source of

HEALTH OR HYPE?
the pill

Oral contraceptives can affect the absorption of certain nutrients within the body – and increase the need for vitamins B$_1$, B$_2$, B$_6$, B$_{12}$, C, E, folic acid, and the mineral zinc. If you take the Pill, eat plenty of fruit and vegetables to ensure that you obtain lots of these nutrients. B$_6$ supplements are often used because B$_6$ metabolism can be affected by the Pill, causing side effects similar to PMT.

zinc, and zinc is known to be one of the key nutrients involved in the production of sperm. Low levels of zinc have been linked both with poor libido in women and with a low sperm count in men. You can obtain zinc from shellfish (particularly oysters), wholemeal bread, brown rice, dark green leafy vegetables, lean red meat and turkey.

Selenium This mineral is vital to ensure the production of healthy sperm. Lean meat, offal, brown rice and porridge oats are good sources.

Manganese The metabolism of the female hormone oestrogen depends on manganese. It follows that a deficiency of manganese will significantly reduce fertility in women. Spinach, chestnuts, tea, oats, wholegrain cereals, wheatgerm, raisins,

Fertile folates *Watercress is a particularly good source of folic acid, one of the B vitamins which helps to keep your reproductive system in working order.*

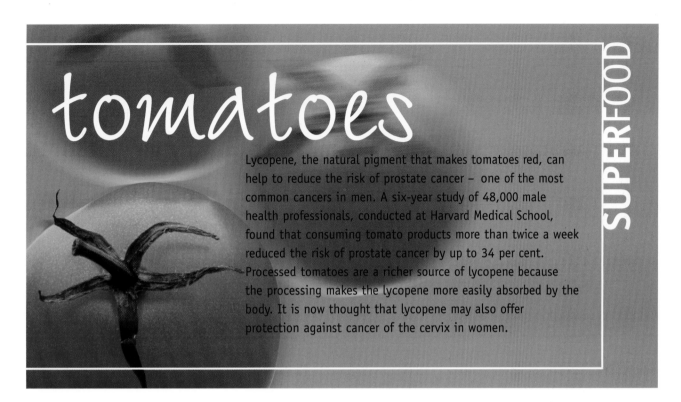

tomatoes

SUPERFOOD

Lycopene, the natural pigment that makes tomatoes red, can help to reduce the risk of prostate cancer – one of the most common cancers in men. A six-year study of 48,000 male health professionals, conducted at Harvard Medical School, found that consuming tomato products more than twice a week reduced the risk of prostate cancer by up to 34 per cent. Processed tomatoes are a richer source of lycopene because the processing makes the lycopene more easily absorbed by the body. It is now thought that lycopene may also offer protection against cancer of the cervix in women.

blueberries, pineapple, beans, peas and nuts are all good sources of manganese.

Essential fatty acids Linoleic acid is important for sperm production. Sunflower and vegetable oils and nuts contain plentiful amounts.

Phytoestrogens Chemicals of plant origin that resemble the female hormone oestrogen are abundant in soya beans and soya products such as soya drinks and tofu. They may also help protect against prostate and other cancers by preventing the growth of tumours (see page 187).

Antioxidants Fruit and vegetables are high in antioxidants which may lower the risk of cervical cancer (see page 118).

Arginine An increased sperm count and the ability of sperm to move are both helped by the mineral arginine. Protein foods such as lean meat, eggs, beans and pulses, nuts and seeds and dairy products such as cheese are good sources.

UNWANTED SIDE EFFECTS

Your diet can also help to protect you against some of the unwelcome effects of an active sexual life. Cystitis, for example, is probably the most common urinary tract infection (or UTI) in women. It is popularly known as 'honeymoon cystitis' because it can result from frequent and vigorous sexual intercourse.

Cystitis is caused by a bacterial infection of the bladder or the urethra, resulting in a painful burning sensation on urination. The symptoms of cystitis can be relieved effectively by drinking at least 3 litres (5 pints) – of water a day, which helps to flush the bacteria out of the bladder and dilutes the urine, which makes it less acidic and not so painful to pass. Sufferers should avoid strong tea, coffee and citrus juices, which can irritate the bladder lining. Fresh cranberries and cranberry juice can also help – as a preventative measure, drink between 350 and 500 ml (12-18 fl oz) daily. It is now believed that increasing

Cranberries and blueberries contain a natural antibiotic that prevents *E. coli* bacteria, responsible for causing cystitis, from sticking to the bladder walls.

GINKGO BILOBA *improves blood flow to the brain and other organs and there is some evidence to suggest that it may also help to correct male erectile dysfunction and impotence. Supplements of ginkgo biloba are available from health food stores.*

REDUCING CAFFEINE *is particularly important for men who suffer from impotence. This is because a high daily intake can have the effect of restricting the flow of blood to the penis. Caffeine is found in tea, coffee and cola drinks.*

OYSTERS *are rich in zinc – a deficiency in this mineral has been linked with a lack of the male sex hormone testosterone. Some studies have shown that, for those men who have low zinc levels, eating foods high in zinc and taking zinc supplements can help to alleviate the problem.*

EAT TO BEAT impotence

vitamin C intake may assist by reducing the growth of bacteria. In addition, naturopaths recommend an infusion of fennel seeds.

Improving your diet may also help to overcome other problems, such as yeast infections (see page 78) and prostate problems (page 186), as well as certain longer-term medical problems such as high blood pressure, prolonged stress or high cholesterol levels, all of which are known to reduce sex drive.

MALE IMPOTENCE

A man's ability to get or sustain an erection can be affected by physical or psychological factors. Fatigue, stress, and depression are common causes. Impotence can also occur as a side-effect of a physical disorder such as diabetes mellitus, atherosclerosis and certain neurological problems. Medications may also affect a man's erection – beta blockers, antihypertensives and antidepressants are frequent causes.

In many cases, changes in diet can result in significant improvements. Blood circulation to the penis can be impaired by the build-up of cholesterol and fatty deposits (see pages 54-56), and a low-fat diet may help to improve blood flow.

Where the problem has a hormonal cause, eating foods rich in zinc and vitamin B_6 may help to boost the production of male sex hormones. Too much alcohol can weaken the strength of nerve signals to the penis and suppress the manufacture of male sex hormones, so it's best to limit alcohol consumption to one drink a day.

DO APHRODISIACS WORK?

Food and sexual prowess have been linked throughout history. Casanova was reputed to eat 70 oysters a day; the Romans fed chickpeas to their stallions to improve their performance; and the *Kama Sutra* recommends honey to increase sexual arousal. Hundreds of different

foods, herbs and spices – from anchovies to aniseed – are claimed to have aphrodisiac properties.

Aphrodisiacs are named after Aphrodite, the Greek goddess of love, who was said to be born from the sea, which perhaps explains why seafood has the reputation for possessing aphrodisiac qualities. Chillies and other spices are also believed to increase sexual performance – perhaps because they produce similar physiological effects to those experienced during sex, such as a raised pulse and sweating.

In ancient times, many people believed in the law of similarity, reasoning that food or roots such as ginseng and asparagus that resembled genitalia must possess sexual powers. Foods that are symbolic of life or procreation such as eggs, caviar, figs, pomegranates, nuts and seeds are often reputed to increase fertility. Such claims are based on folklore rather than fact, however, and there is no scientific

evidence to prove that any of these foodstuffs really do improve sexual performance. But food, like sex, is a sensual pleasure involving smell, taste, texture and appearance, and if you are in the right frame of mind, with the right person, even a meal of baked beans on toast can be an effective aphrodisiac.

The foods of love The following foods have all been claimed to enhance sexual pleasure. While there is no scientific proof of this, they contain many beneficial nutrients – and there is certainly no harm in experimenting with them.

Prunes The Elizabethans served prunes in brothels as they considered them to be effective aphrodisiacs.

Ginseng The word ginseng means 'man root' and the plant's reputation probably arises from its visual similarity to male genitalia.

Aniseed In Ancient India, aniseed was mixed to a paste with honey and rubbed into the sexual organs.

Onions and garlic In the belief that these enhanced sexual stamina and desire, celibate Egyptian priests were forbidden from eating these foods.

Ginger Some people believe that this aromatic root stimulates sexual desire and increases the flow of blood to the penis.

Carrots The ancient Greeks believed that carrots were highly aphrodisiac. They also ate the seeds and foliage to boost sexual performance.

Artichokes There is an old French saying that goes, 'Artichokes, like wine, are good for ladies – when gentlemen eat them.'

Aubergine This vegetable is a renowned aphrodisiac in India. The *Kama Sutra* suggests rubbing the juice of the aubergine on your partner's body to increase desire.

MENUPLAN
to enhance your sex drive

These foods will not only keep you active during the day – but will energise you throughout the night as well.

MORNING BOOST Blend blueberries with unsweetened soya drink for a great start to the day; or have oat porridge with a swirl of low-fat yoghurt and berry fruits. Add a handful of raisins or chopped fresh fruit to wholegrain cereals for extra manganese. Serve with soya drink.

LIGHT LUNCHES For extra zinc eat a wholemeal sandwich or roll filled with lean meat, chicken or prawns and watercress; or crab pâté spread on toast. Heat up a can of tomato soup: it's quick, easy and provides lots of lycopene. Or pile some prawns into half an avocado, drizzle with olive oil and fresh lemon and season with a twist of pepper.

EVENING MEALS Lean meat, chicken or fish with plenty of dark green leafy vegetables and rice will keep your libido healthy. Finish with fresh fruit or a soya yoghurt. Or try Mango and Champagne Sorbet (recipe overleaf) for a special dessert.

DRINKS AND SNACKS Bananas or peanuts boost your B_6 intake; and carrot or other pure fruit juices provide antioxidant vitamins; make smoothies with soya drink and fruit; and eat soya yoghurt.

A blueberry muesli — the perfect way to start the day

Blueberry Muesli
Pour 100 ml (4 fl oz) semi-skimmed milk over 55 g (2 oz) sugar-free muesli, stir in 1 level teaspoon demerara sugar, 2 teaspoons wheatgerm and 80 g (3 oz) blueberries. Serve with a spoonful of no-fat Greek yoghurt. Serves 1

NUTRIENTS PER SERVING: Calories **300** Carbohydrate **52 g** (sugars **23 g**) Protein **13 g** Fat **6 g** (saturated **1 g**) Fibre **7 g**

mango and champagne sorbet

This special occasion dessert gets a lift from champagne, but a dry sparkling wine makes a good substitute. The sorbet looks elegant served in glasses, rather than dessert dishes. You can also serve it with amaretti biscuits.

preparation time: **15 minutes**

freezing time: **about 5 hours**

serves **4**

NUTRIENTS PER SERVING	
calories	114
carbohydrate	34 g
(sugars)	33 g
protein	2.5 g
fat	0.3 g
(saturated)	0
fibre	3 g

4 ripe mangoes, puréed to give about
  500 ml (18 fl oz) purée
250 ml (9 fl oz) champagne or dry
  sparkling white wine
Juice of 1 lime
50 g (1¾ oz) icing sugar
2 egg whites
Lime slices, to garnish

1 Place the mango purée in a large bowl and pour in the champagne and lime juice. Sieve in the icing sugar and mix the ingredients together well.

2 Pour the mixture into a shallow, freezerproof plastic container, cover and freeze for about 3 hours, until half-frozen and mushy.

3 Put the egg whites in a large, dry bowl and whisk them until stiff. Spoon in the mango mixture and fold together lightly with a metal spoon.

4 Pour the mixture into a freezerproof container, cover and freeze for about 2 hours, or until firm. Serve straight from the freezer, with *langue de chat* biscuits, and garnish with lime slices.

stuffed **artichokes** with **prawns**

Artichokes taste wonderful and eating them encourages you and your dining partner to use your fingers in the most sensuous way. This dish makes a special starter for a supper party. It's a little fiddly to prepare but the effort is well worth the spectacular result.

preparation time: **20 minutes**

cooking time: **20 minutes**

serves **2**

Zest and juice of 1 large lemon
2 globe artichokes, trimmed, and stalks and
    any tough outer leaves removed
1 tablespoon olive oil
1 large clove garlic, crushed or finely
    chopped
3 spring onions, finely chopped
175 g (6 oz) peeled, cooked tiger prawns,
    shelled, but tails left on
4 plum tomatoes, quartered, deseeded and
    cut into small dice
Salt and black pepper
Lemon-flavoured olive oil, to serve

1 Put the lemon juice in a large pan of water and bring to the boil. Lower the artichokes into the boiling water. Cover the pan and cook the artichokes for about 20 minutes, or until you can easily pull a leaf away from the base.

2 Remove the artichokes from the pan and set aside, upside down, to drain and cool. Slice off the top and scoop out the hairy choke.

3 Heat the olive oil in a pan, add the garlic and cook over a medium heat for 4 minutes. Add the spring onions and cook for 2–3 minutes. Add the prawns and cook for a further 2 minutes, stirring continuously. Stir in the tomatoes, lemon zest and seasoning.

4 Spoon the prawn mixture into the artichokes. Drizzle with a little lemon-flavoured olive oil, and garnish with extra lemon zest, if you wish. Serve immediately.

NUTRIENTS PER SERVING	
calories	200
carbohydrate	11 g
(sugars)	8 g
protein	26 g
fat	8 g
(saturated)	1.5 g
fibre	2 g

halibut **with watercress** pesto

The watercress in this pesto is a fresh-tasting alternative to basil – the clean, peppery flavour harmonises beautifully with the halibut, whether it is grilled or griddled. Served with a mixture of roasted vegetables, it makes a superb dish for supper à deux.

preparation time: **15 minutes**

cooking time: **30 minutes**

serves **2**

2 halibut steaks, each about 200 g (7 oz)
Salt and black pepper
FOR THE PESTO
85 g (3 oz) watercress
2 tablespoons pine nuts
55 g (2 oz) freshly grated Parmesan cheese
5 tablespoons olive oil
3 cloves garlic
Watercress leaves, to garnish

1 Place the halibut under a moderately hot grill or on a lightly oiled griddle pan, season with salt and pepper and cook for 4–6 minutes on each side, or until cooked through.

2 To make the pesto, place the watercress, pine nuts, Parmesan, olive oil and garlic in a food processor and process to a purée. Serve the salmon with the pesto, and a mixture of roasted vegetables.

NUTRIENTS PER SERVING	
calories	665
carbohydrate	1 g
(sugars)	1 g
protein	49 g
fat	52 g
(saturated)	11 g
fibre	1 g

Building strong defences

Certain foods give a powerful boost to your immune system – they are wonderful allies in protecting you against colds and flu, as well as helping you to avoid serious illnesses such as cancer. Using food to build up your body's defences makes you better equipped to combat infection.

Your immune system thrives best on a varied, well-balanced diet, plenty of exercise, good sleep and a positive attitude to life. But there are several foods that are particularly helpful in strengthening your resistance; these can make your immune system super-efficient. Knowing how your body's defences operate, and choosing the best foods to boost them, gives you a head start.

HOW IMMUNITY WORKS

Your immune system is made up of bone marrow, thymus glands, lymph nodes and spleen, also your skin, lungs and gastrointestinal tract. Together, these constitute an

elaborate defence system which protects your body against invasion by foreign substances such as bacteria and viruses.

The major players in your immune response are the white blood cells. There are several different types of white blood cell, each with a specific role to play. Phagocytes – made by the bone marrow – are responsible for digesting bacteria and deactivating toxins (for example from septicaemia or blood poisoning). Other white cells, called lymphocytes, produce antibodies. These are involved in identifying and killing substances that your body identifies as foreign

(such as blood cells from an incompatible blood group), as well as providing general immunity.

Sometimes the immune system can become over-eager and attacks the body's own cells – a condition known as auto-immunity. This can cause problems such as rheumatoid arthritis, in which the joints become swollen and stiff and, in severe cases, deformed (see page 332).

The immune system may also occasionally identify normally harmless foods such as strawberries

Safe from attack Eating plenty of antioxidant foods gives a great boost to your immunity, creating an effective barrier against infection.

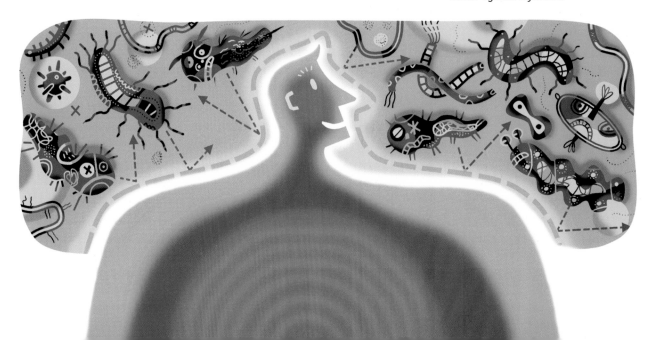

A POTENT BLEND *Combine immune-boosting foods such as vegetables rich in beta carotene. Adding puréed carrot, sweet potato and pumpkin to mashed potatoes will improve your resistance to infection.*

1 *Blend red peppers, carrots, passata, lemon juice and pepper to make a tangy fresh drink.*

2 *Purée fresh or frozen raspberries or else strawberries to make a delicious fruit coulis.*

3 *Use red and yellow peppers, tomatoes and finely chopped chilli and garlic to make a spicy salsa and serve it with roast meat or fish.*

4 *Use watercress instead of lettuce in sandwiches.*

5 *Blend strawberries or raspberries with a carton of live yoghurt and a little milk for a delicious fruit smoothie.*

6 *Sweet potatoes are delicious baked and have plenty of beta carotene and vitamin E.*

7 *Dried apricots make a great snack and are a rich source of beta carotene.*

SEVEN WAYS TO boost your immune system

or shellfish as foreign invaders and produces antibodies to that particular food, resulting in an allergic reaction (see page 124).

Stress, poor diet and nutritional deficiencies make you susceptible to infection. But you can counteract these factors by eating foods that strengthen your immune system.

Immunity-boosting foods

Certain foods are widely known for their protective properties. **Oriental mushrooms** such as shiitake (see page 119), oyster, enoki and tree ear are renowned for improving immunity and are associated with longevity in Asian cultures. Shiitake and oyster varieties are available in supermarkets.

Live yoghurt contains *Lactobacillus acidophilus* bacteria: these stimulate cells that fight bacteria and increase the production of the antiviral agent gamma-interferon. As a result, people who eat live yoghurt regularly have 25 per cent fewer colds than those who eat it rarely or never. **Garlic** has been used throughout history to treat colds and flu; now folklore has been backed up by science. Garlic contains a chemical called allicin, which is responsible for its characteristic smell and taste. A powerful antibiotic, allicin has

both antiviral and antifungal powers. Enthusiasts claim that garlic must be eaten raw in order to reap its full benefits, but it is not yet known if allicin is deactivated by cooking.

The essential nutrients

Your immune system requires specific vitamins to be effective. **Fruit and vegetables** are the most accessible all-round sources of these vitamins. Spinach, watercress, carrots, sweet potatoes, broccoli, peppers and mangoes all provide beta carotene, while citrus fruit such

bodyworks

as oranges, lemons, grapefruit, mandarins, kiwi fruit, raspberries and strawberries, supply vitamin C.

ANTIOXIDANTS

All fruit and vegetables contain a group of phytochemicals (plant chemicals) known as antioxidants. Without these chemicals you will become vulnerable to illness (even cancer and heart disease) within a few months. The body produces its own antioxidants, but you also need to obtain them from food.

Free radicals Antioxidants neutralise harmful substances produced by your body. Called free radicals, these are normal by-products of your metabolism (such as breathing). Their creation is also triggered by cigarette smoke and environmental pollutants, and your immune cells release them in response to invading bacteria and viruses. Left unchecked, free radicals can upset the healthy functioning of body cells. The immune system produces its own antioxidants to prevent cell damage. But you can improve this function by eating foods rich in antioxidants.

The major protectors

The first line of defence against invasion by foreign bodies is the skin and the mucous membranes that line the gastrointestinal tract.

Vitamin A is the main antioxidant needed to keep skin and mucous membranes healthy. It ensures that immune cells develop properly, combats the effects of ageing and disease and also protects against skin cancer. Foods rich in vitamin A include liver and kidneys, oily fish, full-fat milk, egg yolk, cheese, margarine and butter.

Beta carotene Orange, red, yellow and dark green fruit and vegetables such as melons, carrots, apricots, pumpkin, broccoli and mangoes are rich in beta carotene, which your body converts into vitamin A.

Vitamin C strengthens immunity by increasing the numbers of your immune system cells and boosting their ability to kill bacteria and viruses. Best sources are citrus fruit such as oranges, lemons, grapefruit.

Vitamin E prevents damage caused by oxidation of polyunsaturated acids in cell membranes. It also helps to maintain the structure of the immune cells and tissues and improves the functioning of your lymph tissue. Seeds and seed oils, margarine, avocados, nuts, wheatgerm, wholemeal bread, and egg yolks will boost your levels.

Zinc is crucial for the production of antibodies and for a healthy immune system. Even a mild deficiency can increase your susceptibility to infection. Oysters and other shellfish, pulses, pumpkin seeds and wholemeal bread are good sources.

Iron is an essential component of haemoglobin and many enzymes involved in the metabolism of energy. An iron deficiency will lower your immunity to infection by reducing the activity of white cells. Red meat, liver and offal, egg yolks, pulses and

Strengthen your defences Regular exercise is one of the best ways of boosting your immunity to infections. Ideally, you should aim to achieve at least 30 minutes continuous physical activity every day.

shiitake

Shiitake mushrooms contain a compound called lentinan, which is thought to protect against cancer in two ways. It prevents normal cells from developing into tumours and also inhibits the growth of tumours. Fresh shiitake mushrooms are readily available in supermarkets – they have a meaty, slightly smoky flavour and are delicious in stir-fries or sautéed with a little oil and garlic. They are also available in dried form.

dark green leafy vegetables such as spinach are all rich in iron.

Some other helpful vitamins and minerals are vitamin B_6, folic acid, pantothenic acid, selenium, copper magnesium, nickel and tin. But stick to recommended levels of these (see page 341). Too much of a particular vitamin or mineral can inhibit the functioning of your immune system.

FOODS TO COMBAT CANCER

Two out of five people will develop cancer at some time in their life. As up to one-third of all cancers are linked to poor diet, the right foods can significantly reduce the risk.

Wiser choices It is now thought that a change in eating habits could prevent nine out of ten deaths from cancer of the bowel and halve the number of deaths from breast cancer.

The relationship between diet and cancer is complex: some foods are protective, others increase risk. But there is no doubt that changing the focus of your diet towards fruit and vegetables helps to boost the body's natural defences. Keep your fruit bowl full and on display – seeing it will stimulate your tastebuds. Buy fresh fruit and vegetables on a 'little and often' basis, and store them in the fridge or a cool place to minimise vitamin loss. And eat them within two or three days of purchase.

Fibre and cancer protection

One simple way to lessen the risk of cancer is to increase your intake of fibre (see page 76 for ways of doing this). A fibre-rich diet protects you against bowel cancer and possibly breast cancer as well.

Fibre comes in two forms, soluble and insoluble. Insoluble fibre speeds up the rate at which waste is passed through the body, reducing the time that any cancer-causing substances remain in contact with the intestine.

Echinacea

There are many herbal remedies that are believed to strengthen the immune system. But the most popular and widely researched is echinacea, a herb native to North America.

Traditionally used by American Indians to treat a variety of conditions, from the common cold to snake bites, echinacea is thought to stimulate the immune system. It helps the body to fight infections by increasing the number and activity of infection-fighting white blood cells. Echinacea is now widely used as a means of preventing the onset, severity and duration of the common cold.

MENUPLAN
five-a-day anti-cancer foods

Introduce at least five servings a day from the following selection of foods to your daily menu – and vary your choices throughout the week. Fresh, frozen, canned and dried fruits and vegetables, and fruit juices all count as part of your five servings.

Each day choose five items from the selection below — one serving is equivalent to 85g (3oz):

ONE APPLE, PEAR, PEACH, ORANGE OR BANANA Pile slices of these on to your high-fibre breakfast cereal or have fruit as regular snacks.

TWO MEDIUM-SIZED FRUITS such as kiwi, plum, or tangerine. These make good snacks in between meals.

THREE PIECES OF DRIED FRUIT such as apricots and prunes. They're easy nibbles for car or train travel.

Take five fruits and give your immune system a boost

ONE AVOCADO OR GRAPEFRUIT HALF These make a good first course for lunch or supper. Garnish your avocado with prawns for extra nutrient value.

ONE CUP OF FRUIT such as strawberries, raspberries, cherries or grapes. Add any of these to breakfast cereals or include them in a colourful fruit salad or a fruit kebab for dessert.

TWO OR THREE TABLESPOONS OF FRUIT SALAD or stewed fruit — eat as a dessert or with breakfast.

TWO TABLESPOONS OF LIGHTLY COOKED VEGETABLES Remember to cook these the healthy way. Vegetables retain cancer-protection properties if they are steamed, stir-fried or griddled.

ONE BOWL OF SALAD Include this in all your main meals such as lunch or supper.

ONE GLASS OF FRUIT JUICE Deliciously refreshing, fruit juice is good at any time of day.

Soluble fibre is fermented in the colon, producing chemicals that help to combat cancer. Researchers are also investigating the protective action of fibre on levels of oestrogen in the body. High levels of the hormone are a known factor in the development of breast cancer.
Soya and cancer There is growing evidence to suggest that soya has an important role to play in preventing certain cancers, including breast, prostate and colon (see pages 184-185). In Far Eastern countries, where soya is a staple food, breast cancer accounts for only 70 deaths per 100,000 women, as compared with 225 deaths per 100,000 in the United Kingdom. Similarly, there is a reduced incidence of prostate and colon cancer in countries where soya is prevalent in the diet.

The natural pigment lycopene (see page 111) is highly concentrated in tomatoes, and has impressive cancer-fighting properties. Lycopene is also found in pink grapefruit, watermelon and guava.
Tea Powerful antioxidants called flavonoids are the active anti-cancer agents in tea. Green tea is considered to be particularly beneficial (see page 219) and is now believed to lower the risk of some digestive and urinary tract cancers.

WHAT TO AVOID

You should not ruin your enjoyment of life by becoming over-anxious about what you eat. But it is important to know which foods place you at risk of cancer.

Red meat Eating over 140 grams (5 ounces) a day increases the risk of certain cancers, particularly cancer of the colon. Average consumption of red meat in the United Kingdom is 90 grams (3¼ ounces) a day. If you regularly eat more than this amount, try to cut down, and aim to have red meat only twice a week.

Other foods to watch Cured and smoked meats and fish should be eaten only occasionally – two or three times a month rather than every week. The same cautionary approach applies to pickles and charred foods (particularly charred fatty foods). These contain specific substances that are known to play a role in causing cancer.

Alcohol and cigarettes You are at risk of cancer of the mouth, throat, larynx, oesophagus and liver if you drink heavily. Stick to the safe guidelines recommended on page 97. If you smoke as well, the chances are even higher: the best thing you can do for your health is to stop smoking (see page 69).

Cut down on fat A diet high in fat (especially saturated fat) increases your vulnerability to cancer of the breast, bowel, pancreas and prostate. Unsaturated fats such as olive oil and foods rich in omega-3 fatty acids, such as oily fish provide excellent protection (see page 56).

Almost one-third of the fat you eat comes from oil, butter, margarine or low-fat spreads. While you should keep your total fat intake to about a third of your diet, saturated fat should be firmly restricted to around ten per cent of total energy (see the Five Food Groups, pages 11-15).

If you are watching your weight, don't assume that you should use butter because it has slightly less Calories (37 per teaspoon) compared with olive oil (45 Calories per teaspoon). Unsaturated fats are always a healthier choice. The message is clear: use fat sparingly; choose lean cuts of meat, trim off visible fat, and use fat-free methods of cooking, such as steaming (below), griddling, poaching as well as *en papillote* (see page 260).

steaming

The health benefits of steaming

RETAINS NUTRIENTS Steaming retains the nutrients in food. For example, broccoli can lose over 60 per cent of its vitamin C when it is boiled, but only 20 per cent when steamed. It is also a healthy, low-fat cooking method – frying food in just 1 tablespoon of oil adds 135 Calories.

VARIETY You can steam fish, poultry, puddings, sponges, couscous, custard and dumplings as well as vegetables.

The method Steaming is easy – put the food in a perforated pan or colander and fit it over a pan of boiling water. Cover with a close-fitting lid – the steam cooks the food. Use stacking sets of stainless steel steamers or Chinese bamboo.

Preparation Some foods should be covered before steaming – wrap fish in a parcel of kitchen foil and fit sponge puddings into heat-resistant pudding bowls with clip-on lids.

pork and shiitake mushroom stir-fry

This authentic stir-fry is quick, easy and full of flavour. Shiitake mushrooms add their deliciously smoky aromas – and are renowned for their immune-boosting properties. They are available in larger supermarkets and from some greengrocers.

preparation time: **10 minutes**

cooking time: **9 minutes**

serves **4**

NUTRIENTS PER SERVING	
calories	237
carbohydrate	7
(sugars)	6
protein	28 g
fat	11 g
(saturated)	2.5 g
fibre	3 g

2 tablespoons sesame or vegetable oil

450 g (1 lb) pork tenderloin, finely sliced

2 cloves garlic, crushed

2.5 cm (1 in) fresh root ginger, peeled and finely chopped

1 bunch of spring onions, cut into thin slices 3 cm (1¼ in) long

200 g (7 oz) baby sweetcorn, halved lengthways

225 g (8 oz) shiitake mushrooms

3 tablespoons black bean sauce

1 tablespoon runny honey

225 g (8 oz) pak choi, trimmed (use Savoy cabbage if pak choi is unavailable)

Noodles to serve

1 tablespoon sesame oil, to garnish

Finely sliced spring onions, to garnish

1 Heat 1 tablespoon of oil in a wok or large frying pan, add the pork and stir-fry over a high heat for 3 minutes or until browned. Remove from the pan and set aside.

2 Wipe the wok clean with kitchen paper, add the remaining oil and heat. Once the oil is hot add the garlic and ginger and stir-fry for 1 minute. Add the spring onions, sweetcorn and mushrooms and continue cooking for 2–3 minutes.

3 Return the pork to the pan and stir in the black bean sauce, honey, 3 tablespoons of water and the pak choi. Cook for 3 minutes or until the sauce is bubbling and hot.

4 Cook the noodles according to the packet instructions. Drain, then stir in the sesame oil.

5 Place the noodles and pork in a bowl and garnish with spring onions.

chicken with sweet pepper relish

Try this light, aromatic way of cooking chicken with a rainbow of colourful peppers. Serve it on a bed of polenta or couscous. The relish would also make a good accompaniment to grilled or griddled fillets of lean pork.

preparation time: **15 minutes**

cooking time: **40 minutes**

serves **4**

3 red peppers, halved and deseeded
2 yellow peppers, halved and deseeded
2 orange peppers, halved and deseeded
85 g (3 oz) reduced-fat soft cheese
Salt and black pepper
4 skinless chicken breasts
8 slices of Parma ham
2–3 tablespoons sweet chilli sauce

1 Place the peppers under a hot grill for about 10–15 minutes or until the skin is black. Cover with a clean wet cloth or place in a plastic bag and allow to cool for about 10 minutes. Remove the skin from the peppers and blot dry with absorbent kitchen paper.

2 Place 1 red pepper in a food processor or blender and pulse until roughly chopped. Transfer to a bowl, add the cheese and mix well. Season to taste.

3 Using a sharp knife, make a lengthways slit in each chicken breast and spoon in a little of the cheese mixture. Wrap 2 slices of ham around each chicken breast and enclose in a foil parcel. Cook at 190°C (375°F, gas mark 5) for 30 minutes or until the chicken is cooked.

4 To make the relish, slice the remaining peppers into thin strips and transfer to a bowl. Stir in the chilli sauce and mix well. Remove the chicken from the foil parcel, allow to rest for 5 minutes then slice and serve with the pepper relish.

NUTRIENTS PER SERVING	
calories	346
carbohydrate	22 g
(sugars)	22 g
protein	37 g
fat	11 g
(saturated)	4.5 g
fibre	6 g

carrot and ginger soup

The pungent flavours of ginger, garlic and orange add instant appeal to a familiar ingredient. Make this vibrantly colourful soup with a home-made stock – it tastes better and it is also healthily low in salt.

preparation time: **15 minutes**

cooking time: **40 minutes**

serves **4**

2 tablespoons olive oil
1 medium onion, peeled and finely chopped
1 clove garlic, crushed or finely chopped
5 cm (2 in) piece fresh root ginger, finely
*   chopped*
600 g (1 lb 5 oz) carrots, peeled and
*   roughly chopped*
700 ml (1¼ pints) vegetable stock
*   (recipe on page 338)*
Zest and juice of 2 large oranges
Salt and black pepper
Chives, chopped, to garnish

1 Heat the oil in large pan, put in the onion, garlic and ginger, and cook over a medium heat for 3-4 minutes. Add the carrots and continue cooking for a further 5 minutes, stirring occasionally. Pour in the stock, orange juice and zest, season and bring to the boil. Reduce the heat, cover and simmer for 30 minutes or until the carrots are soft.

2 Purée in a food processor until smooth. Return to the pan and reheat gently. Garnish with the chopped chives.

NUTRIENTS PER SERVING	
calories	122
carbohydrate	16 g
(sugars)	14 g
protein	2 g
fat	6 g
(saturated)	0.9 g
fibre	4 g

FOOD ALLERGIES

Most people enjoy foods such as dairy products and cereals as a problem-free part of a healthy diet. However, for those who have over-sensitive immune systems, substances found in these foods can cause an allergic reaction.

If you have a food allergy, this need not spoil your pleasure in food – you can still eat really well. With a little imagination, your meals can be both delicious and satisfying. The solution is simply to be willing to experiment, and to broaden your repertoire of ingredients and recipes.

What is a food allergy?

Any food can provoke an allergic reaction, but some are more common than others. Wheat, cow's milk, shellfish, peanuts, eggs and citrus fruit are all known to trigger allergic responses in susceptible individuals.

In their cases, the immune system over-reacts to a normally harmless food or ingredient by producing antibodies. These trigger the release of histamine and other chemicals into the blood stream, resulting in an allergic reaction. Even the tiniest amount of a food to which someone is allergic will cause a reaction.

Allergic symptoms The type of reaction varies from swelling of the lips to asthma, eczema, nettle rash (urticaria), vomiting and diarrhoea. In the most extreme cases, a severe reaction called anaphylactic shock develops, resulting in breathing difficulties, a sudden drop in blood pressure and – very rarely – in death. Avoiding the culprit food is the only way to avoid such reactions.

Family patterns Food allergies can strike at any age but are most common in children. They can be temporary (eight out of ten children grow out of a food allergy by the age of five years) or lifelong conditions. Allergies run in families, so children of parents who have a food allergy are more likely to inherit the problem. Weaning a child too early has been linked with food allergies and parents of young babies should be aware of this (see page 137).

Other conditions such as stress, poor diet and ill health can both increase susceptibility, and make existing allergies worse.

Food intolerance

You may have an adverse reaction to a particular food, but test negatively for allergy. When this happens, the term 'intolerance' rather than allergy is used. Intolerance may be caused by a problem with certain digestive enzymes in the body. Different kinds of these are needed to break down specific foods. But some people fail to make the enzyme required to digest a particular food. Lactose intolerance (see opposite) is a good example of this.

In less straightforward cases, food intolerance may cause similar symptoms to allergies, such as a rash or headache. These may be the result of a reaction to specific chemicals present in food, such as caffeine in coffee and tea, or substances known as vasoactive amines in cheese and chocolate. In these circumstances, the immune system may be involved in some way, but precisely how and why is not known.

what's the trigger?

A wide range of ailments are known to be caused by certain foods.

Asthma – milk and dairy products, eggs, fish, nuts, certain food additives, particularly tartrazine (E102), sulphur dioxide (E220) and sodium benzoate (E211).

Eczema – cow's milk and dairy products, eggs.

Digestive problems such as diarrhoea, bloating – milk and dairy products, wheat and grains, yeast.

Irritable bowel syndrome – wheat and dairy products.

Urticaria (hives or nettle rash) – almost any food can cause urticaria in susceptible people, including strawberries, shellfish, papaya and food additives, notably tartrazine (E102) and sodium benzoate (E211).

Sinus problems and rhinitis (constantly runny nose) – wheat, eggs, food colouring (particularly azo dyes), salicylates (found in aspirin, some fruits such as strawberries) and sodium benzoate (E211).

Migraine and headaches – cheese, chocolate, citrus fruits, caffeine and red wine are common trigger foods for migraine and headache.

Testing for food allergy

Estimates vary, but it is believed that three in every ten people in the United Kingdom suffer from a food-related allergy or intolerance. And these conditions can be difficult to diagnose. If symptoms occur almost immediately after a particular food is eaten, it is easier to identify the culprit. But there is often a delay between eating the food and the onset of symptoms. Also, the same food can provoke different symptoms in different people.

Skin prick tests are often used by specialists to help identify allergies. The surface of the skin is scratched or pricked with a needle containing a small amount of the suspected food. If an allergic reaction occurs, the skin becomes red and slightly swollen. These tests are not 100 per cent reliable, but are useful guides.

Exclusion diets The most reliable way to diagnose an allergy or intolerance is to eliminate the suspected food from the diet. This should only be done under medical supervision. If symptoms improve, you are either allergic to, or intolerant of, that particular food.

Several foods may be excluded at once, and each has to be carefully reintroduced, one at a time, in order to establish which is the cause of the problem. If you omit several foods from your diet, or a single food group such as dairy products, it can result in a serious nutritional deficiency. This is just one of many good reasons to seek medical advice.

Problems with dairy products

Dairy products can cause a number of serious problems. The inability to digest milk is one of these. The medical name for this is lactose intolerance, a condition in which the body fails to produce an enzyme called lactase, necessary for digesting lactose, a natural sugar in milk.

Seven per cent of babies and children under five years suffer from an intolerance to cow's milk. But milk and dairy products can cause problems for adults too. Without lactase, lactose cannot be digested. Instead, it passes unchanged into the large intestine where it is fermented by bacteria there, causing bloating, abdominal pains and diarrhoea.

The inherited condition called lactase deficiency, which becomes apparent shortly after birth, is very rare. A temporary lactose intolerance, after you have suffered a stomach upset such as gastroenteritis, is much more common.

Some people have an allergy to the protein in cow's milk; this is less common than lactose intolerance, but may cause similar symptoms. It can occur at any age.

If you have a lactose intolerance, you may be able to cope with very small quantities of milk and other dairy foods without any ill effects. But in more severe cases, avoidance is the only strategy, and you'll need to use alternatives such as soya and other lactose free products.

Exploring the options Browse around your local health food store and experiment with the various products – pour soya milk over cereals or use coconut milk in a milk shake. Alternatives do exist – some people with cow's milk protein allergy can substitute sheep's or goat's

Alternatives to dairy foods *If you have to avoid dairy products there are various lactose-free alternatives. These are available at larger supermarkets and health stores and include soya milk (above left), coconut milk, oat drink, soya margarine, and non-dairy olive oil spread (above right).*

milk, and other products such as cheese and yoghurt made from these. **Severe lactose intolerance** You may have to avoid milk in any form – including sheep's and goat's milk. You should also steer clear of dairy products such as cream and soft cheese. However, butter and hard cheese are safe to eat, as they contain very little lactose. And natural yoghurt rarely causes problems.

Many processed foods contain lactose or traces of cow's milk protein, as do some artificial sweeteners and medicines. Check all labels carefully and avoid products that contain lactose.

These are the words you should look for in the list of ingredients: casein or caseinate, hydrolysed casein or whey, lactose, non-fat milk solids, lacalbumin, lactoglobulin, skimmed milk powder, whey, ghee, monosodium glutamate (MSG).

Allergy to cereals

In vulnerable people, an allergy to gluten, a protein in cereals such as wheat, oats, barley and rye damages the tiny, hair-like projections that line the small intestine (called *villi*). These are responsible for the absorption of nutrients.

This condition is called coeliac disease; damage and inflammation to the upper part of the small intestine can cause weight loss and vitamin and mineral deficiencies, such as anaemia. A strict avoidance of all foods that contain gluten brings about a rapid improvement and is usually the only treatment necessary. **Foods to avoid** If you have to follow a gluten-free diet, you will not be able to eat wheat, oats, barley, rye and all products made using them

where to get your calcium

Milk and dairy products provide a large amount of calcium in most diets, so you will have to get it from other sources if you are unable to eat these foods.

Non-dairy sources of calcium include canned fish such as pilchards and sardines, dark green leafy vegetables such as spinach, white bread, apricots, sesame seeds, baked beans and hard water. To enhance your calcium intake, combine ingredients creatively: for example, sprinkle a spinach salad with sesame seeds, and garnish it with croûtons.

If you think you're not getting enough calcium from a dairy-free diet, ask your doctor if you should take a lactose-free supplement.

such as pasta, couscous, cereals, cakes and biscuits. Gluten is often hidden in the ingredients of foods so you should always read the labels. Look out for items such as modified starch and flour-based binders and fillers. Also, be careful to avoid drinks such as lemon barley water and brewed beverages made with barley such as beer and stout.

An experienced dietitian will help you to plan your meals, and will also direct you to specialist organisations. And look in gluten-free cookbooks for recipe ideas. Replace prohibited foods with plenty of potatoes, pulses, rice, corn and nuts.

Tips for the cook When you are on a gluten-free diet, you need to invent ingenious strategies to give variety to your cooking. In fact there are lots of

Gluten-free and delicious Enjoy the oriental flavours in this fragrant Tom Yam Soup. It is made with fresh stock which is healthily low in salt and won't trigger allergic problems. The recipe is on page 128.

different ingredients to use for baking and thickening, and with clever improvisation, you can achieve some really good results. Visit your local health food shop and ask for the gluten-free products, as well as any leaflets that are available and advice on what products they can obtain for you.

Cooking with gluten-free flour

The gluten in flour makes bread rise and produces its characteristic texture. Dishes that are made using various types of gluten-free flour (see below), many of which are available from good health food shops, will not have quite the same texture as those made using wheat flour. With a little practice, however, you will soon be able to produce 'alternative' bread and cakes .

Gluten-free grains and flours, such as rice flour and ground rice, are available as brown or white rice flour. Use them to make biscuits.
Potato flour also called potato starch or farina – is good for baking and is an excellent thickener for sauces.
Soya flour is an excellent source of protein and B vitamins. It has a strong flavour and is best used in combination with other flours.
Cornflour or cornstarch is made from maize. It is a good thickening agent for sauces and can also be used to make cakes, bread and biscuits.
Chickpea flour, also called gram flour or besan flour has a pleasantly strong flavour and is widely used to make Indian breads. It is a good source of protein and vitamins.
Arrowroot is an excellent thickening agent useful for gravies and sauces.
Chestnut flour has a distinctive flavour and can be used successfully for baking cakes and biscuits.
Sago flour has little flavour and is similar to rice flour in texture. Use for puddings and thickening stews.
Tapioca Like sago flour, tapioca is almost pure starch. Use for puddings and for thickening.
Buckwheat flour has a strong, distinctive flavour – it is often used to make buckwheat pancakes. For general baking use it is best mixed with other gluten-free flours.
Maize is gluten-free and is made into cornflour and a wide range of products. These include polenta (try the instant variety sold in supermarkets), popcorn and corn syrup which is used as a sweetener.

tom yam soup

Fragrant lemon grass and kaffir lime leaves from Asian food stores add freshness to this feast of Oriental flavours. If you're allergic to shellfish, replace the prawns with chicken. Cut two cooked and skinned chicken breasts into thin slices and add at step 3.

preparation time: **10 minutes**

cooking time: **15 minutes**

serves **4**

NUTRIENTS PER SERVING	
calories	190
carbohydrate	25 g
(sugars)	1 g
protein	16 g
fat	2.5 g
(saturated)	0.4 g
fibre	1 g

115 g (4 oz) rice noodles
2 teaspoons vegetable oil
2.5 cm (1 in) root ginger, peeled and finely chopped
2 lemon grass stalks, peeled and finely chopped
1 red chilli, deseeded and finely chopped
1.4 litres (2½ pints) home-made chicken stock (recipe page 338)
4 kaffir lime leaves
140 g (5 oz) small mushrooms, thinly sliced
85 g (3 oz) baby sweetcorn, sliced
4 spring onions, finely sliced
280 g (10 oz) cooked and peeled tiger prawns, with tails on
3 tablespoons fish sauce
juice of 2 limes
3 tablespoons chopped fresh coriander
Finely shredded spring onion and red chilli, to garnish

1 Prepare the rice noodles according to the packet instructions.

2 Heat the oil in a large saucepan, add the ginger, lemon grass and chilli and cook for 1 minute. Add the chicken stock, lime leaves, mushrooms, sweetcorn and spring onions. Bring to the boil, then reduce the heat and simmer for 10 minutes.

3 Stir in the noodles, prawns, fish sauce and lime juice and continue cooking for a further 2 minutes. Add the coriander.

4 Remove the lime leaves, divide the soup between 4 serving bowls, garnish with the shredded spring onions and chilli, and serve.

tiger prawn and mangetout stir-fry

This crunchy stir-fry has lots of colour, texture and flavour, and is quick to make. You can serve it with plain rice or rice noodles. Keep a bag of tiger prawns in the freezer, and use those if you don't have time to buy fresh.

preparation time: **5 minutes.**

cooking time: **7-9 minutes**

serves **2**

NUTRIENTS PER SERVING	
calories	200
carbohydrate	10 g
(sugars)	10 g
protein	21 g
fat	7 g
(saturated)	1 g
fibre	3 g

1-2 tablespoons rapeseed or sunflower oil
½ red pepper, deseeded and sliced
½ green pepper, deseeded and sliced
4 salad onions, sliced
100 g (3½ oz) mangetout peas, washed and trimmed
200 g (7 oz) peeled tiger prawns
2.5 cm (1 in) piece of fresh ginger, grated
2 cloves garlic, crushed.
2 tablespoons dry sherry

1 Heat 1 tablespoon of oil in a wok or large non-stick pan over a high heat.

2 Fry the peppers, onions and mangetout for 4-5 minutes, stirring all the time. Add the prawns, and fry for another 2-3 minutes. Sprinkle in the ginger and garlic and a little extra oil if they start to stick. Stir-fry for 1 more minute.

3 Remove from the heat, add the sherry and serve with rice or rice noodles.

lemon **polenta** cake

Bake this light, pretty, lemon-scented cake as a celebration of what you can enjoy when you are following a gluten-free diet. Served with fresh strawberries and blueberries, it's perfect for a tea-time treat or dessert.

preparation time: **15 minutes**

cooking time: **45-50 minutes**

serves **8**

175 g (6 oz) butter
175 g (6 oz) caster sugar
2 large eggs, beaten
150 g (5½ oz) ground almonds
85 g (3 oz) polenta
½ teaspoon gluten-free baking powder
zest of 2 large lemons
2 tablespoons lemon juice
FOR THE LEMON SYRUP
85 g (3 oz) caster sugar
zest and juice of 1 large lemon
icing sugar to dust and fresh strawberries
   and blueberries to serve

1 Preheat the oven to 180°C (350°F, gas mark 4). Line the base of a 17 cm (6½ in) spring-release cake tin with non-stick baking parchment and lightly grease the sides.

2 Cream the butter and sugar until light and fluffy. Gradually beat in the eggs. Fold in the almonds, polenta, baking powder, lemon zest and juice and mix them thoroughly.

3 Spoon the mixture into the prepared tin and bake for 45–50 minutes or until a skewer inserted into the centre comes out clean. Set aside to cool.

4 To make the syrup, place the sugar, lemon zest and juice and 2 tablespoons of water in a small pan and heat until the sugar dissolves. Simmer for 5 minutes, then remove from the heat.

5 Remove the cake from the tin and transfer to a serving plate. Using a cocktail stick, prick the cake in several places. Drizzle over the syrup. Dust the cake with icing sugar before serving.

NUTRIENTS PER SERVING	
calories	466
carbohydrate	43 g
(sugars)	35 g
protein	7 g
fat	30 g
(saturated)	13 g
fibre	1.5 g

building strong defences

PART TWO

Journey through the years

From birth to a grand old age, food makes all the difference. Right from the start, folates from green, leafy vegetables and other foods are crucial for a baby's healthy development; and growing children need the right nutrients to build strong bones and provide abundant energy. With the passing years, your nutritional needs change – and, by fine-tuning what you eat to each stage, you can feel and look your best at any time of your life.

Only the best will do

Every parent wants to give their baby and toddler a good start in life – and this means choosing the right food from the beginning. By providing your child with a balanced diet and establishing healthy eating habits during the early years, you are giving them a firm foundation for years to come.

When you hold your newborn baby in your arms for the first time, you will find it difficult to believe how quickly such a tiny creature will grow; in fact babies more than double their birth weight in the first six months of life. Although this rate of growth slows down slightly at the toddler stage, babies continue to gain weight steadily. During these early years, babies and toddlers need much higher levels of nutrients than adults.

BABIES – DOWN TO BASICS

Unlike adults, for whom a low-fat, high-fibre diet is best, babies and toddlers have small stomachs and need highly concentrated sources of energy and nutrients to fuel their growth. Fat is the most concentrated form of energy, and a good supply is essential for babies. Breast milk contains special polyunsaturated fatty acids that are crucial for the development of the brain, the central nervous system and the eyes. Until babies are weaned, breast or formula milk will provide them with all the energy they need.

Building blocks

Babies need three times as much protein as adults per unit of body weight. This vital nutrient is used to build all the cells and tissues that enable your child to grow. Breast or formula milk supplies all the protein babies need in the first six months of life. But as they begin to eat more solid food and drink less milk, protein must be provided from other sources. Meat and/or pulses should be introduced to the weaning diet by six months. After six months, you can start introducing fish and well-cooked eggs.

Essential minerals Iron is an essential component of haemoglobin, the red pigment in blood which transports oxygen to all cells

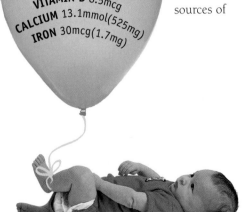

0-3 MONTHS
ENERGY(kcal)
545(male) 515(female)
PROTEIN 12.5g
VITAMIN C 25mg
VITAMIN A 350mcg
VITAMIN D 8.5mcg
CALCIUM 13.1mmol(525mg)
IRON 30mcg(1.7mg)

4-6 MONTHS
ENERGY(kcal)
690(male) 645(female)
PROTEIN 12.7g
VITAMIN C 25mg
VITAMIN A 350mcg
VITAMIN D 8.5mcg
CALCIUM 13.1mmol(525mg)
IRON 80mcg(4.3mg)

7-9 MONTHS
ENERGY(kcal)
825(male) 765(female)
PROTEIN 13.7g
VITAMIN C 25mg
VITAMIN A 350mcg
VITAMIN D 7mcg
CALCIUM 13.1mmol(525mg)
IRON 140mcg(7.8mg)

in the body. Without enough iron (see the balloons below), anaemia will develop, causing fatigue, lack of energy, loss of appetite and slowed physical and mental development. Babies are born with a store of iron which lasts around six months. From then on, you should ensure that they eat plenty of iron-rich foods. Before six months, feed iron-enriched cereals to weaning infants to supply them with this essential nutrient. After six months, well-cooked eggs can be given, and after ten months you can offer red meat, liver and liver pâté, oily fish, and dark green vegetables such as peas, broccoli, spinach and sprouts, and dried fruit.

The tannin in tea prevents iron from being absorbed, so avoid giving young children tea to drink, even after weaning. **Calcium** is vital for a baby's growing skeleton, also for healthy teeth, muscles, heart, nerve function and blood clotting. Breast and formula milk will usually supply all the necessary calcium in the early months of a child's life. However, as your child grows up, milk products such as cheese, yoghurt, fromage frais, custard and other milk puddings are good calcium-rich choices.

Essential vitamins Give your baby vitamin drops ACD from six months if breastfed, and after formula milk is no longer given if bottle-fed.

Vitamin A (also known as retinol) is crucial for healthy skin and eyes. It converts light into electrical signals in the retina of the eye.

Orange-coloured fruit and vegetables such as carrots, peaches and apricots are good sources of vitamin A, as are milk, full-fat dairy foods, eggs, margarines and liver. If you are breastfeeding, you may need to increase your consumption of vitamin A above the reference intake of 600 micrograms (see page 341). **Vitamin C** is needed for growth and tissue repair. It also boosts iron absorption, so you should accompany iron-rich foods with those rich in vitamin C, especially if you are feeding your child a vegetarian diet.

The richest sources of Vitamin C are citrus fruits, kiwi fruit, mango, pineapple, guava, tomatoes and green peppers. Other sources are potatoes, sweet potatoes, fresh fruit and vegetables such as broccoli, spring greens and brussels sprouts. **Vitamin D** is essential for the absorption of calcium from food, and a deficiency can cause the bone disorder known as rickets. Plentiful amounts of Vitamin D are contained in oily fish, liver, fortified cereals and margarine. It is also found in milk and butter. Most of our vitamin D is made from the action of sunlight on skin (see page 46), so toddlers should spend plenty of time outside, especially in the summer, to build up a store of the vitamin. Make sure that they are protected from sunburn with a hat and/or sunscreen.

10-12 MONTHS
ENERGY(kcal) 920(male) 865(female)
PROTEIN 14.9g
VITAMIN C 25mg
VITAMIN A 350mcg
VITAMIN D 7mcg
CALCIUM 13.1mmol(525mg)
IRON 140mcg(7.8mg)

1-2 YEARS
ENERGY(kcal) 1230(male) 1165(female)
PROTEIN 14.5g
VITAMIN C 30mg
VITAMIN A 400mcg
VITAMIN D 7mcg
CALCIUM 8.8mmol(350mg)
IRON 120mcg(6.9mg)

a daily routine for babies and toddlers

4–6 MONTHS

ON WAKING Breast or bottle-feed.

BREAKFAST Non-wheat baby cereal mixed with breast milk or infant formula; breast or bottle-feed.

LUNCH Vegetable purée with puréed meat or pulses; breast or bottle-feed or cooled boiled water.

TEA-TIME Puréed fruit; breast or bottle-feed.

BED-TIME Breast or bottle-feed.

7–9 MONTHS

ON WAKING Breast or bottle-feed.

BREAKFAST Cereal and milk; breast or bottle-feed.

LUNCH Puréed or mashed meat fish or pulses; mashed potato and vegetables; yoghurt or milk pudding; cooled, boiled water in a cup.

TEA-TIME Egg and toast fingers or pasta and cheese dish; a few vegetable fingers — baby sweet corn or soft cooked carrots; pieces of ripe fruit or mashed banana; breastfeed or offer a drink of baby milk from a cup.

BED-TIME Breast or bottle-feed.

10–12 MONTHS

BREAKFAST Breakfast cereal with milk; toast fingers; baby milk from a cup or breast milk.

LUNCH Chopped meat, fish or pulses; potato, rice or pasta; mashed or chopped vegetables; yoghurt or milk pudding; water or diluted fruit juice.

TEA-TIME Sandwiches or pasta and cheese; slices of tomato, cucumber or green pepper; stewed or dried fruit or pieces of ripe fruit; cup of baby milk.

BED-TIME Breastfeed or baby milk in a cup.

TODDLERS (1-3 YEARS)

BREAKFAST Breakfast cereal and milk; diluted fruit juice.

MID-MORNING Snack such as bread sticks and cheese cubes; milk drink.

LUNCH Meat, fish or pulses with potato, rice or pasta; vegetables; yoghurt or milk pudding; water or diluted fruit juice.

MID-AFTERNOON Scone, tea bread or pancakes (see below); pieces of fruit; water to drink.

TEA-TIME Pasta or rice dish with ham, eggs, or cheese, or sandwiches with tuna, peanut butter or liver pâté; vegetable and fruit pieces; milk to drink.

Pancake treats

Pancake batter: mix one beaten egg, 150 ml (5 fl oz) of full-fat milk, 40 g (1½ oz) wholemeal flour and 1 teaspoon of sunflower oil in a blender or food processor for 2-3 minutes until the mixture is smooth and thick. Let it stand for 1-2 hours. Coat the base of a heavy frying pan with a thin layer of sunflower oil, pour in spoonfuls of the batter (one dessertspoonful will make a small pancake). Fry over medium heat until golden on both sides. Fill with jam, ricotta or honey. Makes about 20 pancakes.

NUTRIENTS PER PANCAKE Calories **21** Protein **1 g** Carbohydrate **1.5 g** (sugars **0.5 g**) Fat **1 g** (saturated **0.5 g**) Fibre **0**

Toddlers will love these scrumptious home-made pancakes

why breast is best

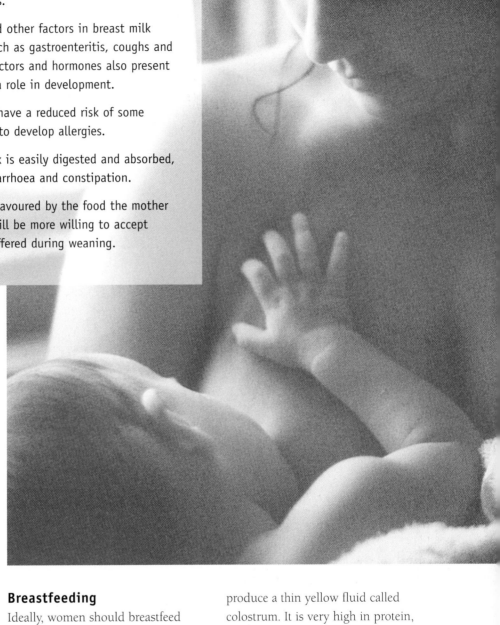

The perfect formula Breast milk contains all the nutrients a baby needs in exactly the right quantities.

Powerful protection Antibodies and other factors in breast milk protect the baby from infections such as gastroenteritis, coughs and colds, and ear infections. Growth factors and hormones also present in breast milk are believed to play a role in development.

A healthy future Breastfed babies have a reduced risk of some chronic diseases and are less likely to develop allergies.

Gentle on your baby As breast milk is easily digested and absorbed, breastfed babies suffer less from diarrhoea and constipation.

An easy transition Breast milk is flavoured by the food the mother herself eats and a breastfed baby will be more willing to accept these family foods when they are offered during weaning.

Water your baby

Babies and toddlers have a large surface area of skin in relation to their body size, so they can lose a lot of water by sweating, especially in hot weather. Give frequent drinks to prevent this loss of fluid.

The best drinks are milk and water. Sugary squashes and drinks blunt the appetite and are bad for teeth even if they haven't come through yet. Fruit juices are a good source of vitamins, but their sugar and acid content can also damage a child's teeth; to avoid this, dilute them well and restrict to meal times.

EARLY FEEDING

Until babies are at least four months old, they will get all the protein, fats, carbohydrates, vitamins and minerals needed for healthy growth in the form of breast or infant formula milk. Indeed, the digestive system is not sufficiently mature to handle anything else before this time.

Breastfeeding

Ideally, women should breastfeed their baby if at all possible (see above), but those who are unable or prefer not to breastfeed can meet all their baby's nutritional needs with formula milk.

The correct balance of nutrients and fluid is provided naturally in breast milk. During the 72 hours after your baby is born, the breasts produce a thin yellow fluid called colostrum. It is very high in protein, minerals and vitamins A, D and B_{12}, and low in fat and energy. Most of the protein present is contained in the form of immunoglobulin A; this is believed to prevent infection and also block any allergens passing from the baby's gut into the bloodstream.

Towards the end of the first week, the composition of the milk changes.

When the baby starts to nurse at the beginning of each feed, the first milk produced is thin, low in fat and very thirst-quenching. As the feed continues, the milk becomes richer in fat and protein. These two types of milk are commonly called foremilk and hindmilk respectively. Both ensure the healthy development of your baby.

Bottle feeding

Alternatives to breast milk are made according to strict guidelines and resemble breast milk as closely as

Early independence Children may make a mess when feeding themselves but it's good to encourage them to experiment.

possible. Formula milks are generally made from cow's milk (although alternatives based on soya beans, goat's milk and organically produced cow's milk are available). They are adapted by reducing the protein and salt content and adjusting the levels of other nutrients. Formula milk is packaged in powdered form or ready-

mixed cartons or bottles; but whichever type you use, it is vital that you follow the manufacturer's instructions. Do not add more powder than recommended: your baby will get too much protein and fat and not enough water.

What to avoid You must never give unmodified cow's milk to infants under 12 months. It is too low in vitamin D and iron, and too high in protein and salt, which can put strain on a baby's kidneys; it can also cause gastrointestinal bleeding. Full-fat cow's milk can be introduced after twelve months.

Formulas for later Follow-on milks are marketed for ages six months to two years on the basis that their higher iron content will help to prevent anaemia; but if babies are eating a well-balanced diet including iron-rich foods these are unnecessary.

WEANING YOUR BABY

After four to six months, as they become increasingly active, babies have more need of calories, iron, zinc vitamins A and D and other nutrients than milk alone can provide. At this time you can start weaning or introducing solid foods. By now babies have good head control and can sit up to receive solids; they can also learn how to move food from the tongue to the back of the mouth for swallowing.

When should you start? Babies give signals which indicate that they need to eat more – you'll notice a change in feeding habits. Your baby may appear dissatisfied after each feed or demand more milk than usual. Another sign is waking up for a night-time feed, having previously slept through. When the first tooth appears, usually at around six

months, this is a further indicator of the need for solids.

Introducing solids Eating solid foods is no easy task for an infant – simply learning that food can come on a spoon and that it needs to be moved to the back of the mouth for swallowing takes time. So you need to be patient. Avoid introducing solids when your baby is desperately hungry or upset; instead, offer some milk first to provide temporary satisfaction and then try one or two teaspoons of a relatively liquid baby food (see below for ideas). Do not add salt or sugar.

Babies will start chewing when they develop teeth, but until then 'solids' is a bit of a misnomer. When you first wean your baby you will need to offer quite soft, liquid foods. Once these are happily accepted, you can gradually water them down less. Good foods to start with are:
• Wheat-free baby cereal mixed with baby milk. Baby rice fortified with iron is most commonly used, but iron-fortified cornmeal, tapioca or millet cereal are also good options.
• Vegetable purées: try potato with a little carrot, cauliflower or broccoli, swede or parsnip and peas.
From about six to nine months, you can consider extending the range:
• Puréed meat or pulses added to vegetable purée increase iron and protein.
• Puréed fruit such as apple, pear, mango, apricot, peaches or avocado.

INTRODUCING ADULT FOOD

Babies introduced to a wide variety of foods from 6 to 12 months have fewer feeding problems over the next couple of years than those fed on a limited, bland range of foods. This is a time when most babies are happy

to experiment with flavours and textures – some toddlers relish strong-tasting foods such as gherkins and salami.

After six months, begin to offer soft, lumpy food. It takes a while for your baby to learn to control lumps in the mouth, so don't be surprised if they come back out. New skills take time to acquire. Move on to mashed and then chopped food as quickly as your baby allows. Offer meat, fish, pulses, vegetables, fruit and cereal.

Self-feeding

Finger foods can be introduced from about seven months – the shapes and colours make interesting objects for babies to explore. Start with softer foods: pieces of ripe fruits such as pears, bananas, melon, apricot, avocado, halved seedless grapes, mango, papaya, peach and kiwi fruit are popular favourites. Try them with cubes of hard cheese, cooked pieces of chicken or turkey, quarters of hard-boiled egg, rice cakes, bread sticks, toast fingers and cooked pasta shapes.

Lightly cooked vegetable sticks are also suitable and, as your baby becomes more competent at chewing, you can introduce crunchy raw vegetables such as tomatoes, cucumber, carrots, and peppers. Toddlers should be encouraged to take all drinks from a cup after 12 months. Use of the bottle after this age can cause tooth decay and may also affect the development of your baby's mouth and speech.

Allergies and intolerances

If you or your partner suffers from a food allergy, your baby might develop one too. Even if there is no family history of allergies, it is unwise to introduce certain foods too early. The foods that most commonly trigger allergies are chicken's eggs, cow's milk and wheat. Others include nuts, soya and shellfish. Avoid feeding your baby wheat, eggs and fish under the age of six months; after this age, the gut is better equipped to cope with these foods.

only the best will do

purée

COOKFORHEALTH

The benefits of purées for babies

NUTRITIOUS AND PURE Purées are perfect for babies – you know what is in the food and there are no additives. You can freeze any leftovers in ice cube trays to use as required.
VARIETY You can purée most foods, including fruit, vegetables, meat, fish and poultry.

The methods Use a food processor or liquidiser. Thin the purée by adding milk, fruit juice, or water. From 4 to 6 months, babies prefer a smooth, semi-liquid purée; thereafter, you can use less liquid. You can also mash food with a fork (cooked apple or pear); press it through a plastic sieve with a spoon (cooked lentils or cooked apricots); or mash it with a potato masher (cooked parsnip, swede, pumpkin or squash).
Preparation Peel fruit and vegetables, remove any pips and cook if necessary (steam, boil or roast). Remove fat, skin or bones from meat or fish and cook (grill, steam, boil or roast).

taking control of
FUSSY EATING

Many toddlers go through phases of turning their nose up at certain foods, or even refusing to eat at all. This can be both worrying and infuriating, but remember, they have a store of most nutrients, so it won't harm them if they don't eat properly for a while. In fact, they often need less food than you might think.

As good as a feast One of the frustrations of being a toddler – or the parent of a toddler – is that communication is very much a hit-and-miss affair. Since babies cannot express themselves in words they have to resort to other means of getting the message across. These may include turning their head away, pushing the plate away, spitting food out and struggling to get down from the table. All these can look like bad behaviour but they are simply ways of saying 'I'm not hungry'.

Lack of appetite could be because they are not growing very rapidly at this point. Most youngsters grow in spurts, so they will have periods when their desire to eat fluctuates. It may be that your child has filled up on snacks or milk. Sweet drinks in particular raise the blood sugar level and curb the appetite.

Offer some fruit or a few vegetable sticks if your child is hungry, and the next meal is not due for some time. If they become too tired or too hungry, children may be too upset to eat. Three small meals and two nutritious snacks spaced at regular intervals can help to counter this.

Using food as a weapon
Toddlers sometimes use food as a handy means of seeing how far they can push you. This is when you should stay very calm. Don't force your child to eat – otherwise you'll

As toddlers mature, they will begin to experiment with their likes and dislikes — and this can make for frustrating mealtimes. Your youngster will probably show more interest in running around rather than eating, but try not to create a fuss, as this will only make you both bad-tempered.

FOOD IS FUN Toddlers will happily tackle spaghetti, crunch on crudités, decorate themselves with their dinner or prefer to play with your nose rather than eat – just keep your sense of humour at all times.

turn mealtimes into battlegrounds. Accept the message that the child has had enough to eat, and quietly remove any leftover food. Also, deal with an outright refusal to eat without panicking – offering an alternative meal will only encourage further attempts to use food to manipulate you.

Fussy eating

Toddlers can be faddy about certain foods – they have an acute sense of taste and smell at this age. But forcing a child to eat something may result in a lifelong dislike of that food. If a child objects to certain textures such as fibrous or chewy meat, soggy or stringy vegetables, or

soups with croûtons, offer other foods from the same food group to ensure a balanced diet. Serve fruit and raw vegetables if a child won't eat cooked vegetables. And if a toddler refuses to drink milk, add it to mashed potato, scrambled eggs, pancakes, milkshakes and smoothies . Extra cheese can also substitute for milk.

Making mealtimes happier There are many positive steps you can take to help ease mealtime frustrations. Eat regularly as a family because children learn good eating habits by observing and imitating adults.Enjoy your meals in a slow, relaxed, happy manner but do not let them drag on for too long – about half an hour is a reasonable time.Involve your children by letting them help with the preparation of meals, for example allowing them to set the table with bright mats, plates and cups.

pumpkin and apple purée (5–6 months)

Wedges of bright yellow pumpkin are available in large supermarkets and shops selling Caribbean food – and many babies love this combination. If you can't get pumpkin, try using 2 large carrots, washed, peeled and diced, instead.

preparation time: **10 minutes**

cooking time: **25 minutes**

serves: **4**

NUTRIENTS PER SERVING	
calories	13.6
carbohydrate	5.3 g
(sugars)	4.3 g
protein	1 g
fat	3.75 g
(saturated)	1.6 g
fibre	0.2 g

300 ml (10 fl oz) water
115 g (4 oz) pumpkin flesh, diced
2 medium eating apples, peeled, cored and diced

1 Put the water in a saucepan and bring to boil. DO NOT ADD SALT.

2 Add the pumpkin to the boiling water and simmer for 5 minutes.

3 Add the diced apple and cook gently for 15 minutes until very soft.

4 Drain and mash with a potato masher.

5 Spoon the mixture into an ice cube tray. Two ice cubes will make one portion. Cool the rest quickly, cover with cling film, label and freeze for up to one month.

Note If you want an even finer purée, save 100 ml (3½ fl oz) of the cooking liquid and liquidise with the pumpkin and apple.

minced lamb with apricots (6–9 months)

This is a delicious, easy to prepare recipe that can be adapted for babies and adults. For a smoother texture, mash with a fork, or liquidise, adding a little more stock if necessary. The nutrient per serving amount is for a 25 g (1 oz) baby portion.

preparation time: **15 minutes**

cooking time: **20 minutes**

serves **4**

NUTRIENTS PER SERVING	
calories	27
carbohydrate	1 g
(sugars)	0.1 g
protein	2 g
fat	1.5 g
(saturated)	0.5 g
fibre	0.2 g

2 tablespoons vegetable oil
1 small onion, chopped finely
400 g (14 oz) minced lamb
60 g (2¼ oz) ready-to-eat dried apricots, chopped finely
1 yellow pepper, deseeded and chopped finely
200 ml (7 fl oz) home-made unsalted stock (recipe page 338) or unsalted vegetable water

FOR ADULT PORTIONS
1 tablespoon Worcestershire sauce
¼ tablespoon paprika
salt and pepper
1 tablespoon plain flour (made into a paste with 5 tablespoons water)

1 Heat the oil in a saucepan, and gently fry the onion until soft.

2 Add the meat and brown lightly, stirring occasionally.

3 Add the apricots, pepper and stock and mix well.

4 Cover and allow to simmer gently for 15 minutes, or until the meat is tender.

5 Take out baby's portion.

6 Add the Worcestershire sauce, paprika, seasoning and flour mixture and stir for one minute until the sauce thickens.

tuna pasta (toddlers)

This is a delicious way of encouraging toddlers to eat fish with the rest of the family. The tuna blends into the sauce and there is hardly any fishy smell. Alternatively, you could replace the tuna with finely chopped mushrooms and ham.

preparation time: **25 minutes**

cooking time: **5 minutes**

serves **4 adults**

2 tablespoons olive oil

2 tablespoons tomato purée

2 tablespoons pesto sauce

2x185 g (6½ oz) cans of tuna in oil, drained

300 g (11 oz) penne, cooked in boiling salted water and drained

50 g (1¾ oz) grated mozzarella cheese (available in packets in the supermarket)

1 Heat the olive oil in a large saucepan and stir in the tomato purée and pesto sauce, then add the tuna.

2 Add the cooked pasta in three stages, mixing well at each stage so the tuna, sauce and pasta are well blended.

3 Continue to heat, stirring continuously until the pasta is heated thoroughly.

4 Serve in individual bowls, sprinkled with the grated cheese.

NUTRIENTS PER SERVING	
calories	370
carbohydrate	15 g
(sugars)	1 g
protein	31 g
fat	17 g
(saturated)	5 g
fibre	1 g

only the best will do

Growing in leaps and bounds

You will be doing your children a great favour if you can instil in them an appreciation of good food. The key to success in this is eating together as a regular part of family life. And if they succumb to the lure of junk food occasionally, don't worry – a taste for excellent food can last a lifetime.

Helping children to establish a healthy relationship with food, so that they see it as a pleasurable aspect of life, is one of the arts of good parenting. The way to do this is not to lecture them about what's good and what's bad. Your own attitude to food is the best role model – if you take positive delight in choosing and cooking the best ingredients, it will be easy and natural for them to participate.

Develop their love for quality food while they are still young, and the chances are that they will reap the benefits throughout their lives.

APPRECIATING GOOD FOOD

A surprising number of children are keenly interested in cooking and want to learn as much as they can about it. The lure of becoming a television chef or maybe of running their own restaurant is undoubtedly influencing their career options.

If your child shows a keen interest, there is a wide choice of cookery and food programmes that you can watch together, as well as excellent cookery books to read. All this information is easily available – and will encourage young people to explore the world of food.

Getting them involved

One way to inspire your children to take an interest in food is by inviting them to join you in planning meals, buying the food and cooking. They will enjoy trying out easy-to-make meals such as pasta and tomato sauce, meat and vegetable kebabs with rice, or a pizza base decorated with tomato sauce, sliced vegetables and grated cheese. And get them to cook flapjacks, fruity muffins or apple crumble for dessert.

Chocolate fever The influence of television on children's food choices is widely recognised. During school holidays, advertisements for high-fat, high-sugar products are shown more frequently, exposing children to extra pressure. Try to discourage your children from random grazing on snack foods while they are watching television, but be realistic – they are only human.

Employ subtle strategies and serve foods that will satisfy growing appetites without being full of fat. Shift the emphasis of family meals to vegetables and carbohydrate foods such as potatoes, rice, pasta, noodles and polenta, and have plenty of fresh fruit available. All these are low in fat and high in nutrients.

If your children enjoy burgers, make healthy versions at home. Try the recipe for an Italian-style Veggie Burger (see page 152), or make ordinary burgers from best quality mince and serve them in a wholemeal bun with a crunchy, delicious salad. This is just the sort of food that children enjoy learning to cook themselves.

Refining the appetite Let your children decide when they have eaten enough – they are growing in spurts and their appetites will vary naturally from time to time. Children who are forced to finish everything on their plate may lose their ability to self-regulate their appetite. This may lead to obesity in later life.

SOLID FOUNDATIONS

A regular pattern of meals helps to establish a sense of order and calm; ideally meals shouldn't be chaotic and rushed. Offering a wide variety of foods is also essential if children are to get a full range of nutrients.

As with adults, a balanced diet for children and adolescents is based on the Five Food Groups (see pages 11-15) and the proportions of these that they eat. If you follow this sensibly, your children will thrive. You can

So that's how it's done The love of food and cooking may begin at a very young age. A carefully supervised session helping the children to roll out pastry is an enjoyable way of getting them familiar with the basic skills.

check the overall calories for growing children on page 16 – and adjust the size of the servings from each of the food groups to suit your child.

Cereals and potatoes These should be the basis of each meal or snack. Children will eat about five servings of foods such as bread, cereals and pasta each day, but adolescents need more than this. These foods are high in the B vitamins needed for growth. Some adolescent boys may need up to 12 servings a day.

An apple a day Aim for five servings of fruit and vegetables a day. Large amounts are unnecessary for children, they simply need different fruit or vegetables every day. If your children refuse to eat vegetables because they are going through a fussy eating phase, don't be drawn into a pitched battle about it – let them have all their five servings as fruit. Encourage their appreciation of vegetables by cooking them in imaginative ways: put them in stir-fries, or in the Hearty Minestrone Soup (the recipe is on page 153).

Milk and dairy foods Remember to choose the best milk for your child: under-fives should always drink whole milk as they need the energy provided by the extra calories and

fat-soluble vitamins. Semi-skimmed milk is a good overall choice after five years, but if your child tends to be underweight, carry on serving full-fat milk. Adolescent girls who are watching their weight can drink skimmed milk – but keep a quiet watch, and make sure that they do not become underweight.

The daily three servings of milk and dairy foods can be put together in various ways:

• Serving one is a 200 ml (7 fl oz) glass of milk.

• Serving two is chosen from a pot of yoghurt, fromage frais or a milk pudding.

• Serving three is chosen from cheese in a sandwich, on a pizza or on pasta.

This is one serving more than is recommended for adults, to provide enough calcium for growing and developing bones. And teenage boys grow so fast, you may well find that they need at least four servings a day.

High-protein foods Two servings a day of foods from the protein group provide enough protein and minerals such as iron, zinc, and magnesium for growth and tissue repair. Choose as wide a range as possible and buy the best quality that you can afford. Serve fresh meat such as chicken, turkey, lamb, pork and beef, and fresh fish. Remember that beans and pulses contain excellent protein.

Fast foods such as good quality, low-fat sausages, chicken nuggets, burgers, and fish cakes are fine occasionally – they are often high in fat, but do contain some protein.

How much fat and sugar? Fat and sugar are a normal part of your child's diet. Butter and cream, for example, supply essential fatty acids. However you should keep an eye on

high-fat extras such as crisps and snacks as they contain large amounts of salt but very few nutrients. Also, watch the amounts if your child is becoming overweight. Sugary sweets and snacks provide energy, but again, few nutrients. Avoid making sweets a battleground – and don't ban them altogether. Your child may feel resentful if other children eat them.

Popular combinations Children and adolescents will happily enjoy dishes which use combinations of food

from two or more food groups at a time. For example, a portion of shepherd's pie contains a serving of meat and a serving of potato and can also include a serving of vegetables if some onions or mushrooms have been cooked with the meat. Italian dishes such as meat lasagne and ham or pepperoni pizza are very popular with children and adolescents. Both contain a serving from each of the four main food groups and are excellent choices.

THE GROWTH SPURT

Up until ten years children's growth is fairly steady. After this a definite speeding up occurs, usually between 11 and 15 years in girls and 13 and 16 years in boys.

During this period, daily calorie and nutrient requirements will increase significantly. Girls need between 1845 and 2110 Calories, and boys between 2220 and 2755 Calories. Eating larger quantities of a balanced diet would be fine, but this rapid growth occurs at a time when young teenagers are starting to rebel – and this may be expressed in their food choices. Teenagers may devour large amounts of crisps, chocolates, hamburgers and fizzy drinks.

Increased demands Boys' energy requirements during the growth spurt are very high and many parents are completely staggered by the extent of their appetites. Be prepared to go shopping more often and try to keep high-energy snack foods at the ready. Stock up on extra breakfast cereals, bread, milk and cheese to provide these pit-stop snacks – often demanded within an hour or two of a hearty meal.

Calcium in action

Growing bones need a good supply of calcium. Even after children stop growing taller, plenty of calcium is still vital, as it continues to be deposited into the bones, making them strong and resilient. This

Calcium-rich combinations Potatoes are high in vitamin C, beta carotene and potassium, but also contain useful amounts of calcium. And they go wonderfully well with other calcium-rich foods: think of a spoonful of soured cream or yoghurt on a baked potato, or crème fraîche mixed into mashed potato or a new potato salad. Sesame seeds (above right) are another good source of calcium, either whole or turned into tahini paste – an essential ingredient of authentic hummous.

Building strong, healthy bones Milk and milk products are the best-known sources of calcium, but this very valuable nutrient can also be found in some unexpected places. There is lots of calcium in ice cream, the basis of Knickerbocker Glory with Strawberry and Orange Sauce (left), but this children's favourite also has calcium-rich chopped nuts sprinkled over it. The recipe is on page 153.

milk

Milk is a superbly nourishing food – it is easily digested and contains a range of valuable vitamins and minerals. It is a good source of protein and the calcium it contains is readily absorbed by the body. Milk and milk products such as cheese and yoghurt are major sources of calcium, essential for building healthy bones and strong teeth in growing children.

Milk has essential B vitamins as well as phosphorus and zinc (which boosts the immune system). Children under five years should only be given whole milk; from then onwards, skimmed or semi-skimmed milk (with reduced fat content) is fine.

process continues right up to their early twenties. It is now known that if you have a high density of calcium in your bones when you are young, you are less likely to suffer from osteoporosis (thin, easily-fractured bones) later in life. To read more about building strong bones, turn to pages 44-53.

Healthy levels Children drink significantly less milk than a generation ago – instead they are choosing sugary soft drinks, colas and squashes. Fashionable body image may have an influence on this – some adolescent girls avoid eating dairy foods such as cheese, yoghurt and milk, in the hope that this will prevent them putting on weight.

The result is that many children and adolescents do not get enough calcium from their food. Encourage your children to consume lots of milk, cheese or yoghurt: teenagers should have at least three 200 ml (7 fl oz) glasses of milk a day; and either 40 grams (1½ oz) of cheese or 125 ml (4 fl oz) of yoghurt to meet their daily needs.

Strong, healthy teeth

Your child's teeth can be damaged by sugary foods and drinks from the earliest stages (see page 51). And a regular routine of brushing and flossing as well as frequent check-ups at the dentist should be established as soon as teeth appear.

Dentists recommend brushing twice a day with just a smear of fluoride toothpaste. Young children swallow a lot of toothpaste if a large amount is squeezed onto the brush; also, too much fluoride can cause permanent staining of the teeth.

A sweet tooth Sugary foods are certainly a major factor in causing problems with teeth. But it is the frequency with which these foods are eaten that increases the number of dental caries. These are holes in the teeth made when sugars are converted into acids by bacteria in the mouth. The acids dissolve the protective enamel of the teeth. Low-sugar snacks such as fruit, filled rolls, pitta bread with a dip, and crackers with Marmite or cheese are better choices to eat between meals.

Avoid sugary drinks Milk and water are ideal drinks between meals rather than acidic, sugary soft drinks and squashes. Always dilute fruit juice as it is naturally very acidic, and can attack the tooth enamel.

Independence and food

Adolescence is a time of emotional and social change as well as the physical changes of growth and puberty. Your children begin to seek peer approval and your parental influence diminishes. This applies to eating habits as much as any other aspect of their lives. They will begin to spend more time away from home and will buy more of their own food.

Popular snacks Adolescents may change from eating three regular meals a day to more or less constant snacking. If these 'pit-stop' meals are high-fat, fast and convenience foods, they may not get enough of essential nutrients – iron, calcium, zinc and B vitamins in particular. The best that parents can do in most cases is to reinforce the emphasis on healthy eating by giving them good, fresh,

alternative calcium sources

Calcium is a valuable nutrient for the growing body – but it isn't just present in milk and cheese. There are various other foods that contain it, and these may be of special interest if you are following a vegetarian or lactose-free diet. You can obtain calcium from:

• Yoghurt

• Fromage frais

• Fortified soya products such as soya drink, yoghurt, cheese and tofu

• Apricots (especially dried)

• Nuts – especially almonds (but avoid immature almonds, as they contain compounds that are potentially poisonous); Brazil nuts, hazelnuts

• Sesame and sunflower seeds

• Dark green leafy vegetables (such as spinach, chard, spring greens, cabbage)

• Watercress

• Prawns

• Anchovies

• Sardines

• Tahini (sesame paste)

• White bread (it is enriched with calcium)

nutritious food at home while giving them the freedom to conform to peer pressure outside.

The moody blues Adolescent girls are very susceptible to mood swings, particularly just before menstruating. There is some evidence to suggest that extra B vitamins, particularly vitamin B_6 (pyridoxine), will help with this. The best sources of this vitamin are liver, wholegrain cereals, bananas, pulses and sunflower seeds. Irregular eating patterns and missed

meals may be the reason behind mood swings. Some girls become anxious and moody after a few hours without eating as a result of the drop in blood sugar levels. Encourage a more regular eating pattern, though this may be difficult for adolescents who are in and out of the home.

Keep blood sugar stable High-fibre foods and foods with a low glycaemic index (see page 79) will tend to keep blood sugar levels stable. Choose granary-style breads

Playground food *Taking time out to enjoy a healthy snack is essential for young girls who need to keep their energy levels high. If your children do not have school lunches, give them nutritious food to take to school. Lunch-box suggestions include: small cartons of milk; fruit juices; sandwiches with their favourite fillings; yoghurt; fresh or dried fruit; some mixed nuts, plain popcorn; pasta or potato salad; crudités and salads.*

FRESH PEPPERS *These are rich in vitamin C and beta carotene, plant chemicals that help to build and renew skin cells and keep your skin healthy and looking good. Peppers change from green to red or yellow as they ripen, but their nutrient values are similar whatever colour they are.*

1 *Keep your skin clean and free from infection with antiseptic face washes.*

2 *Drink plenty of fluids – aim for at least eight glasses of water and fruit juices a day.*

3 *Alcohol, tea and coffee are all diuretics which increase the loss of water from the body in urine. Have less of these or increase the amount of water you drink to compensate.*

4 *Eat plenty of fruit – especially citrus fruits – and fresh vegetables to provide Vitamin C which is vitally important for skin repair.*

5 *Take more zinc, also vital to skin repair. Best sources are meat, nuts, cereals, milk and green vegetables.*

6 *The essential fatty acids found in oily fish are very important for healthy skin, so eat fresh salmon, trout, mackerel, herrings and sardines, or have them in fish fingers, pâtés or fishcakes.*

7 *To improve the skin condition psoriasis, eat plenty of foods rich in beta carotene. It is most abundant in red and yellow vegetables and fruits such as carrots, tomatoes, peppers, apricots and mangoes.*

SEVEN WAYS TO **banish skin problems**

made with wholegrains and cereals such as pasta and basmati rice – and try to use more pulses and lentils. Flapjacks and oat cereals also help to keep blood sugar constant.

The pressure to be thin When they see images of tall, slim supermodels in fashion advertising, many girls become unhappy with their own body shape. Three out of five say

they would like to be slimmer. But most young girls attempt to slim in ways that are counter-productive. They skip meals, but then snack on high-fat foods such as crisps, biscuits, chocolate and ice cream.

The end result is to increase their overall calorie intake. They mistakenly believe that high-carbohydrate foods such as bread,

potatoes, breakfast cereals, rice and pasta are fattening. In fact the opposite of this is true. These foods contain virtually no fat unless it is added separately. Weight for weight, they are low in calories and are satisfyingly filling because they contain fibre. By cutting down on these foods which are rich in B vitamins, zinc and iron, would-be

slimmers are deprived of many essential nutrients. They also become hungry and are then tempted to snack on high-fat, low-nutrient foods. The weight inevitably goes on again in a relentless cycle.

Getting enough iron

Lack of iron is surprisingly common among young people – 25 per cent of preschool children in the United Kingdom are thought to be deficient in this mineral. Adolescents and people who diet are particularly vulnerable.

When girls begin to menstruate their iron stores are depleted by blood loss each month (see page 60). This may lead to anaemia, a deficiency of the blood pigment haemoglobin which transports oxygen around the body.

Lack of iron causes a fall in haemoglobin levels, and reduces the amount of oxygen in the tissues. This can cause problems such as fatigue and impaired concentration at school. Add iron to the diet, and these problems may be resolved. The richest and most easily absorbed sources are from liver, kidneys and red meat. Other foods that contain good amounts of iron include eggs, red kidney beans, canned fish, dried fruit and green leafy vegetables.

Iron-rich foods are more readily absorbed by your body if you eat food containing vitamin C at the same time. Citrus fruit and fruit juices are the best sources, but a medium-sized potato supplies a useful amount. It is also important to remember that tea reduces iron absorption and it is best not to drink it with meals – this applies to everyone, children, teenagers and adults alike.

Learning about alcohol

Many teenagers begin drinking alcohol well before they are 18 years old. Although there is an increasing amount of information in the media about the dangers of drinking too much, it is difficult to prevent young people drinking when all their friends are pressuring them to conform. Some may learn the consequences the hard way by being involved in alcohol-related accidents, or by becoming pregnant. Arming

Wholewheat pasta is an ideal choice if you are avoiding eating meat. It is low in fat, high in fibre and B vitamins, has carbohydrates for energy and also contains protein.

them with useful facts may help them to cope:
• Don't drink on an empty stomach. Alcohol is absorbed very quickly into the blood if you do this.
• Eat a small meal or snack before you begin drinking – this will slow down the absorption, especially if the food contains some fat.
• Suggested snacks include a sandwich, a slice of pizza, crackers with cheese or some nuts or crisps.
The immature liver Young people have low levels of the enzymes which break down alcohol in their liver. The alcohol level in their blood will consequently rise more quickly than in older people who drink regularly and have a ready supply of enzymes. The novice drinker's liver will eventually produce these enzymes but this takes time and will only begin once alcohol levels are

already rising. Chinese and other ethnic groups have lower levels of these enzymes and are therefore more vulnerable. Also, alcohol has more effect on girls than boys, because of differences in body composition.

How much is enough? The amount of alcohol that each individual can cope with varies considerably, but on average one unit of alcohol in the blood is broken down in an hour. Adolescents should be cautioned against consuming alcohol at a greater rate than this. There is one unit of alcohol in a small can of lager, one glass of wine, or one measure of spirits.

Few people realise that the alcohol content in their blood can continue to rise for up to two hours after they have stopped drinking. It is often on the way home that they, or a friend, may become aggressive and get involved in a fight, or even become so ill that they collapse.

Choosing to be vegetarian

Many young people decide to stop eating meat and fish. This may be because of a concern for animal welfare, or because they think it is a healthier option and will also help them to keep slim. As meat and fish are rich sources of many nutrients – especially protein, iron, zinc and B

enjoy more pulses

Use hummous made from chickpeas and tahini as a dip for crudités or as a sandwich filling.

Include dhal made from lentils in vegetable curries or with rice dishes such as vegetable pilau.

Choose soups made with beans such as minestrone. Also choose lentil-based soups such as lentil and tomato.

Substitute red kidney beans for meat in pasta dishes such as lasagne.

Serve rice and beans together – you can use any bean you like – aduki, blackeye, cannellini or red kidney. These can all be bought ready-cooked in cans if you don't have time to pre-soak and cook them yourself but choose ones without added sugar and salt.

Spice up a can of baked beans with some curry or chilli powder.

Create bean salads by mixing two or three varieties together, such as red and white kidney beans with blackeye beans.

Discover the soya bean – products such as tofu and Textured Vegetable Protein (TVP) can be used as direct substitutes for meat in many traditional dishes. They both have much less flavour than meat and so are better suited to highly flavoured chillies or casseroles with plenty of herbs.

Include more nuts and seeds – add them to salads: try walnuts or pine nuts in a green salad. Add extra nuts to breakfast cereals.

Add chopped nuts to puddings such as crumble toppings and meringues.

Use peanut butter for sandwich fillings.

Choose snack bars, cakes and biscuits containing nuts and seeds.

vitamins, it is imperative that some thought is given to the foods that must be included to replace these key nutrients.

What to eat instead Pulses, nuts and extra eggs are ideal replacement foods and should be eaten twice a day. However, inexperienced vegetarians may not be used to eating pulses and will need some encouragement and ideas on how to eat more of these on a daily basis.

Parents – survival tips

It is not easy to compete with the lure of fast or convenience foods. Try cooking similar foods in your kitchen but in healthier forms.

• Make burgers with very lean mince meat, wholegrain breadcrumbs, herbs and minced onions and bind with an egg. Grill or oven-bake.

• Chicken nuggets can be made by dipping pieces of chicken in a whisked egg white, rolling in bread crumbs and cooking in the oven.

• Make chunky chips by cutting your own potatoes quite thickly (larger chips absorb less fat), frying in oil, and blotting on kitchen paper.

• Buy low-fat sausages to grill.

Add more vegetables There are various ways to sneak extra vegetables into your children's food:

• Chop vegetables such as peppers, courgettes and mushrooms into any ready-made sauce you have, and simmer until soft. Purée to disguise them if necessary.

• Crunchy and colourful, stir-fried vegetables are more popular than steamed or boiled – flavour them with tasty soya sauce.

• Serve vegetable crudités with favourite dips such as hummous, tzatziki and guacamole.

• Make varied kebabs – try chicken

pieces with peppers, mushrooms, baby corn and cherry tomatoes.

• Serve vegetable soups more often – they are so easy to make.

Boost carbohydrates Encourage youngsters to tuck in to generous servings of starchy foods.

• Pasta, rice or potato should comprise about one third of the whole meal – or more if possible.

• Always use thick-sliced bread for toast and sandwiches.

• Serve buns, scones, teabread, pancakes and muffins instead of biscuits and cakes.

Disguise the ingredients Liver is an excellent source of nutrients, but some children refuse to eat it.

• Use liver sausage in sandwiches or serve liver pâté with toast.

• Similarly, serve oily fish such as mackerel (smoked is best) puréed and made into a pâté.

Pile on the fruit Fruit should be a regular part of every meal – buy seasonal and locally grown produce for the finest quality and flavour. Many children will readily accept fresh fruit because it is so easy and fast to eat. If your child does not like eating breakfast, offer some fruit, including dried fruit, instead.

Let them do the cooking

Encourage teenagers to feel at home in the kitchen by letting them cook simple family meals. They may become confident enough to entertain their friends to a complete meal – so try giving them the use of the kitchen for an afternoon and evening so that they can show off their new talents.

You may be left with a kitchen that looks as if a bomb has hit it, but avoid recriminations, or you will discourage them from trying again.

MENUPLAN
for school days

If your children take packed lunches to school, you'll need to provide them with foods rich in calories, plus calcium and vitamins to keep them going through the day.

AT BREAKFAST As an extra calcium boost, serve a separate glass of milk (or a smoothie) in addition to the milk poured over breakfast cereal. Encourage fruit at breakfast too — a glass of diluted fruit juice or fresh fruit sliced on the cereal helps to absorb calcium easily.

FOR SCHOOL BREAKS Pack a pot of yoghurt with a small snack such as a wholemeal roll or bagel with cheese.

AT LUNCHTIME Cold pizza slice with extra cheese sneaks in more calcium, and scatter vitamin-rich vegetables on top; include boxes of salads or some raw vegetables such as cherry tomatoes, carrot sticks or cucumber slices. Finish with a chocolate biscuit and fresh fruit.

AFTER SCHOOL Deliver extra milk in the form of 'treats' such as milk shakes, smoothies or hot chocolate, depending on the weather.

IN THE EVENING Base meals on pasta or rice or potatoes. Serve meat or fish with stir-fried vegetables or in a meat sauce such as bolognese (simmered with extra vegetables). Serve a home-made Italian-style Veggie Burger or Hearty Minestrone Soup (recipes overleaf); fruit or rice puddings (see index for recipes); as a special treat Knickerbocker Glory with Strawberry and Orange sauce (recipe overleaf).

AFTER SPORTS Water, milk, or diluted fruit juice. Banana or a small snack.

EXTRAS bowls of cereal and milk; baked beans on wholemeal toast; extra slices of bread.

Fresh rolls and bagels make a great snack at school break.

italian-**style** veggie **burgers**

Risotto rice, tomatoes and Parmesan cheese give these nutritious burgers an Italian flavour. They're fun and filling when served in a warmed ciabatta roll with slices of fresh tomato, red onion and lettuce leaves – and a dash of ketchup.

preparation time: **15 minutes, plus 10 minutes cooling and 30 minutes chilling**
cooking time: **45 minutes**
serves **6**

NUTRIENTS PER SERVING	
calories	325
carbohydrate	27 g
(sugars)	5 g
protein	10 g
fat	18 g
(saturated)	4 g
fibre	4 g

1 tablespoon olive oil
½ tablespoon butter
1 clove garlic, finely chopped
1 onion, finely chopped
1 carrot, finely chopped
2 teaspoons dried oregano
1 teaspoon dried thyme
85 g (3 oz) risotto rice
200 ml (⅓ pint) hot water
7 tablespoons canned chopped tomatoes
25 g (1 oz) freshly grated Parmesan cheese
400 g (14 oz) canned chickpeas, drained
1 egg
Salt and black pepper
Wheatgerm, for rolling
Sunflower oil, for frying

1 Heat the olive oil and butter in a large, heavy-based saucepan. Add the garlic, onion, and carrot and cook for 5–7 minutes over a medium heat, until softened. Add the herbs and rice and stir to coat them in the oil and vegetable mixture. Cook for 1 minute.

2 Mix the hot water and tomatoes, then add a third of the liquid to the rice mixture. Cook for 8–10 minutes, stirring frequently, until the liquid has been absorbed. Add another third of the liquid and repeat the process. Add the remaining liquid and repeat the process again, until the rice is tender but still retains a little bite. Mix in the Parmesan and leave for 10 minutes to cool.

3 Transfer the mixture to a food processor, then add the chickpeas and egg. Season to taste and blend until fairly smooth. Refrigerate for 30 minutes.

4 Spread a layer of wheatgerm on a plate. For each burger, place 3 tablespoons of the mixture on the plate and shape into a flattened round. Sprinkle with more wheatgerm to coat. Repeat this process to make 6 burgers. Heat enough oil to lightly cover the base of a frying pan, then fry the burgers for 4 minutes on each side, or until crisp and golden.

hearty minestrone soup

This classic Italian bean and pasta soup is substantial enough to be eaten as a meal in itself – serve it with a mixed green salad and crusty bread. A scrumptious mix of beans, pasta, and vegetables, it is delicious made with your own stock (see recipe page 338).

preparation time: **10 minutes**

cooking time: **37 minutes**

serves **4**

5 tablespoons olive oil
1 onion, chopped
1 stick celery, chopped
1 large carrot, chopped
1 bay leaf
1.2 litres (2 pints) vegetable stock
400 g (14 oz) tomato passata
175 g (6 oz) pasta shapes, such as farfalle
    or conchiglie
400 g (14 oz) canned haricot beans,
    drained and rinsed
Salt and black pepper
250 g (9 oz) spinach, washed and thick
    stalks removed
40 g (1½ oz) Parmesan cheese, finely grated

1 Heat the olive oil in a large, heavy-based saucepan. Add the onion, celery and carrot and cook over a medium heat for 8–10 minutes, stirring occasionally, until the vegetables have softened.

2 Add the bay leaf, stock and passata, and bring to the boil. Reduce the heat, cover, and simmer for 15 minutes, or until the vegetables are tender.

3 Add the pasta and beans, bring the soup back to the boil and simmer for 10 minutes, or until the pasta is tender but still *al dente*. Stir occasionally to prevent the pasta sticking.

4 Season to taste, add the spinach and cook for a further 2 minutes, or until the spinach is tender. Serve in individual bowls, sprinkled with the grated Parmesan.

NUTRIENTS PER SERVING	
calories	450
carbohydrate	54 g
(sugars)	10 g
protein	18 g
fat	19 g
(saturated)	4 g
fibre	9 g

knickerbocker glory with strawberry and orange sauce

This dessert looks temptingly indulgent, and will delight your children while providing them with valuable calcium. For special occasions, add a swirl of melted chocolate topping.

preparation time: **10 minutes**

cooking time: **15 minutes**

serves **4**

250 g (9 oz) strawberries, halved
Juice of 1 orange
1 teaspoon finely grated orange zest
    (optional)
1 tablespoon unrefined caster sugar
25 g (1 oz) chopped mixed nuts, lightly
    toasted in a dry frying pan
8 scoops of vanilla dairy ice cream
Grated chocolate, to serve

1 Put the strawberries, orange juice and zest, if using, in a food processor and blend until smooth. Transfer the mixture to a saucepan and add the sugar. Cook over a medium heat for 10–12 minutes, until thickened. Leave to cool.

2 To serve, place a spoonful of the strawberry and orange sauce in the bottom of a tall glass. Add two scoops of ice cream and another spoonful of fruit sauce. Sprinkle over a quarter of the nuts and grated chocolate. Repeat the process to make four sundaes.

NUTRIENTS PER SERVING	
calories	310
carbohydrate	38 g
(sugars)	35 g
protein	6 g
fat	15 g
(saturated)	8 g
fibre	1 g

The **time** of **your** life

When you're young and single you may have little time to buy and prepare food; you're too busy living life to the full and making the most of all the possibilities open to you. Dashing from work to social events is fine, but it demands a lot of energy. Eat the right foods and you'll easily last the pace.

If you work hard and play even harder, you're trying to cram a lot into your schedule. But as long as you're smart about the food you eat, you'll have plenty of energy to enjoy life to the full.

FOOD FOR YOUR LIFESTYLE

Sometimes a handful of bar snacks nibbled with your drinks may have to make up for a skipped evening meal. But drinking without eating adequate food is not good for you (see page 284). Buy a fortifying snack: something as simple as a cheese salad sandwich on wholemeal bread will counteract the bad effects.

Selecting bar snacks If you are grabbing something to eat from a bar menu, choose meat, fish or shellfish tapas or canapes – they are rich in protein and vitamins. Avoid high-fat, crisps crackers and pretzels. And use vegetable sticks to scoop up dips instead of corn chips.

Salted nuts are high in fat, so moderate the amount you eat if you are watching your weight. On the other hand, nuts provide valuable nutrients – peanuts, pistachios, or cashews are a better choice than other high-fat, low-nutrient snacks such as crisps.

Don't miss breakfast

Late nights and a rushed morning routine leave little time for preparing breakfast at home. Instead, buy a healthy snack on the way to work. This could be a filled roll, sandwich or bagel, or a flapjack. Choose a low-fat yoghurt, latte or milky cappucino and pure fruit juice to make a well-balanced meal that will keep you going for a few hours.

A good lunch The middle of the day may be your best opportunity to eat a substantial meal, especially if you know that you won't be eating later. A lunch based on pasta, potatoes, rice, wholemeal bread, couscous or any other complex carbohydrate is ideal. Accompanied by vegetables and salad, it will give you sustained stamina for the rest of the day.

Fast foods Takeaway foods are easy and quick when you don't have much time to cook. But you should choose the healthiest options (see overleaf). Also, avoid high-fat snacks such as croissants and chocolate bars. These raise blood sugar levels quickly, but levels fall quickly too, leaving you fatigued and hungry.

Make up the deficit At weekends you may need to catch up on missed sleep. After a long lie-in, a satisfying

brunch will compensate for a missed breakfast (look at the Menu Plan, opposite page, for some ideas).

Special nutrients

The varied range of foods described in the Five Food Groups (see pages 11–15) will equip you to handle the most hectic pace. Some nutrients are particularly important at this stage of your life.

MENU**PLAN**
weekend brunches

Make up for any meals that you missed during the week by enjoying one of these satisfying brunches. They are quick, tasty and help to set you up for the week ahead.

Get the most out of life Choose foods that provide you with a long-lasting energy so you can enjoy life to the full – day and night.

BASIC BRUNCH Omelette or scrambled eggs with fresh herbs, served with grilled lean bacon, tomatoes and granary toast. Have a milky drink or a smoothie (see index for recipes). Or try kedgeree or Smoked Haddock Risotto (recipe page 168). Follow this with fresh fruit or ice cream or sorbet with a fruit coulis.

SCANDINAVIAN-STYLE A selection of cold meats, smoked fish and rollmops; ham, smoked salmon and pâtés; a platter of cheese and a choice of breads and crispbreads. Follow with fruit or fruit juice.

MEDITERRANEAN-STYLE Cold soup such as gazpacho; or charred tomato and pepper; roasted mediterranean vegetables served with pasta; follow with melon and berry fruits.

Mix many kinds of foods for tasty brunches

DRINKS Sip plenty of mineral water with slices of citrus fruit; fresh orange juice with sparkling white wine; barley water; or try non-alcoholic elderflower champagne.

Calcium You need to have milk, cheese or yoghurt three times a day. This is because your bones continue to use calcium for new growth until you are 25 to 30 years old (see page 45). Weight-bearing exercises such as dancing, walking and running are great for strong, healthy bones, so try to build them into your schedule.
Iron To help combat fatigue (see pages 251-252), eat foods rich in

iron. Choose liver, lean red meat, dark poultry meat, oily fish (salmon, sardines, mackerel and tuna) fortified breakfast cereals, eggs, green leafy vegetables, nuts and pulses.
Vitamin C Eat plenty of citrus fruit and vegetables for antioxidant protection (see page 118). And when you're out drinking, have a glass of

fruit juice every so often to top up your vitamin C levels, and to combat the nutrient-depleting effects of alcohol and cigarette smoke.

Sip water throughout the day – at least eight glasses. If you have time, cook a quick meal such as a stir-fry with rice (see index for recipes) before you go out drinking.

choosing a
TAKEAWAY

Takeaway food makes a quick, convenient meal when you don't have time to cook. And as long as you're careful about what you order, fast food needn't be harmful to your health. The best policy is to choose dishes which are lowest in fat, salt and sugar and highest in nutrients.

Indian takeaway Boiled rice, chapattis and naan bread provide healthy carbohydrates (but poppadoms are often fried, so eat these in moderation). A meat or fish dish such as tikka or tandoori will provide high levels of protein, iron and zinc. But remember that lamb is higher in saturated fat than chicken or beef. If you don't eat meat, choose rice with a lentil dish such as dhal. Accompany it with a vegetable side dish such as aloo gobi (cauliflower and potatoes) or a spinach (saag) dish for a balanced meal. Avoid oily foods such as korma, masala and pasanda sauces; pilau rice; deep-fried foods such as onion bhajees, samosas, prawn puri and fritters such as pakora and wada.

Chinese or Thai Base your order around plain or steamed rice or noodles. Stir-fried, chop suey, yellow and black bean sauce dishes are healthily low in fat. But avoid high-fat foods such as fried rice, spring rolls, anything in batter, crispy duck and sweet and sour sauces. Satay sauce is also high in fat but rich in magnesium and zinc. For dessert choose lychee, or another fruit, or sorbet.

Pizzas The right pizza makes a good, well-balanced meal. The cheese topping supplies calcium and protein but it is high in fat, so don't order extra cheese. Choose a small, thick-based pizza for extra carbohydrates, and order extra vegetables or a side salad. Avoid fatty meats such as

TAKEAWAY FOOD IS FAST AND CONVENIENT; IT CAN ALSO BE HIGH IN FAT AND SALT AND LOW IN FIBRE AND VITAMINS. BUT YOU CAN OVERCOME THIS PROBLEM BY MAKING THE MOST OF THE HEALTHIEST ITEMS ON OFFER. CHOOSE CAREFULLY AND SELECT A WELL-BALANCED MEAL WHICH AVOIDS POTENTIALLY HARMFUL INGREDIENTS.

FAST TRACK *If you eat takeaway foods such as burgers, pizzas, Indian dishes and hot dogs on a regular basis you'll need to keep an eye on what they contain. You can still enjoy them: just avoid the main high-fat, high sugar pitfalls.*

pepperoni and garlic bread (also high in fat). Pan-fried and stuffed-crust pizzas also have extra fat, so avoid these.
Burgers Choose a small, plain burger and skip the fatty melted cheese and mayonnaise. Use a little ketchup (it is rich in protective lycopene but also high in salt and sugar) and order a small portion of chips. A side salad boosts vitamins and antioxidants. Drink fruit juices instead of coke and a glass of milk rather than a milkshake.
Fish and chips Fish provides excellent protein and minerals. If you are watching your weight you may prefer to discard the deep-fried batter or breadcrumb coating.

Ask for a small portion of chips – thin and crinkle-cut chips are higher in fat than thick-cut ones.
Jacket potatoes Salmon or tuna fillings contain vital fatty acids – these protect your heart and improve your skin. Shellfish is rich in minerals, while baked beans are high in fibre. To avoid extra fat, ask for a low-fat spread, or a very small portion of butter, and avoid mayonnaise. Order salad, preferably undressed, and a piece of fruit.
Kebabs Shish, shashlik and chicken kebabs are made with lean meat, but doner and kofte kebabs use minced lamb which has a much higher fat content.
Sandwich bars Ask for thick-sliced wholemeal bread or baps or bagels to maximise the carbohydrate and B vitamins. Choose lean chicken, meat, shellfish or low-fat cheese fillings with salad and low-calorie dressings.

pork escalopes **with** citrus salsa

The sharp flavour of a citrus dressing, with chilli added if you like, makes a clean-tasting accompaniment to the escalopes. Serve them with lightly steamed green beans and carrots and with a rocket salad drizzled with olive oil and lemon juice.

preparation time: **15 minutes, plus at least 1 hour marinating**

cooking time: **10–12 minutes**

serves **4**

NUTRIENTS PER SERVING	
calories	240
carbohydrate	4 g
(sugars)	4 g
protein	32 g
fat	10 g
(saturated)	4 g
fibre	1 g

FOR THE SALSA

2 oranges, segmented and finely chopped

1 lemon, segmented and finely chopped

1 bird's eye chilli, finely chopped, (optional)

1 spring onion, finely sliced

2 teaspoons parsley, finely chopped

FOR THE ESCALOPES

4 pork escalopes, each about 150 g (5½ oz)

Black pepper

4 sprigs thyme or lemon thyme leaves, chopped

1 Make the salsa by mixing together the chopped oranges, lemon and chilli (if used), pressing them slightly with a fork to release the juices.

2 Add the spring onion and parsley. Set aside for at least 1 hour to allow the flavours to amalgamate.

3 Heat the grill to high. Season the escalopes with pepper and sprinkle with the thyme. Grill for 5–6 minutes on each side, until the juices run clear.

4 Serve the escalopes immediately on warm serving plates, topped with a spoonful of salsa.

speedy gazpacho

This chilled soup is a powerful blend of flavours and nutrients. Raw onion and garlic and finely chopped fresh chilli provide their own kick. But if you like it extra-hot, blend in some chilli powder with the garnish on the bowl.

preparation time: **10 minutes**

serves **4**

½ cucumber, diced
2 large red peppers, deseeded and chopped
1 large red onion, roughly chopped
1 large garlic clove, roughly chopped
6 large basil leaves
700 g (1 lb 9 oz) tomato passata
1 tablespoon olive oil
4 tablespoons red wine vinegar
300 ml (½ pint) cold chicken or vegetable stock (recipes page 338)
Juice of ½ lemon
Black pepper
TO GARNISH
Basil leaves, torn
1 chilli, finely chopped
½ cucumber, finely diced
1 small green pepper, deseeded and diced
Croûtons

1 Put the cucumber, red peppers, onion, garlic and basil in a food processor and blend for 1 minute. Add the passata, oil and vinegar and blend until smooth.

2 Stir in the stock and lemon juice and season to taste with pepper. Pour into a large bowl, cover and chill for 2–3 hours.

3 Garnish the bowl of soup with the basil and chilli (if using) and serve the cucumber and pepper dice and the croûtons in separate bowls.

NUTRIENTS PER SERVING	
calories	120
carbohydrate	18 g
(sugars)	17 g
protein	5 g
fat	4 g
(saturated)	0.5 g
fibre	4.5 g

mediterranean **grill**

Enjoy this mixed grill accented with the flavours of the warm south. Sumptuous as it looks, it contains fewer calories than a conventional mixed grill. A fresh tomato salad and baby new potatoes, garnished with basil, would be a good accompaniment.

preparation time: **5 minutes**

cooking time: **20–25 minutes**

serves **2**

1 small aubergine, thickly sliced
1 courgette, thickly sliced diagonally
1 red pepper, deseeded and quartered
10 button mushrooms
1 tablespoon olive oil
Black pepper
4 lean pork sausages flavoured with herbs
200 g (7 oz) rump steak, trimmed of fat
Fresh basil leaves and parsley, to garnish

1 Preheat the grill. Place the vegetables on a baking tray and lightly brush with olive oil. Season with black pepper and

cook under the grill for 5 minutes. Turn them over, brush lightly with oil and return to the grill for a further 5 minutes, or until they are brown. Cover with kitchen foil and keep warm.

2 Pierce the sausages with a fork, place in the grill tray and cook until brown, turning occasionally. Add the steak and cook for 4–5 minutes each side.

3 Serve the vegetables, steak and sausages on a warmed plate, garnished with the basil and parsley.

NUTRIENTS PER SERVING	
calories	470
carbohydrate	117 g
(sugars)	11 g
protein	31 g
fat	31 g
(saturated)	11 g
fibre	6 g

Starting a family

Planning a new baby is exciting for every couple: it can also provide an opportunity for both partners to maximise their fertility by choosing a healthier diet and lifestyle. Certain foods are invaluable in helping to conceive a child and enjoy a happy, trouble-free pregnancy.

Prospective parents rarely ask themselves if they are in the best physical condition to conceive a child and sustain a pregnancy. But the health of both partners has a direct impact on their fertility. It can make all the difference between whether having a baby is a pleasure or a problem.

Generally, a balanced range of nutritious foods combined with regular, moderate exercise is sufficient to maintain good sexual and reproductive health. But with infertility in both men and women on the increase, would-be parents need to scrutinise their diets and lifestyles as never before.

Be patient You may decide to make some positive changes to increase your chances of conceiving a baby. If so, you should be aware that any improvements will not happen overnight: it can take up to three months to bring your body to peak levels of health and fertility.

Your efforts will be worth while, however: the advantages of being in good health before starting a family

are far-reaching. A baby conceived by a mother eating a healthy diet is less likely to suffer heart disease and diabetes in middle age.

BOOSTING FERTILITY

When partners make the momentous decision to have a baby, and then find they are not able to conceive, the disappointment can be utterly overwhelming. Infertility can affect both men and women, and may be due to various medical conditions.

Poor nutrition can contribute to infertility and, in some cases, may even be the sole cause. Many couples, rather than using fertility treatments, have been able to conceive by changing the foods they eat, improving their overall nutrition, and following a healthier lifestyle.

A change of lifestyle

Drinking alcohol to excess affects fertility in men and women in several ways. It lowers sex drive and affects sexual performance in both partners. And it can depress hormone levels in men and women,

A perfect combination Scallop and Bacon Kebabs are rich in zinc, B vitamins and selenium, and make an ideal meal if you are planning to have a baby. The recipe is on page 168.

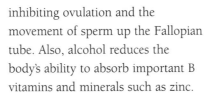

The right choice One or two well-cooked eggs a week provide zinc to boost fertility and won't raise your cholesterol levels. Pine nuts (above right) are another good source of zinc – eat them as snacks or scattered over a spinach salad.

inhibiting ovulation and the movement of sperm up the Fallopian tube. Also, alcohol reduces the body's ability to absorb important B vitamins and minerals such as zinc.

Deficiencies in Vitamin B_6 and folic acid have been linked to infertility. And zinc is one of the most important nutrients for sperm production. A deficiency results in lower sperm counts – men drinking over four units of alcohol a day are at risk of reduced sperm levels.

Ideally, a couple hoping to conceive a child should stop drinking or cut down drastically. They should certainly keep to safe drinking guidelines (see page 97).

Are you overweight? Obesity causes infertility and it also lowers libido in both sexes. If you need to lose weight, you should follow a diet low enough in calories but high in all the essential nutrients (see pages 91-99) to ensure your own and your baby's good health when you do conceive.

Quit smoking Cigarette smoking not only affects overall health (see page 69) but also lowers fertility in

women, because both direct and passive smoking can contribute to irregular menstruation.

Boosting the sperm count
A man produces sperm all the time but the number and quality of sperm are influenced by the food he eats. A low sperm count or poor-quality sperm are well-known causes of male infertility. To produce healthy sperm, men should eat a healthy, balanced diet. This should include foods rich in essential fatty acids (such as oily fish and polyunsaturated oils), vitamins A, B, C and E, and the minerals zinc and magnesium. Two of these nutrients, vitamin C and zinc, have a highly specific role.

Vitamin C When sperm enters a woman's body she produces antibodies that make the sperm clump together; this makes it more difficult for them to fertilise the egg. Vitamin C reduces this reaction, and improves the chances of conception.

Zinc Although the amount of zinc present in the body is very small, it is crucial to a man's fertility. Zinc is

concentrated in male sex glands and sperm and helps to produce sperm and male hormones.

Men lose some zinc in sweat and urine. If zinc stores become low, levels of sperm and male hormones decrease and fertility is lowered. The body needs only tiny amounts which can be obtained from many sources (see Mineral Rich Foods opposite). Supplements may push levels over the RDA (recommended daily allowance) of 15 milligrams. As zinc protects the body against infection, an imbalance may reduce this action. And taking excessive amounts may cause fever, nausea and vomiting.

A healthy blood supply Hardened arteries (atherosclerosis) can affect a man's potency. The supply of blood to the penis and testes may be impeded, and this can cause problems with sperm production. To maintain the health of your arteries, follow a heart-friendly diet (see pages 56-63), and ensure that you eat oily fish at least twice a week.

Improving female fertility

A woman is born with all her eggs (ova) already formed in her ovaries. Each month during ovulation, one (or more) of her eggs ripens and is released ready for fertilisation. But the hormones controlling this process can be upset by several factors such as poor diet, stress and extreme physical exercise. The resulting hormonal imbalance may cause infertility or impaired fertility.

The effects of dieting A survey of women attending London fertility clinics showed that half of them had been trying to lose weight. But their diets were very low in key nutrients which affect hormonal imbalance and may cause failure of ovulation.

Women need to maintain at least 18 per cent body fat if they hope to conceive. Those who are under this level and severely underweight may stop menstruating completely. This is because stores of body fat regulate the hormones that control ovulation and menstruation.

Get active Restricting the amount you eat in order to lose weight is not a good idea when you are also trying to conceive. Increase your physical activity instead – this will have the added benefit of making you fitter. If you join a gym, use it regularly – aim to get at least 30 minutes continuous exercise a day. Daily sessions of walking, skipping, dancing, jogging and swimming are

MILK *acts as a soothing balm for many women plagued by morning sickness. It is particularly effective served ice-cold from the fridge. For easier digestion, drink it skimmed or semi-skimmed: or try it whisked to a light froth, flavoured with a little vanilla.*

1 *Take small, frequent sips of low-fat milk throughout the day.*

2 *Eat little and often: nibble dry biscuits, toast, oat cakes or rice cakes.*

3 *Ginger is a great help in combating nausea. Every couple of hours, snack on a ginger biscuit;* *or eat slivers from a piece of fresh or preserved ginger. Regular tastes of ginger beer are good too.*

4 *If you enjoy yoghurt, a few spoonfuls at frequent intervals can help.*

5 *Take regular sips of mineral water and eat small pieces of fresh fruit.*

FIVE WAYS TO calm morning sickness

Tender asparagus spears are not only delicious, but also boost fertility in men and women. They are rich in vitamin C to aid conception and contain folates vital for a baby's earliest stages of growth.

all simple but effective ways of increasing physical activity.

Caffeine Recent findings indicate that high levels of caffeine decrease blood levels of the hormone prolactin. Imbalances in prolactin are associated with infertility, so you should cut down on caffeine-rich tea, coffee and cola drinks.

The effects of contraception Some women remain infertile for months after they stop taking the Pill or using the copper IUD. This may be due to a zinc deficiency or a hormonal imbalance, or both. A diet rich in zinc, manganese and vitamin B_6 can help to restore fertility.

Manganese and vitamin B_6 help to break down oestrogen. This is crucial to conception, as raised oestrogen levels prevent pregnancy. Women using a copper IUD may have high levels of copper, but low stores of zinc, magnesium and manganese.

MINERAL-RICH FOODS

Oysters and shrimps are the best sources of zinc, but you can get plenty from other shellfish (crabs, mussels, lobster), sardines, turkey, duck, goose, game and lean meat. Hard, crumbly cheeses such as Parmesan, Cheshire and Cheddar are helpful sources, as are eggs, wholegrain foods and brown rice. You can also enhance your fertility

by snacking on nuts: they provide zinc, magnesium, manganese and vitamins E and B_6. Hazelnuts, almonds and sunflower seeds contain plenty of vitamin E, while sesame seeds, Brazil nuts and pine nuts are rich in zinc.

If you can't resist chocolate, eat a few chocolate-coated Brazil nuts. And toss pine nuts or sesame seeds into salads. Peanut butter on toast or on a sandwich will give you a great boost of magnesium and zinc.

Eating lean meat is a good way to obtain magnesium, zinc, and B vitamins. Pork and bacon are especially high in zinc, and dark poultry meat from the leg and thigh has more zinc than the breast meat.

Liver and liver pâté All women planning a pregnancy, or who are already pregnant, should try to avoid liver and liver pâté. Their vitamin A content is very high, and this may damage the foetus.

However, liver is rich in zinc, magnesium, and vitamin B_6 as well as vitamin A, and men who are trying to increase their fertility may wish to include it in their diet. There is a delicious recipe for Pan-fried Lamb's Liver on page 176.

After her baby has been born, liver and liver pâté are excellent, nourishing foods for a new mother, especially if she is breastfeeding.

Eat at least five servings of fruit and vegetables a day if you want to maximise your fertility – citrus fruit is particularly high in vitamin C for healthy sperm. Eat green, leafy vegetables for manganese and antioxidants; red and orange fruit and vegetables for beta carotene.

Beans and pulses provide some manganese, and you can also obtain it from wholegrain cereals: they are richer sources of magnesium, manganese and vitamin B_6 than

HEALTH OR HYPE?
food cravings

During pregnancy you may crave a food that you've never liked until now. But there is no proof that this is a response to your body's nutritional needs: it may be due to hormonal changes. You may crave fruit, fruit juices, chocolate, a spicy chutney or dairy products. Cravings for non-food substances such as clay, chalk, or coal (called *pica*) are rare but can be dangerous: they can cause anaemia and blood poisoning, and are associated with poor foetal development.

*A **picture of health** Your prospects of enjoying a blooming pregnancy will be greatly improved if you eat the right foods. A jar of live, natural yoghurt provides calcium and B vitamins and improves your digestion.*

refined varieties. Buy wholegrain bread that has been leavened with yeast. Your body can absorb more magnesium from this than from unleavened bread such as pitta.

Oily fish contain essential fatty acids: eat salmon, tuna, mackerel or sardines at least twice a week. Eggs provide essential fatty acids and vitamin A, while milk and yoghurt provide calcium and magnesium.

THE ROLE OF FOLATES

During its first weeks in the womb, your baby needs a good supply of folate, one of the B vitamins. This vitamin is crucial to the development of the brain and spinal cord. Without an adequate supply of folate your baby may develop neural tube defects or spina bifida, a condition in which the spinal cord and nerves are damaged. For more information on the early development of the nervous system, turn to pages 36-37.

Apart from those with epilepsy (see below) all women planning a pregnancy should eat plenty of high-folate foods (see opposite).

Supplements In addition, a daily supplement of 400 micrograms of folic acid is needed. This is easy to absorb and you should start taking it three months before conception and until the 12th week of pregnancy.

Folic acid is now widely available in supermarkets and pharmacies. You can take folic acid instead of your usual multivitamin supplement. Many multivitamin formulations contain high levels of vitamin A, so it is best to avoid these in the first few weeks of pregnancy.

Some breads and breakfast cereals are fortified with folic acid (the packaging has a white 'F' on a blue background to indicate this). In the United States all flour contains supplements of folic acid. Health experts are currently considering recommending the same policy for flour manufacturing in the United Kingdom.

Caution: Women who suffer from epilepsy and are on anti-convulsant therapy should consult a doctor before taking folic acid supplements.

Top folate foods

Breads and breakfast cereals fortified with folate, avocados, asparagus, beetroot, broccoli, Brussels sprouts, spinach, green beans, black-eyed beans, yeast and beef extract and all nuts and seeds provide abundant folate. Other good sources include potatoes, parsnips, cauliflower, peas, cabbage, soya beans, baked beans, hummous, blackberries, citrus fruit and dates, brown rice, wholemeal bread, wholegrain pasta and eggs.

Folate-friendly cooking Folate is easily destroyed when foods are overcooked, so steam or cook vegetables in small amounts of water. They should be as fresh as possible – folate levels decrease if they are stored for any length of time.

Watch the alcohol

Excessive amounts of alcohol during pregnancy can cause birth defects. But there is little evidence to show that small amounts are harmful. To be on the safe side, avoid all alcohol during the first few months of pregnancy and thereafter limit your intake to one unit of alcohol a day, preferably with a meal. If you choose to avoid alcohol, try fruit juice cocktails instead. The simplest are the most delicious – just mix your favourite fruit juice or elderflower cordial with sparkling water. Or buy a juicer so you can make your own drinks from fresh fruits.

FOOD AND PREGNANCY

When you are pregnant you may be tempted to cast caution to the winds and stop worrying about what you eat. Your rationale may be that you will get larger anyway, and you may even persuade yourself that you should 'eat for two'. In one sense this is true. You need to put on enough weight to store as body fat which will provide energy for breastfeeding.

But you won't need extra calories for the first six months of pregnancy. And in the last three months, you will only need about 200 extra Calories daily – a sandwich made with two medium slices of wholemeal bread and 55 g (2 oz) chicken breast meat is a rough equivalent of these extra calories.

The best nutrients

Everything that you eat is passed to the foetus, so you should eat a wide range of healthy foods to ensure that your baby has the best start. And choose fresh rather than processed foods whenever possible: the fewer additives you consume, the safer your baby will be.

How much protein? A little extra protein is recommended during pregnancy, but most women eat more than enough. A small portion of lean meat, fish, eggs, pulses, or nuts twice a day is sufficient. If you are vegetarian, your protein and iron intake may be lower. You should always eat pulses in combination with cereal foods such as pasta, couscous and rice, and you may consider taking an iron supplement.

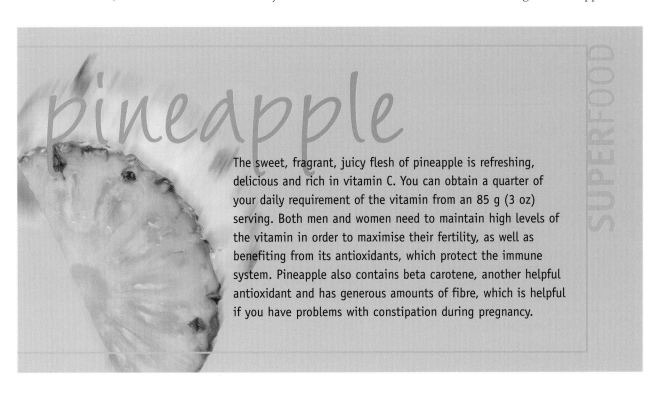

pineapple

SUPERFOOD

The sweet, fragrant, juicy flesh of pineapple is refreshing, delicious and rich in vitamin C. You can obtain a quarter of your daily requirement of the vitamin from an 85 g (3 oz) serving. Both men and women need to maintain high levels of the vitamin in order to maximise their fertility, as well as benefiting from its antioxidants, which protect the immune system. Pineapple also contains beta carotene, another helpful antioxidant and has generous amounts of fibre, which is helpful if you have problems with constipation during pregnancy.

MENUPLAN
for pregnancy

Boost your energy, maximise your nutrients and enjoy a healthy pregnancy.

FOR BREAKFASTS A cereal fortified with iron and folic acid, or a Swiss-style variety with nuts and dried fruit. Pour over semi-skimmed milk and add fresh fruit. Drink fruit juice. At weekends, have a poached or scrambled egg and grilled lean bacon with wholemeal toast and fruit or juice.

MID-MORNING Eat fresh fruit such as apricots and oranges for beta carotene. Or try an Apricot Smoothie (recipe page 202).

FOR LUNCH Choose oily fish such as mackerel or salmon pâté on wholemeal bread. Accompany with a green salad and pine nuts or sunflower seeds. Or have a small jacket potato with a low-fat filling.

EVENING MEALS Base meals on pasta, rice, couscous or potato and include plenty of orange or red vegetables, such as carrots or peppers. Have a little lean meat or shellfish. Or Scallop and Bacon Kebabs (recipe overleaf). Almond and Apricot Ricotta Tart (recipe overleaf) is a delicious dessert.

SNACKS Brazil nuts or a low-fat yoghurt with nuts sprinkled over or a piece of hard cheese for calcium.

After the first three months of your pregnancy, you will not need a folic acid supplement. But you should continue eating high-folate foods.

Calcium levels Your body absorbs calcium more efficiently when you are pregnant, and you need to consume at least 700 milligrams daily. You can easily achieve this by having milk, cheese or yoghurt twice a day – a 225 ml (8 fl oz) glass of milk contains 297 milligrams of calcium. If you prefer not to eat too many dairy products, choose soya drinks and yoghurts.

Vitamin D Most of your body's store of vitamin D is made from the action of sunlight on your skin (see page 46). You need more vitamin D when you are pregnant, but if you spend a few hours outdoors every day, you will usually make enough. However, if you have a dark skin, live in Northern Europe or cover your skin for religious reasons, you may not absorb enough sunlight, especially during winter. To compensate for this, eat some vitamin D-rich foods every day. Oily fish, taramasalata and eggs all have high levels. Also, use margarine rather than butter, as it is fortified with vitamin D.

Vitamin A During the last three months of your pregnancy you can consume a little more vitamin A. But proceed with caution. Eat plenty of orange and red fruit and vegetables such as apricots, peppers and carrots. These are all high in beta carotene which is converted into vitamin A by your body as and when you and your baby require it. But don't forget that liver and liver products such as pâté should be

Fit for motherhood *Exercise regularly while you are pregnant, as this will provide natural support for your growing baby by strengthening your abdominal muscles. It also prepares your body for labour. Avoid over-strenuous routines as you get larger.*

avoided throughout your pregnancy (see page 163), as they contain very high levels of vitamin A.

Iron Your doctor can check if you have adequate iron levels at the beginning of your pregnancy. If these are satisfactory, you will not need to take a supplement. Iron absorption is enhanced during pregnancy, so eat foods rich in iron such as red meat, dark poultry meat, eggs, pulses and nuts. Also, tea interferes with your body's ability to take up iron, so it is better to drink it between meals rather than with food.

Vitamins C and E New research shows that high levels of vitamins C and E can reduce the risk of pre-eclampsia. This rare but serious complication in pregnancy causes a severe rise in blood pressure. The richest sources of vitamin C are citrus fruits, peppers, strawberries, kiwi fruit, pineapple and tomatoes. To obtain plenty of vitamin E, eat avocados, safflower and sunflower oils, sunflower seeds, almonds, hazelnuts, butter and margarine.

Ups and downs

The hormones circulating in your body during pregnancy may cause some discomfort.

Morning sickness Nausea and vomiting affect many women during the first three months of pregnancy. This usually happens in the morning, but some women feel nauseous throughout the day. After 12–16 weeks the symptoms subside, but they may last longer. Look at the box on page 162 for tips on how to cope with the worst effects.

Strange sensations Distinct changes in taste and smell may occur during pregnancy. A soap or a herbal tea that was previously innocuous may

food safety in pregnancy

Certain foods contain substances that can harm your baby – do not eat these. Take extra care with household hygiene, food storage, and food preparation (see pages 22-23) to avert potential problems.

Soft and blue-veined cheese such as Camembert, Brie and Stilton should be avoided. They harbour a bacteria causing listeriosis, which may cause miscarriage or still birth.

Raw and undercooked meat may contain a parasite which causes toxoplasmosis. This infection usually has no ill effects unless it is passed on to your baby. Then it can cause a range of severe problems, including eye and brain damage. Make sure that you cook meat thoroughly, and wash your hands and work surfaces after handling raw meat. If you have a cat or dog be aware that the parasite is carried in their faeces. Wear gloves when gardening or changing cat litter and wash your hands after handling pets.

Unwashed fruit and vegetables You may acquire toxoplasmosis from unwashed fruit and vegetables. Rinse these thoroughly, ensuring that no traces of soil are present.

Peanuts The number of children allergic to peanuts is increasing; it is now thought that they become sensitive to peanut proteins while in the womb. If you or your partner have a food allergy, hay fever, eczema or asthma, avoid eating peanuts while you are pregnant.

suddenly make you feel queasy, and you may have to avoid these now.

Constipation Hormones can make your intestines relax, and this may result in constipation and piles (haemorrhoids). Drink at least eight cups of fluid daily and increase your fibre intake by eating extra fruit, vegetables and wholegrain cereals. Dried fruit, especially prunes, are an excellent natural laxative. Exercise gets your muscles working and this helps to ease constipation.

Indigestion and heartburn When the baby is large enough to press on your stomach you may experience discomfort. Sometimes the acid in your stomach leaks into your oesophagus causing heartburn, and

you may also have problems with indigestion (see page 82). There are several things you can do to avoid these problems: cut out fatty foods; avoid large meals – eat frequent, small, nutritious snacks; don't eat late at night; prop up the end of your bed; and sip soothing drinks such as cold water, or ginger or peppermint tea.

Fitness and weight gain Keeping active in the early months of pregnancy is important. You should not put on more than the average weight-gain of 12 kg (28 lb) over the nine months. The fitter you are, the better you will cope with your changing shape and the stress of labour.

scallop and bacon kebabs on a bed of rocket

If you are planning a pregnancy, include these delicious kebabs in your range of supper dishes. They should help to boost your fertility, because the scallops are rich in zinc. The flavours of scallops and bacon complement each other perfectly.

preparation time: **5 minutes, plus 30 minutes marinating**

cooking time: **8–10 minutes**

serves **2**

NUTRIENTS PER SERVING	
calories	320
carbohydrate	2 g
(sugars)	0.5 g
protein	20 g
fat	26 g
(saturated)	4.5 g
fibre	0

4 large scallops with coral
4 rashers unsmoked streaky bacon, rinded and cut in half
55 g (2 oz) rocket
2 tablespoons chopped chives
Cherry tomatoes, to garnish
FOR THE MARINADE
1 tablespoon olive oil
1 tablespoon lime juice
Black pepper
FOR THE DRESSING
2 tablespoons balsamic vinegar
3 tablespoons olive oil
Black pepper

1 Put the scallops in a dish. Mix together the marinade ingredients, pour over the scallops and turn them to coat. Put in the fridge for 30 minutes to marinate.

2 Roll up the bacon pieces. Thread the scallops and bacon rolls alternately on 2 kebab skewers. Grill for 4–5 minutes on each side, until lightly cooked.

3 Mix together the dressing ingredients. Arrange the rocket on 2 serving plates and put the skewers on top. Sprinkle over the chives and garnish with the tomatoes. Pour over the dressing.

smoked haddock risotto

Creamy arborio rice and fine quality naturally smoked, undyed haddock make a superb combination of flavours. Because the fish is already salty, use your own vegetable stock made without salt (see the recipe on page 338).

preparation time: **10 minutes**

cooking time: **45–55 minutes**

serves **4**

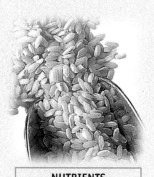

1.2 litres (2 pints) unsalted vegetable stock
600 g (1 lb 5 oz) undyed smoked haddock
1 tablespoon unsalted butter
1 tablespoon olive oil
1 small onion, finely chopped
450 g (1 lb) arborio rice
1 teaspoon ground turmeric
300 ml (½ pint) dry white wine
Juice of ½ lemon
1 tablespoon chopped parsley, to garnish

NUTRIENTS PER SERVING	
calories	630
carbohydrate	92 g
(sugars)	2 g
protein	34 g
fat	7 g
(saturated)	2 g
fibre	0

1 Bring 600 ml (1 pint) of the stock to the boil in a frying pan. Reduce the heat, add the fish and poach for 5 minutes, until it is opaque. Remove the fish from the pan and flake the flesh, discarding the skin and bones. Set the flesh aside. Strain the liquid and add it to the remaining stock.

2 Heat the butter and oil in a heavy-based pan. Add the onion and cook for 3 minutes. Add the rice and turmeric and cook for 2 minutes, stirring. Pour in the wine and lemon juice. Bring to the boil, reduce the heat and simmer for 5–10 minutes, until the wine is absorbed. Gradually add the stock. Simmer, stirring, for 20–25 minutes, until the rice is tender.

3 Stir in the fish. Put the risotto into a serving dish and garnish with parsley.

avoided throughout your pregnancy (see page 163), as they contain very high levels of vitamin A.

Iron Your doctor can check if you have adequate iron levels at the beginning of your pregnancy. If these are satisfactory, you will not need to take a supplement. Iron absorption is enhanced during pregnancy, so eat foods rich in iron such as red meat, dark poultry meat, eggs, pulses and nuts. Also, tea interferes with your body's ability to take up iron, so it is better to drink it between meals rather than with food.

Vitamins C and E New research shows that high levels of vitamins C and E can reduce the risk of pre-eclampsia. This rare but serious complication in pregnancy causes a severe rise in blood pressure. The richest sources of vitamin C are citrus fruits, peppers, strawberries, kiwi fruit, pineapple and tomatoes. To obtain plenty of vitamin E, eat avocados, safflower and sunflower oils, sunflower seeds, almonds, hazelnuts, butter and margarine.

Ups and downs

The hormones circulating in your body during pregnancy may cause some discomfort.

Morning sickness Nausea and vomiting affect many women during the first three months of pregnancy. This usually happens in the morning, but some women feel nauseous throughout the day. After 12–16 weeks the symptoms subside, but they may last longer. Look at the box on page 162 for tips on how to cope with the worst effects.

Strange sensations Distinct changes in taste and smell may occur during pregnancy. A soap or a herbal tea that was previously innocuous may

food safety in pregnancy

Certain foods contain substances that can harm your baby – do not eat these. Take extra care with household hygiene, food storage, and food preparation (see pages 22-23) to avert potential problems.

Soft and blue-veined cheese such as Camembert, Brie and Stilton should be avoided. They harbour a bacteria causing listeriosis, which may cause miscarriage or still birth.

Raw and undercooked meat may contain a parasite which causes toxoplasmosis. This infection usually has no ill effects unless it is passed on to your baby. Then it can cause a range of severe problems, including eye and brain damage. Make sure that you cook meat thoroughly, and wash your hands and work surfaces after handling raw meat. If you have a cat or dog be aware that the parasite is carried in their faeces. Wear gloves when gardening or changing cat litter and wash your hands after handling pets.

Unwashed fruit and vegetables You may acquire toxoplasmosis from unwashed fruit and vegetables. Rinse these thoroughly, ensuring that no traces of soil are present.

Peanuts The number of children allergic to peanuts is increasing; it is now thought that they become sensitive to peanut proteins while in the womb. If you or your partner have a food allergy, hay fever, eczema or asthma, avoid eating peanuts while you are pregnant.

suddenly make you feel queasy, and you may have to avoid these now.

Constipation Hormones can make your intestines relax, and this may result in constipation and piles (haemorrhoids). Drink at least eight cups of fluid daily and increase your fibre intake by eating extra fruit, vegetables and wholegrain cereals. Dried fruit, especially prunes, are an excellent natural laxative. Exercise gets your muscles working and this helps to ease constipation.

Indigestion and heartburn When the baby is large enough to press on your stomach you may experience discomfort. Sometimes the acid in your stomach leaks into your oesophagus causing heartburn, and

you may also have problems with indigestion (see page 82). There are several things you can do to avoid these problems: cut out fatty foods; avoid large meals – eat frequent, small, nutritious snacks; don't eat late at night; prop up the end of your bed; and sip soothing drinks such as cold water, or ginger or peppermint tea.

Fitness and weight gain Keeping active in the early months of pregnancy is important. You should not put on more than the average weight-gain of 12 kg (28 lb) over the nine months. The fitter you are, the better you will cope with your changing shape and the stress of labour.

scallop and bacon kebabs on a bed of rocket

If you are planning a pregnancy, include these delicious kebabs in your range of supper dishes. They should help to boost your fertility, because the scallops are rich in zinc. The flavours of scallops and bacon complement each other perfectly.

preparation time: **5 minutes, plus 30 minutes marinating**

cooking time: **8–10 minutes**

serves **2**

NUTRIENTS PER SERVING	
calories	320
carbohydrate	2 g
(sugars)	0.5 g
protein	20 g
fat	26 g
(saturated)	4.5 g
fibre	0

4 large scallops with coral
4 rashers unsmoked streaky bacon, rinded and cut in half
55 g (2 oz) rocket
2 tablespoons chopped chives
Cherry tomatoes, to garnish
FOR THE MARINADE
1 tablespoon olive oil
1 tablespoon lime juice
Black pepper
FOR THE DRESSING
2 tablespoons balsamic vinegar
3 tablespoons olive oil
Black pepper

1 Put the scallops in a dish. Mix together the marinade ingredients, pour over the scallops and turn them to coat. Put in the fridge for 30 minutes to marinate.

2 Roll up the bacon pieces. Thread the scallops and bacon rolls alternately on 2 kebab skewers. Grill for 4–5 minutes on each side, until lightly cooked.

3 Mix together the dressing ingredients. Arrange the rocket on 2 serving plates and put the skewers on top. Sprinkle over the chives and garnish with the tomatoes. Pour over the dressing.

smoked haddock risotto

Creamy arborio rice and fine quality naturally smoked, undyed haddock make a superb combination of flavours. Because the fish is already salty, use your own vegetable stock made without salt (see the recipe on page 338).

preparation time: **10 minutes**

cooking time: **45–55 minutes**

serves **4**

NUTRIENTS PER SERVING	
calories	630
carbohydrate	92 g
(sugars)	2 g
protein	34 g
fat	7 g
(saturated)	2 g
fibre	0

1.2 litres (2 pints) unsalted vegetable stock
600 g (1 lb 5 oz) undyed smoked haddock
1 tablespoon unsalted butter
1 tablespoon olive oil
1 small onion, finely chopped
450 g (1 lb) arborio rice
1 teaspoon ground turmeric
300 ml (½ pint) dry white wine
Juice of ½ lemon
1 tablespoon chopped parsley, to garnish

1 Bring 600 ml (1 pint) of the stock to the boil in a frying pan. Reduce the heat, add the fish and poach for 5 minutes, until it is opaque. Remove the fish from the pan and flake the flesh, discarding the skin and bones. Set the

flesh aside. Strain the liquid and add it to the remaining stock.

2 Heat the butter and oil in a heavy-based pan. Add the onion and cook for 3 minutes. Add the rice and turmeric and cook for 2 minutes, stirring. Pour in the wine and lemon juice. Bring to the boil, reduce the heat and simmer for 5–10 minutes, until the wine is absorbed. Gradually add the stock. Simmer, stirring, for 20–25 minutes, until the rice is tender.

3 Stir in the fish. Put the risotto into a serving dish and garnish with parsley.

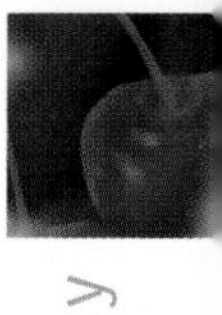

almond and apricot ricotta tart

This tart combines the creaminess of ricotta with the crunchiness of chopped almonds in a sweet pastry case. If you don't have time to make your own pastry, use ready-made shortcrust pastry instead.

preparation time: **15 minutes, plus 20–30 minutes chilling time for the pastry**
cooking time: **25–30 minutes**
serves **8**

FOR THE PASTRY

225 g (8 oz) plain flour
115 g (4 oz) butter, diced
1 tablespoon caster sugar
3–4 tablespoons cold water, to mix

FOR THE FILLING

250 g (9 oz) ricotta cheese
2 egg yolks
50 g (1¾ oz) caster sugar
½ teaspoon almond essence
225 g (8 oz) canned apricot halves in juice, drained
55 g (2 oz) almonds, roughly chopped

1 Put the flour in a large bowl and rub in the butter with your fingertips until the mixture resembles breadcrumbs. Add the sugar. Use a knife to mix in sufficient water to make a soft dough and chill for 20–30 minutes. Heat the oven to 180°C (350°F, gas mark 4). Roll the pastry out on a lightly floured surface and use to line a 20 cm (8 in) flan tin. Line the pastry with kitchen foil, weigh down with baking beans and bake for 15 minutes. Remove the foil and bake for a further 5-10 minutes, until golden brown and cooked through.

2 Place the ricotta cheese in a large bowl. Mix in the egg yolks, sugar and almond essence. Pour the mixture into the pastry case, arrange the apricots on top, and sprinkle over the almonds.

3 Return to the oven for 4–5 minutes. Serve warm or cold, with low-fat Greek yoghurt or half-fat crème fraîche.

NUTRIENTS PER SERVING	
calories	350
carbohydrate	34 g
(sugars)	12 g
protein	8 g
fat	21 g
(saturated)	10 g
fibre	1.5 g

New **mother**, new **baby**

As a new mother, you have to cope with enormous demands on your energy and endurance, especially if you are breastfeeding. This is the time to ensure that you get maximum nourishment from your diet. Choosing the right foods to keep both yourself and your baby healthy is the best answer.

For most women, labour is both a lengthy and an exhausting process. You expend an enormous amount of energy giving birth and will have lost a lot of fluid by the time your baby is born. You may also have missed some meals.

Your first priority is to replenish your depleted fluid levels. Drink some water, juice, barley water or a fruit squash. And try to eat some food as soon as you feel up to it. A high-energy, high-carbohydrate snack such as a flapjack, sesame bar, sandwich, biscuits or cake is fine.

THE FIRST DAYS

As you recover from the birth and start getting used to your baby's needs, make sure that someone else is responsible for providing you with regular, nourishing meals.

You need plenty of iron-rich foods to boost your reserves. Lean meat or oily fish, eggs, dried fruit, pulses, nuts and green vegetables can help to replace the iron you have lost during and after labour. You should also consume vitamin C (citrus fruits are a good source) to help your body to absorb iron.

Adjusting to breastfeeding

The ideal food for a new baby is breast milk (although you may decide to feed with formula milk). For more information on early feeding, turn to page 135.

During the first 72 hours after your baby is born, you will produce a thin, yellow nutrient-rich fluid called colostrum. By the third day the composition of your breast milk will have changed. At the beginning of each feed, the first milk you produce is thin, low in fat and thirst-quenching. As the feed continues, your milk becomes richer in fat and protein. These different types of breast milk are called foremilk and hindmilk respectively. They are both important for your baby's healthy development.

Mutual support *There are many ways in which a father can share the load, especially during the first weeks. These include shopping, cooking, nappy changing and household chores.*

Mother's milk Breastfeeding mothers need extra fluid to produce enough milk for their baby. Make sure you have plenty to drink and take regular sips throughout the day. Water or milk are fine, or try different diluted fruit juices.

Your baby may wake and feed very frequently throughout the day and night. Over a 24-hour period this is exhausting: you will certainly lack sleep, and your breasts may be uncomfortably heavy and distended. **Feeding patterns** It takes a lot of time and patience to establish a regular feeding routine, especially with a first baby. Some take quite a while to settle down. Eventually, though, the intervals between feeds will lengthen and you will begin to feel more relaxed as your supply of milk adapts to the baby's demands. **Drinking for two** During the early months of breastfeeding you will produce about 500 ml (18 fl oz) of milk daily. This increases to around 800 ml (1⅓ pints) in the later stages of lactation. You will therefore need to consume plenty of extra fluid: try to drink about 2-2½ litres (3½-4½ pints) daily. Preferably, this should be water, milk and diluted fruit juices. It is a good idea to keep a glass of water at hand so you can take sips every time you feed your baby.

Foods to avoid

Some mothers claim that if they eat certain foods such as spices and orange juice, their babies have

diarrhoea-like symptoms. This has not been proved, but you can try cutting back on these foods if you think they are affecting your baby.

Avoid peanuts if you or your partner have a history of allergies (see page 137). And keep your alcohol intake low: it can pass into your breast milk and may make your baby sleepy and unable to suckle efficiently. An occasional drink will relax you and will not harm your baby. One unit a day is a reasonable guideline (a glass of wine is one unit). Caffeine can also enter breast milk and make your baby nervous and irritable so avoid coffee and other high-caffeine drinks.

Some drugs (including nicotine) can reach your baby through your breast milk. Avoid smoking completely, and check with your doctor before taking any medication.

Nutrients and breastfeeding

As a nursing mother, you need high-quality foods to maintain your milk supply. Try to eat plenty of fruit and vegetables, dairy foods, oily fish, lean meat, pulses, nuts and wholegrain foods. These will provide all of the vitamins, minerals, protein and energy that you need.

Although a deficient diet is unlikely to affect the quality of your milk, it can reduce the quantity you

produce and may also affect your health. This is because your body uses its own reserves of nutrients to achieve the proper composition of breast milk if you are not consuming enough in your daily diet.

Current advice for a breastfeeding mother is to increase the vitamin and mineral content of your diet to a substantial degree (see the chart opposite). For example, women who are not breastfeeding need about 700 mg of calcium daily. But this requirement increases dramatically when you are breastfeeding. You then need about 1250 mg every day – equivalent to 1.2 litres (2 pints) of milk or about 175 g (6 oz) of Cheddar cheese. This amount helps ensure that your baby has healthy bones and teeth and it also supplies enough for your own needs.

Extras for nursing mothers It is not difficult to meet your increased nutritional requirements. To obtain more protein, vitamin B_{12}, zinc and phosphorus, simply eat slightly larger portions of meat, fish, pulses and milk. Or spread meat or fish pâtés, hummous or taramasalata on wholemeal toast.

Breastfeeding women excrete less calcium than usual, so milk, yoghurt or cheese three times a day will supply enough calcium. Full-fat milk, cream and yoghurt provide vitamins A and D. And two extra slices of wholemeal bread or an extra serving of breakfast cereal daily will satisfy your extra requirement of the B vitamins thiamin, riboflavin and niacin, and the minerals magnesium and selenium. Eating plenty of fresh fruit, red and orange vegetables as well as dark green leafy vegetables will ensure that you have enough Vitamins A, C and folate.

Fortifying snacks Choose easy-to-eat finger foods while breastfeeding, such as vegetable tartlets, or make Apple and Cranberry Bars (see recipe on page 316).

MENUPLAN
for new mothers

All mothers need to eat regular, healthy meals to maintain energy levels throughout the day. Follow these guidelines, making sure that you have plenty of fresh fruit and vegetables.

BREAKFAST Wholegrain breakfast cereal enriched with folic acid and iron. Add fresh or dried fruit. A slice of wholemeal toast with some butter and your favourite spread. Drink some diluted fruit juice.

LUNCHTIME A sandwich is quick, filling and can be delicious; try the Open Sandwich (recipe overleaf) or Red Onion and Rosemary Focaccia (recipe page 293); Alternatively, make a pasta or couscous salad with leftover pasta, chopped red or orange peppers (for vitamin A) and any other combination of chopped raw vegetables. Accompany with a high-protein food such as cold meat or sprinkle some chopped nuts in the salad. Follow with fruit and ice cream.

DINNER Any dish containing meat, fish or pulses combined with a starchy food and vegetables. Try Pan-fried Lamb's Liver with Orange Balsamic Dressing (recipe overleaf). Finish with a dessert to keep your energy levels up for feeding during the night. Try Lemon Polenta Cake (recipe page 129) or Exotic Fruit Cheesecake (recipe page 101).

SNACKS Eat regular snacks such as fruit, nuts, sandwiches and yoghurts during the day.

Vitamin D is made by the action of sunlight on the skin (see page 46). If you don't spend time in the sun every day or have a dark skin which you normally keep covered, take a supplement. The best food sources are margarine, oily fish and eggs.

Health clinics in the United Kingdom often provide inexpensive vitamin drops. These contain the crucial vitamins A, D and C and are recommended for breastfeeding mothers and children under five.

Coping with tiredness

Accept all offers of help so that you have as much time as possible to rest. Ask your partner to bring you some toast and jam and a milky drink after an early morning feed, as these help you to go back to sleep. Try not to hurry breastfeeding or bottle-feeding. Set aside this time to sit quietly and peacefully so you can concentrate on feeding and bonding with your baby.

Finding time to prepare food for yourself each day may seem impossible. Your baby may demand a feed every time your own meal is on the table. Tiredness can reduce your appetite and it is easy to get into the habit of eating less. But this is the very time when you need to be eating well and regularly:

Don't skip meals Irregular eating patterns and insufficient food reduce your nutrient levels and lower your blood sugar. This may make you more irritable and less able to cope with pressure. A self-perpetuating cycle can build up: you will feel increasingly tired if you are not getting sufficient nutrients. If you are

EXTRA DAILY NUTRIENTS FOR BREASTFEEDING MOTHERS

NUTRIENT	PER DAY	% INCREASE
Calories	500	26
Protein	11 g	24
Thiamin	0.2 mg	25
Riboflavin	0.5 mg	45
Niacin	2 mg	15
Vitamin B$_{12}$	0.5 mg	33
Folate	60 mcg	30
Vitamin C	30 mg	75
Vitamin A	350 mcg	58
Calcium	550 mg	80
Phosphorus	440 mg	80
Magnesium	50 mg	19
Zinc	6 mg	86
Copper	0.3 mg	25
Selenium	15 mcg	25

The percentage increase is compared with the reference nutrient intake for non-lactating women

breastfeeding, your milk supply may be affected. Your baby will become increasingly hungry, irritable and demanding, and may even lose weight – this will make you even more anxious.

Action plan To combat fatigue and make your daily routine easier, stock up on a variety of nutritious snacks.

• Choose different kinds of bread and rolls to make appetising sandwiches. Try focaccia or ciabatta with Italian ham, mozarella cheese, olives and sun-dried tomatoes.

• Eat wholewheat crackers or crispbread with pâtés or dips.

• Chop up raw vegetables and keep them in the fridge. They are good to eat by themselves or with dips.

• Don't forget fruit: an apple, pear banana or handful of grapes is a perfect snack. Treat yourself to a wide variety of fruit.

• Use fresh fruit to make delicious

Quick and nourishing Mothers need feeding too. Snack on wholemeal toast spread with pâté (above) to give yourself a lift, or make an appetising Bresaola and Lamb's Lettuce Ciabatta. The recipe is on page 177.

smoothies – try an Apricot Smoothie (recipe page 202).

• Packets of dried fruit and nuts make quick, nutritious snacks.

• When you cook rice, pasta or couscous, make extra so you will have some for the next day to use as the base for a salad.

• Cook meals that are easy to eat with a fork while cuddling a restless baby. Try Easy Smoked Fish Pie (recipe page 203) or Pea and Lemon Risotto (recipe page 188).

• Stews and casseroles can be made in advance: prepare them while your baby sleeps and cook them in a slow oven. Bake some potatoes as well.

• Buy bags of ready-prepared stir-fry ingredients and add frozen prawns for a tasty, nutritious meal.

• Keep a selection of ready-made pasta sauces and fresh pasta in the freezer. You can defrost and cook them very quickly.

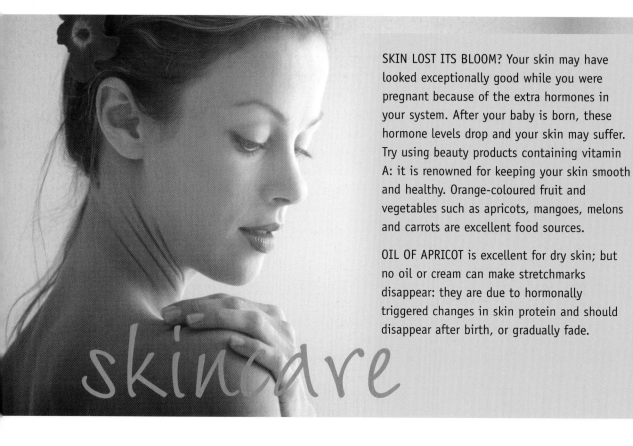

skincare

BEAUTYFOODS

SKIN LOST ITS BLOOM? Your skin may have looked exceptionally good while you were pregnant because of the extra hormones in your system. After your baby is born, these hormone levels drop and your skin may suffer. Try using beauty products containing vitamin A: it is renowned for keeping your skin smooth and healthy. Orange-coloured fruit and vegetables such as apricots, mangoes, melons and carrots are excellent food sources.

OIL OF APRICOT is excellent for dry skin; but no oil or cream can make stretchmarks disappear: they are due to hormonally triggered changes in skin protein and should disappear after birth, or gradually fade.

More than usually tired

It is very common for new mothers to experience an emotional low after childbirth. This is known as the 'baby blues' and is caused by a drop in hormone levels. Feelings of weepiness, moodiness and anxiety may last for more than a week.

In some cases, this may develop into postnatal depression, a serious condition characterised by feelings of apathy, loss of interest in your child, yourself and other people. If you feel that this may be happening to you, consult your doctor immediately. There is a wide range of treatments available, including antidepressants, counselling and supplements.

Mothers who bottle-feed

There are various reasons for choosing not to breastfeed. You may have to return to work soon after the birth, or take essential medication that could harm your baby if it is passed on in breast milk.

You should not worry that your baby will be nutritionally deprived – formula milks do provide all the vitamins, minerals and nutrients that your baby will need. For more information on feeding your baby on formula milk, turn to page 136.

Energy for yourself In common with all new mothers you need all your resources of energy and endurance to meet the demands of caring for your baby. Your diet should include plenty of fruit and vegetables, low-fat dairy foods, oily fish, lean meat, pulses, nuts and wholegrain foods. However, unlike mothers who are breastfeeding, you do not need to consume extra nutrients and calories.

During your pregnancy, you will have stored fat on your hips and thighs. The energy from this is normally used during breastfeeding. But as you won't lose the extra weight this way, you need to ensure that you do not consume excessive calories after your baby is born.

Base your meals around starchy ingredients such as bread, rice, pasta and potatoes, and try to cut down on fats (see page 62). Use low-fat cooking techniques such as grilling or griddling rather than frying.

Eat plenty of fresh fruit and vegetables: these boost your fibre levels and keep your blood sugar steady. And avoid sugary snacks such as biscuits and confectionery. They cause surges in your blood levels of insulin. This prevents you from using up the weight gained during pregnancy. Accept that you will lose the extra weight gradually and eat regular, nourishing meals to keep yourself healthy and fit for parenting.

Getting back into shape

Most women gain about 9-12 kg (20-28 lb) during pregnancy. After your baby is born you will lose a lot of this, but may still be about 5 kg (11 lb) heavier than before.

Within six weeks, your uterus will have shrunk considerably and you will lose a further 1.5 kg (3 lb 5 oz). The remaining weight is concentrated in fat stored on your hips and thighs. If you are breastfeeding, this should disappear gradually, but you will probably not lose the remainder until you stop breastfeeding.

Prolong breastfeeding If you gained a lot of weight during pregnancy or were overweight to begin with, you should try to breastfeed as long as possible. But you should avoid going on a diet while breastfeeding, as this may reduce your milk supply.

Dieting has even caused some women to give-up breastfeeding early, mistakenly thinking that they can't produce enough milk.

Exercise is best The best way to lose the extra weight on your hips and thighs is by getting plenty of exercise. You need to tone up all your muscles, especially those stretched and weakened during pregnancy. Before your six-week check-up with your doctor, do some gentle exercises for your pelvic floor and abdominal muscles. Your midwife or a physiotherapist will advise you on how to do these. After your check-up you can start an exercise programme to increase your overall levels of physical activity.

A happy alternative A bottle-feed can be enjoyed by father and baby. He can either use formula milk or his partner's expressed breast milk.

pan-fried lamb's liver with orange balsamic dressing

Liver should be avoided during pregnancy because of its high vitamin A levels, but it is invaluable for exhausted new mothers. The balsamic and orange sauce gives an aromatic flavour to a classic dish.

preparation time: **10 minutes**

cooking time: **25–30 minutes**

serves **4**

NUTRIENTS PER SERVING	
calories	500
carbohydrate	46 g
(sugars)	14 g
protein	31 g
fat	22 g
(saturated)	5 g
fibre	4 g

1 tablespoon polyunsaturated margarine
2 medium spring onions, sliced
100 ml (3½ fl oz) semi-skimmed milk
600g (1 lb 6 oz) potatoes
Salt and black pepper
1 tablespoon olive oil
1 large red onion, sliced lengthways
400 g (14 oz) lamb's liver, cut into thin
* strips*
Strips of orange peel, to garnish
FOR THE SAUCE
3 tablespoons balsamic vinegar
2 small oranges, cut into segments

1 Melt the margarine in a small saucepan. Add the spring onions and sweat them gently. Add the milk and heat through. Remove from the heat and cover.

2 Cook the potatoes in boiling water until tender. Drain, season and mash, using the onion milk to soften them. Keep warm in the oven.

3 Heat the olive oil in a heavy-based frying pan. Add the red onion and fry until lightly browned. Remove from the pan and keep warm. Add the liver to the pan, adding a little more oil, if necessary. Quickly fry the strips of liver, turning them frequently, for about 5–6 minutes, or until just cooked. Remove from the pan and keep warm.

4 Make the sauce: add the vinegar and orange segments to the pan, stirring to deglaze it, and heat through. Place spoonfuls of the creamy mashed potato on 4 serving plates, top with the onion and liver, and pour over the hot balsamic sauce. Serve at once, garnished with orange zest.

bresaola and lamb's lettuce ciabatta

This open sandwich is high in taste, low in fat and contains essential iron for recuperating mothers. Bresaola is a cured Italian beef, cut into paper-thin slices, and is available from large supermarkets and delicatessens.

preparation time: **10 minutes**

serves **2**

1 small ciabatta loaf
Olive oil for drizzling
6 slices bresaola
115 g (4 oz) prepared lamb's lettuce
½ red pepper, deseeded and cut into strips
6 black olives
Black pepper
Salad dressing of choice

1 Heat the oven to 180°C (350°F, gas mark 4). Cut the ciabatta in half and drizzle lightly with oil. Bake in the oven for 4–5 minutes, until warmed through.

2 Roll the bresaola into tubes. Put the warm bread on a serving plate. Place half the lamb's lettuce on top, add the bresaola, and garnish with half the red pepper and all the olives. Season with black pepper.

3 Mix together the remaining red pepper and lamb's lettuce in a bowl, and pour the salad dressing over the top. Serve the ciabatta and salad immediately.

NUTRIENTS PER SERVING	
calories	425
carbohydrate	53 g
(sugars)	6 g
protein	20 g
fat	13 g
(saturated)	2 g
fibre	1.5 g

roast pepper and tomato soup

The vibrant colour of this simple-to-prepare soup makes it a dramatic starter, and its deep, intense flavour is very satisfying. It is meant to have a thick texture, but you can add water or stock if you prefer a thinner soup.

preparation time: **10 minutes**

cooking time: **35 minutes**

serves **4**

675 g (1 lb 8 oz) firm, ripe tomatoes, halved
4 red, yellow or orange peppers, deseeded and quartered
1 large onion, cut into 8 pieces
3 cloves garlic
4 large sprigs fresh marjoram or thyme
2 tablespoons olive oil
2 tablespoons sun-dried tomato purée
Salt and black pepper

1 Heat the oven to 200°C (400°F, gas mark 6).

2 Place the tomatoes, pepper quarters, onion pieces and garlic in a large roasting tin. Add the herbs, season with black pepper and drizzle with olive oil.

3 Roast in the oven for 30 minutes, until the edges of the vegetables are soft and they are beginning to brown and darken. Remove any stalks from the herbs, leaving the leaves.

4 Put the vegetables, herbs and any cooking liquid in a blender or food processor and blend until smooth. Add the tomato purée, and season to taste.

5 If the soup seems too thick, thin it with a little boiling water or vegetable stock. Serve piping hot.

NUTRIENTS PER SERVING	
calories	160
carbohydrate	22 g
(sugars)	20 g
protein	4 g
fat	7 g
(saturated)	1 g
fibre	6 g

The **prime** of **life**

Feeling at ease with yourself is one of the rewards of being an adult – you don't need to be a slave to every lifestyle fad. On the other hand, you may become too relaxed and acquire classic 'middle-age spread'. If you eat intelligently, however, you won't lose your shape as you grow older.

Your attitude to food and nutrition may require some adjustment as you progress through your adult life and into the middle years. It's a time when many people take their health for granted and don't pay enough attention to seeking out the foods that are most beneficial for fitness.

For some people, any weaknesses in health may become particularly apparent towards the middle and late forties. At this stage, the wear and tear of time and the effects of smoking and alcohol may begin to affect your body, especially if you haven't been eating healthily.

You are now more vulnerable to heart problems, cancer, high blood pressure and other more serious conditions. So good nutrition, combined with regular exercise and giving up smoking, is of paramount importance. At this point you still have a chance to make a real difference to your future well-being.

FOODS FOR YOUR FUTURE

Incorporating certain foods into your diet will help to protect you against major illnesses such as cancer and cardiovascular disease and ensure that you are fit and healthy later in

life. It is never too late to start changing eating habits for the better. Your overall aim should be to control your weight, reduce the amount of fat (especially saturated fat) you eat, have at least five servings of fruit and vegetables a day, eat more carbohydrate foods such as pasta, and cut down on salt.

• The World Cancer Research Fund says that five or more portions of fruit and vegetables daily may prevent 20 per cent of cancer cases.

• Eating more fruit and vegetables also protects against heart disease – the United Kingdom's main killer.

• Fruit and vegetables are rich in antioxidants (see page 118) which help to protect cells against cancer-inducing free radicals.

• People who regularly eat spinach and other green leafy vegetables are much less likely to get cataracts (clouding of the lens of the eye).

• These greens also help to protect against an eye disease called age-related macular degeneration, which is a build up of dead cells in the eye. Until the 1990s, this condition was virtually unknown in people under 64. It now affects younger people and is the most common cause of sight loss in the United Kingdom.

Dish up the fish

Oil-rich fish such as mackerel, fresh tuna, salmon and sardines are immensely helpful in protecting you against heart disease because they are rich in omega-3 fatty acids. A regular intake of these can reduce your risk of heart attacks and strokes.

Omega-3 fatty acids help your heart in various ways – by thinning your blood, making it less sticky and liable to clot; lowering blood pressure and cholesterol levels and by encouraging the muscles lining the artery walls to relax, thereby improving blood flow to your heart.

These fatty acids also have an anti-inflammatory effect, which can help to relieve some of the symptoms associated with rheumatoid arthritis (see page 332) and psoriasis (see page 31), a chronic skin condition characterised by scaly patches on the elbows, knees, shins and scalp.

Prevention is best

Some people have a family history of heart and arthritis problems. If you are one of these you will find it very beneficial to include oily fish in your diet in specific quantities:

• To help prevent heart disease, eat at least two servings of fish a week,

Foods to combat cancer *Purple grape juice (above) and Brazil nuts (left) are rich in cancer-fighting substances. Selenium is the active ingredient in Brazil nuts, flavonoids in purple grape juice. Brazil nuts have been linked with the prevention of stomach cancer, but you don't need to eat more than two or three a week, as they are also high in calories.*

one of which should include an oily fish such as mackerel, tuna, salmon, sardines or anchovies.

• If you have arthritis or psoriasis you'll need to eat between four and six servings a week.

Whether you eat your fish as smoked salmon or canned sardines, it doesn't matter – the omega-3 fats are not destroyed by cooking or canning. The only exception is canned tuna which has few omega-3 fats. Choose fresh tuna instead.

As an additional nutritional bonus, eat up the bones of canned fish such as pilchards and sardines. These are an ideal source of calcium.

Extra heart-protection In addition to fish, there are other foods that help your heart to stay healthy:

• Nuts can help to prevent heart disease; this may seem surprising, because nuts are high in fat. But apart from Brazil nuts (and coconuts which are lightly saturated), this is mostly unsaturated fat, which helps to improve blood cholesterol levels.

• The nuts highest in healthy, non-saturated fats are walnuts, almonds and hazelnuts. They should always be eaten unsalted and/or dry-roasted without oil. For maximum benefit, try to eat 25 grams (one ounce) of

a little exercise can help a lot

Even a small increase in physical activity makes the world of difference to the health of your heart, respiratory system, muscles and joints. You don't need to be a marathon runner to get the benefits of exercise – just make simple changes to your routine.

Take the stairs instead of the lift.

Walk part of the way to work every day.

Wash your car by hand rather than using a drive-in car wash.

Do some gardening jobs every day.

Paint a room for satisfying, creative activity.

Clean your windows yourself instead of hiring a window cleaner.

Simple changes such as these all lead to an increase in your energy expenditure. It is useful to see exactly how much difference they can make:

Weeding your garden for 30 minutes, four times a week, over a year expends extra energy that is equivalent in weight to over two and a half kilos (about six pounds).

Walking briskly for between 20 and 30 minutes every day uses up energy that is equivalent to about five kilos (about 12 pounds) of fat a year.

these nuts at least five times a week. The benefits are substantial – the risk of heart disease has been found to be 35 per cent lower in people who eat these types of nuts regularly.

• Soya beans and soya products (see pages 184-185) provide excellent protection against heart disease and other illnesses, including cancer.

• If you enjoy red wine, you'll be glad to know that it may help to protect your heart. There is some debate about how (see page 58), but a glass a day may combine benefit and pleasure. Red wine and purple grape juice are rich in flavonoids, antioxidant compounds which help to prevent heart disease and strokes.

Middle-age spread

Becoming overweight can literally be fatal. It increases the risk of heart disease and diabetes, and also exacerbates problems with joints. Gaining weight is not an inevitable

consequence of growing older, but it can seem that way. Even if you are sure that you are not eating more than usual, the extra flab seems to creep up on you in insidious ways.

This gradual increase doesn't happen by magic, even if you are convinced that this is the only possible explanation. A more likely reason is that your levels of activity are declining as the years progress. What happens is that physical activity (and the amount of energy

you use) decreases rapidly with age. Even if you have been eating the same amount of food all along, the fact that you are not moving around as much means that you are not using up the food you eat in the same way. This excess energy is then stored in your body as fat.

Make it a pleasure The secret of keeping in shape during the middle years is to find an activity that you enjoy and feel comfortable with. It shouldn't demand a dramatic change

in your lifestyle because this makes it all the more difficult for you to adjust. Be realistic: start slowly, and gradually build up the frequency and length of time that you exercise.

If you enjoy activities such as walking or a round of golf, you are three times more likely to avoid middle-age spread and seven times less likely to become obese. So the extra activity really is worthwhile.

Feel good, look good Although exercise burns calories it also has a much more important effect – it helps to preserve and develop muscle tissue in your body.

Muscle tissue is lean and plays a much more active part in your body metabolism than fat. This means that muscle tissues use up more calories than those in fat. Consequently, the more of this kind of tissue you have, the more calories your body burns. Exercise also helps your body to stay firm and well toned and this has a positive effect on your posture, self confidence and self-image.

HRT – the weight of evidence

Most doctors would claim that hormone replacement therapy (HRT) is not associated with weight gain, but many women taking HRT feel otherwise. Whether becoming heavier is a side effect of HRT, or a common feature of the menopause and ageing, is still not clear. Some women find that their breasts are fuller when taking HRT, so this may explain the feeling of extra weight.

The progestogen effect Some types of progestogen, one of the synthetic hormones used in HRT, may cause fluid retention and bloating. This can make it look as if you have put on weight. In some women these progestogens can trigger a marked

increase in appetite, and this may be another clue to why they may be piling on the extra pounds.

Where the weight goes A woman's body shape changes naturally at the menopause; the drop in oestrogen levels means that body fat is more likely to accumulate around the middle of her body than on the hips and bottom, a pattern of 'apple-shaped' obesity linked with an increased risk of cardiovascular problems (see page 57).

HRT helps to prevent this change in body shape, returning it to a more normal pattern of fat distribution. This may be one of the reasons it is associated with a reduced risk in heart disease.

A time of change

The menopause usually begins around the age of 50 years, although it can occur earlier or later. As levels of oestrogen and progesterone begin to fall, periods become irregular and eventually cease. At least 75 per cent of women in the United Kingdom experience one or more symptoms associated with the menopause and 30 per cent say that they are severe.

These symptoms may include hot flushes, night sweats, loss of confidence, aching joints and muscles, mood swings, depression, irritability, fatigue, dizziness, panic attacks, insomnia, palpitations, vaginal dryness, painful intercourse and loss of sexual desire.

Oestrogen loss accompanying the menopause also accelerates the loss of calcium from the bones, and increases the risk of osteoporosis (see pages 45-49). Calcium loss also leads to changes in blood fats that increase the risk of heart disease.

continued on page184

Discover vegetables *Eating fresh vegetables such as Swiss chard (above) is a highly pleasurable way of consuming the immunity-boosting nutrients antioxidants, vitamin C and iron. All dark green leafy vegetables are especially rich in plant chemicals which help protect against major illnesses including cancer and heart disease.*

handling the
MENOPAUSE

If you're not taking HRT, there is an excellent alternative strategy that helps you to handle common menopausal symptoms. It simply involves choosing the right foods.

Follow a diet that is low in fat, particularly saturated fat. This helps to prevent a rise in HDLs in the blood that increase the risk of heart disease (see page 56). A low-fat diet also helps to prevent weight gain.

A high-fibre diet will help to prevent constipation (see page 74) – soluble fibre is particularly good as it helps to reduce high blood cholesterol levels.

Fruit and vegetables provide the antioxidants – vitamins A, C, E and beta carotene – that help to reduce the risk of cancer and heart disease (see page 118).

Eat plenty of calcium-rich foods – declining oestrogen levels accelerate the loss of calcium from the bones. The

National Osteoporosis Society recommends that menopausal women who are not taking HRT should aim for an intake of 1500 milligrams of calcium daily, but only 1000 milligrams for women taking HRT.

Two glasses of skimmed or semi-skimmed milk and three slices of Cheddar cheese provide 700 milligrams; ten dried figs 269; 115 g (4 oz) skinned grilled chicken 179; and 25 g (1 oz) toasted almonds 148.

Good sources of calcium include dairy products, canned fish eaten with their bones (such as sardines and pilchards), oranges, watercress, broccoli, dried fruits (especially figs and apricots) and sunflower seeds.

Vitamin D is essential for absorbing calcium. Eggs, oily fish, butter and fortified margarine are good sources.

Controlling your caffeine levels will help you to

The MENOPAUSE IS SOMETHING THAT ALL WOMEN EXPERIENCE. SOME SAIL THROUGH BLITHELY, AND FIND IT A LIBERATING AND POSITIVE EXPERIENCE. OTHERS HAVE PROBLEMS. IF YOU DECIDE NOT TO TAKE HRT, TRY HANDLING MENOPAUSAL SYMPTOMS BY CHOOSING YOUR FOODS WISELY AND GETTING LOTS OF EXERCISE.

MENOPAUSE NEEDN'T BE A MISERY *Enjoy plenty of exercise and feast on foods rich in calcium such as cheese, and sumptuous salads full of antioxidants. If you become depressed, St John's Wort may provide relief.*

manage symptoms such as anxiety and mood swings. Caffeine increases the intensity and number of hot flushes.

Reducing the amount of salt you eat will help you to relieve water retention. Also, be aware that a high salt intake can increase the loss of calcium from the bones, with the associated risk of osteoporosis. Use herbs, spices and other flavourings such as garlic, lemon juice, mustard or vinegar to add flavour to your food.

Choose foods that are rich in plant-based oestrogens. Examples are soya beans and soya products, chickpeas,

lentils, also some nuts and berries (see overleaf).
Drink plenty of water and other fluids – aim to drink at least eight glasses a day.

Try to keep the amount of protein you eat within the proportions recommended in the Five Food Groups (see page 12). A high intake can accelerate calcium loss.

What's the alternative?
Herbal remedies and supplements that may help to relieve menopause symptoms are:
- Hot flushes – Black Cohosh or Red Clover.
- Depression/mood swings – Hypericum (St John's wort).
- Insomnia – Camomile, Lime Blossom or Valerian tea.
- Loss of libido – Hypericum (St John's wort).
- Fluid retention – Hawthorn or Dandelion.
- Fatigue – Vitamin B complex, Ginseng (600 mg daily).

Although hormone replacement therapy (HRT) can help redress many of these problems and offers relief from some of the symptoms, not all women can or want to take it (see preceding pages for an alternative approach).

THE SECRETS OF SOYA

The soya bean has astonished nutritional experts with its range of health-protective virtues. It is a powerhouse of disease-fighting compounds, including various kinds of antioxidants known to protect against cancer (see page 118).

In the USA, the Food and Drug Administration has authorised a new health claim for those foods that contain a minimum of 6.25 grams of soya protein per serving. Food manufacturers can now state on the label that '25 grams of soya protein a day, as part of a diet low in saturated fat and cholesterol, may reduce the risk of heart disease'.

Active ingredients Researchers have been developing an overall picture of how the different compounds in soya beans act against various diseases. For example, they have highlighted the importance of a group of hormone-like substances called phytoestrogens. These are found in soya beans, lentils, chickpeas, and alfalfa. Soya beans and foods made from them are by far the best sources.

A substance in soya beans called genistin has a particular role in inhibiting the development of breast and prostate cancer – both these

A touch of luxury This creamy Broccoli and Stilton Soup is rich in cancer-fighting compounds and also has high levels of calcium. The recipe is on page 188.

cancers are more prevalent in the middle years of life. In Japan, where the incidence of breast and prostate cancers is comparatively low, the average daily intake of the protective nutrients contained in soya products is 20 to 50 times greater than a typical Western diet.

An easier menopause

There is increasing evidence that soya can help to reduce many of the unpleasant symptoms associated with the menopause. A specific group of phytoestrogens (called isoflavones) plays a crucial part in this. Isoflavones have a similar structure to human oestrogen, and bind onto oestrogen receptor sites in the body in a way that mimics the effect of natural oestrogen.

Many problems experienced during menopause are caused by the decline in oestrogen levels in middle age, so these soya-derived hormones may offer the promise of a viable alternative to HRT in the future.

Cook's tips

If you are unfamiliar with soya products, you'll be impressed with the range currently available in large supermarkets, health stores and in Chinese and Asian grocery shops. Look around, and do a little research to discover what's on offer. Browse through oriental recipe books for different ways to use soya – you may find some in your local library. You will probably come across the following ingredients:
• Edamame are fresh soya beans in their pods, harvested when they are young and tender. Steamed and salted they make a delicious snack.
• Tofu, or bean curd, is made from puréed, pressed soya beans. It is

low in fat and is also a very good source of protein. It is generally displayed in the dairy products section of large supermarkets.

There are two kinds of tofu – firm and silken. Firm tofu has a texture similar to cheese; it can be marinated and used to make kebabs or cut into cubes and added to stir-fries. Silken tofu has a texture similar to set yoghurt; use it to make dips, salad dressings, sauces or desserts. When buying tofu, smell it to make sure

that it isn't sour – if it is packaged it will have a freshness date stamped on the wrapping.

At home, rinse the tofu, and put it in the refrigerator in fresh cold water. Change the water daily, and eat the tofu within three or four days.
• Textured vegetable protein (TVP) is a meat substitute made from soya bean flour. TVP is low in fat and rich in protein. It is also versatile – you can buy it as dehydrated chunks or 'mince', or incorporate it into dishes

such as burgers, rissoles, patties and sausages.

• Soya drink – usually called 'soya milk' – is available unsweetened or sweetened. It comes in a variety of flavours. Look out for brands with added calcium. Soya drink is cholesterol-free, lactose-free and available in low-fat form. Use it exactly the same way as you would cow's milk – enjoy it as a drink, pour it on cereals, use it in cooking or to make smoothies.

One 250 ml (9 fl oz) glass of soya drink will provide you with about 4 to 10 grams of soya protein and around 20 milligrams of isoflavones, depending on the brand.

• Tempeh is a thin cake made from fermented soya beans that has a mushroom-like, slightly smoky flavour. You can use it as a really tasty substitute for meat – grill it, or add it to stews, pasta sauces or even casseroles.

• Isolated soya protein is a protein-rich powder which can be mixed into drinks and sauces to boost the protein content. It is almost pure protein: 25 grams of the powder (one ounce) contains within it 24 grams of protein.

soya

Soya beans contain an amazing range of health-protective and disease-fighting compounds. For example, they are very rich in isoflavones, a group of hormone-like substances that behave in a similar way to natural oestrogen. Soya beans and foods made from them are the richest sources of isoflavones, which are known to combat heart disease, cancer and other serious illnesses.

Isoflavones function in a number of ways: they fight heart disease by working in combination with soya protein; they improve the balance of cholesterol in the blood; they also make blood less sticky and so less likely to clot.

They help to protect against osteoporosis in two ways: they work with the high levels of calcium also present in soya and are so similar to oestrogen in their action that they maintain the healthy levels of oestrogen and calcium which keeps bones strong and resistant to breaking.

Soya also contains several types of antioxidants that help to protect you against various forms of cancer, including breast, prostate and colon cancer.

SUPERFOOD

The oriental way *Tofu, or bean curd, makes great stir-fries. It is an immensely versatile food. Try the recipe for Marinated Tofu Stir-fry with Satay Sauce and Wild Rice on page 53.*

Soya flour is made from ground, roasted soya beans – 25 grams (one ounce) contains between 10–14 grams of protein. It is available in full-fat or low-fat form and can be used as a substitute for white flour in recipes such as muffins and cakes. Soya flour has quite a strong flavour, so you may prefer to mix it with another type of flour – try substituting 20–30 per cent of wheat flour with soya flour.

• Miso is the seasoning that gives the traditional Japanese miso soup its distinct flavour. It is made from fermented soya beans and is used mainly as a seasoning. Miso is very salty, and should be used sparingly.

• Soya puddings and ice creams are available in a wide range of flavours.

prostate and breast cancer

Prostate and breast cancers are prevalent during the mature years – and while women are generally aware of this, men are still not sufficiently alert to the risk of prostate cancer.

Both men and women should have regular checks; also, following a cancer-protective diet will decrease these risks significantly.

Population studies show that the incidence of breast and prostate cancer is much lower in countries such as Japan which has a high consumption of soya and soya products.

Prostate Cancer		Breast cancer	
USA	17.5 per 100,000	USA	22 per 100,000
UK	17.1 per 100,000	UK	27.7 per 100,000
Japan	4.0 per 100,000	Japan	6.6 per 100,000

Figures taken from the America Cancer Society – facts and figures 1996

broccoli and stilton soup

This rich, dark green soup is a popular classic – it combines the fresh flavours of the vegetable with a tangy, salty, note introduced by the cheese.

preparation time: **10 minutes**

cooking time: **25 minutes**

serves **6**

NUTRIENTS PER SERVING	
calories	190
carbohydrate	11 g
(sugars)	3 g
protein	12 g
fat	11 g
(saturated)	6 g
fibre	4 g

1 tablespoon vegetable oil
1 onion, finely chopped
1 large potato, finely diced
1 litre (1¾ pints) vegetable stock (recipe
    page 338)
Salt and black pepper
675 g (1½ lb) broccoli, broken into florets
140 g (5 oz) Stilton cheese, crumbled, plus
    extra to garnish

1 Heat the oil in a large pan, add the onion and cook gently for 3–4 minutes. Add the potato and continue to cook for 10 minutes, stirring occasionally.

2 Add the stock, season to taste and bring to the boil. Add the broccoli, reduce the heat and simmer for 5–10 minutes, or until just tender.

3 Transfer the soup to a food processor or blender and purée until smooth. Return the soup to the pan, stir in the cheese and reheat until just warmed through but do not boil.

4 Transfer to bowls, garnish with a little cheese and serve with wholemeal rolls.

pea and lemon risotto

This light, melt-in-your-mouth risotto has the fresh taste of lemon and is very easy to prepare. Cook it for an informal supper dish. The peas are a good source of fibre.

preparation time: **15 minutes**

cooking time: **30 minutes**

serves **4**

NUTRIENTS PER SERVING	
calories	400
carbohydrate	51 g
(sugars)	4 g
protein	19 g
fat	13 g
(saturated)	8 g
fibre	5.5 g

400 g (14 oz) frozen or fresh peas
25 g (1 oz) butter
1 onion, finely chopped
200 g (7 oz) arborio rice
1 litre (1¾ pints) hot vegetable or chicken
    stock (recipes page 338)
Grated zest and juice of 1 lemon
85 g (3 oz) grated Parmesan cheese, plus
    extra shavings to garnish
Salt and black pepper

1 Cook the peas in a large pan of boiling salted water for 3–5 minutes, or until tender. Drain and cool under cold water.

2 Melt the butter in a large saucepan, add the onion and cook over medium heat for 5 minutes, or until soft. Add the rice and stir well to ensure that every grain is coated. Continue to cook, stirring, for 1–2 minutes.

3 Add enough hot stock to cover the rice and continue to cook over medium heat, stirring frequently. Once the stock is absorbed, add more and continue adding hot stock in this way until the rice is cooked – it should be tender on the outside but firm on the inside.

4 Add the peas, lemon zest and juice and warm through. Stir in the Parmesan, and season to taste. Serve immediately, garnished with Parmesan shavings.

timely **teacake**

The ingredients in this delicious tea-time treat include many that are known to be helpful in alleviating menopause symptoms. Linseeds, also called flaxseeds, are a good source of protein and may be found in health food stores.

preparation time: **10 minutes, plus 30 minutes standing**

cooking time: **1½–2 hours**

makes **2 cakes (8 slices each)**

100 g (3½ oz) soya flour
100 g (3½ oz) wholemeal flour
100 g (3½ oz) porridge oats
100 g (3½ oz) linseeds
50 g (1¾ oz) sunflower seeds
50 g (1¾ oz) sesame seeds
50 g (1¾ oz) flaked almonds
2 pieces stem ginger, finely chopped
200 g (7 oz) ready-to-eat dried apricots
1 teaspoon ground mixed spice
750 ml (1 pint 7 fl oz) soya drink
TO DECORATE
Apricot jam and toasted flaked almonds

1 Place all the dry ingredients in a large bowl and mix well. Add the soya drink, mix well and allow to stand for 30 minutes. If the mixture seems a little too stiff add a little more soya milk.

2 Heat the oven to 190°C (375°F, gas mark 5). Line 2 x 450 g (1 lb) loaf tins with baking paper.

3 Divide the teacake mixture between the tins. Put the tins in the oven and bake for about 1½–2 hours, or until a skewer inserted into the centre comes out clean.

4 Allow to cool in the tins for 5 minutes then turn out on to a wire rack to cool completely. Then brush with a little warm apricot jam and sprinkle with toasted flaked almonds.

NUTRIENTS PER SLICE	
calories	200
carbohydrate	16 g
(sugars)	6 g
protein	9 g
fat	12 g
(saturated)	1 g
fibre	4 g

Holding **back** the **years**

Ageing well is an art – nowadays, people are staying fitter, feeling better and living longer than ever before. Although genes play a role in the ageing process, the food you eat at this time of life can make all the difference to your retirement years.

As you approach retirement age, you should take the time to think about yourself, and what you want from life. To get the most out of each day, you need to be as fit and healthy as possible. The answer is simple: stay active and eat really well, and you'll be full of vitality and zest for life, now and in future years.

ENJOY YOUR FOOD

Eating is one of life's great pleasures, and the key to good living is to choose food that is both healthy and delicious. Meals do not have to be expensive or entail elaborate cooking. A tasty snack can be just as nutritious as a cooked dish. Convenience foods available from supermarkets can also have positive health benefits: look for fruits canned in fruit juices, tuna in spring water or sunflower oil, and vegetables canned without salt.

Wise choices To stay at peak levels of fitness, follow the guidelines in the Five Food Groups (pages 11-15). This way, you'll ensure the widest possible range of nutrients. Even if you do not have any specific health problem, various changes that are a natural part of ageing will have a direct effect on your body.

VITAMIN B_{12} *deficiency has been linked to memory loss and senility, so eat plenty of liver, kidney, oily fish, meat, eggs, dairy products and fortified breakfast cereals.*

VITAMIN B_1 *enhances memory function, so include lean meats, such as pork, and eggs in your diet.*

SUNFLOWER SEEDS *and other foods rich in vitamin E (seeds, nuts, wheatgerm and leafy green vegetables) all improve memory.*

EAT TO BEAT memory loss

Subtle changes

At this time of your life, your body becomes less efficient at absorbing and using several vitamins and minerals. And long-term use of prescription drugs may reduce your uptake of certain nutrients.

You may also find that your appetite has decreased – but your need for vitamins and minerals stays the same, and may even increase. It is therefore even more important that the food you eat is nutritious.

Without noticing it, you may have become less active, resulting in a slower metabolic rate. Consequently, your body needs fewer calories, and, if your energy intake isn't reduced, you will gain weight.

Danger signs Being overweight increases your risk of serious illness, including diabetes, heart disease and high blood pressure. It also puts extra stress on your joints, making conditions such as arthritis more painful. If you have noticed that you

***Masterly toast** Sardines become a sophisticated dish if you serve them on lightly browned wholemeal French bread rubbed with garlic. Canned sardines (with or without tomato sauce) are just as good as fresh ones: not only are they rich in fish oils, but you can eat the bones, making them a great source of calcium.*

have become heavier, act now. You may have to cut down on calories, or it may be a simple matter of increasing your levels of physical activity. Try to get around 30 minutes of continuous exercise every day: go for a walk, do some gardening, or enjoy a pleasurable, active pastime such as dancing.

Avoiding diabetes One in ten people over 60 years develops diabetes (see page 102). At this age, you are more likely to contract the the non insulin-dependent type – and changing your diet is often enough to control it.

There are two ways to protect yourself against diabetes: by keeping your weight down and taking regular exercise. The risk of becoming diabetic is five times greater for people with a body mass index of over 30 (see page 17). Regular physical activity reduces this risk by as much as 40 per cent.

The latest findings on obesity point out that the way you carry excess weight is crucial. 'Apple-shaped' obesity – in which excess weight is carried around the waist – increases vulnerability to diabetes. For more on the health issues of being overweight, see pages 57-58.

Dealing with hypertension

Circulatory problems are also more common at this stage of life: high blood pressure, or hypertension, increases your risk of both stroke and heart attack. Obesity is a known factor in hypertension, another good reason to watch your weight.

Eat less salt Most people in the United Kingdom consume about 12 times more salt than they actually need. Limiting your salt intake can actively reduce high blood pressure.

About 75 per cent of the salt in your diet comes from processed foods, and cutting back on these will reduce your intake substantially.

A banana a day Eating potassium-rich foods can actively help to lower your blood pressure. These include fruit and vegetables (especially bananas, nuts, tomatoes and avocados). For more information about high blood pressure and for more ways to cut down on salt, turn to pages 58-60.

A good digestion

Some older people are plagued with constipation (see pages 81-82). The solution is easy: eat plenty of foods rich in insoluble fibre, such as wholegrain cereals, pulses, fruits and vegetables, and drink at least 1.7 litres (3 pints) of water a day.

Diverticulitis When the build-up of pressure in the large bowel forces its lining through weak points in the bowel wall, small pockets are formed. These are called diverticuli and do not cause symptoms by themselves. However, if they become infected and inflamed, they may cause pain in the lower abdomen. Diverticulitis affects around half the United Kingdom population over the age of 60 years.

A high-fibre diet combined with plenty of fluids is the best way to prevent diverticular disease. Small seeds in foods such as kiwi fruit, strawberries, tomatoes and jam can at times become trapped inside the diverticuli, so these are best avoided.

Healthy bones and joints

Osteoporosis (thinning bones) is more prevalent with age. In the United Kingdom, one in four women over 50 and 1 in 12 men over 70 are affected. Eat plenty of foods rich in calcium and vitamin D (see page 194), but moderate amounts of high-protein foods such as meat, fish and pulses. Combined with high levels of salt, protein leeches calcium from the bones, increasing your risk of osteoporosis. To read more about keeping your bones strong, turn to pages 44-53.

Supple and mobile Osteoarthritis, a degenerative condition that causes inflammation of the joints, affects most people over the age of 60, although some do not notice any symptoms. It usually develops in the knee and hip joints, and can cause pain, stiffness and loss of mobility. Obesity aggravates symptoms, so keeping your weight down is crucial. For more on arthritis, turn to pages 332-337.

More fish Oily fish and fish oils have anti-inflammatory properties that reduce pain and allow greater movement in arthritic joints. To both prevent and control arthritis, you should eat oily fish such as mackerel, herring, salmon, pilchards, kippers, sprats, sardines or tuna at least twice a week.

Do you need supplements? If you don't eat fish, you should take fish oil supplements, such as cod liver oil. If you are trying to combat osteoarthritis, it will be at least three to six months before they take effect. To be of real benefit, fish oil capsules must be taken in high doses and

Bring light into your life
Staying indoors deprives you of sunlight – your body needs this to make vitamin D for strong, healthy bones. Get out and about as much as possible and eat plenty of oily fish – they're a great source of Vitamin D. Also, their omega-3 fatty acids protect your heart and keep your joints supple.
Potassium-rich bananas keep your nerves and muscles strong, and if you're a bit more forgetful than you used to be, consider taking a Vitamin B$_6$ supplement – it may help to keep you alert.

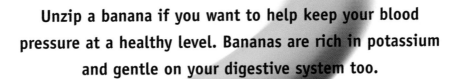

Unzip a banana if you want to help keep your blood pressure at a healthy level. Bananas are rich in potassium and gentle on your digestive system too.

those bought from pharmacies may not be sufficiently concentrated. Check with your doctor, and do not exceed the recommended dose.

All in the mind Some people claim that fish oil supplements may help to reduce the risk of Alzheimer's disease. Others believe that vitamin E can help to delay its onset. This devastating illness is characterised by confusion, memory loss, depression and progressive dementia. It affects one in ten people over the age of 65 and one in five over 80.

There is still no cure or effective treatment for alzheimer's, but some limited evidence suggests that the herbal remedy ginkgo biloba may delay the development of the disease, as it helps to improve blood flow to the brain. Other herb and food-based remedies are currently being examined. Keeping your brain active and stimulated may also be helpful. To read more on enhancing your memory, turn to pages 264–269.

Taste sensation Your senses of smell and taste become less acute with age. But if you are tempted to use more salt, you risk raising your blood pressure. Instead, try garlic, lemon juice, mustard or vinegar to add variety and flavour. Look after your teeth and, if you wear dentures, make sure they fit well so you can enjoy your food without discomfort.

FOOD FOR A LONG LIFE

For flourishing health, you need foods that contain active ingredients to boost your immune system and keep you robust and active.

Vitamins B_6 and B_{12} As you get older, your absorption of these is reduced, so you will need to take supplements. Meat (especially pork), liver, fish, eggs, wholegrain cereals, wholemeal bread, bananas, pulses, brown rice, nuts and yeast extract are good sources of these vitamins.

Vitamin C is a great antioxidant: it boosts your immune system, promotes wound healing and increases your absorption of iron. Citrus fruit, tomatoes, potatoes, sweet peppers and broccoli contain abundant amounts.

Vitamin D helps you to absorb calcium and keeps your bones healthy. Many older people in the United Kingdom are deficient in vitamin D, which is made by the action of sunlight on the skin.

YOUR NUTRITIONAL NEEDS

Daily intakes of important nutrients for men and women aged 50 years and over

NUTRIENT	MEN	WOMEN	NUTRIENT	MEN	WOMEN
Protein (g)	53.3	46.5	Phosphorus (mg)	550	550
vitamin			Magnesium (mg)	300	270
B_1 (mg)	0.9	0.8	Sodium (mg)	1600	1600
B_2 (mg)	1.3	1.1	Potassium (mg)	3500	3500
Niacin (mg)	16	12	Chloride (mg)	2500	2500
B_6 (mg)	1.4	1.2	Zinc (mg)	9.5	7.0
B_{12} (mcg)	1.5	1.5	Copper (mg)	1.2	1.2
Folate (mcg)	200	200	Iodine (mcg)	140	140
A (mcg)	700	600			
C (mg)	40	40			
D (mcg)	10*	10*			
mineral					
Calcium (mg)	700	700**			
Iron (mg)	8.7	8.7			

* Over 65
** The National Osteoporosis Society recommends that post-menopausal women taking HRT maintain an intake of 1000 mg calcium a day while post-menopausal women not on HRT should consume 1500 mg/day.

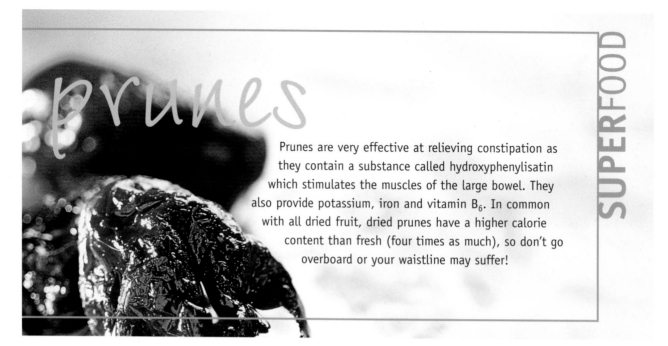

prunes

SUPERFOOD

Prunes are very effective at relieving constipation as they contain a substance called hydroxyphenylisatin which stimulates the muscles of the large bowel. They also provide potassium, iron and vitamin B$_6$. In common with all dried fruit, dried prunes have a higher calorie content than fresh (four times as much), so don't go overboard or your waistline may suffer!

When the weather is fine make sure that you get outside for at least 30 minutes each day. If you go for a daily walk in the sunshine, the exercise will be doing you good too. Use a sunscreen when the sun is hot.

You should also eat foods rich in vitamin D. These include oily fish, eggs and dairy products. And eat margarines – they are fortified with extra vitamin D. Choose those made with heart-friendly oils such as olive, sunflower, safflower and soya.

It may be that you are unable to get out of the house much. In this case supplements can be a real help: a daily combined supplement of calcium and vitamin D has recently been shown to reduce bone fractures by 30–40 per cent in elderly housebound women.

Vitamin E To keep your immune system healthy, top up your vitamin E intake from seeds and seed oils, nuts, wheatgerm, wholemeal bread and leafy green vegetables.

Your mineral requirements You need to make sure that you avoid mineral deficiencies – these are more common in older people.

Potassium and magnesium Long-term use of medication such as diuretics can speed up the loss of potassium and magnesium. Low levels cause depression and may result in muscle weakness. Bananas, meat, potatoes, oranges, and dried fruit are rich in potassium and nuts, bananas, apricots and soya beans will provide good amounts.

Zinc and copper Both minerals boost your immune system and promote healing. Levels are often low in elderly people, so eat zinc-rich foods such as oysters, meat, liver, pumpkin and sunflower seeds. And get copper from liver, kidneys, nuts and cocoa.

Calcium As you get older, you need to be aware that your body is less efficient at absorbing calcium. Dairy products are one of the richest sources – but other calcium-rich foods include canned fish such as pilchards and sardines, white bread, apricots and baked beans.

Using bran The phytate in wheat bran hinders the absorption of calcium, iron, zinc and copper, so avoid sprinkling raw bran over your food. Instead, buy good quality, high-fibre cereals – these contain the right balance of bran.

Healthy fluid levels

It becomes even more vital to drink enough fluids as you get older. You need at least eight glasses a day (see pages 79-80). Fruit juice, water, herbal tea and squash all count. But avoid too much coffee, strong tea and alcohol – these act as diuretics, and may cause you to dehydrate.

At this point in your life, you are less sensitive to thirst and more vulnerable to dehydration. In extreme cases, mental confusion diagnosed as the onset of senility has been reversed by increasing fluids. Drinking plenty of liquids in conjunction with a high-fibre diet also helps to prevent constipation.

Protein is essential for the repair and maintenance of tissue. You need two

to three servings of protein foods daily from a wide range of foods, including lean meat, chicken, fish, dairy foods, beans and pulses.

Smart shopping

Writing a weekly meal plan helps you to balance your diet and avoid wasting money – so make a list. If you live alone, consider sharing the shopping and cooking with a friend.

Time your buys Buy fruit and vegetables in season – they are cheaper and fresher. But frozen fruit and vegetables are a good alternative, as they are still vitamin-rich.

Compare prices Supermarkets now give the price of items per kilogram. Loose produce is nearly always cheaper than pre-packaged. And look out for any special offers.

Go lean Don't pay for fat – buy the leanest meat, and bulk out dishes such as shepherd's pie by adding root vegetables or pulses.

Avoid processed foods Cut back on meat pies, burgers and sausages – they are high in salt and fat.

Stocking your larder Keep some basic foods in your store cupboard so you can still make a meal even if you don't get to the shops. Include:
• Long-life milk, milk powder or evaporated milk.
• Long-life fruit juice, canned peas, pulses, sweet corn, tomatoes, soups, fruit in natural juice, and dried fruit.
• Instant mashed potato, rice, pasta and breakfast cereals. Couscous and polenta make a change.
• Canned fish and meat such as tuna, pilchards, sardines and ham.
• Baked beans and canned spaghetti.
• Stock cubes, yeast extract, herbs and spices.
• Canned milk puddings, custard.
• Cocoa or drinking chocolate.

MENUPLAN
keeping active

To stay active in the later years, choose foods that keep you fighting fit and on the move. Take a look at these meal ideas and create a menu that suits your lifestyle.

GREAT BREAKFASTS Fruit makes a fine start to the day — add it to your favourite muesli. A few prunes or prune juice will help to keep things on the move and a glass of fruit juice will help boost your vitamin C levels. And enjoy a poached egg on wholemeal toast occasionally.

LIGHT LUNCHES Canned sardines, baked beans or cheese on toast all make a quick, tasty lunchtime meals; alternatively, have a baked potato filled with mashed tuna or cottage cheese; or vegetable soup with a wholemeal roll or sandwich.

Wholemeal spaghetti is delicious sprinkled with chopped herbs and olive oil

MAIN MEALS Eat at least two servings of fish a week – one of these should be an oily fish. Buy these canned or look out for inexpensive buys such as fresh sardines or herrings. White fish provides low-fat protein – try Easy Smoked Fish Pie (recipe page 203). Add a small can of baked beans to the mince in shepherd's pie or spaghetti bolognese – it makes the meat go further and boosts the fibre. Feast on generous amounts of vegetables, fresh, frozen or canned.

HEALTHY DESSERTS Choose fruit desserts, or a milk-based pudding, or low-fat yoghurt for extra calcium (see index for recipes).

SNACKS If you have a small appetite, you may prefer to eat little and often, but snacks should never be used as a substitute for proper meals. Enjoy ready-to-eat dried fruit, fresh fruit, teacakes, malt loaf, milky drinks, crumpets, and toast and honey.

spinach and feta **frittata**

Frittata is Italy's answer to the omelette, although this version also has a touch of Greece, in the form of feta cheese. Since feta is already quite salty, you will need to add very little or no extra salt when you season the recipe.

preparation time: **10 minutes**

cooking time: **10–12 minutes**

serves **2**

NUTRIENTS PER SERVING	
calories	330
carbohydrate	3 g
(sugars)	3 g
protein	17 g
fat	27 g
(saturated)	10 g
fibre	1 g

150 g (5 oz) fresh young spinach
4 eggs, beaten
4 tablespoons semi-skimmed milk
Freshly grated nutmeg
Salt and black pepper
1 tablespoon vegetable oil
85 g (3 oz) feta cheese, roughly chopped

1 Wash the spinach and remove any tough stalks. Place the spinach in a large pan, add 1 tablespoon water and cook for 2–3 minutes, or until just wilted. Drain well, squeezing out as much liquid as possible, then roughly chop.

2 Whisk together the eggs, milk, nutmeg and seasoning. Heat the oil in a small non-stick frying pan. Add the spinach and cook over a medium heat, stirring occasionally, for 1–2 minutes.

3 Pour the egg mixture into the pan, sprinkle over the cheese and cook for 4 minutes, or until the bottom of the frittata is just set.

4 Put the pan under a preheated grill and cook for a further 4–5 minutes, or until the top is just firm to the touch.

hot bananas with pecan nuts and maple syrup

This simple, vitamin-rich dessert is very quick to make and looks and tastes delicious. Fromage frais, natural yoghurt or vanilla ice cream all make very good accompaniments, served either in spoonfuls with the dessert, or in a separate bowl.

preparation time: **5 minutes**

cooking time: **2–3 minutes**

serves **4**

40 g (1½ oz) unsalted butter
6 bananas, thickly sliced diagonally
6 tablespoons maple syrup
25 g (1 oz) pecan nuts, lightly toasted
Grated dark chocolate, to garnish
Fromage frais, natural yoghurt or vanilla ice cream, to serve

1 Melt the butter in a large, heavy-based frying pan. Add the banana slices and cook for 1 minute over a medium heat, turning them once to coat them well with the butter.

2 Add the maple syrup and continue to cook the bananas for 1–2 minutes, until slightly softened.

3 Divide the banana slices among 4 dessert dishes. Add the pecan nuts and sprinkle with grated chocolate. Serve with fromage frais, natural yoghurt or ice cream.

NUTRIENTS PER SERVING	
calories	320
carbohydrate	50 g
(sugars)	45 g
protein	2.5 g
fat	13 g
(saturated)	6 g
fibre	2 g

broccoli and pasta bake

Simple macaroni cheese is given an extra boost by the addition of fresh broccoli. The Parmesan cheese in the sauce gives a delicious flavour, but if you prefer, you can also use your favourite hard cheese, such as Cheddar or Double Gloucester, instead.

preparation time: **5 minutes**

cooking time: **25 minutes**

serves **2**

FOR THE CHEESE SAUCE
15 g (½ oz) butter
25 g (1 oz) plain flour
200 ml (7 fl oz) skimmed milk
40 g (1½ oz) Parmesan cheese, grated
Salt and black pepper
FOR THE PASTA
55 g (2 oz) macaroni or other pasta shapes
225 g (8 oz) broccoli, divided into small florets
15 g (½ oz) wholemeal breadcrumbs
25 g (1 oz) grated Cheddar cheese

1 Make the cheese sauce: melt the butter over moderate heat in a heavy-based saucepan. Stir in the flour and cook for 1-2 minutes, until foaming. Add the milk gradually, stirring constantly until the sauce boils and thickens. Season and simmer for 2 minutes. Stir in the Parmesan cheese and set aside.

2 Cook the pasta in lightly salted boiling water until just tender. Drain well. Lightly steam the broccoli until tender. Place the pasta and broccoli in a shallow flameproof dish. Pour over the sauce and mix well.

3 Mix the breadcrumbs and cheese together and sprinkle over the pasta. Put the dish under a medium hot grill and cook for 10 minutes, or until lightly browned and heated through.

NUTRIENTS PER SERVING	
calories	400
carbohydrate	41 g
(sugars)	8 g
protein	24 g
fat	17 g
(saturated)	10 g
fibre	4.5 g

Enjoying a grand old age

Nowadays old age is not something to be dreaded. On the contrary, the Third Age, as it is often called, is a time of relaxed, fulfilled maturity rather than passive decline. Discover new ways of extending your activities as well as your life-span, and enjoy the foods that boost your health and strength.

Thanks to advances in health care, improved diet and better standards of living, expectations of ageing have been transformed. However old you are, you can get the maximum enjoyment out of this stage of your life. This means keeping as fit and mobile as possible, taking a lively interest in what goes on around you and paying attention to what you eat. You need food that gives you protection from the wear and tear of ageing, supplies lots of energy and also pleases your taste buds. By accepting the natural physical and emotional changes that are happening to you with grace and humour, you can help yourself to enjoy a healthy and happy old age.

A POSITIVE APPROACH

Food is no longer regarded simply as a fuel that enables us to survive. On the contrary, it is a major factor in our quality of life. The older you are, the more important it is to take a lively interest in what you eat. Nutritious food actively helps to combat the effects of ageing: it helps wounds to heal quickly; it keeps tiredness at bay; it maintains the strength of muscles and gives you energy to get through your day.

Restoring your appetite Some older people find that they simply don't have the same relish for food that they once used to enjoy. There are logical reasons for this. For instance, if you are living on your own because you have lost your partner, cooking and eating for yourself may simply feel like too much trouble.

GINGER, *in its various forms, improves circulation. Add ground ginger to slices of fresh melon. Grate fresh ginger into a cup of hot water for an infusion that helps circulation and prevents nausea. Suck a few pieces of crystallised ginger or eat a ginger biscuit.*

SPICES THAT WARM *Cinnamon, cloves and cardamom are warming spices. They contain substances that improve circulation, so adding them to drinks and foods can alleviate the effects of chilblains. This problem is aggravated by cold, and afflicts many elderly people.*

CINNAMON, CLOVES AND CARDAMOM *(left) are useful aids to good digestion. Add all three to warmth-inducing hot toddies. Give baked apples a flavour boost with cinnamon and cloves. And try the delicious recipe for Cinnamon Rice Pudding (page 202).*

EAT TO BEAT chilblains

Good companions Daily exercise with your dog is an effective way of improving your health. Walking stimulates your appetite, improves your circulation and also helps you to avoid putting on unwanted extra weight.

Food and friendship Sharing a meal with another person can revive your interest in food and in life in general. So, why not share your meals (and shopping) with a friend who is in a similar situation?

Many elderly men may not have had much experience of cooking. If this is true in your case, you may find it surprisingly enjoyable to explore the wide variety of foods and products sold in supermarkets, shops and markets. It's a good idea to plan a well-stocked larder (see page 195) and to shop for bargains. Remember, too, that it is never too late to join a cookery class, or to start enjoying food programmes on television.

Keeping on the move

You may find that your appetite is not so keen if you're not moving about as much. This is a natural result of getting older, but the less active you become, the more vulnerable you are to problems such as diabetes, heart disease and high blood pressure. The answer is to increase your physical activity.

Even the gentlest exercise helps – just walking about the house can get your body's systems moving. If you feel that a gentle stroll is not enough, try out activities such as dancing, swimming, yoga and gentle stretch routines. Your local library will have details of what classes are available.

If you miss regular companionship, consider getting a dog or cat. A dog makes a particularly lively pet – taking it for regular walks in the fresh air and sunshine will help you to feel good and also boosts your levels of vitamin D.

EATING TO SUIT YOURSELF

You may enjoy keeping to a set routine of eating three meals at regular times every day. That's fine, but there are other alternatives. For example, you can happily graze your way through the day by eating a variety of small, nutritious meals and snacks – the Menu Plan on page 201 has several good ideas.

food poisoning

Food poisoning is unpleasant at any age, but when you're older, the effects can be much more serious, even life-threatening. Follow these tips to keep your food fresh and safe to eat:

Before you buy, look at the dates on packaging and make sure that foods are still within their 'best before' or 'use by' date.

If you're buying chilled or frozen food, make sure you're able to get it home and into the fridge or freezer within a reasonable time.

Keep raw and cooked foods separate. Never prepare raw and cooked food using the same equipment (knives, chopping board etc), unless it has been thoroughly washed first. Keep cooked and raw foods separate in the fridge, with raw food at the bottom.

Check that your fridge is working at the correct temperature. This should be 1–5°C. Never put hot food into the fridge, it causes the temperature to rise and bacteria may multiply.

Always wash your hands with hot soapy water before handling food and again between handling raw and cooked meats. Cover any cuts on your hands with waterproof plasters.

Make sure that food is properly cooked Be very careful with chicken. To test, insert a skewer into the thickest part of the meat – the juices should run clear with no sign of blood. Reheat leftovers thoroughly.

Avoid raw eggs or lightly cooked eggs or dishes made using them. Always cook eggs thoroughly – until the yolk is solid.

Wash dish cloths and tea towels regularly. Ideally, boil them: a dishcloth can contain up 100 billion bacteria after a week's use.

Citrus fruits Lemons and other citrus fruits give zest to food, help to improve resistance to infection and to keep your skin, bones and teeth in good condition.

• Two portions of meat, poultry, fish, eggs, beans or nuts.
• Four portions of fruit and vegetables, including at least one piece of citrus fruit and one portion of a dark green leafy vegetable such as spinach or spring cabbage.
• Four servings of carbohydrate foods such as a couple of slices of bread, a bowl of cereal, rice or pasta. Choose wholegrain breads and fibre-rich breakfast cereals to avoid constipation (see page 74).

Special treats A small glass of sherry or your favourite tipple 30 minutes before you eat can help to stimulate your appetite. Check with your doctor or pharmacist whether any medication you are taking may interact with alcohol.

Tempt your taste buds The number and sensitivity of your taste buds decreases with age and you may experience a diminished sense of smell and taste as you get older. But don't fall into the trap of adding extra salt to your food and risking

This way you'll still benefit from a wide range of nutrients from the Five Food Groups (see pages 11-15).

Many elderly people don't drink enough. Consequently, they risk becoming dehydrated, and this may lead to confusion. Between six and eight glasses of water a day is ideal. You can also drink fruit juices (including prune juice which helps to keep your bowel movements

regular), and milky drinks (to provide calcium). If you enjoy tea, avoid drinking it with meals because it inhibits iron absorption.

Whether you're nibbling on snacks and small meals or preparing three meals a day, as a general daily guide you need to consume:
• At least two glasses of milk or a dairy product such as a piece of cheese or a pot of yoghurt.

Natural healing The anti-inflammatory, aromatic oils in fresh rosemary leaves are released in warm water. Soaking aching joints in this brings effective relief.

problems such as raised blood pressure. Use herbs, garlic, spices and lemon juice to add flavour.

Get the benefits All the vitamins, minerals and foods that are recommended in the previous chapter (pages 192-194) are just as beneficial at this later stage of your life. Fruit and vegetables are especially valuable: they provide protective antioxidants and also contain soluble fibre which helps to prevent constipation, haemorrhoids and diverticular disease. If you have diabetes, eating foods rich in soluble fibre such as beans, pulses, oats, fruit and vegetables can help you to keep your blood sugar levels stable and reduce high blood cholesterol levels.

SMART STRATEGIES

Advancing age can sometimes bring problems that can affect your ability to eat and enjoy meals. Often there are simple ways to help improve matters. Arthritis or rheumatism can make simple tasks such as opening

cans and peeling vegetables difficult. There are various utensils which help make these jobs easier. Special cutlery and crockery are also available. For more information on arthritis, turn to pages 332-337.

Dental checks

You want to enjoy your food, but if you have dentures you may have difficulty chewing and swallowing. Visit the dentist regularly – as you get older the shape of your mouth and gums change and your dentures may need to be replaced. Badly fitting dentures can cause mouth ulcers and sore spots and make it uncomfortable to eat foods such as toast and crispbread

Hand and foot soak

Aches and pains in your hands and feet may be a problem, particularly if you have arthritis. For a soothing soak, pour some comfortably warm water into a bowl or foot bath. Add a tablespoon of ground ginger and a few sprigs of rosemary (or three or four drops of essential oil of rosemary). Soak your hands or feet for about 15 minutes and just relax.

For more information on arthritis, turn to pages 332-337.

MENU**PLAN**
graze all day

If you prefer to eat small meals and snacks throughout the day, try these ideas.

KEEP the fruit bowl filled.

HAVE PLENTY of nibbles in the form of nuts and dried fruit

MAKE CRUDITÉS from a variety of fresh, raw vegetables.

TRY TOAST TOPPERS of sardines, baked beans, scrambled eggs or hard-boiled eggs.

BAKE A POTATO and eat it with a small can of baked beans.

MAKE different-flavoured smoothies for variety (see Apricot Smoothies overleaf and the recipe index (pages 342-343) for other recipes).

GRILL KIPPERS with some tomatoes.

ENJOY a wholemeal muffin with cream cheese and chives.

Add smoked salmon to scrambled egg for a luxury snack

apricot smoothies

Smoothies make quick, easily digestible snacks and are very simple to prepare. If your appetite is poor, or you have been ill, use full-fat milk and yoghurt to increase the calories.

NUTRIENTS PER SERVING	
calories	150
carbohydrate	25 g
(sugars)	25 g
protein	6 g
fat	3.5 g
(saturated)	2 g
fibre	1 g

200 g (7 oz) canned apricots in natural juice, drained
150 g (5 oz) apricot yoghurt
150 ml (5 fl oz) chilled milk
1 tablespoon muesli to garnish (optional)

1 Place the apricots, yoghurt and chilled milk in a liquidiser or food processor and blend for 1 minute, or until completely smooth.

preparation: **2 minutes**

serves **2**

2 Divide the mixture between 2 large glasses and sprinkle over the muesli if desired.

3 Serve at once, while the smoothies are still cold.

cinnamon rice pudding

A traditional treat, rice pudding is given a spicy boost with a touch of fragrant cinnamon. This would make a good accompaniment to cooked fruit such as stewed or baked apple. Save any leftovers to eat for breakfast.

NUTRIENTS PER SERVING	
calories	260
carbohydrate	52 g
(sugars)	36 g
protein	8 g
fat	3 g
(saturated)	2 g
fibre	1 g

40 g (1½ oz) pudding rice
20 g (¾ oz) caster sugar
1 medium cooking apple, peeled and cubed
2 tablespoons sultanas
375 ml (13 fl oz) semi-skimmed milk
Pinch of ground cinnamon

1 Heat the oven to 150°C (300°F, gas mark 2). Place all the ingredients in a 600 ml (1 pint) shallow oven-proof dish and stir well.

preparation: **5 minutes**

cooking time: **1½ hours**

serves **2**

2 Transfer the baking dish to the oven and bake for 1½ hours, or until the rice is soft.

3 Set aside to cool a little, and serve the pudding on its own or with stewed apples or poached pears.

4 Alternatively, chill in the refrigerator and serve cold.

easy **smoked** fish **pie**

The delicately smoked haddock in this simple fish pie gives wonderful flavour to a traditional dish. Naturally smoked haddock tastes best: it is available from your fishmonger, or the fresh fish counter of large supermarkets

preparation time: **20 minutes**

cooking time: **50-55 minutes**

serves **2**

*450 g (1 lb) old potatoes, peeled and cut
    into even-sized pieces*
225 g (8 oz) undyed smoked haddock fillet
300 ml (10 fl oz) semi-skimmed milk
1 tablespoon plain flour
Salt and black pepper
Small can sweetcorn (198 g (7 oz), drained
15 g (½ oz) butter
25 g (1 oz) Cheddar cheese, grated

1 Cook the potatoes in boiling, lightly salted water for 15–20 minutes, or until soft. Drain well.

2 Put the fish in a shallow pan, pour over the milk, cover and simmer for 10 minutes, until tender. Remove the fish, flake the flesh discarding the skin and bones. Strain the milk, and set aside.

3 Place the flour in a bowl and gradually whisk in 200 ml (7 fl oz) of the reserved milk. Transfer to a saucepan and slowly bring to the boil, stirring continuously, until the mixture thickens. Reduce the heat and simmer for 1 minute. Season to taste.

4 Heat the oven to 200°C (400°F, gas mark 6). Mix together the flaked fish, sweetcorn and white sauce. Adjust the seasoning. Spoon the mixture into a shallow ovenproof dish.

5 Mash the potatoes with the butter, remaining milk and seasoning. Spoon over the fish mixture. Sprinkle the grated cheese over the top. Transfer the dish to the oven and bake for 25 minutes, or until the top is golden. Serve with steamed broccoli.

NUTRIENTS PER SERVING	
calories	332
carbohydrate	48 g
(sugars)	11 g
protein	17 g
fat	7.5 g
(saturated)	4 g
fibre	2.5 g

enjoying a grand old age

PART THREE

Mind and Body

Food can have a powerful effect on your emotional and mental state. It can influence your mood, memory and sense of stability and calm. Achieving a feeling of well-being means getting the right balance. Choosing certain foods will certainly make you feel better, but you may also need to make other adjustments. Exercise will enhance your physical and psychological health, and making time to relax will help to deal with the effects of pressure.

Grace under pressure

We all suffer from stress at one time or another – this symptom of modern living is virtually impossible to avoid. But eating strategically can help you to cope. The right foods will provide your body with a powerful defence against stress, enabling you to rise to its challenges.

Stress isn't always bad for you – a little tension is exciting and can help you to achieve a personal goal such as competing for a job or organising a special event. But long-term stress is different: it is very damaging, and will eventually take its toll on your health.

Whether stress is caused by the trauma of bereavement, a house move, loss of a job or by a happy occasion, such as a family wedding, the body reacts in the same way, entering what is known as 'fight or flight' mode. This 'ready for action' response encourages the production of the hormone adrenaline, which can induce tension in seconds.

THE STRESS REACTION

Everybody knows the signs of stress: a pounding heart; an increased feeling of alertness; sweating; and butterflies in your stomach. While you are coping with these reactions, the other systems in your body such as your digestion, blood circulation and sex drive are put on hold.

In addition, adrenaline stimulates the release of fatty acids (the main chemical components of fat) and glucose into your bloodstream in order to fuel your muscles; now,

because there is more fat circulating in your system, the cholesterol levels in your blood are raised.

These reactions are not harmful in short bursts, but if your system is subjected to continual stress, you will become exhausted. The adrenal cortex in your brain (your hormone headquarters) will eventually tire of maintaining a state of red alert.

Fast and fresh Because it is rich in stress-busting nutrients, you should make fish a regular item on your menu. You could visit a sushi restaurant or bar to enjoy it at its exotic best.

Stress damage

Long-term stress can produce a wide range of physical symptoms such as headaches, migraines, palpitations, backaches, colds and flu, high blood pressure, sweating, irritable bowel syndrome and muscular tension. None of these is life-threatening, but prolonged stress can increase the risk of more serious health problems,

including strokes, heart disease and cancer. It can upset your mental equilibrium and you may suffer from insomnia, dizziness, irritability, poor concentration, memory-loss, lethargy, depression, and lack of confidence.

Helpful strategies Though stress can cause various kinds of havoc, the right foods can help you overcome these problems. Good nutrition and a varied diet are crucial in coping with stress. Studies have shown that certain foods can relieve its negative effects; and some also provide a beneficial 'feel-good' factor.

The way you eat can make a noticeable improvement in your tension levels. Small, frequent meals, rather than three large meals a day help you to reduce stress by sustaining your energy levels right through the day. This helps your body to cope successfully with physical and mental pressures.

Fight or flight When your body is flooded with adrenaline, your tension levels soar. Taking action relieves this stress, but if this is not possible, you get trapped by conflicting impulses.

Take time to eat Avoid eating on the run: sit down and enjoy your meal, chew your food thoroughly, and don't bolt it. This helps to keep you calm, and also helps you to digest your food properly. As for choosing what foods to eat, focus on those that actively combat stress.

Slow-burn energy Unrefined carbohydrate foods including brown rice, wholewheat pasta as well as wholegrain bread are broken down slowly by the body. They supply long-term, sustained energy, as do oats, pulses and potatoes.

Carbohydrates also have a gentle, calming effect on the brain: they help to transport tryptophan, the amino acid which produces the brain chemical serotonin (see page 244). Also, the more fruit and vegetables you eat, the better – they are

are you stressed?

Everyone reacts differently to stress but most people will have a recognisable pattern. It is useful to learn about your own responses to stressful situations as it can help you to deal with them. These are just some of the effects of stress:

• Do you feel constantly tired?

• Do you find it difficult to sleep at night and wake up in the morning?

• Do you often feel angry and hostile?

• Do you get palpitations?

• Have you experienced rapid weight loss or gain?

• Do you get frequent colds?

• Are you uninterested in sex?

• Are you often close to tears?

• Do you drink and smoke more to help you get through stressful times?

• Do you bite your nails or fidget?

• Do you feel you cannot cope?

• Do you eat to comfort yourself?

• Do you have mood swings?

• Do you suffer from headaches or migraine?

• Do your suffer from memory loss?

excellent providers of the antioxidant vitamins beta carotene, vitamin C and E as well as valuable fibre. Antioxidants help to strengthen your immune system (see page 118) which may be weakened by stress.

Fruit is an ideal alternative to sugary foods; its natural sugar (fructose) is released more slowly in the body, providing stable supplies of energy when you are under stress.

Eat at least five portions of fresh fruit or vegetables a day – a portion may be an apple, a banana, a glass of fruit juice (which contains all the nutrients of fruit but not the fibre) two tablespoons of cooked vegetables or a bowl of salad.

Heart-friendly fish Your heart is put under particular strain by stress. Oily fish, rich in beneficial omega-3 fatty acids, are known to reduce the risk of heart disease. But this protective action is also thought to calm hostile feelings experienced during times of pressure. The best fish to choose include salmon, mackerel, tuna and herrings.

Low-fat is best Avoid foods that contain saturated fat and opt for low-fat protein foods such as fish, lean meat and poultry. Foods high in calcium help to reduce tension, so eat low-fat milk, yoghurt, tofu, reduced-fat cheese, sesame and sunflower seeds, fortified soya drink and dark green vegetables.

Don't get hyped-up

During periods of stress you may forget to eat regular meals. This is a mistake because these are the occasions when good nutrition is most important.

It is very tempting to resort to various stimulants instead, including nicotine and excessive amounts of

caffeine from drinking tea and coffee. But stimulants supply little or no vitamins or minerals: in fact they rob your body of valuable nutrients. Also, stressed individuals may reach for alcohol – which is a chemical depressant and depletes your supplies of vitamins A, B and C, zinc, magnesium and essential fatty acids, and also leads to dehydration. Tea and coffee both inhibit your uptake of valuable minerals such as iron, magnesium and calcium.

It is also important to cut down on sugar. It provides a lot of calories but little nourishment and also suppresses your appetite. Refined sugar, found in biscuits and cakes,

Calming and fortifying *This beautifully textured Butternut Squash and Lentil Soup is high in B vitamins. These help to reduce anxiety and tension and release energy from your food. The recipe is on page 214.*

Antioxidant protection *Orange-fleshed sweet potatoes (below) are a very good source of the immune-boosting anti-oxidant, beta carotene. They are also versatile; steamed, baked or mashed, they have a distinctive, sweet flavour.*

releases its energy very quickly in the body, triggering an abrupt insulin response that can make you light-headed. This initial energy boost is temporary – levels plummet lower than before, resulting in lethargy.

ANTI-STRESS NUTRIENTS

Stress is now known to rob the body of essential vitamins and minerals, yet a healthy diet can help the body fight back. Make sure you compensate for any shortfalls by eating foods that are rich in the following nutrients.

The B-complex group Generous supplies of B vitamins play a crucial role in how well you respond to

stressful situations. These vitamins are necessary for your nervous system to function well. They also help to maintain a healthy digestive system and help to release energy from your cells. This is a crucial function, because your body's demand for energy is increased during times of stress.

B vitamins cannot be stored in the body for very long, so your stores need to be replenished every day. Foods that supply B vitamins include: wholegrains, such as brown rice; yeast extract; dairy produce; lentils and other pulses; liver; green vegetables; seafood; lean meat; eggs; nuts; seeds; and dried fruit.

Vitamin C In a recent population study in the USA, it was found that high doses of vitamin C actively reduced levels of stress hormones in the blood. Like the B-complex vitamins, vitamin C cannot be stored in the body. This is why many nutritionists believe that a person who is under long-term stress

SEVEN WAYS TO relax and enjoy life

1 Eating with a friend is very relaxing – sharing conversation and food at a table makes you eat more slowly, so you can unwind.

2 Exercise is very important. Regular physical activity – at least 30 minute sessions three times a week – strengthens the immune system and promotes relaxation. Low-intensity exercises, such as swimming, jogging or cycling, trigger the body to produce endorphins (natural body chemicals) which produce a sense of well-being and euphoria.

3 Treat yourself to a massage – aromatherapy, reflexology or shiatsu. Massage helps to increase energy and reduce stress.

4 Take deep breaths. Stress causes breathing to become shallow and irregular. Deep breathing increases the amount of oxygen in the blood and slows down the heart rate.

5 Learn how to meditate – this can lower raised blood pressure and help to calm you down.

6 Essential oils such as rose and lavender are relaxing, rosemary and geranium are anti depressant.

7 Set aside at least 20 minutes a day to relax. This doesn't have to be complicated – read a book, go for a walk, listen to music or simply sit quietly.

A GOOD LAUGH *Joking is a great way to combat stress. It makes your body relax automatically, boosts your immune system, and stimulates your system to produce calming endorphins.*

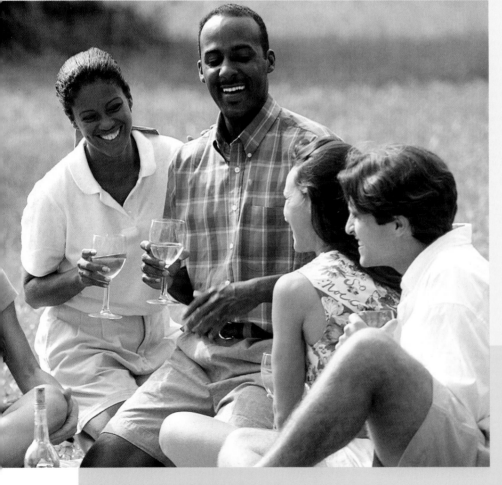

SEVEN WAYS TO relax and enjoy life

requires this nutrient in much greater quantities than the Reference Nutrient Intake (RNI) which is sufficient under normal circumstances (see page 341). Vitamin C also helps to maintain the immune system which is weakened during times of stress.

Foods rich in vitamin C include: citrus fruits (oranges, mandarins, lemons, limes and grapefruit) and berry fruits such as blackcurrants, blueberries, strawberries. Canteloupe melon and kiwi fruit are good sources, also vegetables – broccoli, Brussels sprouts, cabbage, potatoes, peppers and tomatoes.

MINERALS THAT MATTER

There are several other nutrients that help to combat stress, including the following minerals.

Magnesium is excreted in larger amounts when you're under stress; also, a shortage of this mineral activates the stress response. Magnesium deficiency leads to muscle tension and cramps. Magnesium is found in wholegrain cereals, nuts, pulses, sesame seeds, dried figs and green vegetables.

Calcium is needed for the good functioning of the nerves and muscles and, like magnesium, it is needed in greater amounts during times of stress. Choose low-fat sources of calcium such as semi-skimmed or skimmed milk, low-fat yoghurt and cheese, pulses, leafy green vegetables and canned fish.

Low levels of zinc are common among those suffering from stress. It is essential for boosting the immune system and fighting infections. It is found in oysters, red meat, nuts, sunflower seeds, egg yolks, dairy produce and wheatgerm.

Other minerals that enable the body to cope with the demands put upon it during times of stress are:
• Copper, which protects your immune system.
• Potassium, which helps your nervous system to function properly.
• Chromium, which helps to control your blood cholesterol levels and protect your heart and circulation.
• Iron, which is essential to make the haemoglobin in red blood cells. These carry oxygen around the body, to combat fatigue and help to keep your breathing steady.
• Selenium, which protects the immune system and helps to produce and regulate various hormones (including the thyroid hormone).

Make sure that you obtain the recommended levels of these minerals (see page 341). Good sources include wholegrain cereals, dairy produce, pulses, fish and shellfish, eggs, nuts and red meat.

Herbs that help with stress

Some people have used the following herbal remedies as good alternatives to prescribed tranquillisers. These herbs can help the nervous system in various ways. Some are used to sedate; some to stimulate and others to support the immune system, which is frequently a casualty of prolonged stress.

Ginseng is the most widely-known medicinal plant in Chinese medicine. It stimulates the nervous system and strengthens the immune system as well as helping to combat physical and mental stress. Ginseng is a good 'adaptogen' – this means that it will react differently according to each person's needs. Consequently, it will calm you if you are stressed and

stimulate you if you are tired. The Russian variety, Siberian ginseng, is similar in its action: it appears to improve tolerance to stress due to its effect on the adrenal gland. It also increases endurance as well as combating fatigue.

Echinacea is a popular remedy, renowned for its immunity-boosting properties. It can be taken to prevent or speed recovery from colds, flu and general infections.

Goldenseal boosts the immune system by increasing the production and activity of white blood cells.

Kava is an increasingly popular herbal preparation. It is made from

Fight off infections *Prolonged stress makes you susceptible to viral infections such as colds and influenza. Echinacea (purple coneflower) is a well-researched immune system stimulant and is an effective remedy for these conditions.*

the root of *Piper Methysticuma*, a variety of pepper plant grown throughout the Polynesian islands and New Guinea.

It is traditionally used as a cure for sleeping disorders and headaches, and it is also the main ingredient of a drink which is passed around at social gatherings such as weddings and christenings. Everyone sips the brew to share the happy mood it induces. Now sold in tablet form at health food shops, kava is used to reduce stress and anxiety.

Caution Herbal remedies can be potent, so you should ask a doctor before taking them. This is especially important if you have a psychiatric or medical condition, are pregnant, or have high blood pressure.

Drinks to calm you down

There are a number of caffeine-free drinks available. These can be very helpful when you are feeling tense

and anxious. You may also like to try some herbal teas that can have an actively calming affect.

Soothing brews Herbs have a wide range of therapeutic properties, and make simple and effective antidotes to stress. Peppermint tea is safe and renowned for soothing a tense digestive system; camomile tea calms your nerves and can induce sleep (see page 245); and thyme tea boosts your immune system.

Avoid caffeine When you are under stress you should moderate your intake of tea, coffee, alcohol, cocoa and fizzy drinks such as cola. The caffeine they contain is known to increase stress symptoms, and also robs the body of nutrients. This means that, even when you eat nutritious food, your system may not to be able to utilise it well. If you drink large quantities of caffeine-based drinks, it is probably wise to reduce your intake gradually.

Caffeine-addicts can experience severe reactions such as headaches, nervousness and irritability.

Alternatives to coffee Ingredients as varied as chicory, toasted grains or dandelions are used as substitutes for coffee. They are caffeine-free, so you can drink as much as you want without the worry of side effects. Decaffeinated coffee is a useful alternative, You may prefer to try one of the various brands available that remove caffeine from the coffee without the use of chemicals.

Fruit drinks Freshly squeezed fruit or vegetable juices provide rich amounts of vitamin C and beta carotene to improve your immune system. They are healthy alternatives to caffeine and sugar-laden fizzy drinks. Commercial juices are a useful standby but try to avoid juice drinks; these may contain extra sugar and additives – read the labels to check before you buy.

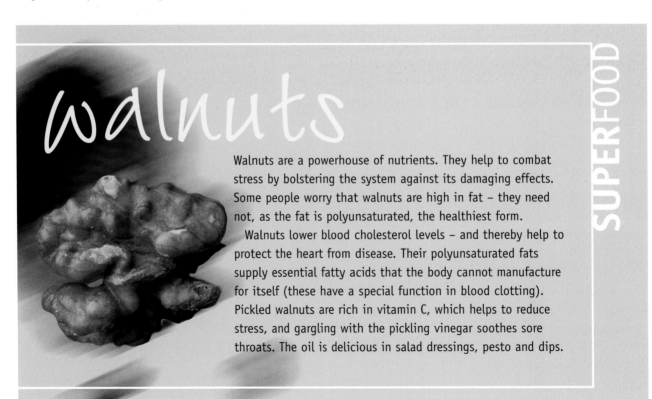

walnuts

SUPERFOOD

Walnuts are a powerhouse of nutrients. They help to combat stress by bolstering the system against its damaging effects. Some people worry that walnuts are high in fat – they need not, as the fat is polyunsaturated, the healthiest form.

Walnuts lower blood cholesterol levels – and thereby help to protect the heart from disease. Their polyunsaturated fats supply essential fatty acids that the body cannot manufacture for itself (these have a special function in blood clotting). Pickled walnuts are rich in vitamin C, which helps to reduce stress, and gargling with the pickling vinegar soothes sore throats. The oil is delicious in salad dressings, pesto and dips.

anti-stress tips

Eat small, regular meals based on carbohydrates, low-fat protein and plenty of fruit and vegetables. Choose carbohydrate-rich foods such as pasta, potatoes or rice for your evening meal, as these help the body to produce cortisol, the anti-stress hormone which helps you to wind down.

ANTI-STRESS BREAKFAST Try Anti-stress Granola (recipe overleaf); or Mini Banana Pancakes (page 285); slice fresh fruit into wholegrain cereals or porridge, and drink freshly squeezed fruit juice; choose wholemeal toast with a high-fruit, low-sugar jam or yeast extract.

LIGHT AND EASY MEALS Eat light, low-fat, high-protein meals, such as griddled or grilled chicken or fish with a baked potato and green salad or steamed vegetables; sandwiches or a soft tortilla with tuna, chicken, hummous or guacamole filling, served with carrot, pepper and celery crudités; sardines on wholemeal toast.

MAIN MEALS Fish is great for stress. Try Monkfish Kebabs with Spiced Couscous (recipe overleaf) or Tiger Prawn and Ginger Stir-fry (page 128) served with buckwheat noodles and sprinkled with sesame seeds; Any pasta with a tomato sauce is good too.

ANTI-STRESS DRINKS Cut down on or avoid coffee, tea, fizzy drinks and cocoa. Drink water, herbal teas and fresh fruit juices instead.

STRESS-RELIEF SNACKS Fresh or dried fruit (apricots, dates and figs are a good source of fibre, vitamins and minerals); pumpkin and sunflower seeds; nuts, particularly walnuts and hazelnuts; rice cakes with hummous or yeast extract; or wholemeal bread with vegetable, nut or bean pâté. Warm pitta bread spread with pesto or olive pâté and thin slices of tomato, red pepper and watercress sprigs.

Guacamole

Scoop the flesh from a large, ripe avocado into a bowl and mash it roughly with a fork. Add half a small onion, finely chopped, a tablespoon of finely chopped coriander, 1/2 teaspoon finely chopped red chilli, and the juice of one lime. Cover and chill for 30 minutes before serving with a tortilla or corn chips. Serves 2

NUTRIENTS PER SERVING: Calories **160** Carbohydrate **5 g** (sugars **1.5 g**) Protein **2 g** Fat **14 g** (saturated **3 g**) Fibre **3 g**

Dip a cornchip in guacamole for a vitamin-rich snack

anti-stress granola

This crunchy fruit and nut mix makes a great start to the day; by making your own cereal mix, you can be sure that you're using the best ingredients to minimise the effects of stress. Serve it with low-fat milk or yoghurt and fresh strawberries.

preparation time: **10 minutes**

cooking time: **55 minutes**

makes **675 grams (1½ lb)**

NUTRIENTS PER 25 G (1 OZ) SERVING	
calories	97
carbohydrate	10 g
(sugars)	4 g
protein	2 g
fat	5 g
(saturated)	0.5 g
fibre	1 g

115 g (4 oz) porridge oats
115 g (4 oz) jumbo oats
55 g (2 oz) sunflower seeds
25 g (1 oz) pumpkin seeds
55 g (2 oz) roasted hazelnuts
25 g (1 oz) almonds, roughly chopped
50 ml (2 fl oz) sunflower oil
50 ml (2 fl oz) clear honey
55 g (2 oz) raisins
55 g (2 oz) dried apricots, roughly chopped

1 Heat the oven to 140°C (275°F, gas mark 1). Mix the oats, seeds and nuts together in a bowl, and set aside.

2 Heat the oil and honey gently in a large saucepan until melted. Remove from the heat, then add the oat mixture and stir well. Spoon the honey-coated mix to two baking trays.

3 Bake for 50 minutes or until crisp, stirring occasionally to prevent the oat mixture sticking to the baking trays. Remove from the oven and mix in the raisins and apricots. Store in an airtight container until ready to use.

rich butternut squash and lentil soup

This richly spiced, wholesome and comforting soup (illustrated on page 209) makes a substantial lunch on its own, served with wholemeal or naan bread. You could also serve it with wholemeal croûtons rubbed with garlic.

preparation time: **10 minutes**

cooking time: **55 minutes**

serves **4**

NUTRIENTS PER SERVING	
calories	340
carbohydrate	56 g
(sugars)	15 g
protein	18 g
fat	7 g
(saturated)	1 g
fibre	7 g

2 tablespoons olive oil
1 large onion, finely chopped
1 large clove garlic, chopped
2 teaspoons ground cumin
1 teaspoon mild chilli powder
½ teaspoon ground turmeric
½ teaspoon ground ginger
Seeds from 3 cardamom pods
Finely grated zest of 1 lemon
1 medium butternut squash, peeled, deseeded and cubed
225 g (8 oz) split red lentils, rinsed
1.2 litres (2 pints) vegetable or chicken stock (recipe page 338)
2 tablespoons lemon juice
Salt and black pepper
4 tablespoons low-fat yoghurt, to garnish

1 Heat the oil in a large, heavy-based saucepan, add the onion and fry gently for 5 minutes, until softened. Add the garlic, spices and lemon zest, then cook for 1–2 minutes, stirring frequently. Add the squash and lentils and stir well to coat them in the spiced oil mixture. Cook for 2 minutes, stirring frequently.

2 Add the stock and bring to the boil. Reduce the heat and simmer for 45 minutes, until the squash and lentils are tender. Pour into a food processor and process until smooth and creamy. Return the soup to the pan and heat through. Add the lemon juice and season. Serve garnished with yoghurt.

monkfish **kebabs** with **spiced** couscous

Lightly spiced with cinnamon and cumin, this Morroccan-inspired dish is rich in vitamins and minerals. Serve with a green leaf salad dressed with olive oil and a squeeze of fresh lemon. Use cod, halibut, salmon or tuna steaks if you can't get monkfish.

preparation time: **15 minutes, plus 1-2 hours marinating**

cooking time: **20 minutes**

serves **4**

FOR THE MARINADE
2 cloves garlic, crushed
2.5 cm (1 in) piece of fresh ginger
2 tablespoons olive oil
1 teaspoon ground cumin
Juice of 1½ lemons
FOR THE KEBABS
900 g (2 lb) monkfish tails, skinned, cut
    into bite-sized pieces
2 courgettes, thickly sliced
2 red onions, quartered, layers separated
FOR THE COUSCOUS
280 g (10 oz) couscous
500 ml (18 fl oz) boiling water
Salt and pepper
2 tablespoons olive oil
2 cloves garlic, chopped
1 teaspoon ground cinnamon
1 teaspoon mild chilli powder
1 teaspoon ground cumin
1 teaspoon ground coriander
1 mango, peeled, pitted and diced
25 g (1 oz) butter
Chopped fresh coriander.
to garnish

1 Mix the marinade ingredients in a shallow dish. Add the monkfish and turn to coat all sides. Leave to marinate for 1–2 hours in the refrigerator.

2 Thread the marinated fish on 8 skewers, alternating with pieces of courgette and onion. Lay the kebabs in a shallow dish and brush with the marinade.

3 Cover the couscous with boiling water and season with salt. Cover and leave for 10 minutes to fluff up. Heat the oil in a large, heavy-based frying pan, and fry the garlic for 1 minute. Stir in the spices and cook for 1 minute. Add the couscous, mango and butter. Season, cook for 2 minutes and keep warm.

4 Heat the grill to high. Grill the kebabs for 3-4 minutes each side. Brush with the marinade after turning. Serve with the couscous, garnished with coriander.

NUTRIENTS PER SERVING	
calories	520
carbohydrate	51 g
(sugars)	14 g
protein	41 g
fat	18 g
(saturated)	5 g
fibre	3 g

grace under pressure

Lifting the spirits

The food you eat affects your mental health as well as your physical well-being. A bad diet can be one of the causes of depression or mood swings. A healthy diet, on the other hand, may be enough to lift your spirits without the need for medication and counselling.

Nobody is happy all the time and it is only natural that we should feel low occasionally. But depression and other mood disorders are more than just a bad case of the blues. If you experience persistent and overwhelming feelings of hopelessness, pessimism, sadness and general loss of interest in life, there may be real cause for concern. These feelings can affect your eating and sleeping patterns, self-esteem and the ability to enjoy life. More serious forms of depression demand the help of a doctor.

Nutrition may not be the whole answer, but there is evidence that diet can affect the balance of mental and physical well being. Many experts now believe that drugs and medication are not always the solution to mild depression and a positive self-help approach can be beneficial in many cases.

RESTORING THE BALANCE

Depression is closely connected with the food you eat. People who are depressed often lose their appetite, feel too low to cook, and fill up on nutritionally empty junk foods. A vicious circle develops: poor eating habits lead to nutritional deficiencies which then increase feelings of depression. Doctors have discovered that many people who suffer from depression are also lacking in particular nutrients.

Eating foods rich in these missing nutrients, combined with lifestyle changes and regular exercise, can produce significant improvements in people suffering from mild to moderate depression. Sometimes, better results have been achieved than with prescribed antidepressants.

Foods to beat the blues

If you are feeling depressed, your first priority should be to eat a nutritionally balanced diet (see the Five Food Groups, page 11-15). You should also increase your intake of the following nutrients, which have been linked with depression.

The B vitamins People who are depressed tend to have lower levels of vitamin B6, which is needed for the production of serotonin, the brain chemical that lifts mood (see page 244 and below). Low levels of vitamins B12, B2 (riboflavin) and folic acid can also cause depression. To boost your B vitamins, eat lean meat and poultry, fish, eggs, nuts, seeds, soya beans, bananas, low-fat

A powerful combination *The restorative effect of vitamin C in kiwi fruit (above) lifts your mood and replenishes your body. But you also need vigorous exercise (left) to trigger natural body chemicals that act as antidotes to the blues.*

dairy produce, fortified cereals and leafy green vegetables.

Vitamin C is also depleted in people suffering from depression. Eat plenty of fresh, raw fruits and vegetables: citrus fruit, strawberries, guavas, kiwi fruit, blackcurrants and peppers are excellent sources.

Iron A deficiency in iron may lead to depression. Iron is also essential in the production of the brain chemical serotonin (see page 244 and below). Women who take the birth-control pill are more prone to depression if their iron levels are low.

Foods rich in iron include red meat, egg yolk, liver, red kidney beans, chickpeas, wholegrains, fortified breakfast cereals, nuts, pulses and green leafy vegetables. But if you are pregnant or trying to conceive you should not eat liver (see page 163).

Selenium People who are deficient in the antioxidant mineral selenium also experience feelings of depression and anxiety. Selenium is found in meat, fish and shellfish, wholegrains, avocados and dairy produce.

Zinc Essential for the body to convert tryptophan into serotonin (see page 244 and below), zinc is found in oysters, red meat, poultry, eggs, dairy foods, peanuts and sunflower seeds.

Other minerals that help to fight depression include magnesium and manganese. These are found in wholegrains, pulses, dried figs, vegetables, nuts and seeds.

Omega-3 fatty acids Research is still in its early stages, but depression has been linked to omega-3 deficiency. Scientists suggest that these fatty acids may be able to suppress the signals that are responsible for sudden mood changes. Omega-3 oils may offer new possibilities for treating manic depression. Oily fish such as salmon, herrings, mackerel, tuna and sardines are the richest sources of omega-3 fatty acids.

Refresh your spirits with fennel. With its delicate aniseed flavour and crunchy texture, it is a perfect accompaniment to fish, boosts your body's supplies of antioxidants, and fortifies your immune system.

MOOD AND SEROTONIN

As well as being essential for normal sleep (see page 244), the 'feel good' brain chemical serotonin helps to brighten your mood and control some types of depression. The amino acid tryptophan, found in protein foods such as turkey, chicken, game, cauliflower, broccoli, milk, cheese, lean red meat, eggs, soya beans, fennel and bananas is needed for serotonin production. To maximise your intake, eat some carbohydrate at the same time (see page 245).

the role of antioxidants

As well as helping to prevent diseases such as cancer, antioxidants may be useful for helping people who are vulnerable to bouts of depression. This has been highlighted in recent studies. Vitamin C in particular can help those with mood disorders. After two years of taking supplements of antioxidant nutrients, patients were found to be significantly less depressed than those who were taking a placebo.

Eat small, regular meals to keep your blood sugar levels on an even keel and avoid high-fat, sugary snacks. Instead, try snacking on unsalted popcorn or pretzels, home-made ice lollipops made with real fruit, crumpets with yeast extract or peanut butter, and muffins with high-fruit jam.

In addition, you may want to try the following ideas:
• Eating one or two ripe bananas a day can increase levels of the mood-enhancing chemical serotonin.
• If you dislike oily fish, take a daily fish oil supplement.
• Just one Brazil nut a day can help to make you feel good. They are a very good source of selenium.
• Use more chillies in your cooking: capsaicin, the substance which makes chillies hot, stimulates the release of endorphins, the body's 'feel good' chemicals.

Life-style factors

Though nutritional deficiencies are common in people suffering from depression, these are not always the result of unwise eating habits. Alcohol, caffeine and cigarettes are very efficient at stealing nutrients from the body. An excess of these stimulants (they are also called anti-nutrients), has been linked with depression and low mental energy.

Cigarettes Smoking lowers vitamin C levels in the body, and this can contribute to depression. In addition, it interferes with serotonin receptors in the brain, making them less sensitive to the mood-enhancing serotonin that is available.
Alcohol is a depressant – it interferes with the brain-cell processes and disrupts sleep. It also produces a fall in blood sugar levels, resulting in cravings for sweet, sugary foods. The subsequent extremes of high and low blood sugar levels tend to aggravate any emotional problems.
Caffeine is a mood enhancer, so it can make matters worse for those susceptible to anxiety and mood swings. The combination of caffeine and refined sugar seems to cause even more dramatic mood changes.

THE ALTERNATIVE WAY

Herbal medicines have been used for centuries as a treatment for anxiety and depression. In fact, some herbs are currently even more popular than the prescription antidepressants in some countries.
St John's wort is the most widely used alternative remedy for treating mild to moderate depression. And in Germany it is one of the leading medicines prescribed by doctors. This is because St John's wort (*Hypericum*) has had a success rate

that is on a par with synthetic anti-depressants. Known as the 'sunshine' herb it has been found to have a positive long-term affect on anxiety. It lifts the mood and can enhance your ability to handle your daily life. Symptoms such as extreme sadness, hopelessness, exhaustion and poor sleep also decrease.

As an antidepressant, St John's wort should be taken for between four to six weeks so that you can gauge its effectiveness. Take it at mealtimes and never exceed the manufacturer's recommended dosage. Because there is some concern that it may interfere with the action of other medications, you should always consult your doctor before taking it.

Caution People with fair skin should avoid exposure to strong sunlight if taking St John's wort, as the remedy can make the skin light-sensitive. It may also be advisable to avoid red wine, yeast, cheese and pickled herrings. St John's wort should not be taken in conjunction with other prescription antidepressants, or during pregnancy or lactation.

Ginkgo biloba Active compounds found in ginkgo biloba have been shown to reduce feelings of depression, particularly in older people. It may also help to restore mental and emotional stability. Ginkgo appears to help the brain to function; and may help to improve memory, concentration, circulation and alertness (see page 267).

It has been suggested that ginkgo should be taken for one month to find out if it is beneficial. But you should not exceed the recommended dosage specified on the label.

Kava Like St John's wort, kava (see page 211) is an alternative treatment for depression, anxiety and insomnia. Claimed to be as effective as prescribed antidepressants, kava has been used for centuries: according to some herbalists it is 'the king of the herbal stress relievers'. Available in tablet form from health food shops, it is a muscle relaxant, mood lifter and libido enhancer.

Valerian The usefulness of valerian for treating anxiety and nervous disorders has long been known. It is also an established treatment for insomnia and has been shown to be particularly effective if taken in conjunction with St John's wort.

Homeopathic remedies You should seek professional advice from your doctor or a homeopathic practitioner before taking homeopathic remedies. Homeopathic medicines have unfamiliar Latin names, but some have been found to be highly effective in treating depression. They are now widely available, and can be bought at chemists without the need for a prescription.

continued on page 222

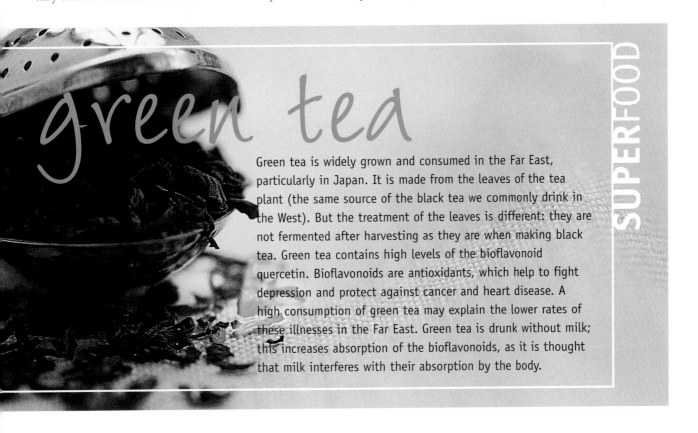

green tea

SUPERFOOD

Green tea is widely grown and consumed in the Far East, particularly in Japan. It is made from the leaves of the tea plant (the same source of the black tea we commonly drink in the West). But the treatment of the leaves is different: they are not fermented after harvesting as they are when making black tea. Green tea contains high levels of the bioflavonoid quercetin. Bioflavonoids are antioxidants, which help to fight depression and protect against cancer and heart disease. A high consumption of green tea may explain the lower rates of these illnesses in the Far East. Green tea is drunk without milk; this increases absorption of the bioflavonoids, as it is thought that milk interferes with their absorption by the body.

all about
MOOD FOODS

Certain foods are known to have a direct effect on your mood. Some can make you calm; some will stimulate you while others may make you jittery and anxious.

The effects of caffeine

Coffee beans are high in caffeine, a mild stimulant used for centuries. Scientists have found that caffeine changes the brain chemistry in a similar manner to modern anti-depressant drugs. Its molecules block the action of a neurotransmitter which shuts off mood-raising chemicals and keeps 'good mood' chemicals circulating in the brain. Mainly found in coffee, caffeine is also present in smaller but significant amounts in tea, some cola drinks, cold and pain relief tablets, and chocolate.

Caffeine can cause problems, however, so use it in moderation. Too much can produce palpitations, tremors,

sweating and insomnia. Children may have problems sleeping if they drink chocolate or cola before bedtime.

Medical advice is to drink no more than six cups of tea or coffee a day; researchers have also found that, for the most effective mood-lift you should drink one cup early in the morning, then no more until late afternoon. The caffeine boost from the first cup of coffee is strong enough to last for several hours.

People who have a tendency to experience mood swings and anxiety may find that caffeine actually makes their symptoms even worse. If you suffer from depression and consume lots of caffeine (for example, more than the recommended amount of tea and coffee mentioned above) it may help to cut down. But be cautious: caffeine can easily become addictive, so suddenly cutting it out of

DO YOU INSTINCTIVELY REACH FOR A CUP OF COFFEE AND A CHOCOLATE BISCUIT WHEN YOU'RE FEELING LOW? IF YOU DO, IT'S NOT BECAUSE YOU ARE WEAK-WILLED: THERE IS A PERFECTLY RATIONAL EXPLANATION. BOTH CONTAIN CHEMICALS WHICH WILL INCREASE YOUR ENERGY LEVELS AND MAKE YOU FEEL GOOD.

PLEASURABLE EFFECTS *Coffee, chocolate and other foods high in caffeine help to create a happy, sociable mood, and can smooth relationships with other people. But as caffeine is known to be addictive, you should be careful where children are concerned. An occasional sweet treat is fine; but it should neither be used to reward good behaviour nor withheld as a punishment.*

your diet abruptly may well result in a range of unpleasant withdrawal symptoms such as headaches, restlessness, shaking and irritability.

The chocolate high

Chocolate is another mood-changing food. As well as giving an instant boost to your blood sugar level, it is particularly rich in tryptophan and is highly efficient at boosting both your of serotonin and endorphin levels. Endorphins are the body's natural painkillers – so the

combined effect of an uplifted mood with a decreased sensitivity to pain can add up to a powerful formula for making you feel both happy and stimulated.

The uplifting effect of chocolate can also be attributed to a substance called phenylethyamine (PEA), which occurs naturally in the brain and is released when we feel happy. And chocolate contains theobromine, another stimulant. There may be a psychological factor – chocolate may make you happy if you were given it as a reward or as a comfort food when you were a child.

Milk chocolate has some nutritional value, as it contains some protein and minerals. Plain chocolate has some iron and magnesium, and all chocolate contains potassium. But it is high in fat and calories and should not replace more nutritious foods.

If you suffer from irritability and depression, try *Natrum. mur.* Other formulas that are recommended for anxiety, depression, and exhaustion are *Sepia* and *Acid. Phos.* (Many homeopathic remedies are listed in these abbreviated forms.)

EXERCISE FOR HAPPINESS

The benefits of exercise when you are feeling depressed are very well documented: it has even been suggested that it is the most powerful antidepressant available. Regular exercise is essential, as it encourages the release of 'feel-good' endorphins into the body, boosting your mood and lifting your spirits.

People who exercise frequently are known to have high self-esteem; they are also generally happier than those who engage in very little physical activity. The best exercises for combating depression are strength-training routines such as weight-lifting, or aerobic activities: these include running, jogging, aerobic work-outs, cycling, cross-country skiing, swimming and tennis. Brisk sessions of walking or climbing the stairs will also help.

Try half an hour of moderate exercise three days a week or 20 minutes of aerobic exercise five times a week. A little activity is better than none at all. Exercises such as pilates, t'ai chi and yoga are all beneficial as they help to improve your energy.

Seasonal Affective Disorder

People who feel unusually depressed or low during the dark winter months may be suffering from Seasonal Affective Disorder or SAD.

TURNIPS – THE ROOTS OF HEALTH *Winter is a time when many people feel low. Green vegetables may not be as abundant in the cold months, but there are plenty of root crops such as turnips (left), swedes and celeriac. These hardy vegetables are rich in nutrients that keep you healthy and help to raise your spirits.*

1 *Base your meals on carbohydrate foods such as potatoes, rice and pasta, and eat frequent, small amounts. Be sure to include plenty of fruit and vegetables, but try to eat saturated fats and protein in moderation.*

2 *Exercise regularly – aim for at least 30 minutes of continuous activity three times a week. Walking is a great form of exercise.*

3 *Cut down on sugar and refined foods.*

4 *Limit your intake of alcohol, tea, coffee, fizzy drinks and chocolate.*

5 *Avoid stimulants such as cigarettes and drugs.*

6 *Try an aromatherapy massage, acupuncture, shiatsu or reflexology.*

7 *Food allergies and intolerances may cause depression. See a doctor or qualified nutritionist.*

8 *Consider taking a multivitamin and mineral supplement if you feel that your diet is inadequate.*

9 *Some herbal and homeopathic remedies may help to relieve the symptoms of depression. But always consult a qualified practitioner first.*

10 *Think positively – if self-help measures are unsuccessful, you can get help from a trained counsellor who can help you to regain a more optimistic outlook.*

TEN WAYS TO **beat the blues**

This winter depression usually occurs when daylight hours decrease and particularly affects people who live in northern regions such as Scandinavia where the days are very short in winter.

Reduced hours of daylight are thought to lead to low levels of serotonin in the brain, causing depression, lethargy, an increased need for sleep, carbohydrate and chocolate cravings and a lack of libido. If SAD is the cause, these symptoms subside in March with the arrival of spring and longer days.

Lightening things up

The majority of SAD sufferers respond to light therapy, either through increased exposure to sunlight or by sitting in front of a special light box. This emits a full-spectrum light which mimics sunlight, and should be used for a few hours a day. Such boxes are becoming increasingly available, and can be purchased by mail order. Doctors often recommend taking a winter holiday in a sunny climate. Plenty of fresh air and exercise are also highly beneficial.

If you have problems with carbohydrate cravings, these can be satisfied by basing your meals around pasta, rice, beans, potatoes, wholegrains and bread along with generous helpings of fruit and vegetables and moderate amounts of protein. This is far more effective than eating high-fat and sugary sweets, biscuits and cakes – they will raise your blood sugar levels quickly, but they then fall equally fast, leaving you more depressed.

Foods rich in tryptophan (see above) are helpful in relieving the depressive symptoms associated with

A natural high *Make the most of a sunny winter day – go for a brisk run with an energetic pet. The light glittering from frosty surfaces increases the mood-enhancing effects of the exercise, so you'll feel thoroughly elated when you get home.*

SAD – remember to eat some carbohydrate with these foods to improve your tryptophan absorption.

Researchers have found that the herbal remedy St John's wort (see page 218) can help. Alcohol worsens symptoms in some people, so you may prefer to avoid it.

PREMENSTRUAL SYNDROME

Recent research has found that tearfulness and moodiness are perfectly normal during a woman's cycle and are generally caused by changes in hormone levels. But

premenstrual syndrome (PMS) produces physical and mental changes including mood swings, depression, headaches, water retention and stomach cramps.

Women who suffer from PMS often have lower levels of serotonin in the brain. Some practitioners suggest eating more foods that contain vitamin B_6 such as meat, fish, wholegrains and leafy green vegetables. Evening primrose oil and vitamin E can also be helpful, as well as cutting down on your intake of caffeine, salt and alcohol.

MENUPLAN
to brighten you up

When you're feeling low, food can transform the way you feel. Use the following ideas to cheer yourself up and enhance your mood.

BREAKFAST BOOSTERS *Eat a boiled or poached egg and wholemeal toast with yeast extract or peanut butter; eat half a grapefruit as well, or have a fresh fruit cocktail.*

LUNCHTIME LIFTS *Try a chicken or tuna fish salad with a baked potato or wholemeal bread; or a bowl of vegetable soup with a low-fat cheese, fish or chicken sandwich.*

EVENING MOOD ENHANCERS *Eat a starchy pasta, noodle or rice dish or a slice of pizza served with a green salad, sprinkled with toasted sunflower and pumpkin seeds. Or have Griddled Venison with Cranberry and Orange Sauce (recipe page 227) to boost your tryptophan levels.*

HAPPY SNACKS *Keep carbohydrate levels up throughout the day with a couple of small low-fat snacks. Choose from wholemeal bread, a fruit scone or muffin, rice cakes, low-salt and sugar popcorn, breadsticks or crackers. Don't be tempted by high-fat butter or margarine — instead use low-fat spreads, with jam, yeast extract, hummous, or low-fat cream cheese. Try and drink at least eight glasses of water a day.*

AND SO TO BED *Drink a calming camomile infusion or a warm milky drink.*

Enjoy a helping of noodles before bed to calm your mood

Using diet to treat PMS

Making some simple changes to your diet can help to alleviate many of the symptoms associated with PMS. Try the following four-step approach:

Step one Before trying any other measures, you should make sure that you are eating a healthy, balanced diet. The best way to achieve this is by following the structure outlined in the Five Food Groups (see pages 11–15). In particular you should:
• Cut back on the fat you eat, particularly saturated fat.
• Reduce your intake of foods high in refined sugar and salt.
• Eat more fruit, vegetables and foods high in carbohydrate and fibre.
• Drink plenty of fluids – try to drink eight glasses of water a day.
• Reduce your caffeine intake – drink no more than five cups of tea, coffee or cola in a day.
• Avoid alcohol.

It may take up to three months for any changes to take effect, but if there is no improvement after this time, move on to the second step.

Step two Symptoms such as mood swings, headaches and fatigue may be caused, or aggravated, by erratic blood sugar levels. During the last two weeks of your cycle try eating a carbohydrate-rich snack or meal every two or three hours.

Ideas for snacks include: a slice of wholemeal toast, low-fat cereal bar, bagel, wholemeal muffin, wholemeal scone, breakfast cereal, ready-to-eat dried fruits or a banana. Aim for three meals plus three high-carbohydrate snacks daily. If there is no improvement in your symptoms after one month move to step three.

Step three In addition to the basic healthy diet recommended in step one, you could try taking the

following nutritional supplements:

• Gamma-linoleic Acid (GLA) from evening primrose oil or starflower oil. Between six and eight 500 mg capsules are required daily. GLA supplements have been shown to be very helpful in reducing breast tenderness associated with PMS, and evening primrose oil is now available on prescription for those suffering breast tenderness.

• Magnesium: 250–300 mg daily – symptoms of magnesium deficiency resemble those of PMS and many women who suffer from PMS are found to have low blood levels of magnesium.

• Vitamin B$_6$: 50–100 mg daily. Do not exceed the recommended dose as taking high dosages has been known to cause nerve damage in some people. Vitamin B$_6$ supplements are believed to help alleviate symptoms such as depression, irritability, headaches and fatigue.

• Calcium: 1000 mg daily.

How long to wait for results? It can take anything up to four months before your system starts to respond to these additional supplements, but if you find that there is still no improvement after this time, you should stop using them.

Step four Symptoms of PMS may also be aggravated by a food allergy or intolerance (see pages 124-125).

Pinpointing the culprit foods can be difficult and it is important to seek the advice of your doctor or a State Registered Dietitian. An exclusion diet which involves leaving out several foods at a time should be professionally supervised. Otherwise you risk becoming deficient in important nutrients.

Further investigation Gut dysbiosis – an overgrowth of the yeast *Candida albicans* in the digestive tract – may cause PMS symptoms. If you haven't noticed a tangible improvement after trying the first three stages visit your doctor and ask about a test for an overgrowth of yeast and/or a possible food allergy.

Healing scents *Essential oil of lavender is widely used in aromatherapy: it is effective in several ways – it stimulates the mind, helps to lift the spirits and also relieves stress by relaxing the body.*

aromatherapy

Aromatherapy is widely recommended to help with depression. The essential oils used in the therapy are pure substances extracted or distilled from flowers, herbs, fruit or trees. They can be extremely powerful, so they are used in minuscule quantities. Just a few drops of essential oil in a bath can relax tense muscles and at the same time, stimulate the body and mind. You can also sprinkle some on to an essential oil burner to scent an entire room and create an aromatic, peaceful environment.

When using an essential oil as part of an aromatherapy massage session, it is important to blend it with a mild 'carrier' oil (almond is a good choice). Otherwise it may irritate your skin. It can then be safely massaged over the body or rubbed onto the temples to induce relaxation and relieve headaches. The oils below can all help when you are feeling low; but it is also important that you like the scent, so sample them before you buy.

Rosemary traditionally known as the herb for remembrance, rosemary has a reviving, uplifting effect on the brain. It can clear the head, making it easier to concentrate and focus.

Bergamot and camomile are soothing anti-depressants and blend well with each other and other oils.

Neroli is expensive but has renowned relaxing properties.

shellfish and rocket pizza

Peppery rocket and mixed seafood from your supermarket are served on a layer of piquant tomato sauce, adding both colour and flavour to this pizza. You can make your own dough for the base (see recipe page 339) or buy one ready-made.

preparation time: **1 hour, 15 minutes or 20 minutes if using a ready-made base**

cooking time: **20 minutes**

serves **4**

NUTRIENTS PER SERVING	
calories	334
carbohydrate	36.9 g
(sugars)	4.2 g
protein	24 g
fat	10.8 g
(saturated)	1.5 g
fibre	2.8 g

1 tablespoon olive oil, plus extra for greasing and drizzling

1 clove garlic, crushed

300 g (10½ oz) tomato passata

1 teaspoon sugar

½ teaspoon chilli flakes

Juice of 1 lemon

Salt and black pepper

Half of recipe quantity pizza dough (page 339)

450 g (1 lb) frozen seafood cocktail, defrosted

Large handful fresh rocket leaves

1 To make the topping, heat the oil in a heavy-based frying pan, add the garlic and fry for 1 minute.

2 Add the passata and sugar and simmer for 5-7 minutes, until thickened. Stir in the chilli flakes, lemon juice and seasoning. Set aside.

3 Heat the oven to 220°C (425°F, gas mark 7). Knead the prepared pizza dough lightly, then roll out to form a round about 1 cm (½ in) thick. Place on a lightly oiled baking tray and push up the edges into a shallow rim.

4 Spoon over the tomato sauce and top with a layer of mixed seafood. Season, and drizzle over a little olive oil.

5 Bake on the top shelf of the oven for 10–12 minutes, until the base is crisp and golden. Scatter the rocket over the pizza and serve immediately.

griddled **venison** with **cranberry** and orange **sauce**

Lean, low-fat venison steaks have a rich, gamey flavour which is highlighted by the sweet-sour citrus sauce. They are very easy to cook, and make a quick dinner party dish. Serve on a bed of polenta, or with steamed baby potatoes and a green salad.

preparation time: **15 minutes, plus 1 hour marinating**

cooking time: **20 minutes**

serves **4**

4 venison steaks, each about 140 g (5 oz)
FOR THE MARINADE
4 tablespoons olive oil
4 teaspoons soya sauce
2 tablespoons maple syrup or honey
½ teaspoon paprika
FOR THE SAUCE
115 g (4 oz) light soft brown sugar
125 ml (4 fl oz) fresh orange juice
1 star anise
½ teaspoon mixed spice
225 g (8 oz) cranberries, defrosted if frozen
Zest of 1 orange, cut into matchsticks
¼ teaspoon salt

1 Mix together the ingredients for the marinade in a shallow dish. Place the steaks in the dish and coat both sides with marinade. Refrigerate for 1 hour to marinate, turning after half an hour.

2 To make the sauce, place the sugar, orange juice, star anise and mixed spice in a heavy-based pan. Stir over a gentle heat until the sugar dissolves. Add the cranberries and half the zest. Cook gently until soft. Season and set aside.

3 Brush a griddle pan with olive oil and heat until the oil is smoking. Cook the steaks for 4-5 minutes on each side. Put them on a serving dish and keep warm. Pour the marinade into the pan and simmer for a few minutes until reduced and glossy. Pour over the steaks. Garnish with the remaining zest and serve with the sauce.

NUTRIENTS PER SERVING	
calories	400
carbohydrate	40 g
(sugars)	39 g
protein	32 g
fat	14 g
(saturated)	3 g
fibre	2 g

baked apple **crumbles**

Baking is a simple and nutritious way of cooking fruit. These apples are filled with a fragrant, spicy mixture of dates, nuts and stem ginger. Serve them with fromage frais, cream or custard as an uplifting treat.

preparation time: **10 minutes**

cooking time: **45 minutes**

serves **4**

1½ tablespoons clear honey
4 tablespoons porridge oats
55 g (2 oz) ready-to-eat dried dates, pitted and roughly chopped
1 tablespoon sunflower seeds
20 g (¾ oz) pecans, roughly chopped
1 piece stem ginger in syrup, roughly chopped
1 tablespoon soft dark brown sugar
4 cooking apples, such as Bramley, cored and scored around the circumference with a sharp knife

1 Heat the oven to 180°C (350°F, gas mark 4).

2 Heat the honey in a small, heavy-based saucepan. Stir in the porridge oats and cook for 2–3 minutes, until the honey is absorbed by the oats. Set aside and mix in the remaining ingredients.

3 Place the apples in an ovenproof dish and pour in a little water. Fill the cavity of each apple with the mixture. Bake for 40 minutes, until the apples are tender.

NUTRIENTS PER SERVING	
calories	260
carbohydrate	48 g
(sugars)	36 g
protein	4 g
fat	7 g
(saturated)	0.5 g
fibre	5 g

Restoring your appetite

We all lose interest in food from time to time – and this isn't always for negative reasons. It's well-known that falling in love can make all else pale into insignificance, including food. But if you've been eating poorly, whatever the reason, it's important to restore your appetite to good health.

A hearty relish for food is one of life's great pleasures. It is also a reassuring indicator of robust health. So, when you or someone who normally eats well suddenly loses interest in their food, it is correct to be concerned.

A HEALTHY APPETITE

The stimulus to eat is regulated by the appestat, a sensory area centred in the hypothalamus. This part of the brain monitors factors that influence appetite, such as glucose and other nutrient levels in the blood. It receives signals from sensors in the stomach and sends out chemicals that activate or suppress your appetite, depending on whether it receives 'empty' or 'full' messages.

Sometimes appetites malfunction, due to an inadequate diet, ill health, or emotional or hormonal factors. The wrong messages may be sent to the body, resulting in a loss of appetite, or conversely, an increase. A brief period of poor appetite is rarely anything to worry about, but if symptoms persist for over a week, a doctor should be consulted.

What affects your appetite?

Illness can diminish your interest in food – something as common as a cold or an upset stomach can put you off for a day or two. More serious disorders such as irritable bowel syndrome (IBS), ulcers, nausea or indigestion can cause discomfort and pain, and this will often affect the desire to eat.

In such cases, light, regular, nutritious meals are preferable to rich, fatty, refined and processed foods, which tax the digestion. Teas made with herbs and spices such as

POTASSIUM *Eat foods with high levels of potassium, such as bananas, potatoes, dried fruit, avocados, nuts, seeds and pulses.*

MAGNESIUM *Foods rich in this mineral, including wholegrains, nuts,* pulses, dried figs and green vegetables can help build a healthy appetite.

VITAMINS B, C *Eat vegetables, fruit, wholegrains, nuts, pulses, meat, poultry, fish, eggs and dairy foods every day to replenish your levels.*

PUMPKIN SEEDS *(left) are a useful vegetarian source of zinc, deficiencies of which are known to reduce the appetite. Lean red meat, crab and other shellfish have high zinc levels, as do sardines, game, poultry, rice, pulses and nuts.*

EAT TO BEAT a poor appetite

peppermint, fennel, cinnamon, camomile and ginger can offer welcome relief. And live natural yoghurt replenishes the intestinal flora of the digestive system.

The emotional factor Stress, anxiety and depression may result in a loss of appetite and erratic eating habits. Just when they need good, nutritious meals to help them deal with stress, people experiencing emotional problems may lose their enthusiasm for food. Eating little and often can help to revive interest.

Stimulants and drugs Cigarettes, coffee and alcohol all suppress appetite. They reduce the sense of taste and smell, give a misleading 'full' message, and may undermine a healthy interest in food. Prescribed drugs can cause appetite loss, especially if they have side effects such as nausea. Stimulants and drugs may also increase your risk of nutritional deficiencies, leading to a repetitive cycle of reduced energy levels and even poorer appetite.

Vitamins and minerals

If your appetite has been low for more than two weeks, boost your intake of foods containing zinc, magnesium and potassium. You also need to eat foods rich in vitamins B and C every day. These vitamins cannot be stored in the body for long and levels need to be regularly replenished (see the box opposite).

Little and often Try to eat five to six small meals – they are less daunting than large ones – based on complex carbohydrates, such as pasta, bread,

MENUPLAN
eat up!

Stimulate your appetite, and boost your energy levels, with these simple ideas.

FOR BREAKFAST Freshly squeezed fruit juice; tomato juice; a banana chopped and blended in cold milk; Banana Muffins (recipe page 86); pancakes or griddle cakes with honey and nuts.

AT LUNCHTIME Lightly grilled chicken or fish with rice or couscous and steamed vegetables; a soft tortilla with tapenade, hummous or guacamole; a wholesome soup (see Hearty Minestrone page 152). Follow with fresh fruit.

IN THE EVENING Crab Cakes with Chilli Dipping Sauce (recipe overleaf) or any dish with prawns, mussels or oysters (see index for recipes); avocado with tuna and mayonnaise; mashed potatoes with roasted fish, meat or poultry and green vegetables; noodles or rice with stir-fried cabbage, carrot, red peppers, baby corn, mushrooms, sprinkled with sesame seeds; Panettone Pudding (recipe overleaf).

SNACK ON fresh or dried fruit, pumpkin and sunflower seeds, nuts, muffins, crumpets, popcorn, pretzels, rice cakes with banana or peanut butter, bagels or waffles.

Spread feather-light rice cakes with peanut butter

*A **staple food** Half the word's population eat rice as their main food. It is grown in water-filled fields or 'paddies'. Its mild flavour and soothing texture make it a valuable food for people who are reluctant to eat, and it is both nutritious and easy to digest.*

potatoes, rice and noodles. If possible, ensure that you have breakfast – even if it's as simple as a smoothie and a piece of fruit such as a banana. This is a good start, supplying the energy you will need to cope with the day ahead.

Although high-fibre foods are a valuable part of your diet, if you haven't been eating heartily for some time, you may find that they cause bloating and trapped wind. Try eating them in smaller amounts until your appetite has improved. You can still obtain easily digested fibre in foods such as mashed potatoes and other root vegetables, vegetable soups, ripe bananas and rice.

What to avoid Fizzy and sugary drinks, tea and coffee all suppress appetite. Instead of drinking large

amounts of alcohol on its own, drink it with a meal and always keep to recommended limits (see page 97). Try to avoid sugary and processed foods, as they lack nutritional value and suppress the appetite.

Other alternatives

Early Chinese physicians prescribed alfalfa leaves to treat many digestive disorders and poor appetite. This practice is also adopted by Ayurvedic practitioners. Alfalfa can be found as sprouted seeds (you can easily sprout your own) or as a herbal supplement.

Colour for stimulation Revive a poor appetite with small amounts of visually appealing, tempting foods. Serve a spoonful of berry fruit with plain yoghurt, for example. See the Menu Plan (previous page) for ideas.

panettone
pudding

This indulgent dessert is just the thing to finish off a meal.

preparation time: **15 minutes, plus 30 minutes soaking**
cooking time: **35 minutes**
serves **4**

275 g (9½ oz) panettone (Italian fruit cake), cut into squares
6 tablespoons chocolate spread
25 g (1 oz) pecan nuts
300 ml (½ pint) skimmed milk
½ teaspoon vanilla extract
1 large egg, beaten
1 tablespoon maple syrup

1 Heat the oven to 200°C (400°F, gas mark 6). Butter a 25 x 20 cm (10 x 8 in) baking dish. Use half the panettone to make a layer in the dish. Add the chocolate spread and sprinkle over the nuts. Top with another panettone layer.

2 Heat the milk and vanilla extract in a saucepan to boiling point. Remove from the heat, whisk in the egg and maple syrup and pour over the cake pressing it flat. Soak for 10 minutes. Bake for 30 minutes, until set.

NUTRIENTS PER SERVING	
calories	550
carbohydrate	65 g
(sugars)	43 g
protein	13 g
fat	27 g
(saturated)	10 g
fibre	1.5 g

crab cakes with chilli dipping sauce

These deliciously light, Thai-inspired cakes are an excellent source of zinc to help to revive the appetite. These tasty morsels can also be served with salsa verde (see page 269).

preparation time: **20 minutes, plus 30 minutes chilling**

cooking time: **25 minutes**

serves **4** (makes 12 cakes)

250 g (9 oz) fresh or canned crab meat
250 g (9 oz) cod steak or fillet, skin and
    bones removed, chopped
2 cloves garlic, chopped
1 medium red chilli, deseeded and chopped
1 stalk lemongrass, peeled and chopped
2 tablespoons finely grated fresh ginger
3 tablespoons chopped fresh coriander, plus
    extra to garnish
1 egg white
Salt and freshly ground black pepper
Sunflower oil, for frying
FOR THE CHILLI DIPPING SAUCE
8 large red chillies, chopped
4 cloves garlic, chopped
2 teaspoons unrefined caster sugar
1 tablespoon rice vinegar
1 tablespoon Thai fish sauce
1 tablespoon olive oil or groundnut oil
1 teaspoon sesame oil
1 tablespoon dark soya sauce
1 small red chilli, chopped, to garnish

1 Place the crab meat, cod, garlic, chilli, lemongrass, ginger, coriander, egg white and seasoning in a blender or food processor and pulse until fairly smooth. Cover and chill for 30 minutes.

2 Make the chilli dipping sauce: put all the ingredients except the soya sauce in a saucepan. Bring to the boil, then cover and simmer for 10–12 minutes. Transfer the mixture to a blender and blend until smooth. Return the sauce to the pan and add the soya sauce. Heat for 2 minutes. Serve hot or cold.

3 Heat a little oil in a heavy-based, non-stick frying pan and place heaped tablespoons of the crab mixture into the pan, flattening with a spatula. Fry for 3-4 minutes on each side, until golden. Cook in batches and keep warm. Serve with fresh coriander, chopped chilli and the chilli sauce.

NUTRIENTS PER CAKE	
calories	91.5
carbohydrate	1 g
(sugars)	0.6 g
protein	8.3 g
fat	6 g
(saturated)	0.6 g
fibre	0

A **healthy** respect for **food**

Food is one of the most powerful forces in life and our attitudes to eating are deep-rooted and complex. From childhood onwards, the influence of our parents, family, friends and images conveyed through the media can affect our eating habits in both positive and negative ways.

When food is a simple, uncomplicated pleasure and is enjoyed as a natural part of being alive, then it provides a solid foundation of good health. But it can also become a fraught emotional issue, bound up with feelings of guilt and anxiety. One of the keys to establishing a healthy relationship with food is to separate it from the arena of the giving and receiving of love and affection. It is this distorted connection that often causes problems.

A HEALTHY START

All parents want to give their child the best nutritional start in life, and most appreciate that good food is essential for growth, development and robust health. But there are frustrating periods when a child simply refuses to eat (see pages 138-139). Foods that are firm favourites one day are rejected the next.

Although fickleness may cause anxiety, children grow and develop at varying rates and have natural fluctuations in appetite. It is perfectly normal for a child to have a ravenous appetite one day, followed by little interest in food the next. When you let children become accustomed to these variations, they can develop a better awareness of when they really feel hungry and when they don't.

Parents need all their resources of patience, calm and humour to guide children towards uncomplicated eating habits and a positive relationship with food. This means avoiding exerting undue pressure to 'clean the plate'.

Children often use food as a way of seeking attention – and refusing to eat may be a direct way of getting a reaction. Punishing or overreacting to such behaviour may only make matters worse. Forcing a child to eat can have a damaging affect on eating habits and it may adversely affect attitudes to food in the future.

Confusing messages

In our pleasure-centred society, hearty meals eaten around the dinner table are viewed as the perfect image of family life. Whether it's a meal at home or a smart dinner party, the message is 'eat-up'. Happiness and love are directly linked with food.

But society also admires a contra-dictory ideal – a slim, lean body with no hint of imperfection. The fashion industry promotes waif-like figures as a desirable image of beauty and success. This is an impossible goal for most people, and sets unrealistic standards for body weight.

Those who are overweight or misguidedly view themselves as being fat, embark on a desperate battle with food. They experiment with diet after diet, experiencing cycles of loss and gain, triumph and failure. The result is low self-esteem and a poor, inaccurate, body image.

Problem triggers Some disturbed eating patterns may be caused by other factors, such as a food intolerance, food allergy or zinc deficiency. For more on intolerance and allergies, turn to pages 124-126. Any unusual reactions to food should be professionally diagnosed. About two per cent of people in the United Kingdom suffer from a food intolerance; but this does not involve the immune system, as it does in a true allergy.

The foods that most commonly trigger reactions are eggs, milk, shellfish such as mussels and oysters, chocolate, wheat, peanuts, soya beans and soya products.

In some cases sufferers will crave the food or foods that are causing the problem. Consequently, they may perpetuate symptoms such as

Living up to the ideal *Eating meals with the family in a happy, relaxed environment is the perfect way to enjoy food – sitting upright at a table also helps your digestive system to work efficiently. But people with eating disorders have lost, or may never have had, this good relationship with food. They need help to restore healthy eating patterns.*

digestive problems, headaches, rashes and hyperactivity. These symptoms improve if the food causing the allergy or intolerance is removed from the diet. If you think you or your child has a food allergy, you should consult your doctor. It is risky to exclude foods without medical supervision, as this may lead to nutritional deficiencies. Something as simple as a zinc deficiency can

lead to diminished appetite and contribute to poor eating patterns. For more on loss of appetite, turn to pages 228-231.

An irresistible force

A food craving is much more extreme than having a favourite food, or buying a treat on impulse. It is more of an overwhelming and unquestioning desire for a certain

food. People who suffer from such cravings are unable to resist the particular food they want, and are willing to go to extraordinary lengths to satisfy their need.

Some people believe that craving is a response to some kind of nutritional deficiency. But there is little scientific evidence to support this, especially as the typical craving is for high-sugar, high-calorie foods,

such as chocolate, cakes, sweets, fried foods and crisps, rather than fresh fruit and vegetables. There are a number of theories about why we crave foods that do not benefit us nutritionally.

Getting comfort from food

High-sugar and high-fat foods are often chosen during times of anxiety, stress or depression – they become an emotional crutch or a love substitute. Sugary foods such as sweets, cakes and biscuits can make us feel good by releasing insulin and by boosting serotonin levels in the brain (see page 245).

Highs and lows The refined sugar found in sweet foods rarely satisfies a craving for long. Also, this type of sugar may upset the delicate balance of blood sugar in the brain. Consequently, the enhanced mood experienced after eating a sugary food is often followed by a marked low, and a craving for more sweets.

Chocolate also gives a rush of satisfaction. It contains caffeine, a well-known stimulant and lifts both serotonin and endorphin levels. The 'high' induced (see pages 220-221) is caused by the response of the natural brain chemical phenylethylamine.

A deep-rooted explanation People may find sweets and chocolates comforting and soothing because they associate them with childhood treats for good behaviour.

Complete satisfaction These sweet potato chips are a justifiable indulgence. Dipped in garlic mayonnaise, they make a great 'comfort food'. And they're healthy, too. Sweet potatoes are rich in fibre, antioxidant vitamin C and beta carotene. The recipe is on page 241.

Another theory is based on human evolution. This suggests that we have always craved foods that are sweet and fatty in order to obtain nutrients for energy and brain development.

Until comparatively recently in our evolution, these have been more readily available in a healthy form, such as meat and fruits. But this inbuilt desire for fat and sugar has now been overridden by an insatiable appetite for processed foods.

This line of thinking is supported by recent research which suggests that a lack of essential fatty acids, found in high levels in foods such as oily fish, seeds, sunflower oil, walnuts and soya beans, may result in food cravings.

Women are more vulnerable to food cravings than men, especially during pregnancy and before menstruation. This has been attributed to fluctuating hormones as well as to low blood sugar levels.

Learning to cope

When a strong food craving persists there are a few self-help techniques that you can try. However, if the condition stays out of control, it may be necessary to seek medical advice.
• Don't completely deny yourself the food you crave, as this may lead to bingeing; instead, allow yourself a little of what you desire. If chocolate is the focus of your compulsion, buy a good quality brand that is high in cocoa solids, rather than a cheaper, sugar-laden alternative.
• If you crave sugary or high-fat foods, look for healthier alternatives. Choose snacks such as fresh and dried fruit, low-sugar cereal bars,

The strength to resist When you are assailed by cravings for sweet foods, choose a healthier alternative. Have a banana instead of a cream cake, and buy a packet of mixed nuts rather than sweets.

natural popcorn and unsalted pretzels. These should keep your blood sugar levels on an even keel.
• Don't allow yourself to go hungry – you may become obsessed with thinking about food and may lose the will-power to fight the craving. Instead, choose satisfying, filling carbohydrate foods, such as pasta, potatoes, noodles and rice to keep hunger at bay.
• Eat small, regular meals to help fight off hunger and craving.
• Snacking is not a sin: as long as you choose healthy foods (see above) you can enjoy your favourite snacks and keep yourself going this way.
• Because people who eat a balanced and varied diet are less likely to experience food cravings, it makes sense to extend the range of foods that you eat, rather than become

stuck in a limited pattern of choice.
• Divert your mind from thinking about food by exercising regularly. The simplest activity is walking: it boosts endorphins, natural brain chemicals that make you feel uplifted, relaxed and refreshed.
• Try to avoid stimulants such as tea, coffee and cigarettes. These may upset your blood sugar levels and consequently increase your cravings for sweet foods.

EATING DISORDERS

Eating disorders are difficult to understand without some personal experience of them. They are far more serious than irregular eating habits such as food cravings. The disorder is often an indication of a complex psychological problem. People with eating disorders are

a positive attitude

Be an inspiring role model Even though you are often tired and under stress, it is worth while trying to set a good example to your children and grandchildren. This means choosing a healthy, varied diet and sharing mealtimes as much as possible. Recent findings show that families with obese children rarely eat together or discuss food.

Base meals on rice, potatoes, noodles or pasta with lean meat, poultry, fish, soya, nuts and pulses. If a child dislikes vegetables, be inventive and experiment with serving them in a variety of guises – you never know when you may hit on a winner.

Encourage children to snack on fresh, dried and preserved fruit rather than high-fat and high-sugar cakes, biscuits and sweets. This does not mean these foods should be completely avoided (this is an unrealistic aim) but eaten in moderation.

Make cooking good fun Include children in cooking and preparing meals – this encourages a healthy interest in food, and they may feel more inclined to eat meals they have helped to prepare.

Don't use food as bribes It is not a good idea to give sweets as a form of reward or approval – this establishes the subconscious connection between sweet food and affection. This can also lead to cravings for sweet foods which may continue into adulthood.

Experiment with new and different ingredients Visually attractive, colourful and tasty food is appealing to children (and everyone else). Opt for a varied range of foods, textures and aromas to stimulate the taste-buds.

often reluctant to seek help and become expert at disguising their condition. Obvious signs may be a preoccupation with food, extreme weight loss, constipation, vomiting, extreme fatigue, muscle weakness, obesity and dental problems.

If you, or a member of your family, displays one or more of these symptoms of an eating disorder, you should seek professional help and advice as soon as possible. An early diagnosis is a vital factor in enabling successful treatment.

Anorexia nervosa, bulimia nervosa and compulsive eating are the three main categories of eating disorder. But it is not easy to pigeon-hole people into one of these groups, as

they may display a number of different symptoms. The following pointers describe the general characteristics of each of these conditions.

Anorexia nervosa

This condition mainly affects teenage girls and young women – it is currently estimated that between one and two per cent of schoolgirls and female university students in the United Kingdom are affected.

Teenage boys and young men account for about ten per cent of all cases of anorexia, but among schoolboys, the numbers may be as high as 25 per cent. People who have to maintain stringent weight limits for professional reasons are

among those at particular risk: these include jockeys, athletes, ballet dancers and fashion models.

It is now thought that the condition may be due to a specific mixture of genetic and social factors, including extreme stress. A genetic malfunction of the appestat, the body's appetite regulator, may be one possible cause. Or the gene involved in the action of the 'feel-good' chemical serotonin, produced in the brain, may make some people more susceptible.

The warning signs Anorexics tend to be perfectionists who often lack self esteem. They are unhealthily preoccupied with food, calories and weight loss, and have an intense fear

of weight gain. They literally starve themselves over a period of time, sometimes to the point of death. There may be periodic self-induced vomiting or the misuse of laxatives or diuretics.

Inaccurate body image

Anorexics equate being slim with being beautiful and desirable; they perceive themselves as being overweight even when they are dangerously thin. They become emaciated, but are unable to appreciate this because they have a distorted picture of their body. Many deny their hunger, and are convinced that they are full after eating a tiny amount of food.

Such prolonged food deprivation leads to malnutrition which affects brain functioning (memory and concentration) and also causes depression. Other effects include hormonal changes, particularly irregular or loss of menstruation, loss of bone density due to a lack of calcium, impaired functioning of the immune system, anaemia, and the growth of fine body hair (the body's attempt to keep warm).

Treatment combines psychological counselling and drug therapy, and may involve a stay in hospital. Dietitians can develop a tailor-made eating programme to help encourage a return to normal eating.

Bulimia nervosa

It is estimated that bulimia will affect 3 out of every 100 women in the United Kingdom at some time in their lives. As with anorexia, boys and young men account for between 10 and 25 per cent of cases. The psychological causes are much the same as in anorexia, but sufferers use

bingeing to compensate for feelings of depression, loneliness and helplessness. Bulimics alternately starve themselves and then secretly gorge on vast amounts of food. They then purge themselves through self-induced vomiting, laxatives or diuretics. This cyclical pattern of behaviour is believed to be more common than anorexia. Purging is a way of regaining control but is also a source of shame and self-disgust. The secretive nature of bulimia

makes the condition extremely difficult to detect, especially when the sufferer maintains a normal weight. It is not unusual for bulimics to maintain an outwardly regular lifestyle and career, but the physical signs do not take long to appear. Habitual vomiting erodes tooth enamel because of the stomach acid, which also causes sore throats.

Fluctuations in weight and digestive disorders are common and depression, anxiety, malnutrition and

Restoring a sense of peace Extreme problems with food such as anorexia nervosa, bulimia and compulsive eating involve both mind and body. The calming effects of techniques such as meditation can help to shift the emphasis from gaining control by means of food to building mental strength through relaxation.

MENUPLAN
establishing good eating habits

Boost your energy levels with small, regular meals based on complex carbohydrates, low-fat protein and plenty of fruit and vegetables. Pasta, potatoes or rice all help to produce cortisol, a hormone which helps to calm you down.

FOR BREAKFAST try the Layered Raspberry and Oat Crunch (recipe overleaf); a wholegrain cereal or porridge; banana fruit smoothie; or wholemeal toast with a high-fruit, low-sugar jam, or with peanut butter or yeast extract.

MID MORNING SNACK on dried or fresh fruit; muffins; crumpets; or a handful of nuts and raisins.

AT LUNCHTIME eat a low-fat, high-protein meal, such as light tofu soup; a wholemeal bread sandwich of tuna, cottage or cream cheese with smoked salmon, slices of turkey with Emmental; or a large mixed salad, sprinkled with toasted sunflower seeds and topped with a poached egg.

IN THE EVENING choose a dish based on complex carbohydrates such as Sweet Potato Chips (recipe overleaf) with garlic mayonnaise, served with grilled chicken or fish; Roasted Red Pepper and Prawn Fajitas (recipe overleaf) with green salad; or a mixed vegetable and black bean stir-fry with rice or soba (buckwheat) noodles.

DURING THE DAY cut-down or avoid coffee, tea, and fizzy drinks. Drink water, herb teas, fruit juices.

SNACK ON fresh or dried fruit; nuts, particularly walnuts; rice cakes, muffins or crumpets topped with peanut butter or yeast extract or mashed banana; mixed seeds, or crudités and hummous.

Chicken soup
Pour 300 ml (½ pint) of chicken stock into a pan, add thin strips of carrots, spring onions (or other vegetables) strips of cooked chicken and some small pasta shapes. Simmer for 5-7 minutes. Serves 2.

Light and nourishing, this chicken soup is made in minutes.

NUTRIENTS PER SERVING: Calories **100** Carbohydrate 52 **g** (sugars **1 g**)
Protein **4.5 g** Fat **3.5 g** (saturated **0.3 g**) Fibre **0.5 g**

Subtle strategies *For people recovering from severe eating problems such as anorexia or bulimia, small portions of a familiar food such as breakfast cereal are less daunting than three large meals a day.*

Emergency supplies *Snacks of sunflower seeds and almonds are a simple way of combating the compulsion of food cravings. They're crunchy, delicious and will help to keep your blood sugar on an even keel.*

fatigue are other signs. Bulimics do not consume food for its nutritional value. Typically, cakes, biscuits, crisps, chocolate and sweets are chosen in preference to healthy foods. Counsellors and dietitians can provide practical advice on how to restore healthy eating patterns and how to introduce a wider variety of foods into the diet.

Helpful strategies Bulimics are encouraged to eat little and often, throughout the day and to base their meals on complex carbohydrates such as rice, pasta and potatoes, low-fat protein and fresh fruit and vegetables. This enables them to

maintain a regular weight without resorting to bingeing and purging. As with anorexia, seeking professional help as soon as possible is a crucial factor in a successful recovery.

Compulsive eating

Binge eaters regularly eat much more than necessary, but they rarely purge or restrict their diets. Consequently, people with this condition (known as compulsive eating disorder) tend to be very overweight.

Around 15 per cent of men and women in the United Kingdom are obese, and about a third of obese people regularly binge on food. It is

now thought that compulsive eating affects considerably more people than anorexia and bulimia. In some cases, bouts of over-eating may be interspersed with dieting.

The condition is usually a result of a psychological problem such as a response to a trauma, rather than simply being a way of satisfying an uncontrollable hunger. As well as the danger to health from being seriously overweight, the mental effects can also be severe. These include guilt, depression, shame and feeling out of control. Compulsive eaters benefit from counselling, and an eating programme to stabilise weight gain.

roasted **red pepper** and **prawn** fajitas

Spicy, marinated prawns and slices of smoky red pepper, encased in a soft, floury tortilla make an ideal dish to tempt a reluctant appetite. They look and smell delicious, are easy to make and provide valuable nutrients

preparation time: **15 minutes, plus 30 minutes marinating**
cooking time: **30 minutes**
serves **4**

NUTRIENTS PER SERVING	
calories	300
carbohydrate	36 g
(sugars)	12 g
protein	19 g
fat	10 g
(saturated)	3 g
fibre	4 g

20 raw tiger prawns, peeled and de-veined, tails removed
2 red peppers, deseeded and quartered
1 yellow pepper, deseeded and quartered
200 g (7 oz) canned chopped tomatoes
½ teaspoon sugar
FOR THE MARINADE
1 teaspoon ground chilli powder
1 teaspoon ground cumin
juice of 2 limes
2 cloves garlic, crushed
2 tablespoon olive oil
3 tablespoons fresh coriander, chopped
Salt and black pepper
TO SERVE
4-8 warm flour tortillas (depending on their size), shredded baby leaf spinach, sour cream and fresh coriander leaves

1 Mix together the ingredients for the marinade and add the prawns. Stir well

to coat the prawns in the marinade. Cover and refrigerate for 30 minutes.

2 Place the peppers under a hot grill for about 15 minutes, or until the skin is black. Put them in a plastic bag, and allow to cool for 10 minutes. Remove the skin from the peppers and blot dry with kitchen paper. Keep warm and set them aside.

3 Remove the prawns from the marinade, then heat the marinade in a large, heavy-based frying pan. Add the tomatoes and sugar and cook for 8-10 minutes over a medium heat, until reduced and thickened. Add the prawns and cook for 2-3 minutes, until pink and cooked through.

4 To serve, fold the mixture into the warm tortillas with the spinach. Top with a sour cream and sprinkle with coriander.

sweet **potato chips** with garlic **mayonnaise**

Sweet potatoes make scrumptious chips and are a welcome alternative to ordinary potatoes. Serve them with garlic mayonnaise or chilli dipping sauce (recipe page 231).

preparation time: **10 minutes**

cooking time: **35 minutes**

serves **4**

Olive oil, for greasing
500 g (1 lb 2 oz) sweet potatoes, peeled and sliced into wedges
5 cloves garlic, unpeeled, the skin of each pierced with the tip of a sharp knife
Sea salt and freshly ground black pepper
6 tablespoons low-fat mayonnaise
Paprika, to garnish

1 Preheat the oven to 200°C (400°F, gas mark 6). Brush a roasting dish lightly with oil. Carefully arrange the potatoes and garlic in the dish. Season to taste.

2 Bake for 30-35 minutes, turning the chips occasionally, until tender and golden.

3 To make the garlic mayonnaise, carefully squeeze the cooked garlic flesh out of each clove (it will be very hot), then mash with the back of a fork or chop with a knife. Mix the garlic into the mayonnaise until combined. Sprinkle the top of the mayonnaise with paprika and serve with the sweet potato chips.

NUTRIENTS PER SERVING	
calories	200
carbohydrate	28 g
(sugars)	8 g
protein	2 g
fat	9 g
(saturated)	0.5 g
fibre	3 g

layered raspberry and **oat** crunch

This breakfast couldn't be more simple, but it looks pretty and appetising, as the raspberries give a luscious swirl of colour, and the oats lend a pleasant crunch.

preparation time: **5 minutes**, **plus 10 minutes standing**

cooking time: **3 minutes**

serves **4**

4 tablespoons clear honey
Finely grated zest of 1 small orange (optional)
500 g (1 lb 2 oz) thick natural yoghurt
225 g (8 oz) fresh or frozen, defrosted raspberries, plus extra to decorate
70 g (2½ oz) porridge oats

1 Mix half of the honey and the orange zest into the yoghurt. Gently stir in the raspberries – do not over-mix. Leave for 10 minutes to allow the raspberries to release their juices, then stir again (the raspberries will give a swirl of colour).

2 Put the oats in a dry frying pan and toast them for a minute. Add the remaining honey and stir to coat the oats. Cook for 2 minutes over a medium heat, stirring, until the oats turn golden and slightly crisp.

3 To serve, spoon a layer of the oat mixture into the bottom of four glasses, then top with the raspberry yoghurt. Sprinkle with another layer of the oats and decorate the top with the extra raspberries.

NUTRIENTS PER SERVING	
calories	180
carbohydrate	31 g
(sugars)	31 g
protein	8 g
fat	4 g
(saturated)	2 g
fibre	1 g

Getting a **good night's** sleep

Insomnia is a frustrating affliction that stalks you at night and leaves you feeling ragged, tired and irritable during the day. The cause can be both physical and emotional. But there is also now evidence that what you eat and drink plays a role in affecting your ability to sleep.

Most people have suffered from sleeplessness at some time in their lives. It can last a few nights or much longer, and may be triggered by a number of factors, including anxiety, chronic pain, depression, pregnancy, stress or the menopause. If you suspect these or any other medical cause for your sleeplessness, you should consult your doctor without delay.

WHY SLEEP MATTERS

Good sleep is critical to both your emotional and physical well being. It is essential for the production of growth hormones – these enable the body to manufacture proteins for growth and cell repair. Sleep also has a direct impact on your mood. Poor-quality or insufficient sleep can lead to extreme fatigue, irritability and even mental instability, while a good night's rest makes you feel rejuvenated and relaxed.

Up to a third of adults in the United Kingdom suffer from some form of insomnia, and as many as half say they are dissatisfied with the quality of their sleep. Your body's needs change with age and you generally require less sleep as you become older. Insomnia manifests

itself in a number of patterns: it may include difficulties in getting to sleep; problems with maintaining sleep, resulting in disrupted sleep and periods of wakefulness; and early morning waking.

What causes insomnia?

Anxiety, depression and stress are believed to be responsible for about 50 per cent of the cases of insomnia evaluated in clinical studies. It is important to consult a doctor if any of these is keeping you awake. But

there are several other factors that may affect how well you sleep. **What food do you eat?** If you cannot pinpoint a specific reason for your inability to sleep, look at your eating habits, since nutrition plays an important role in establishing good sleeping patterns.

As a first step, try keeping a food and drink diary. This will help you to examine the context of your sleeping problems and may also indicate what you are doing right when you do get a good night's

HEALTH OR HYPE?
sleep supplement

When the news emerged in the USA that the amino acid tryptophan plays a crucial part in promoting good sleep, it was immediately hailed as a magic cure for insomnia. Tryptophan appeared on the shelves of health food shops as a 'natural' food supplement; however, some people were found to be taking mega-doses of up to 3000 mg every night – with severe, even deadly, consequences for some. Consequently, the US Food and Drug Administration recalled all products containing tryptophan. Nutritionists emphasise that we can obtain all the amino acids (including tryptophan) we need from small amounts of animal foods such as eggs, milk and meat, and a wide mix of vegetables.

sleep. As a result, you can go on to incorporate the positive elements into your pattern of eating and drinking and remove anything that seems to upset your normal sleep rhythm. It may help to ask yourself the following questions:

How much caffeine? Coffee, tea, cola drinks and chocolate all contain caffeine which can lead to insomnia. It is best to avoid them at night and possibly from about mid afternoon. But cut down gradually because sudden caffeine withdrawal can also cause sleeplessness.

Do you drink alcohol? Although a drink or two with dinner, or a small nightcap, can help to induce sleep, too much may make you wake early in the morning or during the night.

Do you have a sweet tooth? Sugary foods such as chocolate biscuits, cakes and sweets are best avoided just before bedtime as they cause a surge in blood glucose at a time when the body is preparing to rest. Sleep is disturbed as the body concentrates on stabilising its blood sugar levels. Children are particularly sensitive to variations in blood sugar.

Do you eat a late dinner? The digestive system does not work as well at night as it does during the day, so eating a large meal just before bedtime will tax your body and can make it more difficult to fall asleep

Beating your insomnia *You can combine a mix of strategies to combat insomnia. Try eating more foods that are rich in sleep-inducing tryptophan. These include vegetables such as fennel, broccoli and cauliflower, good alternatives if you do not eat meat. Many people find that keeping a diary helps them to keep track of their sleeping and eating patterns.*

Sweet dreams *Eaten after your evening meal, this Buttered Brioche and Apricot pudding will help to ease you into a sound sleep. It is high in carbohydrate but also provides a small amount of low-fat protein, the perfect combination to promote better sleep. The recipe is on page 249.*

or to stay asleep for more than a few hours. For this reason, it is important to eat dinner at least three hours before bedtime. Eating spicy or rich foods at night can prompt digestive problems or heartburn, which may then interfere with sleep.

Slimming on a very low-calorie diet, which leaves you feeling hungry, may also cause you to wake during the night. The brain is stimulated when blood-sugar levels fall below a certain level, and sends signals that it is time to eat. A light carbohydrate snack such as a banana sandwich, wholemeal muffin, flapjack, fresh or dried fruit or a glass of warm milk with a spoon of

honey, eaten before bedtime will help to sustain blood sugar levels and fight off disturbing hunger pangs throughout the night.

Snoring can disrupt your sleep (as well as that of others). You are more likely to snore if you are overweight, or if you have been drinking.
Look at your lifestyle Long working hours and a hectic social life, with little time given to winding down and relaxation, inevitably encourages sleep problems. 'Burning the candle at both ends' leads to exhaustion and eventual burn-out.

Hormonal changes in women such as pregnancy and menstruation, may interfere with normal sleep

patterns. The contraceptive pill and hormone replacement therapy both increase a woman's requirement for vitamin B_6 – and a deficiency of this vitamin has also been linked with insomnia (see below).

Sleep-inducing foods

The foods that you eat in the evening can have a dramatic influence on your sleeping patterns. Those that contain the amino acid tryptophan are particularly significant. Amino acids are the building blocks of proteins and tryptophan is found in all protein foods, especially turkey, chicken, game, cauliflower, broccoli, milk, cheese, lean meat, eggs and

soya beans. Tryptophan is converted in the brain into a neurotransmitter called serotonin. This, in turn plays a vital role in promoting sleep. The time it takes to fall asleep can be reduced by as much as 50 per cent if your serotonin levels are high just before you go to sleep; also, serotonin helps you sleep longer and more soundly.

Clearing the way The production of serotonin relies upon how efficiently tryptophan is delivered to the brain, however. The tryptophan we receive from high-protein foods may not reach the brain at peak levels because other amino acids in the same foods are also competing to get in at the same time.

If carbohydrate foods such as bread or pasta are eaten at the same time as protein foods, the insulin from the carbohydrate drives these competing amino acids into body

cells, leaving a clear passage for the tryptophan to enter the brain cells and raise serotonin levels.

The reason why a milky drink at night helps you to get to sleep is because the natural sugars in the milk (lactose) and the tryptophan in the milk protein helps to convert the tryptophan to serotonin.

Cheese is one of the foods that are frequently mentioned as causing insomnia. It is rich in tryptophan, but may well keep you awake if you eat it on its own. The tryptophan in the cheese not only fails to reach the brain, but the body's energy is diverted into digesting the high protein it contains.

A natural sedative A meal based on carbohydrate foods, such as pasta, potatoes, rice, noodles, bread and fruit, with a very small amount of protein in the form of fish, poultry, lean meat or pulses, can be the

perfect remedy. On the other hand, a low-carbohydrate, high-protein meal, for example, meat, chicken or fish eaten with salad only, may have the opposite effect, and keep you awake.

Drinks for sweet dreams Choose decaffeinated coffee or substitutes based on roasted grains or dandelion. Also, try herbal teas and infusions as a calming alternative to caffeine-laden drinks. Camomile, peppermint, lemon balm and valerian are particularly effective. Honey also acts as a mild sedative and can be added to warm milk or herbal tea as a bedtime drink.

Check the vitamins Is the food you eat low in B vitamins, particularly B_6, B_{12} and niacin? If so, you may find that this is linked with insomnia, especially when you are also under stress. B vitamins play an important role in regulating the production of serotonin. Wholegrains, seafood,

1 *Make a camomile infusion: place a few spoons of the dried herb into a small jug. Pour on* 150 ml (¼ pint) *of boiling water. Steep for a few minutes, then leave to cool slightly. Strain the infusion into a cup and drink before bedtime.*

2 *Valerian is a classic herbal remedy for insomnia. Available in capsule and tablet form, it is taken at bedtime.*

3 *A limeflower or passionflower infusion helps to calm you before sleep (avoid passionflower if you are pregnant).*

4 *Sleep on a pillow stuffed with hops, or make a hop infusion.*

5 *Lavender oil has a known sedative effect. Add it to a bath, use it with massage oil, or dab a little on a tissue, tuck it inside your pillow and inhale the scent during the night.*

6 *Melatonin, a natural brain chemical, may help. It is available in Britain on prescription only.*

CAMOMILE TEA *The dried, daisy-like flowers of camomile are renowned for their sleep-inducing properties. Camomile tea is safe to take during pregnancy (as is lime flower) – normally, herbal teas should be avoided when you are pregnant.*

SIX WAYS TO induce natural sleep

MENUPLAN
for better sleep

What and when you eat may influence the way you sleep. Try these tips to help you to beat insomnia, and promote deep, restful sleep.

FOR BREAKFAST A fruit smoothie (recipe below); poached egg on a toasted muffin; wholemeal toast with peanut butter, high-fruit jam or yeast extract; or fruit compôte (recipe page 79) with natural yoghurt sprinkled with wheatgerm; wholegrain cereals.

LUNCH Sandwiches with a lean meat, turkey, chicken or fish filling; steamed cauliflower with a low-fat cheese sauce; omelette with a green salad.

IN THE EVENING Warm Turkey Salad with Avocado and Lime Dressing (recipe overleaf) is rich in tryptophan. Follow with a high-carbohydrate dessert such as Buttered Brioche and Apricot Pudding (recipe overleaf). Avoid eating rich or spicy meals late at night.

THROUGHOUT THE DAY Drink about eight glasses of liquid to maintain a healthy fluid balance. Between meals, try fresh or dried fruit, a handful of nuts, or a fruit smoothie. Avoid caffeine drinks from mid afternoon.

BEFORE BED Have a light snack such as a banana, or honey sandwich, made with wholemeal bread, a crumpet or muffin or a plain biscuit with a cup of camomile, valerian or lemon balm tea or warm milk.

Fruit Smoothie

Blend together 2 tablespoons of blueberries, raspberries or strawberries, 1 banana, roughly chopped, 150 ml (¼ pint) milk and 1 tablespoon of clear honey for one glass.

NUTRIENTS PER GLASS Calories **270** Carbohydrate **48 g** (sugars **46 g**) Protein **6 g** Fat **6 g** (saturated **4 g**) Fibre **3 g**

liver, eggs, poultry, nuts, beans, lentils, dairy foods, bananas, yeast extract and soya beans are good sources of B vitamins.

A deficiency in magnesium has also been linked with insomnia. Symptoms include nightmares, talking in the sleep and restlessness. Soya beans, wholegrains, nuts, dried fruits, green leafy vegetables and meat are rich in magnesium.

High-strength multivitamin supplements can have a mildly stimulating effect on the body. You should take them in the morning just after breakfast and avoid taking them at night when they may contribute to wakefulness.

Dig deep and sleep well A few hours gardening in the early evening works wonders if you have insomnia. The exercise leaves you satisfyingly tired, and also releases calming endorphins, which help you to unwind and relax, ready for sleep.

Prescription sleeping pills tend to alter natural sleep patterns – so they are best avoided in the long-term. Also, some sleeping pills have side effects: you may become reliant on the drug, experience disrupted sleep and wake up still feeling tired. If you take sleeping pills and wish to stop, it is advisable to seek the advice of your doctor beforehand.

More tips for better sleep

Once you've reassured yourself that you are eating the right foods to help you to sleep well, there are other strategies that can make it easier to relax and drift off:

• Make sure your bedroom is comfortable and conducive to sleep. It should be adequately ventilated and not too hot – sleep quality is reduced above 75°F (24°C). The curtains should be heavy enough to keep the room dark.

• A firm mattress, slim pillow and covers made of natural fabrics are best for sleep.

• Get into a routine of going to bed and getting up at the same time.

• Avoid watching television or listening to the radio in bed.

• Unwind before you go to bed

by soaking in a warm bath with a few drops of lavender, frankincense, basil or clary sage oil. A sprinkling of any one of these aromatherapy oils on the pillow or sheets may also make you pleasantly sleepy.

• Regular exercise, especially if it's in the fresh air, promotes good-quality sleep – a brisk walk for 20 minutes a day could help greatly. It is more effective to exercise in the afternoon or early evening because exercising too late may over-stimulate you.

• If you find it difficult to get to sleep, don't toss and turn or become obsessed with trying to doze off. Instead get up for a while, have a light snack such as toast spread lightly with honey. Read for a while or listen to soothing music.

• Complementary therapies, such as massage and acupuncture relax your body and are therefore very good sleep tonics.

• Meditation is believed to be an even better form of relaxation than sleep.

• Finally, a fish tank may be just what you need to help you get to sleep. It is claimed that fish owners are half as likely to suffer from insomnia.

Some people suffer from involuntary movements in the legs when lying in bed at night and this may interfere with sleep. High doses of folic acid (35–60 milligrams daily) have been found helpful. You can also find it in foods such as broccoli, green leafy vegetables, pulses, wheatgerm, fortified breakfast cereals and bread. **How iron can help** It is now thought that people with this condition are prone to iron deficiency, and a boost in foods rich in iron is recommended. Eat red meat, egg yolk, liver, red kidney beans, chickpeas, wholegrains, fortified breakfast cereals, nuts, pulses and green leafy vegetables.

A taste of honey is not only sweet – it can help soothe you to sleep. A teaspoon stirred into a cup of warm milk is just enough to keep your blood sugar in balance throughout the night.

warm turkey salad with avocado and lime dressing

This quick, easy salad makes a nourishing lunch or light supper dish. It is a good choice if you suffer from insomnia – being a good source of serotonin, it is soothing and will help you to sleep. Turkey is good for slimmers, too, as it is very low in fat.

preparation time: **10–15 minutes**

cooking time: **10–15 minutes**

serves **4**

NUTRIENTS PER SERVING	
calories	290
carbohydrate	10 g
(sugars)	8.5 g
protein	24 g
fat	18 g
(saturated)	4.5 g
fibre	3 g

2 tablespoons olive oil

350 g (12 oz) turkey escalopes, cut into thin strips

1 medium onion, finely sliced

1 teaspoon grated lime zest

2 Little Gem lettuces

175 g (6 oz) cherry tomatoes, halved

1 small yellow pepper, deseeded and cut into strips

Salt and black pepper

Coriander leaves, to garnish

FOR THE DRESSING

1 ripe avocado

150 ml (¼ pint) fromage frais

Juice of 1 lime

2 tablespoons chopped coriander

A dash of Tabasco or chilli sauce, to taste

1 Heat the oil in a large frying pan or wok. Add the turkey and onion. Stir-fry for 10 minutes until the turkey is golden brown and tender, and the onions soft.

2 Sprinkle on the lime zest. Season with black pepper and a little salt.

3 Make the dressing. Place all the ingredients in a blender or food processor and purée until smooth. Season to taste.

4 Arrange the outer leaves of the lettuce on four plates. Scatter on the halved tomatoes and yellow pepper strips. Arrange some of the warm turkey and onions in the centre of each plate and spoon over some avocado dressing. Sprinkle with coriander leaves.

5 Serve with plenty of fresh crusty granary or wholemeal bread.

buttered **brioche** and **apricot pudding**

In this recipe, traditional bread and butter pudding becomes a luxury dessert with milk, fruit and brioche. This is a delicious after-dinner treat – eat it a couple of hours before going to bed to benefit from its calming, sleep-inducing effects.

preparation time: **10–15 minutes**

cooking time: **40–45 minutes**

serves **6**

Sunflower oil, for greasing
300 ml (½ pint) milk
200 ml (7 fl oz) double cream
5 cm (2 in) cinnamon stick
3 large eggs, beaten
115 g (4 oz) caster sugar
3 soft brioche rolls
55 g (2 oz) unsalted butter
115 g (4 oz) ready-to-eat dried apricots,
   cut into quarters
Pinch of ground cinnamon or freshly grated
   nutmeg
2 tablespoons apricot jam

1 Heat the oven to 180°C (350°F, gas mark 4). Lightly oil a 1 litre (2 pint) oblong baking dish.

2 In a small saucepan bring the milk, cream and cinnamon stick to the boil, then remove from the heat. Remove the cinnamon stick. Whisk the milk into the beaten eggs, then stir in the sugar.

3 Cut the brioche rolls into thin slices, butter them on one side and arrange, buttered side up, in the dish. Scatter the apricot pieces over the top. Strain on the egg and milk mixture. Sprinkle with ground cinnamon or nutmeg.

4 Bake for 30–35 minutes or until lightly set. If it browns too quickly, cover with foil for the last part of the cooking. Warm the jam in a small pan and brush the surface. Serve hot.

NUTRIENTS PER SERVING	
calories	**500**
carbohydrate	**47 g**
(sugars)	**39 g**
protein	**9 g**
fat	**32 g**
(saturated)	**19 g**
fibre	**1.5 g**

grilled **asparagus** with **tagliatelle**

Fresh asparagus tips are available in the summer months; buy some and make this simple pasta dish. Served with a mixed salad and crusty bread, it is perfect for lunch or a light supper.

preparation time: **10 minutes**

cooking time: **30-35 minutes**

serves **4**

50 ml (2 fl oz) olive oil
1 clove garlic, crushed
75 ml (2½ fl oz) white wine
85 ml (3 fl oz) canned chopped tomatoes
½ teaspoon dried oregano
6 fresh basil leaves, torn
150 g (5½ oz) asparagus tips
300 g (10½ oz) egg tagliatelle
Salt and black pepper
Freshly grated Parmesan, to serve

1 Heat the oil in a large, heavy-based frying pan, reserving 1 tablespoon. Add the garlic and cook for 1 minute. Pour in the wine and bring to the boil. Cook for a few minutes, until reduced by two-thirds. Reduce the heat, add the tomatoes and oregano, and simmer for 5 minutes. Add the basil and cook for a further 5 minutes, stirring frequently.

2 Brush the asparagus with the rest of the oil. Grill for 6–8 minutes, until tender.

3 Cook the pasta in a large pan of boiling, salted water, according to the packet instructions. Drain and stir the tomato sauce and asparagus into pasta. Season, and scatter with Parmesan to serve.

NUTRIENTS PER SERVING	
calories	**370**
carbohydrate	**59 g**
(sugars)	**3.5 g**
protein	**10 g**
fat	**11 g**
(saturated)	**2 g**
fibre	**3 g**

Restoring lost energy

There is really only one way to recover when you are really tired out: get lots of sleep, and take it easy when you are awake. But when fatigue invades every part of your life you need extra help, especially from the foods that work to revitalise your energy stores.

Most people experience bouts of tiredness, which can usually be attributed to lack of sleep, stress, depression or even something as simple as boredom. Persistent, overwhelming exhaustion is a very different matter. If you have been suffering from this kind of fatigue for several weeks, months or even longer, you may be suffering from chronic fatigue or 'tired all the time' (TATT) syndrome.

TATT syndrome is a general term for groups of symptoms caused by a range of factors. People with illnesses such as post-viral fatigue syndrome or myalgic encephalomyelitis (ME), glandular fever, thyroid disorders (see page 104) and diabetes (see page 102) frequently complain of unusually high levels of tiredness. Extreme fatigue may also be a consequence of food allergies and nutritional deficiencies.

If you suspect that you have chronic fatigue, you should consult a doctor for an accurate diagnosis.

IDENTIFYING THE CAUSE

Several viral conditions, infections, or even a vaccination injection, may trigger chronic fatigue. The root cause can be complex. For example, a gastrointestinal infection caused by an echovirus has been strongly linked to ME.

Symptoms of chronic fatigue include severe muscle weakness and pain during exercise, tiredness and lethargy, flu-like symptoms, mood swings, depression, poor digestion, memory and concentration.

Glandular fever is another viral illness that often precedes ME. It has similar symptoms but sufferers also have a sore throat and painful swollen glands in the neck, and the symptoms go away much sooner.

Other causes If your fatigue does not stem from a viral infection, it may be due to a nutrient deficiency or a food allergy (see pages 124-127). Both problems can be helped by adjusting your diet.

Whatever the cause, eating the right foods can be of immense help in your recovery. Many doctors

Energy from wholegrains *Choose the right nutrients and you can re-energise muscles made weak and sluggish by chronic fatigue. Wholegrain fruit bread can really help because it contains iron, magnesium, B vitamins, and complex carbohydrates, as well as fibre.*

KIDNEYS, steamed pak choi, and griddled peppers make the perfect combination for an iron-rich meal. Drink orange juice to help the body absorb the iron efficiently.

1 *Meat and fish contain good amounts of iron, so have servings of these foods regularly.*

2 *Alcohol in moderation stimulates iron absorption – a good reason for having a glass of wine with a meal.*

3 *Avoid tea, coffee and milk at mealtimes, since all three contain substances which inhibit the body's ability to absorb iron.*

4 *Phytate, or phytic acid, binds with several minerals, including iron, and inhibits their absorption. To ensure maximum uptake of iron from food at meals, avoid including phytate-high wholegrain cereals, nuts and pulses in the meal.*

5 *Vitamin C improves the body's ability to take up iron from food. Have it at mealtimes in the form of orange juice or as citrus fruits in salads or desserts.*

6 *To get enough vitamin C – up to 500 mg daily – you may need to take supplements. Other useful iron supplements are iron tablets and B complex multi-vitamin capsules.*

SIX WAYS TO improve iron absorption

advocate a long-term approach which gives the body time to heal itself. At the same time, follow a varied diet containing a balanced mix of vitamins and minerals.

Nutrients for energy

In many cases of chronic fatigue, a shortage of just one nutrient is enough to sap energy levels. This is why it is essential to pinpoint the possible cause of the problem.
Adequate iron levels One of the first things a doctor will do is test to find out whether you have anaemia,

a common cause of persistent fatigue. Anaemia is a deficiency of the blood pigment haemoglobin, which gives blood its red colour and also transports oxygen around the body. Iron-deficiency anaemia, caused by a lack of iron in the body, leads to a fall in haemoglobin levels. This in turn reduces the amount of oxygen reaching the tissues.

You may not notice the lack of oxygen when you are not moving much, but it could become apparent during periods of physical exertion: walking up a flight of stairs may

leave you feeling exhausted. This is because the extra effort demands more energy, and consequently more oxygen. But if your haemoglobin capacity is reduced, your muscles will not get the extra oxygen they need to function well.

Women who have heavy periods are especially vulnerable to depleted iron levels. They may also feel very tired just before menstruation, because of hormonal changes.

Iron deficiency is common throughout the world. In the United Kingdom pre-school children are

particularly at risk: it is estimated that about 25 per cent are deficient in iron. Teenagers and people who diet are also vulnerable. Such findings highlight the importance of eating iron-rich foods. Red meat, liver, pulses, green leafy vegetables, nuts, wheatgerm and fortified breakfast cereals are all good sources. You can help your body to absorb iron more efficiently by drinking a glass of orange juice with food – vitamin C speeds absorption.

Drinks and foods to avoid To ensure maximum absorption of iron in food, do not drink tea, coffee and milk with meals. The polyphenols in tea and coffee as well as the calcium in milk will block iron absorption.

If you prefer not to eat meat or fish, moderate your intake of unleavened grain foods such as raw bran, pittas and chapattis. These contain high levels of phytic acid, which also blocks iron absorption.

Your mineral intake Magnesium works with the minerals potassium and sodium to generate small electrical currents in muscles, enabling them to relax and contract. If you have even a slight magnesium deficiency, your muscles can be affected, and this could make you feel tired and lethargic.

Good combinations Foods rich in magnesium include nuts, dark green leafy vegetables, fish, seafood, seeds and wholegrain bread and cereals. Magnesium also aids the absorption of potassium, another mineral that enables your muscles to function properly. Bananas, apples, oranges, plums, potatoes, asparagus and yams are high in potassium.

Zinc is a mineral which boosts the immune system and helps to protect against the kind of viral infections that often precede chronic fatigue. Shellfish are the richest source, but dairy foods, meat, pulses, wholegrain bread and cereals also contain zinc.

Essential vitamins Sustained energy levels, increased endurance, reduced fatigue and healthy blood cells are all enhanced by B vitamins, particularly B_6, B_{12} and folic acid. Eating lean meat, liver, fish, nuts, pulses, eggs, wholegrains, seeds and fortified breakfast cereals will greatly boost your intake of these vitamins.

A lack of vitamin B_{12} can lead to pernicious anaemia, a quite different condition from common iron-deficiency anaemia and much rarer. It causes exhaustion and breath-lessness. Vegans and vegetarians who avoid all animal products are at greater risk of vitamin B_{12} deficiency.

Vitamin C helps to produce carnitine, a body chemical that transports fats into muscle cells for increased energy. Eating foods rich in vitamin C, such as citrus fruit and vegetables, will boost energy, as well as improve iron absorption.

A HEALTHY EATING PLAN

The long-term approach to restoring energy levels puts an emphasis on frequent small meals eaten at regular intervals. They should be based on complex carbohydrate foods such as wholemeal bread, pasta, wholegrain cereals, potatoes and rice.

These foods provide steady levels of energy throughout the day (and during the night) and prevent the sharp fluctuations in blood sugar levels which can cause exhausting energy and mood swings. They also contain sufficient fibre to keep the digestive system in good order, avoiding energy-sapping bouts of diarrhoea or constipation.

Establishing better patterns
People who have been severely tired over a long period may have developed eating habits that make their problem worse. They are often too exhausted to prepare and eat food, and often skip important meals such as breakfast.

The classic 'tired all the time' type of fatigue is usually much more pronounced in the morning, even after a full night's sleep, and may decrease as the day continues.

Start as you mean to go on Eating well in the morning replenishes essential nutrients and energy. A breakfast that is based on carbohy-drates enables you to perform better, mentally and physically. Fresh or dried fruit, wholegrain cereals, muesli, porridge and wholegrain bread all give sustained, slow-release energy. They help you fight fatigue better than fatty foods or highly

Regain your zest for life Many factors can sap your energy reserves, from viruses to poor diet. Boost your system with this Spinach, Watercress and Orange Salad, rich in iron and vitamin C. It will put an extra spring in your step when you're in a rush. The recipe is on page 256.

MENUPLAN
to beat fatigue

Eating small, regular meals spaced throughout the day will bring your energy levels back to normal. It will take time, but the results are worthwhile.

SNACKS AND DRINKS Eat frequent, sustaining snacks at regular intervals — a handful of nuts and raisins or unsweetened popcorn; oatcakes or rice crackers; fresh fruit; carrot sticks. Sip water throughout the day (aim to drink at least eight glasses).

Beans means energy — especially on wholemeal toast

ENERGY BREAKFAST
Wholegrain cereals; baked beans on wholegrain toast; a poached egg; a fruit smoothie (see index for recipes); fresh juice or fresh fruit and yoghurt. At weekends make brunch dishes, such as scrambled eggs with smoked salmon or a kedgeree.

LUNCHTIME REVIVAL A small, protein-based meal revives flagging energy — have a bowl of bean and vegetable soup with a wholemeal bap; prawns with noodles, fish, chicken or meat; falafel with hummous, salad and pitta bread; chicken or tuna salad sandwich on rye bread; grilled fish or chicken with Spinach, Watercress and Orange Salad (recipe overleaf); or Baked Mushrooms with Coriander Pesto and Feta (recipe overleaf) with wholegrain bread.

EVENING SUSTENANCE Choose a meal that includes carbohydrate, such as a baked potato with vegetable or meat chilli; Spicy Sardinian Mussels (recipe overleaf) served with pasta or crusty bread and salad; or mashed potato with smoked mackerel and steamed green vegetables.

processed, sugary breakfast cereals. To maintain consistent energy levels throughout the day, try to eat three small meals, plus snacks. This will not only keep hunger pangs at bay, it should also improve your mood and concentration. Choose snacks containing unrefined carbohydrates and fibre, such as wholemeal muffins or scones, fruit bread, cereal bars, fruit or fruit-filled yoghurt.

The post-lunch energy dip You may find that your energy levels fall sharply in the afternoon. This is a recognised part of your daily body rhythm, but experimenting with

what you eat in the middle of the day can make a difference. To increase your mental alertness, try a light lunch which combines some protein with a small amount of unrefined carbohydrate.

Some examples are: a tuna and salad wholegrain sandwich; wholewheat noodles with lean meat; chicken or fish; soup and bread; baked beans on wholegrain toast. You may be very sensitive to refined carbohydrate foods such as white bread and pasta, which encourage the brain to produce the sleep-inducing chemical, serotonin (see

page 244). This affects some people more than others, but if you notice that you feel particularly tired soon after eating these foods, you should avoid having them at lunchtime.

Instead, choose a light meal based on protein – a little lean meat or fish is ideal, especially if accompanied by fruit and vegetables. You can eat a high-carbohydrate meal in the evening, when it may help to send you to sleep.

People who are allergic or have an intolerance to certain foods may experience a variety of symptoms, including headaches, skin reactions,

digestive problems and feelings of tiredness. They may have several symptoms at once, depending on the nature of their allergy. For example, people who are allergic to wheat may have acute eczema, feel tired all the time and also feel physically weak and unable to concentrate.

Wheat and dairy foods are the most common causes of allergies and intolerances. If you suspect that your tiredness is connected to a problem food, you could try eliminating it from your diet for a period. But before doing so, you should consult your doctor, who may suggest that you see a dietitian.

FOODS THAT TIRE YOU OUT

Stable blood sugar levels are the key to maintaining balanced energy reserves (see pages 91-92). The glucose (and caffeine) in a bar of chocolate provide a short, intense energy charge. But they also cause your blood sugar to plummet, often within an hour. This makes you even more tired and perhaps craving foods (usually sweet or fatty) which will generate another fast boost of energy. The result is a damaging 'yo-yo' effect on your system, which can leave you tired and drained.

Glucose and caffeine not only cause unstable blood sugar levels, they also dehydrate the body and inhibit the absorption of vitamins and minerals. If you suffer from fatigue and depression, it may be worth avoiding sugar and caffeine.

Sudden weight loss

Chronic fatigue may be the result of repeated crash diets. Such diets may not provide enough calories to keep you going all day, and they are not effective in the long-term anyway. In addition, they could even deprive you of essential nutrients such as iron, potassium and magnesium, thereby causing exhaustion and muscle weakness. If you are trying to lose weight, you should proceed slowly but surely. Follow a healthy diet and get plenty of exercise (see pages 88-99).

ENERGY BOOSTERS

A nutritionally balanced diet will help to resolve chronic fatigue in the long-term, but there are several ways of giving yourself an immediate lift:
• Exercising may be the last thing you want to do when you're feeling tired, but the more you move your body, the more oxygen it takes in. This, in turn, encourages your energy levels to rise. Choose low-intensity aerobic exercises such as swimming, walking, jogging or cycling. These trigger the production of endorphins, natural brain chemicals, which produce a sense of well-being. A brisk fifteen minute walk once a day will boost your circulation and oxygenate the blood.
• Breathe deeply – many people do not use their lungs well. Shallow breathing results in insufficient oxygen entering your body. Yoga is excellent for teaching you how to breathe correctly.
• Help yourself to get a good night's sleep by avoiding alcohol and drinks that are high in caffeine, such as coffee and tea, and by eating a small carbohydrate snack before going to bed. Turn to pages 242-247 for further advice on sleep problems.
• Get your circulation going with a vigorous rub-down. Soak a rough hand towel in hot water, wring it out and scrub your body from your toes up to your head, using short, energetic movements.

Energy boosts can come from many sources Yams are a good source of the muscle-energising mineral potassium. And try herb teas which contain ginseng, a reviving tonic herb. Ginseng capsules are more powerful in their revitalising effects, but you should not exceed the recommended dose on the packet.

spicy sardinian mussels

An aromatic, steaming bowl of mussels makes a convivial main course. Here, the mussels are cooked in a slightly piquant chilli and tomato liquor. Serve them with plenty of crusty bread to mop up the juice, and with a green salad on the side.

preparation time: **25 minutes**

cooking time: **20 minutes**

serves **4**

20 g (¾ oz) unsalted butter
2 tablespoons olive oil
1 onion, finely chopped
2 cloves garlic, crushed
Juice of ½ lemon
200 ml (7 fl oz) dry white wine
4 tablespoons canned chopped tomatoes
1 tablespoon chopped flat-leaf parsley, plus
    extra to garnish
½ teaspoon dried chilli flakes
2 kg (4 lb 8 oz) mussels, scrubbed and
    thoroughly rinsed
Black pepper

NUTRIENTS PER SERVING	
calories	280
carbohydrate	8.5 g
(sugars)	3 g
protein	23 g
fat	13 g
(saturated)	4 g
fibre	1 g

1 Heat the butter and oil in a large, heavy-based saucepan. Add the onion and cook over a medium heat for 5 minutes, until softened. Add the garlic and cook for a further minute.

2 Turn up the heat to high and pour in the lemon juice and wine. Boil for 2 minutes, or until the alcohol has evaporated. Reduce the heat and add the tomatoes, parsley and chilli flakes. Simmer for 5–8 minutes, until reduced by a third.

3 Add the mussels, cover the pan and cook over a high heat for 5 minutes, shaking occasionally, or until the mussels have opened. Discard any mussels that have not opened.

4 Season with pepper and serve immediately, sprinkled with the remaining parsley.

spinach, watercress and orange salad with citrus dressing

You can buy ready-washed baby spinach leaves and watercress in supermarkets, and make this refreshing salad in minutes. It is an excellent accompaniment for both the dishes on these pages.

preparation time: **5 minutes**

serves **4**

NUTRIENTS PER SERVING	
calories	130
carbohydrate	4 g
(sugars)	4 g
protein	2 g
fat	11.5 g
(saturated)	2 g
fibre	2 g

115 g (4 oz) baby spinach leaves
115 g (4 oz) watercress
1 large orange, peeled, segmented and cut
    into 1 cm (½ in) pieces
FOR THE DRESSING
4 tablespoons extra-virgin olive oil
Juice of ½ lemon
Salt and black pepper

1 Arrange the spinach, watercress and orange pieces in a serving bowl.

2 Mix together the ingredients for the dressing and pour over the salad. Toss the salad to coat the leaves in the dressing, and serve.

baked mushrooms **with coriander** pesto and **feta**

Mushrooms have a succulent, meaty texture when baked, and a rich flavour that is complemented here by the garlicky coriander topping. These are substantial enough to make a satisfying meal: serve with some crusty French bread or ciabatta.

preparation time: **15 minutes**

cooking time: **35 minutes**

serves **4**

200 g (7 oz) spinach, washed, tough stems removed and roughly chopped
60 g (2¼ oz) fresh coriander
3 cloves garlic, crushed
55 g (2 oz) unsalted cashew nuts, chopped
175 ml (6 fl oz) olive oil, plus extra for drizzling
115 g (4 oz) feta cheese, roughly chopped
8 large, flat mushrooms, wiped clean with damp absorbent kitchen paper
Salt and black pepper

1 Steam the spinach for 2 minutes, or until it has wilted. Drain thoroughly and set aside.

2 Place the coriander, garlic, cashew nuts and half the oil in a food processor or blender. Blend until the nuts are coarsely chopped. Add half the feta and the remaining oil and blend until the mixture is a coarse purée.

3 Heat the oven to 200°C (400°F, gas mark 6). Lightly oil a large ovenproof baking dish and put the mushrooms in it, gill side up. Top each one with a spoonful of spinach, then the coriander topping. Sprinkle the remaining feta over the mushrooms. Season well and drizzle with olive oil. Bake for 25–30 minutes, or until tender. Serve hot.

NUTRIENTS PER SERVING	
calories	470
carbohydrate	4 g
(sugars)	2 g
protein	10 g
fat	46 g
(saturated)	10 g
fibre	2.5 g

restoring lost energy

Too **much** of a **good** thing

Many of us have a favourite food or drink that we reach for without thinking. This is fine in moderation, but in excess many foods can have harmful effects. If you have become dependent on certain foods or on alcohol or cigarettes, there are ways to restore the balance.

It is very easy for a pleasurable treat to become a risky habit – this is particularly true of certain foods and drinks. Many bad eating habits begin early in life. Your tastebuds may have been taught to expect a lot of salt or sugar in foods and drinks, or to prefer foods smothered in fat. The customs that prevailed at your family dinner table may linger far into adult life without you being aware of it.

AN ADDICTIVE FORMULA

Family traditions are just one part of the story. For many, food is unconsciously connected with the feeling of being loved and secure. That irresistible urge to buy a large bar of chocolate to eat when you are unhappy may be linked with the fact that your parents used sweets and chocolates as treats, bribes and as rewards for good behaviour.

But as well as the emotional associations, there may be chemical reasons why some foods become a habit. Chocolate may comfort you because it contains substances that actively lift your spirits and improve your mood (see pages 220-221). The sugar in the chocolate boosts your

A savoury sprinkle Instead of depending on your salt shaker buy a herb shaker and combine aromatic herbs and spices (such as coriander seeds, cumin seeds, mixed peppercorns, chilli flakes, dried rosemary, thyme and oregano) into a great-tasting blend. Use an electric grinder or a pestle and mortar to grind them into a fine texture – and experiment with different combinations.

blood sugar, and the tryptophan raises your serotonin and endorphin levels. Serotonin calms you down, and endorphins decrease your sensitivity to pain. For more information on the effects of tryptophan, turn to page 244.

As an extra lift, the chocolate contains phenylethyamine (PEA), which makes you feel happy, and theobromine, which acts as a stimulant. Together, all these ingredients add up to a powerful cocktail – it's not for nothing that some sweet-toothed people call themselves 'chocoholics'.

Everyday habits

You can become dependent on – and even addicted to – very ordinary items of food and drink. An extra sprinkling of salt over your food at mealtimes, an extra lump of sugar in that second cup of coffee or tea or a top-up in that glass of wine.

Public health campaigns have made people aware of the risks of drinking too much alcohol. However the dangers of over-consuming salt, sugar, fat and caffeine are less widely known. And if these are foods that you have come to prefer, the links

Reaping the benefits *Black grapes used to make red wine are rich in antioxidants that protect against heart disease. This is why drinking a moderate amount of red wine is regarded as beneficial for your heart and circulation. But the key word is 'moderate': it is the alcohol produced during wine-making that is the main health hazard.*

between them and health problems may be quite hard to grasp. Among these problems are obesity (see pages 206-215), high blood pressure, heart and circulation problems (see pages 206-215) and stress.

You may have developed a positive liking for sugary, fatty foods – perhaps you add salt automatically, believing that it brings out flavour.

Creative alternatives

Understand the problem, and you are on the way to solving it. Once you identify what makes you over-fond of some foods, and know more about the action of food and drink on your body, you are more likely to

try healthier ways of eating and drinking. When you've been used to familiar flavours and cooking methods, you need lots of ideas to inspire you to try more imaginative alternatives.

For example, you'll need to re-educate your tastebuds so that you won't miss salt. Because this has become such an instinctive part of your cooking routine, be firm with yourself and put the salt shaker at the back of the cupboard. Give your food flavour with different marinades, balsamic vinegars, fruit vinegars, garlic and citrus juices.

If you have a sweet tooth, you may find confectionery snacks hard

to resist, or be inclined to add spoonfuls of refined table sugar to your food and drink. Instead, throw out the sugar bowl and replace it with a bowl piled high with delicious fresh fruit. A piece of fruit contains its own, natural sugars (fructose), antioxidant vitamin C and fibre to keep your system healthy.

Most people eat too much fat – it provides 38-40 per cent of the energy (calories) of the average Western diet. Use your frying pan wisely. Get a good-quality pan with a heavy base, and have a go at dry-frying food such as meat, poultry and fish without adding fat. Simply heat the pan until it is very hot, add

the meat or fish and wait until a light crust has been formed before you continue cooking. Or you could use the *en papillote* method (see below).

If you drink more than six cups of tea or coffee a day you may be already addicted to your daily 'fix' of caffeine (see page 220). You may decide to cut down: but do it gradually, as some people suffer withdrawal symptoms. Sip water throughout the day, and try drinks such as fruit juices and herbal teas.

USING ALCOHOL WELL

It is pointless demonising a particular food or drink – especially alcohol. What matters is whether you make sensible use of it or whether you abuse it.

The benefits Much of the research into the healthy effects of alcohol centres around the antioxidants in red wine. These may delay the onset

Lemons are rich in vitamin C which gives your immune system a great boost. Squeeze plenty of lemon juice into a glass of cold, sparkling water to make a delicious alternative to an alcoholic drink.

of certain cancers, arthritis, and cataracts by reducing cell damage caused by free radicals. Red wine also provides flavonoids such as quercetin and rutin. These plant compounds are believed to block the action of cancer-inducing cells as well as offering protection against coronary heart disease and cataracts and having antihistamine properties.

Moderate alcohol consumption – around two units of wine or beer

(but not spirits) a day – may reduce the risk of heart attacks and some strokes. Women should not exceed 14 units of alcohol a week, men 21 units (see page 97). These amounts should be spread out over a week, not consumed on one night out. You should also try to have two consecutive alcohol-free days a week.

Keep it under control Official figures state that 1 in 25 people in the United Kingdom is dependent on

en papillote

COOKFORHEALTH

The health benefits of cooking en papillote

LOW FAT No added oils or fats are used; flavours are sealed in.
VARIETY Many foods can be cooked this way. Seafood, poultry, vegetables and fruit are the most successful.

The method Cooking in paper or *en papillote*, is easy. Wrap foods loosely, but sealed, in greaseproof paper or foil, then bake or steam. Use moderate heat and a little liquid.
Flavourings The method keeps in the flavours, so you need just a few additions. Herbs, spices, vegetables and fruits all add flavour, also liquids such as stock, citrus juices, wine. Worcestershire and soya sauces and flavoured vinegars.

alcohol and that one in five exceeds safe drinking limits. When alcohol becomes a regular habit, it can lead to serious health problems.

Alcohol addiction

Alcoholism is an illness that has several signs. The amount you drink may increase insidiously; you may have erratic mood changes and memory lapses; you may need to drink early in the morning, or switch from beer to spirits.

Accepting the fact that you are an alcoholic often means abstaining from drink completely. Organisations such as Alcoholics Anonymous (AA) can help with this. If you feel that your drinking has got out of hand, talk to your doctor.

The negative effects You don't have to be an alcoholic to experience the down-side of alcohol. People who drink heavily risk having nutritional deficiencies. This is partly because alcohol is an appetite suppressant; but it also affects the absorption and metabolism of the B vitamins and vitamins A, C and D, essential fatty acids and the minerals calcium, zinc, magnesium and phosphorus.

Despite providing an initial high, alcohol is a natural depressant and induces mood swings that can have dangerous consequences. Drink and drunkenness are a factor in many cases of domestic violence.

Alcohol also loosens inhibitions, and leads to risky behaviour. In 1997, 16,000 people were hurt in drink-driving related accidents and alcohol was implicated in 17 per cent of all fatal road accidents in the United Kingdom.

Drinking too much alcohol can cause heart and circulatory problems and increase the risk of osteoporosis,

diabetes, impotence, and brain and liver damage. Also, according to the World Health Organisation, alcohol is linked to cancer of the throat, mouth, larynx, pharynx, bladder, breast and liver, with the risk being substantially higher among those people who also smoke.

SAY NO TO CIGARETTES

Giving up smoking is the single best thing you can do for your health. It is the highest contributing factor to death and is linked with cancer, nutritional deficiencies, raised cholesterol levels, heart disease and many other ailments.

Cigarettes contain numerous toxins, the most harmful of which are nicotine, benzopyrene and carbon monoxide. These damage cells and cause them to mutate into cancer cells. For more information and advice about giving up smoking, turn to page 69.

Limiting the damage Make sure that your diet includes plenty of fruit and vegetables: these contain high levels of vitamin C and other antioxidants. Vitamin C strengthens the immune system, helping to destroy cancer cells. Smoking and alcohol rob your body of vitamin C – it has been estimated that an extra 50 milligrams of vitamin C are needed for every cigarette smoked.

Diversionary tactics If you need help to stop smoking, various therapies such as hypnotism and acupuncture may help. And you shouldn't worry about putting on extra weight. Increasing your physical activity levels will help you to lose any spare pounds – and you'll benefit from the calming effects of exercise. You might also consider relaxation techniques such as yoga.

MENUPLAN
satisfying alternatives

Use these food and drink ideas to help you to resist temptation.

WHEN YOU CRAVE CHOCOLATE
Snack on fruit: chop an apple or banana into a bowl of yoghurt; make a fruit smoothie (see index for recipes); or try Spiced Fruit Salad (recipe overleaf).

INSTEAD OF SALT
Squeeze lime or lemon juice over food; eat spicy dishes such as Tom Yam Soup (recipe page 128) or Crab Cakes with Chilli Sauce (page 231).

WHEN YOU CRAVE CIGARETTES
Divert yourself with snacks: bowls of plain popcorn; handfuls of nuts or seeds; fruit or vegetable crudités; or breadsticks with hummous or guacamole; Roasted Root Vegetables with Horseradish Sauce for vitamin C and Fresh Tuna Niçoise (recipes overleaf).

INSTEAD OF ALCOHOL
Drink mineral water and a slice of lemon or lime; fruit juices; ginger beer; alcohol-free lager and wine.

TOO MUCH FAT IN YOUR DIET?
Opt for low-fat treats: grilled, griddled or poached chicken or fish; or oven-chips and boulangère potatoes (see page 93).

roasted root vegetables with horseradish sauce

Winter is the time for warm, comforting foods and these root vegetables take on a delicious sweetness when roasted. Sharpened with the bite of horseradish, they make a good accompaniment for roasted or grilled fish, chicken or meat.

preparation time: **10 minutes**

cooking time: **1 hour, 10 minutes**

serves **4**

NUTRIENTS PER SERVING	
calories	390
carbohydrate	35 g
(sugars)	12 g
protein	4 g
fat	27 g
(saturated)	1 g
fibre	3 g

3 raw beetroot, washed but not peeled

2 tablespoons olive oil

1 tablespoon honey

50 ml (2 fl oz) warm water

2 red onions, each cut into 6 wedges

2 sweet potatoes or baking potatoes, sliced into 1 cm (½ in) rounds

Salt and black pepper

FOR THE HORSERADISH SAUCE

200 ml (7 fl oz) crème fraîche

2-3 tablespoons creamed horseradish

Paprika, to garnish

1 Cook the beetroot in boiling water for 35 minutes, or until tender, then drain well. Cut the beetroot into quarters.

2 Heat the oven to 200°C (400°F, gas mark 6). Mix together the olive oil, honey and water in a roasting tin. Add the beetroot and onions and turn in the oil mixture so they are well coated.

3 Transfer to the oven and bake for 15 minutes. Remove from the oven. Add the potatoes to the tin, season, and bake for a further 30–35 minutes, until the vegetables are tender and golden.

4 To make the horseradish sauce, mix together the crème fraîche and creamed horseradish. Pour into a bowl and sprinkle with paprika. Serve the sauce separately.

fresh **tuna** niçoise

This twist on the classic French salad incorporates fresh tuna steaks and a creamy, garlic-scented anchovy dressing. The dish is substantial enough to make a satisfying main course.

preparation time: **10 minutes, plus 30 minutes marinating**
cooking time: **20 minutes**
serves **4**

4 tuna steaks, each about 140 g (5 oz)
2 tablespoons olive oil
Juice of ½ lemon
280 g (10 oz) small new potatoes, scrubbed
175 g (6 oz) fine green beans, trimmed
250 g (9 oz) mixed salad leaves
12 cherry tomatoes, halved
1 small red onion, finely sliced into rounds
85 g (3 oz) pitted black olives
Salt and black pepper
FOR THE DRESSING
2 tablespoons extra virgin olive oil
1 teaspoon white wine vinegar
4 anchovy fillets in oil, drained and
    chopped
1 small clove garlic, crushed
3 tablespoons reduced-fat mayonnaise

1 Place the tuna in a shallow dish, pour over the oil and lemon juice, and season. Turn the steaks in the marinade. Refrigerate for 30 minutes.

2 Steam the potatoes and green beans until tender. Drain and cool. Put the salad leaves, tomatoes, potatoes, green beans, onion and olives in a bowl. Put the dressing ingredients in a blender and process until smooth. Spoon over the salad, and mix well.

3 Heat a griddle pan until hot. Place the tuna steaks on it. Brush with marinade and cook for 5 minutes, turning once (and adding more marinade) until brown outside and slightly pink in the centre.

NUTRIENTS PER SERVING	
calories	515
carbohydrate	19 g
(sugars)	7 g
protein	40 g
fat	32 g
(saturated)	5 g
fibre	4 g

spiced **fruit salad** with vanilla **yoghurt**

This fragrant combination of exotic fruits, vanilla and ginger makes a quick and refreshing end to a main meal. If you have any left over, keep it in the refrigerator overnight and have it for breakfast the next morning.

preparation time: **10 minutes, plus 10 minutes cooling**
cooking time: **7 minutes**
serves **4**

55 g (2 oz) unrefined caster sugar
100 ml (3½ fl oz) water
1 vanilla pod
3 slices of fresh ginger root, peeled
300 g (10½ oz) full-fat Greek yoghurt
1 large mango, peeled and cubed
1 medium pineapple, peeled, sliced and cut
    into chunks
1 Charentais or Galia melon, halved, seeded
    and cubed
Finely grated zest and juice of 1 lime

1 Place the sugar, water, vanilla pod and ginger in a heavy-based saucepan. Bring to the boil, stirring to dissolve the sugar. Simmer for 5 minutes without stirring, until slightly thickened and syrupy. Remove from the heat and cool for 10 minutes.

2 Remove the ginger and discard. Remove the vanilla pod and dry it. Cut the pod in half lengthways and scrape out the black seeds. Mix the seeds with the yoghurt in a serving bowl.

3 Transfer the cooled syrup to a large bowl and stir in the fruits, lime zest and juice. Serve the yoghurt separately.

NUTRIENTS PER SERVING	
calories	300
carbohydrate	53 g
(sugars)	53 g
protein	7 g
fat	7 g
(saturated)	4 g
fibre	5 g

Enhancing your memory

If you have a photographic memory, you are one of the lucky few. The brain stores so much information from the recent and distant past, it is difficult for most of us to remember everything. But food has a surprising influence on memory, and can help the most scatter-brained individuals to sharpen up.

Everyone has occasional lapses in memory; but this doesn't necessarily mean that your brain is not working properly. The pressures of a busy life may place excessive demands on your attention and concentration. For example, you may often misplace items such as door keys, or have trouble recalling names and telephone numbers.

These are irritating but superficial problems – nobody can remember everything that happens to them. And ageing does not necessarily affect your powers of recall; you have a sharper memory in mid life than in childhood. A research study at the University of Kentucky concluded that only five per cent of the cases of poor memory could be attributed to brain disorders such as Alzheimer's disease (see page 267).

From late middle years, however, many people do have problems with memory. Health experts call this age-related cognitive decline (ARCD); symptoms are poor concentration, memory function and language use.

MEMORY MAINTAINERS

Most people, young and old, would like to improve their memories. You can do a lot towards this by ensuring a good supply of blood (and oxygen) to the brain. And maintaining steady blood sugar levels is crucial, because brain cells need glucose to function properly. Even something as simple as not skipping breakfast makes a notable difference. In mental ability tests, the best results were achieved by those tested within half an hour of eating breakfast. This improved performance may be influenced by blood glucose levels: when these are unstable the result may be poor memory and confusion.

Eating unrefined carbohydrates such as wholegrain bread and wholewheat pasta helps to regulate blood sugar levels. These foods take time to digest and glucose is released at a slow, sustained pace.

Super nutrients

A good, all-round diet based on the Five Food Groups (see pages 11-15) is the best way to nourish your brain. But some foods are startlingly efficient at delivering memory-enhancing nutrients. Researchers in the USA have measured levels of oxygen radical absorbing capacity (ORAC) units in foods. They found that those with the highest levels – blueberries, strawberries and

Where did I put it? Keeping track of credit cards, mobile phones and other necessities of modern life places extra strain on short-term memory, making a memory-enhancing diet important.

improve your memory

Challenge yourself Your memory doesn't have to decline as you age. Your brain compensates by using new areas and connections; so keep mentally active and socialise with friends.

Exercise your brain Keep your brain active by learning something new every day – whether its an unfamiliar word or discovering how to use the Internet.

Make lists Help to unscramble your short-term memory by writing down essential reminders rather than trying to keep everything in your head.

Play word games Amuse yourself by doing crossword puzzles or word games. Card games such as bridge or poker also help to keep your mind sharp.

Go down memory lane Look through photograph albums and other mementos to help you recall your past, or you could even write a memoir.

Practise deep relaxation Stress can disrupt your memory. Learn ways to calm down: try deep breathing techniques; meditation; yoga or self-hypnosis.

spinach – all help to stave off memory loss. Other helpful fruits and vegetables include blackberries, plums, broccoli, kale, beetroot, Brussels sprouts and garlic.

Many nutrients directly help the brain to function. Iron, for example, which is involved in supplying oxygen to the brain in haemoglobin. A deficiency of iron affects memory: researchers in the USA tested girls with low iron levels and found that those given iron supplements performed better in memory tests. Foods rich in iron include red meat, liver, nuts, seeds, prunes, figs, apricots, wheatgerm, wholegrain bread, pulses and green vegetables.

Antioxidant vitamins help to protect the oxygen supply in the arteries leading to the brain as well as reducing free radical damage.

Antioxidants are highly effective in boosting memory. Fruit and vegetables provide rich sources.

B vitamins are crucial for brain cell energy. Deficiencies of thiamin (B_1), niacin, B_6, B_{12} and folic acid have been connected with loss of memory, confusion, forgetfulness and other symptoms. Rich sources of B vitamins include wholegrains,

brewer's yeast, meat, poultry, liver, milk, eggs and green vegetables.

Essential fatty acids are needed to develop and maintain the brain. Omega-3 and omega-6 fatty acids are found in oily fish, vegetable oils, olive oil, avocado, walnuts, wheatgerm and soya beans.

Lecithin and choline are needed to produce the brain chemical called

MENUPLAN
for a razor-sharp memory

If you need to give your memory a boost, eat unrefined carbohydrates and foods high in essential fatty acids and protein. And, just as important, don't miss breakfast.

A SUPER START *Choose wholegrain cereal; porridge, fruit juice; wholegrain bread with peanut butter or mashed banana; apricot and ginger compôte; or bananas with natural yoghurt, wheatgerm and honey.*

MIDDAY BOOST *Guacamole with crudités and bread; smoked salmon on toast; scrambled egg on toast.*

SNACKS *Fresh fruit, pumpkin and sunflower seeds, nuts; Date and Orange Oat Cookies (recipe overleaf), fruit bread, malt loaf; dried figs, prunes or apricots; or breadsticks.*

EVENING REVIVERS *Eggs in Rich Chilli Tomato Sauce (recipe overleaf); Fish Steaks with Salsa Verde (recipe overleaf); grilled trout with lemon and fresh herbs; eggs baked with spinach; or omelette filled with chicken and vegetables.*

Snack on a date to improve your memory

DURING THE DAY *Have plenty of water, green tea, herbal teas and fresh fruit and vegetable juices. Go easy on coffee, tea, fizzy drinks and cocoa.*

acetylcholine; it is vital for the rapid functioning of memory and protects the brain against degenerative disease. The main source of choline is fish. Foods rich in lecithin include soya beans, liver, egg yolks, peanuts, peas, trout, wholegrains, cheese and green leafy vegetables.

POWERING THE BRAIN

Eating well will help you to maintain a good memory; but combining a good diet with a healthy lifestyle will amplify these benefits. Physical exercise is one of the best ways to improve your memory. It increases the supply of oxygenated blood and nutrients to the brain, helping it to function efficiently.

Mental exercise is also important. Reading, learning a language, and other mind-expanding activities such as quizzing and puzzling are excellent for stimulating the mind, especially as part of a social activity. Alcohol and smoking sap energy from the brain by damaging brain cells. You should therefore stay within the recommended levels for alcohol (see page 97) and, if you are a smoker, cut down or, better still, quit altogether (see page 69). While caffeine can help to improve mental alertness, excessive amounts may induce tremors and palpitations, raise anxiety levels and affect concentration. Medical advice is that no-one should drink more than six cups of tea or coffee a day.

Lack of sleep can have an adverse effect on concentration and memory. Most adults need seven or eight hours sleep a night, although you may find you need less as you get older. For more information about sleep, turn to pages 242-247.

Stress and anxiety are notoriously bad for the brain, because they rob it of essential nutrients. People who suffer from stress tend to have repetitive thought patterns. These preoccupy the brain at the expense of effective concentration and short-term memory. To find out more about stress, including ways to deal with it, turn to pages 206-215.

Prescription drugs, including sleeping pills, tranquillisers, cough suppressants and pain-relievers, have been found to cause memory loss. If you are taking medications such as these and find that you are becoming forgetful, consult your doctor.

Reducing your calorie intake by dieting may affect your recall – a recent United Kingdom study found that people who dieted to excess were at increased risk of diminished memory. This may have less to do with a lack of calories than the psychological strain of dieting. The effect was similar to that experienced by depressed or stressed people.

It has been observed that women have problems with memory prior to menstruation and also during the

menopause. The exact reason for this is not known, but it is thought to be caused by hormonal changes, especially decreased oestrogen levels. Getting the right nutrients at this time and, perhaps, taking hormone replacement therapy (HRT) may help (see pages 182-183).

Extra help

Various dietary supplements claim to improve memory. If you are taking a prescribed medication, however, it is advisable to check with your doctor before trying them, as they may reduce the efficacy of other medicines. They may even cause unpleasant or even dangerous side effects. Apart from Hupersine A (see right) the following supplements are available from health food stores, in a variety of formulations.

Ginkgo biloba has a good reputation for improving memory, concentration and general mental function. It may also help with the symptoms of confusion. It is a natural vasodilator (it keeps blood vessels open) and helps to oxygenate brain tissue and maintain circulation. This allows more blood to circulate, carrying oxygen and other nutrients all over the body, including the brain. It is also an effective scavenger of the free radicals that may damage cells and tissues. A daily supplement of 120 mg (split into two or three doses) is usually recommended.

Oriental ginseng Chinese, Korean and Siberian ginseng are world-famous medicinal plants which have been found to boost alertness and concentration. Follow the dosage recommended on the packet: taken in excess, ginseng can cause unwanted side effects such as anxiety, irritability and insomnia.

Pick up a punnet Blueberries and raspberries are great memory enhancers. A fresh raspberry coulis (below) is delicious with ice cream. The recipe for a coulis is on page 73

Coenzyme Q_{10} is made in the body; but it is estimated that half the population may lack the nutrients needed to produce it. It is believed to sustain memory and concentration as well as boost energy levels. Daily dosages range from 50 to 100 mg.

Hupersine A, used in traditional Chinese herbal medicine, may help to prevent the breakdown of the brain chemical acetylcholine (see opposite). It is usually supplied by a specialist practitioner, who will advise on dosages and how to take it.

Permanent damage

For some elderly people, memory loss may become a severe illness: senile dementia is associated with poor blood and oxygen flow to the brain from narrowed or blocked arteries – conditions for which ginkgo biloba supplements may be recommended.

Alzheimer's disease results in damage to brain and nerve cells and overall shrinkage of the brain. It is completely irreversible at present, but minor improvements in some patients have been achieved with supplements of coenzyme Q_{10}. Foods naturally rich in this enzyme (offal, spinach, potatoes, yams and soya products) may help.

eggs in rich chilli tomato sauce

Cumin, coriander and chilli add spice to this simple, colourful dish. It is perfect accompanied with crusty bread and a fresh spinach or rocket salad. Jars or cartons of passata (sieved tomatoes) are easily obtainable in supermarkets.

preparation time: **10 minutes**

cooking time: **40 minutes**

serves **4**

NUTRIENTS PER SERVING	
calories	195
carbohydrate	11 g
(sugars)	11 g
protein	10 g
fat	10 g
(saturated)	2 g
fibre	2 g

1 tablespoon olive oil
1 large clove garlic, chopped
1 red pepper, cored, deseeded and finely sliced
2 teaspoons ground cumin
1 teaspoon ground coriander
1 fresh chilli, deseeded and finely chopped
125 ml (4 fl oz) red wine
900 g (2 lb) passata
1 teaspoon dark brown sugar
Salt and black pepper
4 eggs
Chopped fresh coriander, to garnish

1 Heat the oil in a large, lidded, deep-sided frying pan. Add the garlic and pepper and cook over a medium heat for 1–2 minutes, until softened. Stir in the cumin, coriander and chilli, and cook for a further minute. Pour in the red wine, bring to the boil and cook briskly for 2 minutes.

2 Reduce the heat, add the passata and sugar and cook, stirring occasionally, for 15–20 minutes, until the sauce has reduced and thickened. Season to taste.

3 Make four equally spaced hollows in the sauce and break an egg into each one. Cover and cook for 15 minutes, or until the egg whites have set. Serve immediately, garnished with coriander.

date and orange oat cookies

These tasty cookies have a chewy, crumbly texture. Other combinations of dried fruit and nuts such as apricots and almonds or figs and cashews can be used in place of the dates and walnuts, if you prefer.

preparation time: **15 minutes**

cooking time: **20 minutes**

makes **9**

NUTRIENTS PER COOKIE	
calories	280
carbohydrate	37 g
(sugars)	20 g
protein	4 g
fat	14 g
(saturated)	7 g
fibre	2.5 g

115 g (4 oz) unsalted butter
85 g (3 oz) unrefined caster sugar
1 tablespoon clear honey
Finely grated zest and juice of 1 orange
115 g (4 oz) wholemeal self-raising flour
115 g (4 oz) porridge oats
115 g (4 oz) dried, stoned dates, chopped
25 g (1 oz) walnuts, chopped

1 Heat the oven to 160°C (325°F, gas mark 3). Lightly grease a baking sheet. Put the butter, sugar, honey and orange zest and juice in a small saucepan. Cook over a gentle heat until the butter has melted and the sugar dissolved.

2 Put the flour, oats and 85 g (3 oz) of the dates in a large bowl, then add the honey mixture. Mix with a wooden spoon to form a sticky dough. Place nine spoons of the mixture on the prepared baking sheet. Press into rounds 1 cm (½ in) thick. Sprinkle over the remaining dates and walnuts, lightly pressing them into the dough.

3 Bake for 15 minutes, or until golden and slightly crisp. Leave on the baking sheet to cool a little, then transfer to a wire rack to cool completely.

fish **steaks** with **salsa verde**

This dish makes a great after-work meal because it is quick and easy to prepare. The green sauce works well with many kinds of fish and can be made a day ahead. Note that salmon (shown here) and tuna steaks are higher in fat and calories than cod.

preparation time: **10 minutes**

cooking time: **10–15 minutes**

serves **4**

4 fish steaks, such as cod, salmon, halibut, or tuna, each about 140 g (5 oz)
Olive oil or lemon juice for basting
FOR THE SALSA
4 tablespoons olive oil
2 spring onions, chopped
1 clove garlic, crushed
2 shallots, chopped
5 tablespoons fresh coriander leaves
2 green chillies, deseeded and chopped
1 teaspoon clear honey
1 tablespoon white wine or balsamic vinegar

1 To make the salsa verde put all the ingredients in a food processor and blend to a smooth purée. Refrigerate until needed.

2 If using white fish steaks brush them with a little olive oil. Baste oily fish steaks with a little lemon juice. Cook under a preheated hot grill or on a hot griddle for about 5 minutes each side, depending on the thickness of the fish. If you are using a griddle, turn the steaks during cooking to achieve a cross hatch marking.

3 Serve the hot fish steaks with the salsa verde and a green, leafy salad. Cherry tomatoes are also good with this dish.

4 Have plenty of bread – ciabatta or a wholegrain bread with seeds or chopped nuts – on the table.

NUTRIENTS PER SERVING (COD)	
calories	370
carbohydrate	4 g
(sugars)	4 g
protein	26 g
fat	28 g
(saturated)	5 g
fibre	0

Restoring a sense of calm

Children are naturally robust and exuberant. Their boundless energy can leave their parents standing. But some children display more than normal high spirits: extreme or hyperactive behaviour can cause great anxiety to parents. The right foods can play a dramatic role in keeping things calm.

Experts have known since the 1960s that there is a link between food and hyperactivity, and that diet is implicated in delinquency, aggression and other antisocial behaviour. Obviously, social factors are also involved, but food plays a decisive role in helping to form a stable state of mind.

To achieve this balance everyone – young and old – needs a diet that is varied and rich in nutrients (see the Five Food Groups pages 11-15). A well-chosen diet will provide healthy proportions of unrefined carbohydrates, moderate amounts of protein, plenty of fruit, vegetables and fluids (especially water) and limited amounts of processed and refined foods. It should be the foundation of your child's diet.

HYPERACTIVITY

One in ten children is thought to be affected by hyperactivity, also known as Attention Deficit Disorder (ADD) is more common in boys. Symptoms include restlessness, fidgeting, clumsiness, compulsive talkativeness, impatience, irritability, destructive behaviour, poor social skills and temper tantrums. Inadequate nutrition, food allergies, genetic predisposition, imbalances in certain

A MUG OF WARM MILK *sweetened with honey and accompanied by a wholemeal biscuit may help a hyperactive child to sleep. It triggers the production of natural sedative chemicals. Offer the drink about an hour before the child's bedtime.*

EVENING PRIMROSE OIL *supplements contain essential fatty acids that can help to protect the developing nervous system and alleviate behavioural problems.*

EAT TO BEAT hyperactivity

brain chemicals and environmental factors are all possible influences, but no single factor has been identified.

Children may be prescribed powerful medication to control the symptoms of ADD, while the role of food is overlooked. But a balanced diet, low in processed and refined food has been found to help by correcting nutritional deficiencies.

Some children grow out of ADD: but if symptoms continue into adolescence and even into adult life, medication is usually prescribed.

This may be combined with counselling, which often includes the rest of the family, and psychological treatments such as cognitive therapy. Eating foods which are rich in helpful nutrients (see opposite) and avoiding those that are known to cause problems may help too.

Getting the best nutrients

For those who have the classic symptoms of ADD, the following nutrients are particularly relevant and helpful:

More than boisterous *The hyperactive behaviour of children with Attention Deficit Disorder should not be confused with normal play. Feeding your child fresh, unprocessed food can help to create a balanced mood while providing lots of energy for fun and games.*

Essential fatty acids Some types of polyunsaturated fatty acids are not made by the body and must be obtained from foods (see below). Children particularly need them for their rapidly developing brains and nerves. Numerous studies have shown that a lack of essential fatty acids – omega-3 and omega-6 – can lead to behavioural problems.

Conversely, an increase of these acids in the diet has been shown to relieve the symptoms of ADD by improving brain metabolism. Processed foods usually contain saturated or hydrogenated fats that can interfere with the fatty acids needed for mental performance and behaviour; keep these foods to a minimum in your child's diet.

Key food sources Children with ADD often have lower levels of omega-3. This is the primary fatty acid in brain, nerve, eye and heart tissues, and is found in greatest abundance in oily fish such as tuna, herrings, sardines, salmon and mackerel. Two or three portions of these types of fish a week are ideal, but if your child doesn't like fish, use pure fish oil capsules instead.

The United Kingdom Hyperactive Children's Support Group report that rubbing evening primrose oil onto

the body of a child with ADD has a calming effect. This underlines the value of omega-6, found in evening primrose oil, vegetable oils, walnuts, sesame seeds, nuts and olive oil. For more information on essential fatty acids, turn to page 56.

A low intake of thiamin (vitamin B_1) is also known to cause changes in behaviour. People who have low levels of thiamin can become highly aggressive, erratic, impulsive and over-sensitive to criticism. Thiamin is needed to maintain the health of the

central nervous system. Wholegrains, potatoes, nuts, seeds, meat, eggs, brown rice and vegetables are all good sources. Other B vitamins, particularly B_3 and B_6, are also required to assist the brain enzymes that release energy from carbohydrates, to regulate neurotransmitters and to help make the calming brain chemical serotonin. For more about serotonin, turn to page 244.

A lack of the mineral chromium can exacerbate the symptoms of ADD. It is needed to metabolise

Trickle treat Molasses is delicious drizzled over pancakes or cereals. It is made from the liquid left after processing and retains minerals that are lacking in refined sugar. It is sold in health food shops.

sugar and is naturally present in red meat, eggs, seafood, cheese, wholegrains and molasses.

Zinc and magnesium deficiencies have both been linked to children with ADD. The symptoms of magnesium deficiency include restlessness, poor coordination, learning difficulties and fidgeting. Good sources of zinc and magnesium include red meat, nuts, crab, sunflower and sesame seeds, wholegrain cereals, beans, green vegetables and dried figs.

Vitamin C is essential for several brain functions, including the manufacture of neurotransmitters such as serotonin. The best source is fresh fruit and vegetables.

PROBLEM FOODS

While there is agreement that a balanced diet can help to restore diminished levels of essential nutrients, health experts are divided on whether specific foods cause problems in themselves.

The role of sugar Some specialists claim that sugar causes hyperactivity. But other studies claim that, on the contrary, sugary foods (along with other carbohydrates) actually have a calming effect.

Unstable blood sugar Processed sugar loses a large proportion of its chromium, a mineral needed to metabolise sugar and control blood glucose levels. A deficiency in chromium makes the body's insulin

less effective. This may cause bouts of hypoglycaemia leading to aggressive outbursts. People with ADD often have problems metabolising sugar, and researchers have found that upset behaviour that is triggered by sugar is more pronounced when it is eaten first thing in the morning on an empty stomach. Conversely the effects are less obvious when a sugary food is eaten later in the day, and also when it is part of a high-fibre meal.

Restoring the balance

Unrefined carbohydrates such as wholegrain bread, pasta, potatoes (with their skins on) and brown rice help to stabilise blood sugar levels and facilitate the release of serotonin. They are also richer in nutrients than refined carbohydrate foods such as white rice and bread, sweets, cakes and biscuits.

HEALTH OR HYPE?
food additives

In 1994, Australian researchers found that 55 per cent of children in their study who responded positively to the elimination of all foods dyes and additives in their diet, reacted negatively when given a single dye, such as the food colouring tartrazine (E102). The children were more irritable, restless and experienced sleep problems.

Another study at the University of Surrey found behavioural problems in every child consuming tartrazine in their drinks. Four out of the ten children had severe reactions, and three developed eczema or asthma within 45 minutes of having the drink.

Tartrazine is just one of many chemical food additives known to trigger the symptoms of ADD. Others include E110 Sunset yellow, E127 Erythrosine, E219 Benzoic acid, E210, E320, E321 and MSG. You may see an improvement in behaviour if you cut out these additives, so check the ingredients labels on packaged and processed foods before you buy them.

Food allergies Numerous studies connect food allergies to behavioural problems and ADD. The most common trigger foods are wheat, dairy foods, eggs, sugar and chocolate. Tea, coffee and caffeine-laden fizzy drinks such as cola may also cause problems.

Eliminating food allergens has proved highly successful in treating children with ADD. However, you should always consult a doctor or dietitian about taking an allergy test before embarking on any food elimination trial.

DELINQUENCY AND DIET

In 1995, Professor Schoenthale of the Department of Sociology and Criminal Justice in California, published his work on nutritional deficiency among young offenders on remand. He gave them a diet of fresh foods, sometimes added extra supplements, reduced sugar and limited processed foods. He claimed that aggressive, antisocial behaviour improved dramatically.

However, these findings are not regarded as conclusive. Because Schoenthale's young offenders mostly came from deprived backgrounds, had erratic eating patterns and poor diets, there is a question of cause and effect. Health researchers are currently working on more precise studies to examine possible links between diet and violent behaviour.

The theory that environmental pollutants such as lead may cause antisocial (even criminal) behaviour is also under scrutiny. One study has found a correlation between high levels of aluminium and hyperactive behaviour. Also, it is known that many toxins can deplete the body of certain nutrients, including zinc.

MENUPLAN
for steady energy

Hyperactive children need regular amounts of unrefined carbohydrates and fresh, unprocessed foods throughout the day to control blood glucose levels.

FOR BREAKFAST A wholemeal muffin or piece of toast with a poached or boiled egg; wholegrain cereals with fresh fruit; crumpets with yeast extract; pancakes with banana, pecan nuts and maple syrup.

AT LUNCHTIME Cheese and Vegetable Omelette (recipe overleaf); or a quick mixed bean salad; cauliflower, broccoli and macaroni cheese; pizza with salad; prawn and avocado salad; or a smoked salmon, chicken or ham sandwich or bap. Follow this with good-quality ice cream, natural jelly, yoghurt or fresh fruit.

A boiled egg makes a good start to the day

IN THE EVENING Feed your child starchy carbohydrate dishes based on pasta with chicken, vegetables or prawns (see index for recipes); Salmon with Pineapple Salsa (see recipe overleaf), served with rice or pasta; or mixed bean and vegetable casserole with dumplings or potato gratin topping. Choose fruit crumbles, tarts or pies with a spoonful of fromage frais for dessert.

DRINKS & SNACKS Encourage your child to drink plenty of water; but discourage drinks high in caffeine including tea, coffee and cola, as well as orange squash or fruit drinks that contain artificial additives such as tartrazine. For snacks, provide fresh or dried fruit, a handful of nuts or seeds, breadsticks, rice cakes, or a fruit smoothie.

BEFORE BED When your child is restless, offer a light snack such as a banana or honey sandwich, made with wholemeal bread, a crumpet or muffin, or a plain biscuit with a cup of camomile or valerian tea or warm milk with a spoonful of honey.

chickpea and pepper salad

This chunky mix of fibre-rich chickpeas and red peppers is seasoned with plenty of fresh herbs. Chickpeas are popular with children as they have a nutty, slightly sweet flavour and they are convenient too – just use them straight from the can.

preparation time: **10 minutes**

cooking time: **15 minutes**

serves **4**

NUTRIENTS PER SERVING	
calories	160
carbohydrate	20 g
(sugars)	6 g
protein	7 g
fat	6 g
(saturated)	1 g
fibre	5 g

1 tablespoon olive oil

2 red peppers, cored, deseeded and cut into wide strips

400 g (14 oz) canned chickpeas, rinsed and drained

4 tablespoons chopped fresh herbs, such as basil, oregano and flat-leaf parsley

FOR THE DRESSING

3 tablespoons extra virgin olive oil

1 tablespoon balsamic vinegar

Salt and black pepper to taste

1 Oil a griddle pan with the olive oil and heat it. Put the peppers in the pan and cook them for 12–15 minutes, turning occasionally, until softened and blackened. Cool the pepper strips slightly then cut them into chunks.

2 Put the pepper chunks in a serving bowl. Add the chickpeas and herbs and use two spoons to mix them together.

3 Mix together the ingredients for the dressing, and pour it over the chickpeas and peppers. Toss to coat the salad ingredients in the dressing.

pan-fried salmon with pineapple salsa

The whole family will enjoy this quick salmon dish – the fruity, sweet and sour salsa is a perfect foil to the rich flesh of the salmon. If you can't get fresh, use a small can of pineapple, preferably canned in fruit juice.

preparation time: **15 minutes, plus 1–3 hours marinating**

cooking time: **8–10 minutes**

serves **4**

4 salmon fillets, each about 175 g (6 oz)
2 tablespoons olive oil
Salt and black pepper
FOR THE MARINADE
2 tablespoons olive oil
2 tablespoons maple syrup or clear honey
Juice of 1 lime
2 tablespoons chopped fresh coriander
2 tablespoons soya sauce
1 clove garlic, crushed
FOR THE PINEAPPLE SALSA
1 small pineapple, peeled, cored and diced
1 small red pepper, deseeded and diced
1 jalapeno chilli, deseeded and chopped
1 shallot, finely diced
2 tablespoons chopped fresh coriander
Juice of 1 lime

1 Rinse the salmon and pat dry with kitchen paper. Mix together the marinade ingredients in a shallow dish and season to taste. Add the salmon and turn to coat it in the marinade. Cover, and leave to marinate in the refrigerator for 1–3 hours.

2 Mix together the salsa ingredients. Season to taste and refrigerate for 1 hour to allow the flavours to develop.

3 Heat the olive oil in a heavy-based frying or griddle pan. Add the salmon, skin-side down, and cook over a medium heat for 4–5 minutes, turning once. A minute before the end of the cooking time, add the marinade to give the salmon a caramelised glaze. Serve with a heaped spoonful of salsa.

NUTRIENTS PER SERVING	
calories	490
carbohydrate	19 g
(sugars)	18 g
protein	26 g
fat	31 g
(saturated)	5 g
fibre	2 g

cheese and vegetable omelette

This is a cheese omelette with a difference, flavoured with a tasty combination of mint and courgettes. It is simple, fresh and very easy to make. Serve it cut into wedges, accompanied with plenty of crusty bread and a green salad.

preparation time: **10 minutes**

cooking time: **15 minutes**

serves **4**

1 tablespoon olive oil
1 tablespoon butter
2 courgettes, sliced and roughly chopped
5 tablespoons chopped fresh mint
8 eggs, lightly beaten
100 g (3½ oz) Cheddar cheese, diced
Salt and black pepper

1 Heat the oil and butter in a heavy-based frying pan. Add the courgettes and cook for 5 minutes, or until softened and lightly golden.

2 Heat the grill to high. Add the mint to the beaten eggs and season well. Pour the mixture over the courgettes in the pan, then sprinkle over the cheese. Cook over a medium heat for 3–5 minutes, until the eggs are just set and the base is cooked and lightly golden.

3 Put the pan under the grill and cook for 4-5 minutes or until the top of the omelette is lightly golden. Serve it warm or cold, cut into wedges.

NUTRIENTS PER SERVING	
calories	365
carbohydrate	1 g
(sugars)	1 g
protein	22 g
fat	30 g
(saturated)	12 g
fibre	0

PART FOUR

Ways of living

Everyone's circumstances are different, but the way you live has a profound influence on your health. The stresses and strains of daily life affect you whether you are working full time, commuting, handling the pressures of business travel, looking after a family at home, retired from work, or studying. By tailoring what you eat to how you live, and learning how to use leisure well, you can stay fit, flexible and relaxed.

The **way** you **use leisure**

Whether you use your free time to go to the gym, party the night away or take off for a relaxing holiday in the sun, choose the right food to fuel your activities. It adds to your enjoyment and provides an extra 'feel good' factor that makes all the difference.

We all need a break from the relentless demands of work and daily responsibilities, so treasure your free time, and use it to replenish your mental and physical energies. Leisure is wonderfully restorative, and food can help you to enjoy it to the full.

PREPARED FOR ACTION

If sport is your favourite pastime, it's good to know which foods help you to perform best. Many professional athletes have tailor-made diets to bring them to peak fitness levels. You may not be aspiring to world-class standards, but you can pick up many useful tips from the professionals.

Foods for energy The key principle to keep in mind is that certain foods give you fast, quickly released energy, while others sustain you for extensive, long-term activity.

The most important fuel for physical exercise is carbohydrate, as it provides you with a readily available source of energy. When they are digested, carbohydrate foods are broken down into glucose. If your body doesn't use this for energy immediately, any excess is converted into glycogen in your muscles and liver. This stored glycogen is changed back to glucose when your body needs it, and the digestive system helps to keep blood sugar levels in balance. This enables you to exercise without becoming tired.

Everyone should consume more carbohydrate foods, not just sports enthusiasts. As well as providing a good source of energy, they contain

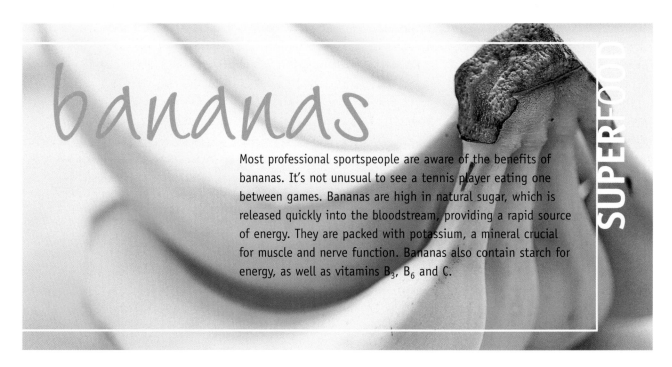

bananas

SUPERFOOD

Most professional sportspeople are aware of the benefits of bananas. It's not unusual to see a tennis player eating one between games. Bananas are high in natural sugar, which is released quickly into the bloodstream, providing a rapid source of energy. They are packed with potassium, a mineral crucial for muscle and nerve function. Bananas also contain starch for energy, as well as vitamins B_3, B_6 and C.

valuable fibre. There are two types of carbohydrate:

Complex carbohydrates (starches) are found in foods such as pulses, lentils and beans, bread, rice, potatoes, yams, pasta, cornflakes and other breakfast cereals and root vegetables such as carrots and parsnips. These carbohydrate foods should form the largest proportion of your diet – about 33 per cent (see the Five Food Groups, pages 11-15).

Simple carbohydrates (sugars) can be found in natural or unrefined form in foods such as fruit and milk, where they are combined with other nutrients. Refined sugar (sucrose) is commonly added to processed foods and confectionery.

You should use sucrose sparingly: it can trigger sudden surges in your blood sugar levels, and may result in unhealthy highs and lows, causing extremes of sudden energy followed by bouts of fatigue.

The sugar in your blood

Foods that make your blood glucose levels rise quickly have a high glycaemic index (see pages 78-79). They include bread, bananas,

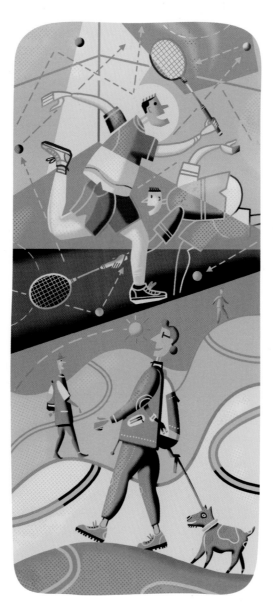

A fast burst or slow and steady?
Your muscles usually have enough glycogen to fuel 1½ to 2 hours of intense physical activity such as a tennis match. But you can boost your body's stores of glycogen in advance if you are planning a prolonged period of exercise such as hill walking. Eating a substantial meal based on pasta or rice a few hours before you set out will prepare your body for sustained effort.

potatoes, cereals and isotonic drinks. An isotonic drink recipe is included in the Menu Plan on page 281. Foods that release energy slowly and steadily have a low glycaemic index. Examples of these include pasta, chickpeas, milk, yoghurt and cheese.

Choosing your food

If you are getting in shape to tackle a strenuous activity, such as a heavy workout at the gym or long-distance running, it's useful to know how to eat beforehand. About two or three hours before you exercise, eat foods with a low glycaemic index, such as wholewheat pasta, lentils and chickpeas. These will be broken

down slowly in your body and provide a stable rise in blood sugar while you exercise. After you've used all this energy, you may need an isotonic drink and a snack food with a high glycaemic index, such as a banana, a raw carrot or a few raisins. These restore your blood sugar levels and refuel your muscles.

Protein for power? Unless you are restricting your diet while slimming, or are seriously involved in power or strength sports, there is no need to eat a high-protein diet when you are training. Usually, it is better to follow a balanced diet, and to obtain extra calories from carbohydrates. Just make sure you include a little

protein at every meal (see the Five Food Groups pages 11-15) and obtain it from a wide range of foods. Either eat fish, lean meat, eggs and dairy products, or, if you are a vegetarian, combine foods such as beans, lentils, cereals, grains, seeds and nuts as a meat-free alternative.

Good fat, bad fat

Not all fats are bad for you – some are essential to your health. Fat cushions your body's organs, and carries vitamins A, D, E and K (they are soluble in water but not in fat). A certain amount is needed to produce oestrogen in women. Around 18-25 per cent of a woman's body weight is composed of fat; and individuals who have less than ten per cent body fat (especially dancers) may have irregular periods or none at all.

wrong – are of fat soluble →

Choose wisely The type of fat you eat (saturated or unsaturated) makes all the difference to your fitness.

• Include oily fish such as salmon, mackerel, sardines or trout in your diet. These contain the essential fatty acid linoleic acid – vital for healthy heart function.

• Choose reduced-fat dairy products rather than avoid them altogether. That way you won't lose out on valuable calcium.

• Use polyunsaturated oils such as olive, rapeseed or sunflower for cooking instead of lard or butter. For more information on fats and your health, turn to page 56.

Vitamins and minerals

If you are eating a varied diet with a wide range of fruits, vegetables, starchy foods, dairy products and protein, you should have plenty of nutrients. Check the Five Food Groups (pages 11-15 for details).

Thirsty work *A vigorous session at the gym is a really satisfying way to wind down and keep yourself in great shape. But you lose a lot of fluid while you're exercising, so have a little to drink at 10-15 minute intervals during your workout. This will slake your thirst and restore your fluid levels. You can choose an isotonic drink, fruit juice, or simple cold water – they all get your body back into balance.*

Iron is particularly important for sportswomen, especially if they are vegetarian or have heavy periods. Choose varied sources of easily absorbed iron to prevent iron deficiency anaemia. Lean red meat, liver pâté, canned sardines and the dark meat from turkey or chicken are all rich in iron. If you have anaemia, your doctor may suggest that you take an iron supplement to boost your levels.

Magnesium loss is very common in high energy sports. If you don't have enough from your food you may suffer from fatigue and muscle cramps. To avoid this, eat lots of seafood, dark green vegetables, nuts, wholegrains and pulses.

Zinc is primarily stored in the bones and muscles and is lost in your perspiration and urine. Seafood, eggs, pulses and wheatgerm provide plenty of zinc to meet your needs.

The importance of fluids

When you exercise, you lose fluids through sweating and it is easy to become dehydrated. The effect on your energy and performance levels can be damaging. To prevent this, drink fluids constantly, before, during and after workout sessions. **How much do you need?** You need at least 1.7 litres (3 pints) of fluids a day, and even more if you're exercising regularly. Water is the best, but you can also include fruit juices, herb or fruit teas, or weak tea. Specialised sports drinks (see recipe opposite) – often known as hypotonic or isotonic drinks – can also be useful. You don't need to

MENUPLAN
to keep going longer

Boost your body's long-term energy capacity by choosing some of these meal ideas on a regular basis. You'll feel good, look good and, above all, you'll be delighted with your new levels of stamina.

KICKSTART BREAKFAST Get a high-carbohydrate launch for the day with thick slices of wholemeal toast and honey; muesli or cornflakes sprinkled with raisins; or try Banana Muffins (recipe page 86). These provide you with energy and useful fibre. Add a glass of orange juice and you're set up for the day.

LIGHT LUNCH Enjoy wholegrain sandwiches with a low-fat filling such as ham, cottage cheese with salad or sliced egg and cress. Follow with fresh fruit or a low-fat yoghurt for dessert, and treat yourself to an oaty snack bar if you are still hungry.

MAIN MEALS Base your evening meals around starchy foods such as potatoes, pasta, rice, polenta or couscous, and bulk these out with fresh vegetables and salads. Eat small amounts of low-fat meat or fish or rather than making it the main focus of the meal. Enjoy fresh fruit or yoghurt for desserts.

ISOTONIC DRINKS These replace lost fluid and energy very quickly after vigorous exercise.

Energy drink
Mix 1 litre (1¾ pints) of apple or orange juice with 1 litre (1¾ pints) of water. Add half a teaspoon of salt and stir. Makes 10 200ml glasses.

NUTRIENTS PER GLASS:
Calories **38** Carbohydrate **10 g** (sugars **10 g**)
Protein **0** Fat **0** Fibre **0**

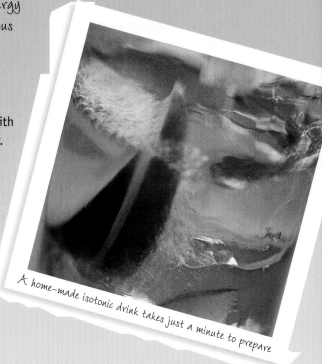

A home-made isotonic drink takes just a minute to prepare

HOW MUCH ENERGY YOU USE – A ROUGH GUIDE*

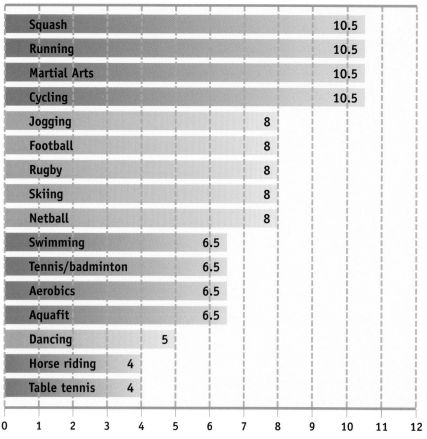

	Average Calories per minute
Squash	10.5
Running	10.5
Martial Arts	10.5
Cycling	10.5
Jogging	8
Football	8
Rugby	8
Skiing	8
Netball	8
Swimming	6.5
Tennis/badminton	6.5
Aerobics	6.5
Aquafit	6.5
Dancing	5
Horse riding	4
Table tennis	4

0 1 2 3 4 5 6 7 8 9 10 11 12

Average Calories per minute

*these figures provide a general guide only – your age, weight and physical fitness all make a difference to the amount of energy you use, as does the vigorousness of the exercise.

spend lots of money on commercial brands, as it's so easy to make your own. They are very effective after periods of prolonged exercise, as they speed up your body's water absorption and quickly replenish carbohydrate levels.

Isotonic drinks contain low levels of salt to replace the sodium and minerals lost through sweating. These drinks are retained in the stomach for only a short time before passing through to the small intestine to be absorbed.

Whatever kind of fluid you use, it is best to sip it little and often rather than waiting until you have a raging thirst. Drink it welll chilled for maximum refreshment.

Eating around your schedule

If you work out regularly, try to fit meals around your exercise schedule. For example, if you prefer to work out early in the morning and miss breakfast, make sure that you eat a carbohydrate snack such as a banana, cereal bar, wholemeal scone later in the morning. Don't rely on a quick fix from a sugar-laden hot chocolate or a high-fat bag of crisps.

If you usually exercise in the early evening, try to have a sandwich in the afternoon and either eat your main meal at lunchtime (keeping it light) or at least an hour after you've finished your session. Have a high-carbohydrate meal such as pasta to refuel your glycogen stores.

pasta with broccoli and walnuts

This colourful pasta dish is simple to prepare.

preparation time: **10 minutes**

cooking time: **15 minutes**

serves **2**

*175 g (6 oz) pasta shapes
175 g (6 oz) broccoli florets
1 tablespoon olive oil
1 small red onion, sliced
½ red pepper, sliced
55 g (2 oz) walnuts
25 g (1 oz) fresh basil leaves
Grated low-fat cheese, optional
Black pepper*

1 Cook the pasta in boiling water until *al dente*. Drain.

2 Steam or boil the broccoli until just cooked. Drain.

3 Heat the oil to hot in a frying pan or wok, add the onion and pepper and stir-fry for 3–4 minutes. Add the walnuts and broccoli and stir-fry for 1–2 minutes.

4 Mix the pasta and basil into the vegetables. Sprinkle over the cheese, if desired, and season with pepper.

NUTRIENTS PER SERVING	
calories	611
carbohydrate	76 g
(sugars)	10 g
protein	20 g
fat	27 g
(saturated)	3 g
fibre	7 g

coriander couscous salad

This mint-scented salad combines the salty tang of feta with the freshness of mint. Like pasta, couscous is made from durum wheat and is a valuable carbohydrate food. It is ideal for supplying long-lasting reserves of fuel for your activities.

preparation time: **5 minutes, plus 30 minutes cooling**

serves **3**

250 g (9 oz) couscous
500 ml (18 fl oz) boiling water
55 g (2 oz) mixed fresh coriander and
   mint, finely chopped
Grated zest of 1 lemon
8 sun-dried tomatoes, drained and chopped
300 g (10½ oz) feta cheese cubes in oil,
   drained, or 300 g (10½ oz) feta cheese,
   cubed
Salt and black pepper, optional

1 Pour the couscous into a large bowl, add the water and allow to stand for 5 minutes.

2 Using a fork, fluff up the couscous and leave to cool for 30 minutes.

3 Stir in the chopped herbs, lemon zest and chopped tomatoes. Add the feta cheese to the bowl.

4 Season with a little salt and plenty of black pepper, if desired. Serve with a fresh, leafy green salad.

NUTRIENTS PER SERVING	
calories	400
carbohydrate	44 g
(sugars)	1 g
protein	13 g
fat	19 g
(saturated)	8 g
fibre	0

the way you use leisure

LATE NIGHTS AND PARTIES

Do you head straight for the pub at night after work and stay until closing time? Or go to night clubs until the early hours? If so, it's easy to allow drinks and nibbles to become substitutes for the nutritious food you need to stay fit and well.

Alcohol's 'empty' calories There are seven calories in every gram of alcohol, almost as many as in a gram of fat (which contains nine). A glass of wine has around 85 Calories, a pint of lager 180. Apart from its calorie content, however, alcohol is 'empty' of nutritional value.

Enjoying a few drinks from time to time is fine; but regular heavy drinking is damaging to your health and can be dangerous (see pages 260-261). Alcohol is absorbed rapidly into your blood stream and distributed through your tissues. It is then broken down by enzymes in the liver. The time this takes varies according to your age, fitness, body weight and the efficiency of your liver. Turn to page 97 for further information about alcohol units and safe drinking guidelines.

Foods that buffer alcohol

A varied, balanced diet will provide all the energy and health-protective nutrients you need to fuel a hectic, round-the-clock life-style.

You should certainly aim to eat at least five servings of fruit and vegetables every day (see the Five Food Groups, pages 11-15). Also, avoid snacking on crisps, chocolate and foods high in sugar, salt or fat.

To keep your energy levels stable, you need to eat meals at regular intervals. This helps to prevent fatigue, and ensures a steady supply of nutrients throughout your body.

Maintaining good fluid levels is crucial too: drink at least eight glasses of water a day, and intersperse these with glasses of fruit juice to give you additional antioxidant protection.

Think ahead You can use food to delay the negative effects of alcohol. For example, before going to a party, try eating a meal based on a high-carbohydrate food such as pasta, rice or potatoes. This will slow down your absorption of alcohol.

The following tips may also help:

• Never drink on an empty stomach.

• Space out alcoholic drinks with glasses of plain water or fruit juice.

• Avoid fizzy drinks such as mixers – they may speed up the passage of alcohol into your blood stream.

• Don't grab a burger on the way home. The combination of greasy food and alcohol may upset your digestive system. Instead, go straight home, drink plenty of water, and eat sensibly the next day.

Handling a hangover Drink at least three glasses of water before going to bed, and more when you get up next morning. Hangover symptoms are mainly caused by dehydration, and the water helps to flush out toxins.

• Eat plain yoghurt, wholegrains or muesli to replenish lost B vitamins

• The herb milk thistle is reputed to help boost liver function. And cynarin, an extract from artichokes has a similar function. Both are available from health food shops.

• Try Apricot Whiz, or Mini Banana Pancakes (see recipes opposite). Bananas are an excellent source of potassium, and are reputed to help the detoxification process.

Drink and gender Women are more vulnerable than men to the effects of drinking: they have lower levels of the enzymes that break down alcohol, a lower body weight and more body fat.

mini **banana** pancakes

**Make these delicious and nutritious pancakes for the ultimate
restorative breakfast. They replenish your energy and set you up for
the day. The mixture makes about 16 pancakes – they can be kept
in the fridge and reheated, or frozen for later use.**

preparation time: **5 minutes**

cooking time: **5-10 minutes**

makes **16 mini pancakes**

*2 small or one large banana, roughly
     chopped*
1 egg
125 ml (4 fl oz) semi-skimmed milk
115 g (4 oz) wholemeal self raising flour
1 rounded tablespoon demerara sugar
Sunflower oil for cooking
Grated nutmeg and caster sugar to serve.

1 Place all the ingredients in a food
processor and process for 30 seconds or
until the mixture is smooth.

2 Heat a tablespoon of oil in a non-stick
frying pan until hot, and gently spoon
in a tablespoon of batter. You may cook
3 or more pancakes at the same time,
depending on the size of your pan.

3 When the pancake is lightly browned on
the underside, turn it over using a fish
slice, and cook on the other side.

4 Repeat until all the mixture is used up.

5 Serve at once sprinkled with caster
sugar and some grated nutmeg.

NUTRIENTS PER SERVING	
calories	**53.5**
carbohydrate	**8.75 g**
(sugars)	**4 g**
protein	**1.75 g**
fat	**1.5 g**
(saturated)	**0.25 g**
fibre	**0.75 g**

apricot whizz

**This delicious, quick breakfast will give you a great boost any
morning, not just when you are feeling hungover. If you prefer,
blend the sunflower seeds with the other ingredients rather than
adding them separately.**

preparation time: **5 minutes**

cooking time: **3 minutes to roast seeds**

makes **1**

1 tablespoon sunflower seeds
3 tablespoons low-fat Greek yoghurt
2 tablespoons freshly squeezed orange juice
*4 large ready-to-eat apricots, roughly
     chopped*
1 teaspoon runny honey
2 drops vanilla essence

1 Gently roast the sunflower seeds over a
medium heat until lightly browned,
moving in the pan frequently. Allow to
cool on kitchen paper.

2 Using a hand blender or small food
processor, blend all the remaining
ingredients until smooth.

3 Serve at once with the seeds sprinkled
on top.

NUTRIENTS PER SERVING	
calories	**160**
carbohydrate	**23 g**
(sugars)	**21 g**
protein	**5 g**
fat	**5.5 g**
(saturated)	**1 g**
fibre	**3 g**

HOLIDAY FOOD

Whether you're taking a break close to home or jetting off abroad, give your taste buds a treat by sampling the local cuisine at your holiday destination. This is also your chance to enjoy a more leisurely approach to your food: devising informal meals and picnics for the family makes a welcome change of routine.

Once you've booked your holiday, take some time to read up on the speciality foods of the region you will be visiting. It adds to the enjoyment of your trip if you have a good idea of what dishes to look for.

Be adventurous Use this opportunity to explore unfamiliar flavours and textures. If you are planning a self-catering break, look up recipes which incorporate local delicacies, write them out (or photocopy them) and take them with you.

But you don't have to deprive yourself or your children of familiar home comforts. You may like to take your favourite brand of tea and coffee, or a box of the family's usual breakfast cereal.

Food for the journey

If you are travelling by car, plane, boat or train, pack some appetising snacks in a cool box or bag – they will keep you going if you are delayed and have to miss a meal. Some biscuits or muesli bars and a few apples are good stand-bys. Travel sickness may be a problem; if so, fresh root ginger is a very effective way to prevent this. Cut a few thin slivers, put them into a plastic bag and take them along with a flask of hot water to make into a tea. Alternatively, pack some good quality ginger biscuits (made with real ginger) to nibble.

Diverting snacks Young children need interesting little treats to keep them occupied. Avoid giving them salty foods such as crisps, which will only increase their thirst. Instead, hand them frequent small snacks – a few grapes or raisins are fine. These help to reduce the boredom of a long journey and will keep them going until mealtime.

Slaking your thirst It is essential to have plenty of fluids available during a journey to prevent dehydration. Take bottles of still water and choose fruit juice rather than sugary, fizzy

Let's go al fresco Eating outdoors is part of the fun of a cycling holiday and adds to the spirit of adventure. Look at the Menu Plan opposite for ideas – pizza slices, pasta salad and filled pitta all provide steady energy to keep you going.

drinks. You should try to avoid over-indulging in alcoholic drinks on long plane journeys – these can dehydrate you very quickly. You will end up feeling exhausted when you arrive. You also risk suffering a hangover in addition to the unpleasant effects of jet lag (see page 308). To avoid this, take sips of water at regular intervals during your flight.

Natural protection

Although changes to your diet are no substitute for sunscreens and other safety measures, you can help to enhance your body's natural defences by increasing your intake of the following nutrients. Start at least a week before you plan to travel:

Vitamin A promotes the growth and repair of damaged tissue and helps to maintain healthy skin. Brightly coloured fruits and vegetables such as red apples, apricots, peaches, carrots and peppers contain beta carotene which the body converts to vitamin A. Dairy products and liver are also good sources.

B vitamins from foods such as fish, poultry, wholegrains, pulses and seeds are also extremely important for maintaining a healthy skin.

Vitamin C will enable you to recover quickly from the effects of sunburn if you boost your intake. To ensure that you keep your levels topped up, eat at least five daily servings of fruit and vegetables including citrus fruits, strawberries, tomatoes and broccoli.

Vitamin E helps to limit damage to your skin cells caused by sunburn. For a meal rich in vitamin E, try an Avocado and Sunflower Seed Salad (recipe overleaf). Sunflower oils and margarines, fortified cereals, fish, eggs, nuts, seeds and wheatgerm are all good sources.

MENUPLAN
holiday picnic ideas

A picnic lunch is great fun for the family – but for the best results, keep it simple. A cool box or bag is the perfect way to carry food, especially in warm weather.

PASTA SALAD Make a simple pasta salad, flavoured with herbs and a little fresh tomato sauce, and add some favourite grilled local sausages or a few pieces of sliced grilled chicken.

PITTA POCKETS Take some pitta pockets and a filling of canned tuna, sliced black olives, lemon zest and fresh tomatoes, seasoned with a drizzle of olive oil, lemon juice and black pepper. To avoid soggy pockets, make up the filling in a separate container before you go, and tuck it into the pitta pockets when you are ready to eat.

Fill scrumptious pitta pockets when you get to the picnic

PIZZA SLICES Make your own Shellfish and Rocket Pizza (recipe page 226) or top a ready-made pizza with peppers, mushrooms and cheese.

DESSERT Something simple — buy a large pot of low-fat natural yoghurt and add chopped pieces of fresh fruit and nuts. Take a whole melon and cut it into slices (remember to take a knife); alternatively, make Lemon Polenta Cake (recipe page 129) and divide it into portions before you set out. Wrap it in foil to keep it moist and fresh.

288

IF YOU GET MILD SUNBURN on holiday, slice a strawberry in half and apply the open surfaces to the skin. The cooling moisture will minimise stinging and throbbing, the surface of your skin won't break and you will recover from the burn quickly.

BEAUTYFOODS

suntime

Water quality

It is essential to find out whether the water in your holiday destination is safe to drink – your travel agent should know. If it is unsafe, avoid it in any form – refuse ice in your drinks and, when eating out, don't eat fruit and raw vegetables that will have been washed in the local water. Instead, opt for fruits with skins that you can peel (so they don't need washing), such as mangoes, melons, bananas, pineapples and oranges.

If you are self-catering, cook vegetables in boiling water and wash salad vegetables in bottled water. Drink bottled water only and use some for teeth-brushing, or use water purification tablets.

Traveller's tummy

To avoid an upset stomach, be extra-vigilant with personal hygiene, exercise caution about the foods that you eat, and follow the guidelines above. Always avoid any foods that look as though they have been on display for a long time.

If you get diarrhoea, try to avoid solid foods for 24 hours, but drink at least 1.7 litres (3 pints) of clear fluids a day so that you don't dehydrate. And eat live yoghurt, which will help to restore the useful bacteria lost from your system.

Children can become dehydrated very quickly – take sachets of oral rehydration salts, or make your own. Mix one teaspoon of salt and eight teaspoons of sugar in a litre (1¾ pints) of bottled water. If symptoms persist for more than four days (two days for children) seek medical help.

Keep things moving Constipation is also common on holiday. It is easy to become dehydrated in a hot climate and this will exacerbate constipation. Drink plenty of fresh fruit juice and water, and limit your alcohol – drink two or three units daily.

Keep up your fibre levels by eating plenty of fruit and vegetables. If wholemeal bread isn't available in your holiday destination, look out for high-fibre alternatives such as dried apricots and prunes.

avocado and sunflower seed salad

This salad is bursting with the antioxidant vitamin E to help protect skin from the sun.

preparation time: **15 minutes**

serves **4**

FOR THE DRESSING
4 tablespoons sunflower oil
Grated zest and juice of 1 lime
½ teaspoon sugar
¼ teaspoon black pepper
FOR THE SALAD
2 large pears
2 large avocados, peeled and sliced
8 sun-dried tomatoes, drained and chopped
Half an iceberg lettuce, shredded
2 tablespoons sunflower seeds, lightly toasted

1 Make the dressing: whisk all the ingredients together.

2 Core and slice the pears and gently stir them into the dressing, with the avocados and tomatoes. Place the lettuce on plates, top with the mixture, sprinkle with sunflower seeds, and serve.

NUTRIENTS PER SERVING	
calories	425
carbohydrate	12 g
(sugars)	9 g
protein	4 g
fat	40 g
(saturated)	6.5 g
fibre	5.5 g

most unsaturated fat, while lamb usually has the least unsaturated.

• Use monounsaturated or polyunsaturated oils and fats for eating and cooking. They are good for your heart and are also higher in skin-protective vitamin E than saturated fats such as butter and margarine.

• Eat salmon, mackerel, sardines, pilchards, herrings and tuna at least twice a week to obtain omega-3 fatty acids. Choose fresh rather than canned tuna. These oily fish provide excellent protection for your joints and also help to lower cholesterol levels. To read more about fatty acids, turn to page 56.

• Vary sandwich fillings: instead of ham, bacon, or sausages, which are high in saturated fat, choose eggs, low-fat cheese, skinless chicken or fish. There are more ideas for sandwich fillings on page 292.

• Tuck quick snacks such as raw vegetables, nuts and fresh and dried fruit into your lunch box.

• Drink plenty of water and other fluids – you need more than the recommended eight glasses a day. Don't count tea or coffee into your daily fluid intake: they are diuretics and stimulate water loss. Working in the heat makes you perspire a lot, so keep bottles of water at hand to prevent dehydration and fatigue.

Working outdoors

It is relatively easy to wrap up and protect yourself against the cold. But it can be more difficult to avoid problems such as sunburn and skin cancer caused by too much sun on your skin. There are over 40,000 new cases of skin cancer reported every year in the United Kingdom: 2000 people die from it annually.

Protect your skin by wearing a hat, covering the back of your neck with a cotton handkerchief or scarf, and by using high factor sunscreens. Eat lots of foods rich in vitamin E which protects your skin cells from the harmful effects of the sun. Good sources include nuts, seeds, eggs, avocados, green vegetables and grain and seed oils. The more fruit and vegetables you eat the better: the antioxidant phytochemicals they contain are known to protect the body against cancer (see page 18).

SHIFT WORK

Your body has its own internal clock, based on a 24-hour ('circadian') cycle. The clock is regulated by hormones, particularly the hormone melatonin. This is secreted by the pineal gland in the brain; its release is stimulated by darkness and it is suppressed by daylight.

The effect of this melatonin action is to programme your body to be active during the day and to sleep at night. Changing to shift work, especially to nights, can play havoc with your internal clock.

Melatonin levels If you are exposed to light during the hours when you would usually be asleep, your body becomes confused. It doesn't produce enough melatonin and may also produce it at the wrong time. Insufficient levels of melatonin in your body can make you lethargic and depressed – a common problem with people working through the night. There can be other problems, too:

• Shift workers' risk of cardiovascular disease is 40 per cent higher than that of other workers. This is because heart beat rates and blood pressure levels function in relation to the body's daily rhythm.

• People working at night also have problems with sleeping. They find it difficult to restore regular sleep patterns when they return to daytime work.

• On average, night-workers eat only a third of their normal daily food intake. They also eat random snacks rather than regular meals; consequently, the foods they eat are low in important nutrients. This may lead to lethargy and loss of concentration, affecting safety standards in the workplace.

• Accidents and mistakes are known to increase during night shifts. This is particularly true of doctors and other health staff working long hours without sleep.

How food helps

The food you eat can help you to manage the transition from one pattern of sleep and work to another. Eating a wide variety of foods is a

Topsy turvy Eating the right food can help you to regulate your sleeping patterns. This is most important if you work irregular hours.

good way to maximise your levels of nutrients – use the Five Food Groups (see pages 11–15) as your guide. Choose low-fat foods and avoid large canteen fry-ups and packets of crisps, especially for your last meal of the shift.

Aim to eat at least two portions of oily fish such as salmon, mackerel or sardines a week: their omega-3 fatty acids will help to reduce your increased risk of heart disease.

If your levels of melatonin are low because of regular night work, you may need to boost your intake of tryptophan. As well as influencing the production of serotonin (see page 244), tryptophan also influences melatonin levels. Foods rich in tryptophan include turkey, chicken, game, cauliflower, broccoli, milk, cheese, lean meat, eggs, soya beans, fennel, bananas and watercress.

Effective foods You can also adapt your food according to whether you want to prepare your body to sleep or to stay awake and alert.

Eating carbohydrate-rich and tryptophan-rich foods together (see page 245) enables the brain to produce more serotonin, which calms you down and makes you sleepy. That is why a snack of a glass of milk and a cracker before bed can help you to get to sleep.

Conversely, foods high in protein reduce serotonin levels. So, eating a high-protein meal such as grilled bacon and egg or a lean piece of steak before you start a night shift may help to keep you awake.

Go easy on caffeine

Coffee and other caffeine-rich drinks are popular drinks with night-shift workers. They use them to stay alert and to concentrate on what they are doing. But this extra caffeine is particularly harmful for these workers. It exacerbates their already increased risk of heart disease, and makes the problem of getting to sleep even worse.

Shift workers should limit their daily caffeine intake to the equivalent of about three cups of freshly brewed coffee, having the last cup several hours before they go to bed.

There are several alternative drinks drinks to replace coffee or tea; they include herbal teas, such as rosehip, mint and peppermint (all taken in moderation), or a simple but refreshing cup of hot water flavoured with a slice fresh lemon or lime.

Sleeping difficulties

The most difficult (and debilitating) problem caused by working during the night is the disruption of your normal sleeping patterns. However, there are various things you can do to help overcome this.

The simplest is to ensure that the room in which you sleep is in complete darkness. If necessary, fit heavier curtains or wear an eye shade. The lower light level stimulates the production of melatonin to help you go to sleep.

If you wish to avoid taking sleeping pills, you may like to try a herbal tea such as camomile or lime flower, which may help you to sleep; and the herbal remedy valerian is also effective (see page 245).

MENUPLAN
for night-workers

Night shifts can severely disrupt your eating patterns – you may either eat too much or miss meals entirely. Here are alternative strategies for helping you to cope.

STRATEGY 1: Fit in with those around you. When you return home from your night shift, you may like to have breakfast with the family. Choose cereal, toast, jam and fruit juice: they are high in carbohydrate which boosts serotonin and helps you sleep. On waking, eat your evening meal with the family: choose high-protein foods such as fish, chicken, red meat or eggs, as these help to keep you alert in the night.

STRATEGY 2: Fit in with your shift structure. This means reversing the normal pattern of your meals.

SHIFT START Eat a high-protein 'breakfast' such as lean bacon and eggs or kippers with wholemeal toast. A cup of coffee or tea will help to wake you up, but don't drink endless cups during a night shift, as the caffeine may disturb your overall sleep patterns and affect your health.

MID-SHIFT If you are very busy on your shift and don't have time for a cooked meal, take sandwiches or soup in a flask, also a cereal bar and a piece of fruit. If you have a work canteen or use a take-away, choose sandwiches made from wholemeal bread and avoid high-fat snacks such as crisps.

END-SHIFT Try not to finish your night shift with a greasy fry-up; instead choose easily digested high-carbohydrate food which will help you get to sleep once you are home. Try tortellini with a simple leaf salad, or grilled salmon with couscous. Eat rice pudding with apricots soaked in orange juice for dessert.

Tomatoes and lean, sizzling bacon help you to stay awake

WORKING FROM HOME

Increasing numbers of people work from home, often sitting for hours at a time in front of a computer screen or taking non-stop telephone calls. Not having to commute to work has many advantages, but it also has its drawbacks.

You simply do not move around as much when you are working from home and this makes you vulnerable to the dangers of obesity and poor health. Lack of physical activity is fourth in the list of risk factors for coronary heart disease after smoking, high blood cholesterol and high blood pressure.

If you work from home your proximity to the kitchen means that it is all too easy to open the fridge to see what's available. Or you may be tempted to take a handful of biscuits to eat at your desk. By contrast, office workers have less direct access to food, and may not have so many opportunities to snack. Their close accessibility to food can be a genuine problem for many people who work

The sharp yet sweet flavour of pink grapefruit works well in juice cocktails. The fruit is also a good source of lycopene, a powerful natural protector against cancer.

at home and they often need to exercise great self-restraint in order to avoid gaining weight.

Food for home workers

It is easy to fall into an unstructured working and eating pattern. You may feel pressured into using all your time for working and slip into the habit of constantly eating at your desk. To avoid this, you may need to rethink the way you work.

• Plan to take proper meal breaks, especially at lunchtime. A light meal such as soup or a salad will make you feel refreshed and provide an energy boost for the rest of the day.

• Stock your fridge with healthy snacks such as raw vegetables and low-fat yoghurts.

• Keep a bowl of fresh fruit on your desk. Apples and bananas are easy to eat, and you could also include some calcium-rich dried apricots, kiwi fruit and seedless grapes.

• Avoid biscuits, cakes and other high-sugar, fatty snacks.

• Don't use food as an antidote to boredom or as a way of coping with a loss of concentration.

Keep well watered To stay fresh and alert, drink at least eight glasses of water during the day. Avoid sugary, high-calorie drinks. Instead, choose

blueberries

SUPERFOOD

Naturally sweet, rich in vitamin C and high in fibre, blueberries make delicious desk snacks. Recent US research studies have suggested they may be helpful in improving eyesight and protecting against eye disorders – good news for people who work for hours at computer screens. Blueberries contain anthocyanins, antibacterial compounds that are highly effective in fighting *E. coli* bacteria, the cause of many gastrointestinal and urinary tract infections. This makes blueberries a useful weapon against recurring infections such as cystitis.

fruit and vegetable juices – they not only slake your thirst, but are also a great way to obtain beta carotene and other antioxidant nutrients. Beta carotene is very good for your eyes – an important benefit if you work at a computer screen. Blueberries (see the box opposite) are also believed to help your eyesight.

Vary your choice If you have a juicer, you can easily make your own fruit or vegetable cocktails. Carrot juice is rich in beta carotene and vitamin C; it also contains folic acid, potassium, magnesium and phosphorus. And cranberry, citrus and pineapple juices are excellent sources of vitamin C.

Natural protection Red peppers contain lycopene (see page 61), a powerful protector against cancer. You can juice them with carrots and a dash of lemon juice to make a healthy, refreshing drink.

Tomatoes are the most concentrated source of lycopene, which is also found in pink and red fruits such as pink grapefruit, guava, watermelon and papaya. All of these make good fruit juice drinks. Keep jugs of fresh juice in the fridge to drink at your desk during the day.

Don't just sit there

Having a sedentary job means that you need to make a conscious effort to build regular physical activity into your daily routine. The current recommendation is that you should have 30 minutes of moderately intense physical activity at least five days of the week. Ideally, the 30 minutes should be done in one session, but two shorter bursts of 15 minutes will do, and may be more manageable for someone working from home.

Stretch your way to health *Take regular breaks and turn your back garden into an exercise area. Daily workouts will help to keep your joints supple.*

Be creative and use your time well:
• While you are waiting for your printer to process long documents, do some sit-ups or star jumps.
• Walk to the post box or post office rather than taking the car.
• Buy a skipping rope and have five minutes of skipping in your garden when you have a break. Skipping is excellent for increasing bone density in the hips and this helps to protect against osteoporosis.
• Take your lunch break at the pool, swim vigorously for 20–30 minutes, and have a light snack afterwards.

• If you work at home because you have school-age children, walk to and from school with them.
• If you have to use a car, park at a distance from the school gate – both you and your children will get some extra exercise.
• Consider buying an exercise bicycle or other exercise equipment, and build in daily time slots around your work to use it. Exercise for five minutes instead of getting yourself a snack from the kitchen. Then drink some water. You'll no longer feel you need a snack.

sizzled **beef** and green **pepper** stir fry

This quickly made supper dish is a light, crunchy mix of vegetables, beef and oriental flavourings. The cup you use does not have to hold exactly 175 g (6 oz) of rice: just be sure to use the same cup to measure the rice and the water it is cooked in.

preparation time: **10 minutes**

cooking time: **18–23 minutes**

serves **2**

NUTRIENTS PER SERVING	
calories	630
carbohydrate	92 g
(sugars)	16 g
protein	27 g
fat	16 g
(saturated)	3 g
fibre	5 g

*1 level cup (about 175 g/6 oz) basmati
    rice, rinsed until the water runs clear*
2 teaspoons cornflour
1 teaspoon mild chilli powder
¼ teaspoon ground cloves
175 g (6 oz) rump steak, thinly sliced
2 tablespoons sunflower or rapeseed oil
2 green peppers, deseeded and finely sliced
15 cm (6 in) piece of leek, sliced
1 carrot, finely sliced
3 stalks lemon grass, trimmed and sliced
2 cm (¾ in) piece of fresh ginger, grated
1 clove garlic, crushed
1 tablespoon dry sherry
½ teaspoon soya sauce
1 tablespoon water

1 Put the rice in a saucepan and add exactly 1½ cups of boiling water. Stir once, cover and bring to the boil. Reduce the heat and simmer for 12–15 minutes, until the water is absorbed.

2 Meanwhile, mix the cornflour with the dry spices and use to coat the meat.

3 Heat 1 tablespoon of oil in a pan until hot. Add the peppers, leek, carrot, lemon grass, ginger and garlic. Stir-fry for 4–5 minutes. Reduce the heat, add the sherry, soya sauce and water to the pan and warm through.

4 Heat the remaining oil in a separate pan until hot. Add the beef slices and stir-fry for 2–3 minutes, until lightly browned all over.

5 Divide the rice between two bowls. Add the vegetables and top with the hot beef strips. Serve at once.

charred fruit platter

Treat yourself to an exotic feast of tangy grilled fruit, coated with a mixture of honey, ginger and lemon juice. Other fruits that are equally delicious grilled this way are pears, apples and kiwi fruit.

preparation time: **10 minutes**

cooking time: **7-8 minutes**

serves **2**

2 tablespoons clear honey
Grated zest of 1 lemon
2 cm (¾ in) piece fresh ginger, grated
4 wedges fresh pineapple, peeled
4 slices mango, peeled
4 slices papaya, deseeded and peeled
2 bananas, peeled and halved

1 Heat the grill to high.

2 Mix the honey, lemon and ginger together and spread liberally over the fruit, coating it well on all sides.

3 Grill the fruit for 7–8 minutes until golden, turning it and basting it with the honey mixture once or twice.

4 The fruit can be served hot with natural yoghurt, or cooled and chilled for serving as a refreshing snack.

NUTRIENTS PER SERVING	
calories	260
carbohydrate	64 g
(sugars)	57 g
protein	3 g
fat	1 g
(saturated)	0 g
fibre	6 g

pink grapefruit and tiger prawn salad

This citrus and tiger prawn combination will make you look forward to lunch. Low in fat and high in taste, it will stimulate your taste buds without inducing a post-lunch slump.

preparation time: **10 minutes**

cooking time: **3 minutes**

serves **2**

6 baby sweetcorns
55 g (2 oz) rocket or other salad leaves
150 g (5½ oz) peeled tiger prawns
1 pink or red grapefruit, segmented
1 stick celery, finely sliced
FOR THE DRESSING
1 tablespoon light oil, such as sunflower
1 tablespoon cider vinegar
1 tablespoon fresh chives
Black pepper, to season

1 Blanch the sweetcorn in boiling water for 2 minutes, then rinse and drain. Cut into 1 cm (½ inch) slices.

2 Put most of the salad leaves into a glass serving bowl. Arrange the sweetcorn, prawns, grapefruit and celery on top, and finish with the remaining salad leaves.

3 Mix the dressing ingredients together and pour over the salad. Serve at once.

NUTRIENTS PER SERVING	
calories	160
carbohydrate	9 g
(sugars)	9 g
protein	17 g
fat	7 g
(saturated)	1 g
fibre	3 g

FOOD FOR STUDENT LIFE

Studying demands a great deal of physical and mental energy as you try to organise your time around lectures, exams and social life. And this may be the first time that you're responsible for looking after yourself.

Choose the best

Exam pressures, limited finances and late nights – these are all much easier to cope with if you maintain your health by eating good food (see the guidelines on pages 11-15).

For some students, it's not always easy to have regular meals. You may be tempted to rely on cheap, fast-food outlets – especially late at night when you're too tired to cook.

Try to eat before you go out so you don't feel ravenous at the end of the evening. A regular diet of junk food will affect both your mental alertness and physical health. Late nights, project deadlines and rushed meals soon lead to vitamin and mineral deficiencies. When exam time arrives, or you have an urgent essay deadline, your body may not have the nutritional reserves it needs to cope with the additional stress on your immune system.

The psychological factor As well as the practical influences on your lifestyle, such as time-pressure and finances, other factors can affect your food habits. For example, how important is food to you? Have you become more interested in food now that you have left home, or do you regard it as something to fill you up quickly and cheaply? Do you restrict your food intake because you want to lose weight or are you eating lots of 'comfort food' to relieve the stress?

How well you function is directly affected by the quality of the food you eat, so get the best nutritional value you can, using tips from the Menu Plan overleaf as a guide. Good health is not just about diet though – alcohol, cigarettes, drugs and lack of exercise all take their toll on your health and alertness.

Fruity solutions

When you don't have time to cook something substantial, fruit is a great alternative. Get into the habit of eating some every day. Raw fruit (and vegetables) are full of flavonoids (commonly known as bioflavonoids).

These nutrients, along with vitamin C, beta carotene and vitamin E, help to fight off disease and give you extra energy. And you don't need to buy expensive fruit to enjoy these benefits – oranges and apples are cheap and vitamin-rich. A can of own-brand fruit cocktail is good too – choose fruit canned in juice rather than syrup which is full of sugar.

Eating vegetarian

If you are vegetarian or vegan you need to take care about what you eat in order to obtain the maximum nutrients from your food. Vegans eat foods from plant origins only, so soya products (including soya drinks) are valuable sources of vitamins and minerals (see pages 184-185).

CONCENTRATE BETTER *with foods rich in vitamin B_1 (thiamin). These include lean meats, such as chicken and fat-free bacon, and eggs.*

CHOCOLATE AND CAFFEINE *also help you focus – eating a piece of chocolate with a cup of coffee will give your brain a boost. The chocolate helps you to concentrate and the caffeine keeps you alert.*

MEMORY FUNCTION *can be enhanced by eating foods high in vitamins B_6 and B_{12} also. You can obtain these vitamins by eating a couple of slices of wholegrain bread and a glass of milk.*

CAULIFLOWER FOR BRAIN POWER *Cauliflower (left), eggs, soya and cabbage all contain choline. This helps to make a neurotransmitter which enables your brain to function well. But you also need vitamin B_5 from liver, eggs and wholegrains to convert the choline into the neurotransmitter.*

EAT TO BEAT exam nerves

Pooling your resources *Students can save precious funds by organising meals that they can eat together, and by making regular shopping lists to share the costs of the food. This way you can buy more, pay less, and eat really well.*

Protein foods Eggs, wholegrains and soya beans are all excellent and inexpensive sources of protein.

Get plenty of iron Fill up on leafy green vegetables such as cabbage, dried apricots and broccoli.

Zinc levels Sprinkle zinc-rich wheatgerm and seeds over meals.

Vitamin B$_{12}$ Eggs and milk are good sources, but as B$_{12}$ is only present in foods of animal origin, vegans will have to obtain it from fortified cereals or supplements.

Calcium Potatoes, sweetcorn and dairy foods provide lots of calcium.

Shopping on a shoestring

You don't have to spend a fortune on food to eat healthily. Here are some money-saving tips for cash-starved budget watchers. Use your funds wisely and you'll still be able to enjoy good, nutritious food.

• Choose supermarket special offers. Most supermarkets regularly offer 'two for one' or half-price deals.

• Look for own brands. Supermarket own-label items are almost always cheaper than big brand names and are usually just as good.

• Share the shopping with a friend or group of friends so you can buy in greater bulk and save money.

• Use your greengrocer or local market stall when buying fresh fruit and vegetables. They are generally much cheaper than supermarkets and often offer better quality.

• Shop late in the evening when supermarkets and market stalls are selling their produce cheaply. There is often a section in supermarkets reserved for reduced-price items.

• Don't shop when you're hungry. You'll be lured into buying more, especially fatty snack foods.

MENU PLAN
exam-week survival tips

Finals test your mental and physical resources to the limit, so follow these friendly guidelines and meet the challenge.

FLYING START *For anti-stress B vitamins and vitamin C, pile slices of fresh fruit onto bowls of muesli or fortified cereals. Use wholemeal bread for toast.*

ENDURANCE AND STAMINA *Choose potato, pasta or rice dishes with plenty of vegetables. Accompany with fresh salads.*

SMART SNACKS *Almonds, Brazil nuts and sunflower seeds may improve your memory.*

THINK DRINKS *Maintain your fluid intake with plenty of water, semi-skimmed milk and fruit juice.*

Forget the stress and enjoy your food *Eating a wholesome sandwich like this with crunchy watercress for freshness saves time when you need to study and gives you long-lasting energy.*

EXTRA SUPPLEMENTS

It is best to obtain your nutrients from a wide range of foods, but if you're not eating a large variety – perhaps you're dieting, or have a food intolerance – it's a good idea to take a daily multivitamin and mineral supplement. These needn't be expensive – supermarket own brands are fine – and one a day could make all the difference to your energy and alertness levels. Smokers are particularly at risk, as their need for the antioxidant vitamins C, E and beta carotene is increased.

Boost your immune system The B vitamins riboflavin, thiamin and niacin are all essential for the release of energy from food, and will therefore help to keep your immune system in tip-top condition. If you don't eat much dairy food, nuts or wholegrains, it may be advisable to take a B group supplement.

Extra vitamin C Your requirement for vitamin C increases in times of stress, and you are then particularly vulnerable to viral infections such as colds. Take 500 milligrams of ascorbic acid tablets daily before and during exam time.

Coping with exam pressure

Don't be tempted to skip a meal because you need to revise. You will feel better and work more efficiently if your body doesn't have to call on your energy reserves. Also, stress may increase your desire to snack – so go with the flow, but choose healthy versions instead of endless packets of crisps.

These snacks will keep you going:
- Citrus fruit for vitamin C.
- Dried fruit, such as figs, raisins and dried apricots for iron and fibre.
- Beans on toast – this is even better if you choose reduced salt and sugar beans, with wholemeal bread.
- A bowl of fortified breakfast cereal with semi-skimmed milk.

Drink hot milk A warm bath and milky drink before bedtime the night before an exam will help you to unwind. Avoid caffeine and smoking before you go to bed.

Cut down on alcohol Limit your intake now and celebrate afterwards.

Ditch the diet This is not the time to try to lose weight – you need energy to help you concentrate.

Eat with friends Why not invite some friends over once a week for a good meal? You could ask them to pool money for the ingredients, or set up a rota system so that everyone takes turns at cooking. Try some of the delicious, inexpensive, as well as nourishing recipes opposite.

chickpea curry with raita

This curry tastes wonderful and is so simple to make. You can use fresh spices but pastes such as korma, madras or vindaloo are easier. For a creamier flavour, add 25 g (1 oz) of creamed coconut towards the end.

preparation time: **10 minutes**

cooking time: **25 minutes**

serves **2**

FOR THE RAITA
150 g (5½ oz) low-fat natural yoghurt
7.5 cm (3 in) piece cucumber, grated
A few mint leaves, chopped
½ teaspoon cumin seeds
Black pepper
FOR THE CURRY
1 tablespoon sunflower oil
2 small onions, chopped
2 cloves garlic, crushed
2.5 cm (1 in) piece fresh ginger, grated
1 heaped tablespoon curry paste
400 g (14 oz) canned chopped tomatoes
400 g (14 oz) canned chickpeas, rinsed
2 tablespoons chopped coriander leaves

1 Combine all the ingredients for the raita and chill until ready to serve.

2 Heat the oil in a frying pan. Add the onions and garlic and fry gently until soft. Add the ginger and curry paste and stir-fry for 1 minute. Add the chopped tomatoes and chickpeas, stirring well. Cover and cook over a low heat for 20 minutes, stirring occasionally.

3 Stir in 1 tablespoon of the coriander and heat again for a few minutes.

4 Sprinkle over the remaining coriander and serve with rice or naan bread.

NUTRIENTS PER SERVING	
calories	370
carbohydrate	48 g
(sugars)	18 g
protein	20 g
fat	11 g
(saturated)	2 g
fibre	10 g

vegetable and coriander soup

Impress your friends with this typical Middle Eastern soup, which is particularly delicious served with lemon juice. It's a hearty meal in itself, and will keep in the fridge for several days.

preparation time: **20 minutes**

cooking time: **45 minutes**

serves **4**

200 g (7 oz) split red lentils
2 tablespoons sunflower or rapeseed oil
1 large onion, chopped
3 cloves garlic, crushed
3 medium potatoes, diced
280 g (10 oz) frozen spinach
25 g (1 oz) fresh coriander leaves, chopped
Salt and black pepper
Juice of 1 lemon

1 Simmer the lentils in plenty of water, according to packet instructions, until soft. Set aside in the cooking water.

2 Heat the oil in a large saucepan. Add the onion and garlic and fry gently.

3 Add the potatoes and fry for about 3 minutes, stirring frequently. Mix in the spinach and coriander, then the lentils with their cooking water. If the lentils have absorbed most of the water, add 300–400 ml (½–¾ pint) water.

4 Season, cover the pan and cook for 40–45 minutes over a low heat, stirring occasionally, until the soup has reached a thick, porridge-like consistency. Add more water if necessary, to prevent the mixture from sticking to the pan.

5 Pour into bowls and serve with a little lemon juice squeezed over the top.

NUTRIENTS PER SERVING	
calories	350
carbohydrate	58 g
(sugars)	5 g
protein	17 g
fat	7 g
(saturated)	1 g
fibre	6 g

Food on the move

Many people regularly travel long distances to work. For some it is the daily commute, for others hours spent in airport lounges or on the 'long-haul'. For railway regulars and corporate high flyers alike, eating the right food helps to combat stress, heighten alertness and improve efficiency.

Rush hour travel is stressful on its own, but combined with the pressures of work, it can become a formula for exhaustion. If you are constantly on the move and don't eat properly, you won't get enough nutrients from your food to cope with the extra demands.

build in some exercise

• Make time to go to the gym once or twice a week, or go to the pool for a swim.

• If you have a bicycle and your workplace is within reasonable distance, use it to commute whenever possible.

• If you commute by train or bus, get off a stop earlier and walk from there to work.

• Running for the train may be a form of exercise, but it is usually done in a panic. Allow extra time to walk briskly to the station knowing that you will arrive in time.

Everyone who commutes knows how delays and overcrowding can quickly build up tension levels. This is because adrenaline, the 'fight or flight' hormone, is released into your bloodstream when you are under stress. An occasional surge of adrenaline does no harm – indeed, it is necessary if you are to perform at your best in many work situations. But constant high levels can deplete your energy reserves.

COMMUTING

You can't stop your body producing adrenaline and there is nothing you can do about it when your train is cancelled or you find yourself at the back of a 5-mile traffic jam. But you can learn how to cope better with these situations: allow plenty of time for your journey, listen to some relaxing music in the car, and read for pleasure on the train rather than do paperwork.

You can also avoid slipping into unhealthy eating habits. These can easily become part of your working life: hurried or missed breakfasts; fizzy drinks and fat-saturated burgers snatched at the railway station; and crisps, chocolate bars or other snacks eaten on the run.

How food can help

In general, a healthy, balanced diet based on the Five Food Groups (see pages 11-15) provides all the nutrients you need. But, as a commuter, you should be aware that some foods are particularly effective in helping you to cope with the pressures of daily travel.

Resistance to infection Travelling in large, closely-packed crowds every day makes you vulnerable to viral and bacterial infections such as colds and flu. The antioxidant vitamins – beta carotene, vitamins C and E – and the minerals zinc and selenium provide a powerful support for the immune system (see page 118). Eat plenty of fruit and vegetables, nuts and seeds and seafood, especially shellfish, and use vegetable oils in cooking, to obtain good supplies of antioxidants.

Energy sources The B vitamins thiamin (B_1), riboflavin (B_2) and niacin all help to release energy from food into your body, where stress may have depleted your reserves. Foods rich in B vitamins include wholegrain foods, yeast extract, dairy produce, lentils and other pulses, liver, green vegetables, seafood, meat, eggs, nuts, seeds and dried fruit.

Anti-stress snack A bag of mixed nuts and dried fruit slipped into your briefcase makes an easy and delicious snack, which, as well as being packed with high levels of energy and protein, is also extremely good for your heart.

Help for the heart Commuting can put your heart under strain because stress makes the heart beat faster and blood pressure rise. Eating oily fish such as sardines, herrings, pilchards mackerel and salmon twice a week helps to protect your heart. They are rich in omega-3 fatty acids which are known to be helpful in treating heart disease (see page 56).

The value of nuts Eating small quantities of unsalted nuts regularly can reduce the risk of heart attacks by 30–50 per cent. This is because:
• Most nuts, though high in calories, contain unsaturated fat. (Coconuts have saturated fat, so avoid them.)

• Nuts contain a high level of antioxidant vitamin E.
• They contain arginine, used to make nitric oxide, which helps to protect heart muscle.

Avoid salty foods Raised blood pressure leads to an increase in the risk of strokes and heart disease. If high blood pressure is a problem, you should cut down on salt and avoid high-fat, high-salt foods such as crisps or chips (see page 59).

Commuting by train Make time for a good breakfast – a glass of fresh orange juice, some banana muffins (see recipe page 86), or a bowl of fortified cereal give a better boost for your energy levels than a hurried snack on the train.

If your journey is long, a banana or an apple, a packet of raisins or unsalted almonds in your briefcase make simple, healthy snacks. Forget about coffee or tea from the station buffet, as the caffeine in them could

add to your stress levels. Choose fruit juices or mineral water instead.

Extra help in winter Supplements such as odourless garlic perles and echinacea (see page 119) can help to give a boost to your immune system. Echinacea should be taken when symptoms first appear: it should not be used continuously, as it is most effective when an infection is acute.

Strategies for car users

Eating a meal before you set out helps you to cope with the stress of driving. But if you have to start your journey without breakfast, take a fruit or cereal bar to eat on the way and a yoghurt and banana for a healthy snack at work.

Keep low-salt savoury biscuits or breadsticks, dried fruit and a bottle of water in the car. Water is most important in summer: take frequent sips – dehydration may cause headaches and affect coordination.

BUSINESS TRAVEL

If you regularly take long-haul flights the excitement of air travel soon wears off. For business travellers, planes mean dehydration, exhaustion and jet-lag. To make matters worse, the chances are that you will have to work efficiently soon after arriving at the airport.

The disruptive effects

Jet lag is the result when your body's internal clock becomes upset from travelling through several time zones. Your 'circadian rhythm' (see page 296) is set by the patterns of daylight and darkness, and time differences across continents can turn night into day too quickly for your body to adjust its rhythm efficiently.

If daylight in your new time zone comes at a time when you would normally be asleep, your brain may not produce enough melatonin, the hormone that regulates sleeping patterns. Insufficient levels can make you lethargic and depressed.

The classic symptoms of jet lag are daytime sleepiness, headache, disorientation, indigestion, poor concentration, clumsiness, insomnia and irritability. And the more time zones you cross, the more noticeable these symptoms become. If you are a typical business traveller you won't have time to adjust to a new time zone. You are more likely go straight from the airport to a meeting. But with some advance planning you can minimise the effects of jet lag, increase alertness and get ready to tackle a busy working day.

Choosing foods that help

If your levels of melatonin are low because of frequent changes of time zones, try boosting your intake of tryptophan, the amino acid that influences your body's production of melatonin, and also releases the brain chemical serotonin (which helps you to go to sleep). Foods rich in tryptophan include turkey, game, chicken, cauliflower, broccoli, milk, cheese, lean meat, eggs, soya beans, fennel, bananas and watercress.

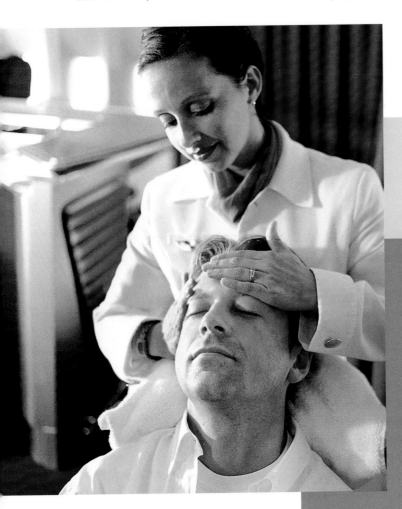

A RELAXING MASSAGE *Enterprising airlines now provide skilled massage for business travellers. This not only reduces stress, it also helps you to relax and fall asleep on overnight flights.*

1 *Eating a simple chicken or turkey sandwich will help to boost your tryptophan levels.*

2 *If you are on an overnight flight, order a milky drink with a plain biscuit to help you sleep.*

3 *Exercise on the days before you fly to boost your serotonin levels.*

4 *Reset your watch to the time zone of your destination as soon as you board the plane. This helps you to be mentally prepared.*

5 *Book a flight that arrives in the morning. You will be more likely to sleep normally the following evening.*

FIVE WAYS TO **beat jet lag**

Ginger helps to combat nausea and digestive discomfort while travelling. Take regular sips of ginger ale during your flight and pack some ginger biscuits or preserved ginger in a small plastic box to nibble.

Melatonin supplements are widely used in the USA, where they are sold over the counter. In Europe, they are not available without prescription. Although melatonin can be effective in countering jet lag, its long-term safety is not known. Also, you need to be accurate in the timing of each dose to ensure that it is effective.

Using light to adjust Your body relies on melatonin to set its body clock. In order to stabilise your levels of the hormone, try to get as much light as possible on the morning you arrive and, if possible, stay in shaded rooms in the evening.

A comfortable flight

Air travel causes problems such as dehydration. To avoid this, drink plenty of water rather than tea and coffee, both of which are diuretics. Watch your alcohol intake, too: it dehydrates you and exacerbates jet lag. To help your digestion, take sachets of mint tea with you and ask for hot water. And to help you sleep, order a milky drink.

Cramps and back pain A sedentary life-style often causes back problems and flying can exarcerbate these. Get up and move around during the flight. Do stretching and twisting exercises or simple yoga exercises where you are sitting. Loosen tight clothing and shoes. If your flight has a stopover, leave the plane and go into the terminal for a walk.

Using the in-flight menu If you travel first or business class, the menu may offer a choice of meals. Airline menus vary a lot, but the panel below shows how to apply some basic principles when ordering an in-flight meal. It makes all the difference to your working day if you choose a breakfast that helps you to stay awake. And you may be able to ensure that meals ordered from the dinner menu are both weight-friendly and a pleasure to eat.

Major airlines provide special meals for people with conditions such as diabetes or coeliac disease. They also offer low-calorie, low-fat and high-fibre meals, but you must order these when booking the flight.

breakfast to stay alert

HOW TO CHOOSE

• Go for protein. The main breakfast options on the menu may be grilled smoked bacon with scrambled eggs, grilled tomato and hash-brown potato *or* smoked haddock kedgeree.

• Choose the bacon, egg and tomato option – its high-protein content helps to keep you awake. Order a fruit juice too, but omit the hash-brown potato, as they contain sleep-inducing carbohydrates. Avoid the kedgeree.

• Avoid carbohydrates. A typical Continental breakfast includes Greek yoghurt with honey, Danish pastry, fresh fruit juice, bread rolls, butter and preserves. Order the yoghurt and juice, but avoid the pastry and rolls.

light options for dinner

HOW TO CHOOSE

• Watch the fat. If the dinner menu offers a Salade Niçoise or Duck Terrine as your choice of starter, order the salad and ask for it to be served with a low-calorie dressing. The terrine is high in fat.

• Your choices for the main course may be grilled breast of chicken with mango sauce, sweet potato and mangetout; *or* seared salmon with hollandaise sauce, buttered new potatoes and seasonal vegetables; *or* wild mushroom ravioli with a cream and Gruyère sauce.

• Choose grilled chicken, or order the salmon or ravioli without the sauce.

• Instead of a sugary, high-fat dessert, choose something simple such as fresh fruit (without cream). Ask for a herb tea or decaffeinated coffee.

CORPORATE ENTERTAINING

There is no doubt that good food can help to keep the wheels of business turning smoothly. But people whose work involves regular corporate entertaining may put their health at risk as a result of eating unwisely.

If you have a demanding, high-level job, you need a nutritious, well-balanced diet to help you to cope with the pressure. Reconciling this with the demands of almost daily business meals requires considerable thought. To come through years of corporate hospitality safely, you need to look after your digestive system, protect your heart and circulation and keep your weight at a healthy level.

To achieve this, you should be well-informed about foods and cooking styles from all over the world. Armed with this knowledge you can handle any menu with confidence, choose a well-balanced meal, pick out the low-fat dishes, and avoid foods that contain hidden salt and other health hazards.

Menu guidelines

To keep your heart and circulation healthy, you should cut down on fatty foods (particularly those high in saturated fats) and keep your weight down. The menu provides useful clues to the fat content of dishes in two main ways:

• A low-fat method of cooking is referred to – 'poached' fish, for instance, or 'griddled' breast of chicken. The panel below explains some of these methods.

• The name of the dish includes descriptive words, often from classic French or Italian cooking, which indicate the ingredients used. The guidelines overleaf will help you to recognise many of these terms, and choose the best low-fat options.

Keeping a healthy balance

When composing a meal from several courses, try to consider the overall balance. Current healthy eating guidelines recommend eating more carbohydrate foods such as pasta, rice or potato dishes. Choose wholegrain rolls or bread rather than white, and ask for a low-fat spread instead of butter.

Balance a carbohydrate-based main course (such as pasta or risotto) with a small serving of protein. You can order fish as a starter – freshly grilled sardines, for example, are a delicious treat and good for your heart. Think of calories too: if your main course is quite high in calories, have a green

how is it cooked?

There are many ways of preparing and cooking food without fat, or with very little. These are the ones most often named on menus.

En papillote Individual portions of well-flavoured food, especially seafood, poultry and vegetables, are wrapped in greaseproof paper or foil and baked.

Griddled/grilled This involves cooking food on a rack so that fats drip off. The heat is intense, so food cooks quickly. With a griddle pan, the heat is beneath the food, with a grill, it is above the food.

Poached Food is cooked in a fat-free, well-flavoured liquid, which is kept at a gentle simmering point, to prevent food becoming tough.

Steamed Food is cooked in the hot steam rising from boiling water, a method which preserves nutrients and maintains food colour.

Braised/casseroled Both techniques involve cooking food slowly in stock or wine. Tougher cuts of meat, poultry and fibrous vegetables become very tender; but the meat may be fatty – ask the waiter.

The king of shellfish Order a fresh lobster in a good restaurant and you will get the whole, splendid shellfish – and the tools needed to tackle it easily. Go easy on any mayonnaise accompaniment.

salad with a low-calorie dressing (or none). Or choose a vegetable starter.

Avoid rich, high-calorie desserts: instead, choose fresh fruit or fruit salads. If there is a cheese board, have small amounts of two or three cheeses, choosing a lower-fat soft cheese as well as a high-fat hard one. Go easy, though – cheese is usually high in calories.

Balance your other meals of the day. If lunch has been substantial, eat a light supper, such as grilled chicken, a salad and mineral water.

Tackling tricky foods

Some people have difficulty knowing how to eat some foods. The more common examples include:

Lobster Crack open the body and claws with the crackers brought to your table. Break the shell apart with your fingers and use the lobster pick to pull out the flesh.

Mussels Pick these up with your fingers and extract the mussel meat with a fork. Put the empty shells in a separate bowl or on the side of your plate. Drink the sauce with a spoon.

Asparagus Use your fingers, not cutlery. And avoid eating your asparagus with high-fat sauces such as hollandaise: instead, choose a light vinaigrette dressing, or even a little melted butter with black pepper. Dip each spear into the sauce, then bite it cleanly through. Leave any woody stems on the edge of the plate.

Alcohol and hospitality

Nowadays, people often avoid alcohol at business lunches, choosing mineral water instead. If you drink alcohol, stay within safe drinking guidelines (see page 97): heavy drinking is not appropriate in business entertaining. Order bottled

Business meals, business deals Take a positive approach to corporate eating and drinking by being well informed about the food and wine you choose. The rewards will be a healthy digestion and heart, as well as improved profits.

water to drink with the meal, even if everyone is also drinking wine. If you're attending a function where there will be alcohol but very little food, have a glass of skimmed milk and a sandwich before you go to ease the effects. You could also alternate glasses of fruit juice or tonic water between alcoholic drinks.

Other tips Avoid nibbling salted snacks with aperitifs and don't add salt to food. Watch out for salt in soy sauces, anchovies and smoked fish. And use the pepper mill: pepper stimulates digestion, eases flatulence and relieves constipation.

Being a good host You can help to maintain your good corporate

relationships by checking whether your guests at restaurants have special dietary requirements. These may be due to conditions such as diabetes or a gluten intolerance, or your guest may be a vegetarian, or follow a low-salt or low-fat diet.

Some religions impose certain food bans or periods of fasting, or require specific practices in the preparation and eating of food which may have to be taken into account.

It won't always be possible to obtain advance warning of every guest's requirements, but thoughtful business executives will choose a restaurant they know well, with a menu that offers plenty of choice.

know what the
MENU MEANS

The names of the dishes on the menu, even if not in English, give clues to their ingredients. As with fast food (see pages 156-157) try to choose the healthiest options:

High-fat dishes Be careful – these use ingredients high in saturated fats such as butter, cream and pastry:

à la king Cooked in a creamy white sauce with vegetables.

alfredo This describes meat or poultry that is cooked in a rich, creamy sauce with ham and mushrooms.

au beurre This means that the food is cooked in butter.

beignet This usually refers to deep-fried cakes/pastries.

coulibiac A hot pastry envelope, usually enclosing fish and other ingredients, which may be high in fat.

croustade Made with a pastry crust.

dauphinoise A classic dish of potatoes cooked in cream and garlic, topped with Gruyère cheese.

en croûte Meat or fish that has been wrapped in pastry.

forestière Usually served with bacon and fried potatoes.

fricassée Light meats such as chicken, turkey or veal cooked in a cream-based sauce.

hollandaise A creamy sauce based on eggs and butter.

mornay A white sauce made with cheese and cream.

Hidden perils These dishes may have extra fat and sugar:

au gratin The dish is topped with breadcrumbs and grated cheese and grilled. Ask for the cheese to be omitted.

crêpe A pancake used for savoury and dessert dishes. Fried and often smothered in sugar.

creole Butter and cream are often used in Creole cooking, so ask before ordering.

dijonnaise Ask if there is extra cream in the mustard sauce.

lyonnaise Avoid extra cream in this onion and herb sauce.

CORPORATE EATING AND DRINKING MAY PUT YOUR HEALTH AT RISK FROM HIGH-FAT, HIGH-CALORIE DISHES ON THE MENU. THESE GUIDELINES WILL HELP YOU TO DECODE THEIR NAMES, SO THAT YOU CAN IDENTIFY DISHES THAT ARE HEALTHILY LOW IN FAT FROM THOSE THAT YOU SHOULD EITHER AVOID, OR APPROACH WITH CAUTION.

BUSINESS ENTERTAINING *To make a healthy selection in a restaurant, take your time when consulting the menu. North African dishes, such as couscous or tagine, tend to be cream-free and therefore a good choice. If you would like a lower-fat version of a dish, ask whether the chef would be willing to adapt the recipe.*

terrine A kind of pâté. Depending on ingredients, it may be high in fat, so check first.

nasi goreng Indonesian term for 'fried rice'. The rice is fried in oil. There are hundreds versions of the dish.

Low-fat dishes You can order these with confidence:

à la fermière Meat or poultry pot-roasted with vegetables.

à la florentine/fiorentina Cooked with spinach.

à la grecque A term usually used of vegetables, prepared Greek-style with olive oil, lemon and herbs.

à la jardinière/giardino Cooked with garden vegetables.

à la niçoise With tomato, tuna, egg, olives and anchovies.

alla arrabiata A hot, chilli-based pasta sauce.

alla cacciatore Braised with tomatoes, herbs, mushrooms.

au jus Literally 'in its own juices' – usually meat.

brochette Meat, fish or vegetables grilled on a skewer.

chasseur Poultry or game cooked with tomatoes, mushrooms and a wine sauce (usually with red wine).

coulis This usually takes the form of a fruit sauce.

marinara A tomato-based seafood pasta sauce.

provençale The dish contains tomatoes, garlic and other Mediterranean ingredients such as olives.

ragoût A casserole of braised meat, poultry or game.

salsa A spicy sauce, often tomato-based.

tagine Meat and vegetable-based stews from Morocco, often served with couscous.

Easing pressure at work

It is normal for all working people, especially working parents, to feel stressed from time to time. Indeed, a certain amount of tension can be invaluable in helping you to meet work targets. But prolonged stress is different: your body needs help from the right foods to relieve its effects.

Stress at the workplace is caused by a combination of factors, including volume of work, time constraints and pressure to perform. Rushed, inadequate meal breaks may encourage you to rely on sugary snacks and caffeine-laden drinks for quick energy. But these only make the situation worse.

STRESS AND YOU

Your body's response to pressure, whether physical or mental, is to release the stress hormone adrenaline into your bloodstream. Your heart beats faster and your blood pressure rises. This 'fight or flight' response (see pages 206-207), a legacy of our caveman past, is intended to boost your physical strength to tackle an enemy, or escape from danger.

However, the largely sedentary nature of modern working life means that the frequent adrenaline boosts you experience do not have positive outlets in physical exertion. Your stress hormone levels may rise higher than normal, and may not return to their previous levels. This can result in raised blood pressure and high

Wholegrains boost energy *The complex carbohydrates in unrefined foods such as brown rice and wholewheat break down slowly in the body, providing necessary sustained energy to help combat stress.*

levels of blood cholesterol. It may also reduce the effectiveness of your immune system and deplete your vitamin and mineral reserves.

You may have classic symptoms of stress (see page 208), and risk becoming less effective at work because of them.

Lifestyle plays a part too: unwise eating and drinking habits and lack of exercise contribute to these negative effects. All this can make you ill, or even damage your long-term health.

Handling pressure There are effective ways of dealing with stress. Work pressure in itself does not cause symptoms such as raised blood pressure. What matters is how you cope.

Some people react to stress by eating unhealthy 'comfort' foods, reducing their physical activity, and increasing their alcohol intake. This can lead to weight gain, and raised blood pressure.

ANTI-STRESS FOOD

To cope with work pressure successfully, you need to improve your diet, moderate the amount of alcohol you drink and get plenty of

exercise. You should also choose foods that are particularly good at combating stress.

When your nervous and immune systems are under pressure, your body quickly uses up its stores of energy. To replenish these stores, you need to increase your intake of B vitamins, because these help to release energy from food and make it available to your body.

Among the best food sources of B vitamins are wholegrains, dairy food, lentils and other pulses, liver, green vegetables, seafood, lean meat, eggs, nuts, seeds and dried fruit.

Strengthening immunity Prolonged periods of stress can weaken your immune system, so you should also eat lots of citrus fruits. These are rich in vitamin C, which boosts your resistance to viruses.

Reducing fatigue Carbohydrate foods such as wholemeal bread, brown rice, potatoes and pasta provide a stable supply of blood sugar to keep your energy levels steady. These foods are much more effective than sugary snacks, as they release a steady trickle of energy rather than a short-term 'hit'.

Banish the salt High levels of salt can lead to raised blood pressure. Limit the amount of bacon, ham, salty snacks, olives and cheese you eat, and avoid ready-prepared meals, which are often high in salt.

The effect on appetite

Pressure can affect your eating patterns. This varies from person to person, but generally speaking, women tend to eat more when they

MENUPLAN
to beat pressure

Although your working day is full of demands that put you under constant pressure, food can be an ally in helping you to rise to the challenge.

START THE DAY WELL Enjoy a bowl of fresh or dried fruit topped with low-fat bio-yoghurt; wholemeal toast with yeast extract and a glass of fruit juice; or a fortified breakfast cereal with semi-skimmed milk and a scattering of sesame seeds, chopped fruit and nuts.

STOP FOR LUNCH Make time for a proper meal break — this could be a wholemeal bread sandwich topped with Brie and grapes, or with low-fat pâté and cucumber; or a bowl of carrot soup with a wholemeal roll.

UNWIND AT NIGHT Plan your meal around a protein-rich main course. Try a simple grilled lean pork chop, which is full of energy-releasing thiamin, or a grilled chicken breast, made tasty with herbs and lemon juice. Both are good with a dressed salad and a baked potato. Lime-marinated cod with salami and mozzarella (recipe overleaf) provides abundant vitamins B and C. Follow with a simple low-fat rice pudding to boost your vitamin B intake even further.

DAILY REMINDERS Throughout the day, drink plenty of water or fresh orange juice instead of coffee or tea. Alternatively, try herb and fruit teas. Take some fruit to work - a banana or an apple is fine. If you have time, prepare a container of chopped kiwi fruit or fresh pineapple to provide a quick burst of energy and vitamin C when you need it.

Pack a desk-top snack of fresh fruits

tension headaches

Headaches at work are usually the result of tension in your neck and shoulder muscles caused by mental or physical stress. Both types of tension lead to pain around the temples, eyes and forehead. If you often have headaches at work, try not to take painkillers. Instead, work out the cause of the stress and deal with the root cause.

• Check your work station – the relation between your chair and desk may be causing poor posture. You can adjust your desk layout, and change the height of your chair, and try tipping the seat so that your knees are below your hips. You should be able to look straight at, or slightly down on, your computer screen.

• Keep a stress diary to help you to recognise the occasions when frustration or anxiety make you tense.

• Relieve muscle tension in your neck and shoulders by breathing deeply and stretching and relaxing these muscles.

• If possible, take a break, including a brisk walk outside.

• Massage essential oil of lavender on your temples to relieve a headache. But be careful – lavender oil is safe to use on its own, but most essential oils should be diluted in a neutral 'carrier' oil such as almond.

feel stressed, and choose sugary foods, such as biscuits or chocolate. Thus, they risk consuming too many calories and too few vitamins and minerals. Men, on the other hand, often eat less when under pressure, but tend to drink more alcohol.

Changing your eating habits A first step towards becoming stress-free at work is to replace biscuits and chocolates with healthier nibbles, such as dried apricots, savoury crackers or packs of raisins and nuts.

Your next step should be to make sure that you have a proper lunch break, however little you feel like eating. This energises you through the afternoon, and you won't need to eat snacks later, when the pressure is off and your appetite returns.

Go easy on caffeine It is tempting to replace lunch with cups of strong coffee when you are up against a deadline. Although the caffeine can keep you going for a while, it may cause problems. It is known to increase blood pressure, and those susceptible to hypertension may find that the combined effects of stress and high caffeine intake have a serious effect on their health.

If you consume food and drink with high levels of caffeine, or take caffeine supplements to help you get through work, you risk having raised blood pressure. Limit your intake of caffeinated drinks to two or three a day and drink plenty of water and fruit juice instead. For more on caffeine, turn to pages 212 and 220.

apple and cranberry bars

Take these fruit-filled bars to work for an energising snack.

preparation time: **10 minutes**

cooking time: **45–50 minutes**

makes **12**

4 dessert apples, peeled, cored and chopped
85 ml (3 fl oz) cranberry juice
70 g (2½ oz) dried cranberries
225 g (8 oz) rolled oats
2 tablespoons light brown sugar
40 g (1½ oz) walnuts, chopped

1 Simmer the apples and cranberry juice in a covered pan for 15 minutes, or until the apples are soft. Purée the mixture in a food processor.

2 Heat the oven to 180°C (350°F, gas mark 4). Base line an 18 x 28 cm (7 x 11 in) shallow baking tin with baking paper.

3 Mix all the remaining ingredients into the purée. Spread the mixture into the tin. Bake for 30–35 minutes, until firm. Cool a little in the tin, then cut into bars. Leave in the tin until cold.

NUTRIENTS PER BAR	
calories	145
carbohydrate	25 g
(sugars)	11 g
protein	3 g
fat	4 g
(saturated)	0
fibre	2 g

marinated cod with salami and mozzarella

Prepare the fish in this simple, zesty marinade in the morning and leave it until the evening when you are ready to cook it. The moist fillets, crispy salami and creamy mozzarella combine beautifully, and taste delicious served on a bed of mixed wild and white rice.

preparation time: **10 minutes plus at least 1 hour marinating**

cooking time: **20–25 minutes**

serves **4**

*4 chunky cod fillets, each about
175 g (6 oz), skinned*
Zest and juice of 2 limes
4 slices Milano salami
4 slices mozzarella
8 slices tomato
Black pepper

1 Place the cod in a container with a lid. Pour lime juice over each fillet and sprinkle over the lime zest. Cover, put in the refrigerator and leave to marinate for at least an hour, but preferably for several hours.

2 Heat the oven to 180°C (350°F, gas mark 4). Transfer the cod fillets to a baking dish, cover and bake in the oven for 15–20 minutes, or until the fish is cooked through.

3 Remove the baking dish from the oven. Top each cod fillet with a slice of salami and place the dish under a preheated grill for 1–2 minutes, until the salami starts to become crispy.

4 Put a slice of mozzarella, topped with 2 tomato slices, on each fillet and return to the grill for another minute.

5 Season with pepper and serve at once on a bed of mixed wild and white rice, spooning some of the cooking liquid from the fish over the rice.

NUTRIENTS PER SERVING	
calories	230
carbohydrate	1.5 g
(sugars)	1.5 g
protein	37 g
fat	9 g
(saturated)	3.5 g
fibre	0.5 g

easing pressure at work

WORKING PARENTS

Juggling children and a career is difficult even for the most organised parent – it takes time and thought to maintain a healthy family diet, and it's very easy for this to slip down your list of priorities in the hurly-burly of daily life. Without careful planning, the demands of your working life may overwhelm all your good intentions to eat well.

Too tired to bother

If you have a long journey to and from work you may find it difficult to get to the shops. What's more, the hard slog of a working day often leaves you feeling too exhausted to cook properly. Many working parents find themselves regularly resorting to the microwave to heat up ready-prepared meals, supplemented with take-away foods.

But once you get out of the routine of cooking meals yourself, you may not get enough variety in your diet – and eating a wide range of foods is the best path to good nutrition. As a working parent, there are good, positive ways in which food can help you to deal with the particular demands of your life – by helping you to combat tiredness, cope with the pressures of work and build good health both for you and your family.

GETTING ORGANISED

When you're busy, it's tempting to buy food on impulse, without having the ingredients of particular meals in mind. But if you simply fill your shopping trolley with whatever looks good on the supermarket shelves, you are likely to find your fridge bare and your cupboard empty when you need to create a meal from

Competing demands *As a busy working parent, time spent with your children is precious. Share mealtimes with them in a relaxed atmosphere; this ensures that the whole family enjoys their food.*

scratch. A more useful approach is to make a list for each shopping trip, and to plan your meals – ideally, at least a week ahead.

Advanced menus Once you get into the habit, you'll find that it's really interesting to develop your meal-plans on a weekly basis. Take a look at the Menu Plan opposite for some ideas for breakfasts, lunches and evening meals that you can mix and match. Just keep in mind the basic guidelines to healthy eating as outlined in the Five Food Groups section (see pages 11-15).

The armchair shopper

Properly thought-out, shopping from home will make endless trips to the supermarket a thing of the past. Why not take advantage of the new home shopping schemes on offer?

You may be able to send your order over the Internet, or phone or fax it to your favourite shop. The time that you spent on those frantic trips to the supermarket after a day's work or on a busy Saturday can now be used to organise your meals and fill in your e-supermarket order form.

As an added bonus, you may find that shopping from home results in lower food bills, as you are no longer tempted to impulse-buy. And if you team up with friends, you may also be able to share delivery charges.

The personal touch Many people prefer to choose their own fruit and vegetables. If you want to look before you buy, get to know your local farm shop, organic box provider or greengrocer. You can buy from these sources and order other essential foods over the Internet.

MENUPLAN
meals for a week

Use the ideas below to plan meals a week ahead. Mix and match recipes into a variety of menus. Thinking ahead makes shopping much easier – and does away with that last-minute panic when you're home from work and can't think what to cook.

BOOSTER BREAKFASTS

CHOOSE VITAMIN-FORTIFIED CEREALS, preferably wholegrain, and avoid sugar or honey-coated versions.

THINK OF FRUIT as a main part of breakfast — slice it into cereals, mix berry fruits into porridge, or make a compôte of dried fruit (recipe page 79).

AT THE WEEKEND enjoy brunches and leisurely breakfasts with wedges of melon, pineapple or papaya, and fresh breads. Or make kedgeree with smoked salmon or smoked mackerel for a nutritious treat.

LUSCIOUS LUNCHES

MAKE OR BUY CRUDITÉS to accompany low-fat dips or hummous and serve with different kinds of bread and rolls to make more interesting sandwiches.

VARY SANDWICH SEASONINGS to excite your taste buds–try red pesto on salami, horseradish with smoked salmon, grainy mustard with Cheddar cheese.

GIVE KIDS VARIETY for their packed lunches including crudités and some fruit.

FEAST ON FRUIT including apples, pears, bananas, grapes, dried apricots, raisins and sultanas.

UNDER 30-MINUTE EVENING MEALS

STIR-FRY STRIPS OF TURKEY STEAK and use to fill a toasted pitta pocket. Serve with a salad of cucumber, tomato, and black olives with olive oil and lemon.

GRILL A PORK CHOP with honey topped with fresh peaches; serve with mashed sweet potato and peas.

COOK PASTA according to the packet instructions and while it is cooking, sauté button mushrooms and courgettes. Add a little low-fat crème fraîche and grated lemon zest and snip over some chives.

SQUEEZE FRESH ORANGE OVER pan-fried chicken breasts, season with fresh tarragon; serve with rice.

MAKE A STIR-FRY from spring onion, pak choi, carrots, bean sprouts and cashews, season with garlic, grated ginger, and soy sauce. Serve with egg noodles.

GRIDDLE MEDITERRANEAN VEGETABLES such as peppers, courgettes, onion and tomatoes with a little olive oil. Season and serve with ciabatta bread.

GRIDDLE LAMB CHOPS with red onion, sliced fennel, and creamy mashed potato.

TOP GRILLED AUBERGINE slices with bacon and serve with hot chilli dip (recipe page 231).

DRIZZLE LIME JUICE over salmon steaks, and microwave. Serve with vegetables and a sauce of horseradish, fromage frais and grated lime rind.

Enjoy these tasty slices of aubergine grilled with bacon

What's in the larder?

Keep a reliable stock of food in your freezer and store cupboard – this way you can always create a nutritious meal at short notice.

Foods for your freezer Double the quantities of favourite family recipes when you cook them and freeze half for later. Also, freeze breads, fish, chickens, peas, sweetcorn, spinach, sliced peppers and herbs, vitamin C-rich summer fruits, low-fat ice creams and sorbets, and stewed apples to make crumbles.

Store-cupboard faithfuls Keep a good stock of cans of tomatoes, kidney and flageolet beans, lentils and chickpeas, canned sardines, tuna and salmon, tomato purée, sun-dried tomatoes, cornflour and flour, a variety of pasta, noodles and rice, couscous, vinegars, oils and mustard, dried fruit and creamed coconut.

CATERING FOR CHILDREN

All parents want to do their utmost to look after their children's health – and this can cause special dilemmas for parents in full-time work.

Where do they eat? Do your children eat with you in the evening, get a meal at an after-school club, eat at a childminder's or have a meal at a friend's house?

Whatever arrangements you make, if most of their meals are eaten away from home, your best strategy is to discuss what your child eats with your child-carers and get them interested and involved in why you are choosing certain foods.

This means planning recipes together, and agreeing on a healthy-eating approach. If your child goes to school, provide a healthy packed lunch, with fresh fruit, crudités, and tasty sandwiches as an alternative to school lunches. This helps them to resist the temptation to opt for chips and burgers from the lunch menu.

Make meals at home with your children enjoyable, nutritious and family-focused. Also, encourage them to get to know about food by helping to cook at the weekend (see page 151). They can try easy dishes such as pizza topped with pineapple, peppers and mushrooms.

Fun to eat Most children love the crunchy, buttery taste of corn on the cob – it's also something that they can learn to cook for themselves.

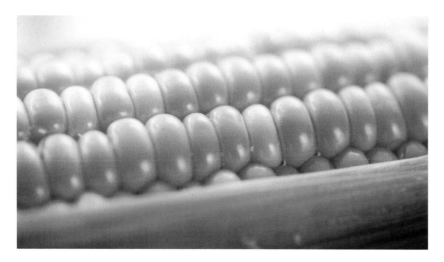

pasta with sage pesto

This pesto has the sharpness of lime and the pungency of sage. Children will love it – and it's a grown-up treat, too.

Preparation time: **5 minutes**

Cooking time: **5–10 minutes**

Serves **4**

*400 g (14 oz) dried tagliatelle
100 g (3½ oz) unsalted
   pistachios, shelled
20 fresh sage leaves
4 tablespoons extra virgin olive
   oil
2 tablespoons lime juice
Salt and black pepper
40 g (1½ oz) Parmesan cheese,
   grated*

1 Cook the pasta according to packet instructions.

2 Meanwhile, blend the nuts, sage and olive oil to a coarse purée in a food processor. Stir in the lime juice, seasoning, and cheese.

3 Mix the pesto into the hot pasta as soon it is drained, and serve immediately. The pesto will keep, covered, in the fridge for 3 days.

NUTRIENTS PER SERVING	
calories	640
carbohydrate	78 g
(sugars)	4 g
protein	20 g
fat	30 g
(saturated)	6 g
fibre	5 g

chicken and mango kebabs with chive couscous

**These spicy kebabs are quick to prepare and taste really special.
Low in fat and high in energy, this is a meal that will give a lift
to tired parents. If nectarines are in season, try using them
instead of the mango.**

preparation time: **10 minutes, plus at
least 15 minutes marinating**

cooking time: **10-12 minutes**

serves **4** (makes 8 kebabs)

*6 medium chicken breast fillets, skinned
and cut into large cubes*
*2 large firm but ripe mangoes, skinned and
cut into large cubes*
Sage or bay leaves
FOR THE MARINADE
Grated zest and juice of two lemons
¼ teaspoon ground cloves
¼ teaspoon ground nutmeg
¼ teaspoon chilli powder
2 tablespoons olive oil
FOR THE COUSCOUS
280 g (10 oz) couscous
500 ml (18 fl oz) boiling water
4 tablespoons chopped chives
Salt and black pepper

1 Put the cubed chicken in a dish, mix
the marinade ingredients together
and pour over the chicken.
Cover, refrigerate and marinate for several hours, if
possible, but not for less than
15 minutes.

2 Heat the grill to high. Thread the
chicken, mango and herb leaves
alternately on to 8 kebab sticks.

3 Cook under the grill for 10–12 minutes,
turning at intervals, until the chicken is
cooked through and the juices run clear.

4 Meanwhile, cover the couscous with the
boiling water and season with salt.
Cover and leave for 10 minutes to fluff
up. Add the chopped chives, season and
fork through until fluffy.

5 Serve the kebabs with the couscous and
a mixed leaf salad.

NUTRIENTS PER SERVING	
calories	590
carbohydrate	62 g
(sugars)	26 g
protein	51 g
fat	16 g
(saturated)	4 g
fibre	5 g

easing pressure at work

Adapting to **circumstances**

You may be a stay-at-home parent or a retired grandparent; or you may have a chronic illness such as arthritis. Whatever your situation, you can positively improve your life by choosing food that will keep you fit and healthy enough to cope with your circumstances.

Many parents are so busy catering for their children's needs that they neglect their own. They are often too tired to make the effort to plan and cook healthy meals for themselves. Consequently, they have insufficient reserves to help them to fight off infections – often caused by viruses that their children bring home from nursery and school. Eating a low-fat, high-fibre diet rich in a variety of fruit and vegetables will provide good antioxidant protection for your immune system.

Parenting is not the sole province of women. Increasing numbers of men stay at home to look after children, and it is just as important for fathers to eat a healthy diet as it is for mothers.

THE ENERGY TO COPE

The foods that are best to keep you fit and healthy are recommended in the Five Food Groups (see pages 11-15). But you may feel particularly run down by the demands of being a parent. In this case you should pay particular attention to those foods that supply extra energy and help you to combat exhaustion.

Getting enough iron If you feel more tired than usual, you may not have sufficient iron stored in your body, and this can result in anaemia. Women who have heavy periods are particularly vulnerable, because they will lose a lot of iron during their monthly bleeds.

If you suspect that you may be iron deficient, ask your doctor for a blood test. You may be prescribed an iron supplement if the results show you are anaemic. You should also eat foods rich in iron including red meat, egg yolks, liver, red kidney beans, chickpeas, wholegrains, fortified breakfast cereals, nuts, pulses and green leafy vegetables. However, if you are pregnant or trying to conceive, you should not eat liver (see page 163).

Food to keep you going

Meals based around carbohydrate foods such as rice, potatoes and pasta help to sustain you throughout the day. Eating a bowl of vegetable soup with a large crusty wholemeal roll at lunch is a much better way to stave off hunger than a slice of white toast or a chocolate biscuit.

You will also need plenty of B vitamins to release the energy from your food. You'll find good sources in wholegrains, yeast extract, dairy produce, lentils and other pulses, liver, green vegetables, seafood, lean meat, eggs, nuts, seeds and dried fruit. A scraping of yeast extract on wholemeal toast is a quick way to boost your vitamin B levels.

Treat yourself A dish of asparagus spears is an excellent boost for your immune system as well as a delicacy. Steaming means the food retains all its nutrients.

spicy meatballs

Adapt this versatile dish for all the family. It has a hot chilli sauce for parents and a milder version for children. Purée the sauce if your child is fussy about vegetables, and serve both versions with spaghetti or rice.

preparation time: **25 minutes plus 30 minutes refrigerating time**

cooking time: **35 minutes**

serves **4**

NUTRIENTS PER SERVING	
calories	270
carbohydrate	21 g
(sugars)	17 g
protein	32 g
fat	7 g
(saturated)	3 g
fibre	4.5 g

500 g (1 lb 2 oz) lean minced beef
2 cloves garlic, crushed
1 onion, sliced
2.5 cm (1 in) piece root ginger, grated
2 tablespoons lime juice
Black pepper
FOR THE MILD SAUCE
1 tablespoon vegetable oil
2 onions, sliced lengthways
3 peppers (any colour), deseeded and sliced
  lengthways
2 cloves garlic, crushed
400 g (14 oz) canned chopped tomatoes
1 teaspoon cumin seeds, crushed
4 tablespoons water
FOR THE HOT SAUCE
1 bird's eye chilli, finely chopped
1 tablespoon chopped fresh coriander
Black pepper

1 Put the minced beef in a bowl. Put the garlic, onion, ginger and lime juice in a blender or food processor, process for a few seconds and add this to the beef, mixing well. Refrigerate for 30 minutes

2 To make the mild sauce, heat the oil in a heavy-based saucepan large enough to hold the sauce and meatballs. Fry the onion, peppers and garlic until lightly browned. Add the tomatoes, cumin and water. Stir well, cover and simmer for 10 minutes, stirring occasionally.

3 Meanwhile, make 24 walnut-sized meat balls from the beef mixture. Place them in the sauce, cover and simmer for 15–20 minutes until they are cooked through. Reserve a portion of sauce and meatballs for the children.

4 Add the chilli and coriander to the remaining sauce, increase the heat and stir for 1-2 minutes. Serve immediately.

Staying in shape

Looking after small children at home places extra demands on your health – you need to be as fit and active as possible. It is easy to put on extra weight by picking at children's meals as well as preparing something for yourself. Snack on fresh fruit – a banana, apple or pear – and a glass of fruit juice if you feel hungry.

If you are overweight, and want to lose the excess pounds, avoid crash diets or cutting down too heavily on food. You will feel even more tired and also risk becoming deficient in several vitamins and minerals.

The best way to shed weight is to get more exercise: book the children into a crèche while you go to the gym, or go for long pram-pushing walks. And make sure your children have lots of exercise, so that they are as tired and ready for bed as you are.

Family mealtimes

Children and parents tend to eat different foods at different times of the day, and may eat together only at weekends. As long as your family meals are healthy, this need not be a problem. Two-in-one shortcuts are useful – with advance planning you can prepare one meal for the

Fit for fatherhood Looking after small children requires physical and mental stamina. Exercise helps on both fronts – why not combine a buggy outing with a vigorous session of speed walking. Aim for 30 minutes continuous activity for maximum benefits.

children and another for yourself to eat later in the evening.

For example Spicy Meatballs (see recipe overleaf) are based on a tomato sauce. This is served plain for children, but chillies and coriander are added for the parents' meal. There are more recipes on pages 152-153.

Shopping with children Taking toddlers to the supermarket can make even the most serene parent desperate with frustration. The following tips make it less stressful.

• Before going out shopping make sure that you have all just eaten. If this isn't possible, give each child an apple to nibble on while they sit in the trolley.

• Alternatively, make your first purchase a packet of breadsticks which they can open immediately.

• Resist 'pester power' from your children; many of the attractively packaged snacks they see advertised on television are high in unhealthy saturated fat and sugar.

• If possible, avoid the aisles which display crisps and sweets, or drive the trolley straight down the middle.

lamb steaks with winter vegetable crumble

A savoury crumble goes well with lamb steaks. It can also accompany a roast or winter casserole, or make a meal in itself – just add some grated cheese to the topping. If you don't have one of the vegetables listed, leave it out and double up on another.

preparation time: **20 minutes plus 1½ hours chilling**

cooking time: **1 hour, 15 minutes**

serves **6**

6 lamb steaks
FOR THE MINT AND TOMATO SALSA
2 shallots, finely chopped
5 ripe tomatoes, chopped
1 tablespoon chopped fresh mint
1 tablespoon balsamic vinegar
1 tablespoon olive oil
FOR THE CRUMBLE
1 tablespoon sunflower oil
1 onion, roughly chopped
½ medium swede, diced
2 large carrots, diced
2 medium parsnips, diced
1 medium white turnip, diced
½ small celeriac, diced
425 ml (¾ pint) vegetable stock or water
3 stalks fresh tarragon
FOR THE TOPPING
50 g (1¾ oz) sunflower margarine
150 g (5½ oz) wholemeal self-raising flour
50 g (1¾ oz) sunflower seeds
Black pepper

1 Combine the salsa ingredients and chill in the refrigerator for 1½ hours.

2 For the crumble, heat the oil in a heavy-based pan. Fry the the onion until soft. Add the vegetables and cook gently for 10 minutes. Add the stock or water and tarragon. Simmer, covered, for 20–25 minutes until the vegetables are tender.

3 To make the topping, rub the margarine into the flour, until it resembles fine breadcrumbs. Add the seeds and pepper.

4 Heat the oven to 180°C (350°F, gas mark 4). Transfer the vegetables to an ovenproof dish and cover with the topping. Bake for 25–30 minutes, or until the topping has browned.

5 Grill the steaks for about 15 minutes, turning once, until they are browned and the juices run clear. Serve with the crumble and mint salsa.

NUTRIENTS PER SERVING	
calories	570
carbohydrate	38 g
(sugars)	13 g
protein	42 g
fat	29 g
(saturated)	8 g
fibre	8 g

summer fruit fool

For an instant dessert, use a packet of ready-mixed summer fruit from your freezer. You could also combine fresh raspberries and strawberries, or blueberries and cherries, whatever is in season. Sieving out the seeds improves the creamy texture.

preparation time: **8 minutes**

serves **4**

250 g (9 oz) summer fruit mixture, thawed
250 g (9 oz) low-fat fromage frais
50 ml (2 fl oz) double cream
2 tablespoons icing sugar, sieved

1 Blend the summer fruits to a purée in a food processor or blender and pass through a sieve to remove any seeds.

2 Lightly whip the cream. Stir the fromage frais and icing sugar into the fruit, and gently fold in the cream.

3 Spoon into tall glasses and chill until required.

4 Serve with dessert biscuits such as *langues de chat*.

NUTRIENTS PER SERVING	
calories	140
carbohydrate	16 g
(sugars)	16 g
protein	5 g
fat	6 g
(saturated)	4 g
fibre	1 g

FREEDOM IN LATER YEARS

Retirement means a radical change of lifestyle, whether you are single or living with a partner. Stopping work may come as an unpleasant shock or even as a feeling of 'bereavement' for some people; but others can't wait to do all the things they have been putting off for years.

One good thing about retirement is that it gives you the time and the freedom to take up new interests or revive old ones. With good health, there is no reason why these pastimes should not be pursued for many years to come – provided you eat well. A healthy diet is one of the essentials for maintaining good health in the later years of life.

Time for a new focus

Retirement gives you a golden opportunity to re-evaluate your priorities, and the way you choose to maintain your body and mind should be one of your main concerns. Now is the time seriously to consider if your diet and lifestyle are as healthy as they should be.

It is well known that older people are more vulnerable than younger ones to such potentially serious health problems as high blood pressure, diabetes and heart disease. To lower your risk of these, try to ensure that your diet includes a wide choice from the Five Food Groups (see pages 11-15), that you eat five portions of fruit and vegetables every day and that you have foods rich in omega-3 fatty acids (see page 56), at least twice a week.

Also, remember to drink plenty of fluids. You should aim to consume at least eight glasses of water or fruit and vegetable juices daily. Many older people drink less than they should because they want to avoid getting up in the night to go to the bathroom. But this can cause real problems: loss of fluids and body salts may cause severe dehydration and even lead to episodes of dizziness and confusion. It is better to drink plenty of fluids, but to have your last drink two or three hours before bedtime.

The pleasures of food

Developing a positive interest in good food is another essential for keeping healthy in retirement. Many people, especially men, spend their adult lives eating food prepared by someone else. Consequently, they seldom experience the pleasure of preparing food themselves.

Easy peasy The main ingredients in this vibrantly colourful bowl of Pea and Lettuce Soup are onions, peas and lettuce. These are all easy to grow in back gardens or on allotments. The recipe is on page 330.

The joys of self-sufficiency
Gardening is a great source of gentle exercise as well as providing you with a steady supply of nutritious raw ingredients. There is much personal satisfaction to be gained from growing, cooking and eating your own food.

Retirement provides an excellent opportunity to improve your cookery skills. There are plenty of courses available for everyone from beginners to aspiring chefs. Or you could get inspiration from watching a good television cook at work. Once you've mastered the basics, why not try baking your own bread or making your own pasta? Both techniques get your fingers working hard as you knead the dough – and the finished products are healthy sources of carbohydrate. Making jams, preserves and chutneys is also satisfying work. They taste much better than shop-bought varieties – and you know what is in them.

GROW YOUR OWN

If the seasonal fruits and vegetables in your preserves and pickles have been grown by you, so much the better. Cultivating your own fruit, vegetables and herbs is economically sound and environmentally friendly. If you do not have a garden, enquire at your local council offices about allotments or local community garden schemes.

When space is really limited, try growing fresh herbs and vegetables in window boxes, pots and planters – visit your local library and browse through the many specialist books that show you how to exploit these small-space growing areas.

Extending your range There is now more time for you to learn about different cuisines. Those delicious meals you may have eaten in a Chinese, Thai, Mexican, Indian or Japanese restaurant, or as ready-prepared dishes bought at the supermarket, could now become part of your home cooking. This is made easier by the range of exotic spices and sauces now available at your supermarket.

You'll probably be surprised at how quickly you feel adventurous enough to cook a deliciously spiced curry for yourself, with a healthy emphasis on fresh vegetables, seafood, chicken and fish.

great food for kids

If you are tempted to stock up on sweets, biscuits and crisps for visits from your grandchildren, think again. A good relationship with your grandchildren shouldn't be dependent on your providing constant supplies of ice cream and chocolate. This could also risk upsetting your own children if they are trying to establish good eating habits in their offspring.

So limit your grandchildren to just one treat for each visit, and make or buy healthier snacks and meals instead. Here are some alternative foods they will enjoy eating and perhaps even help you to make:

Home-made burgers made with very lean mince and served on wholemeal bread rolls.

A dip, such as hummous or cream cheese with some raw pepper and carrot sticks.

A pitta bread filled with mashed tuna and reduced-calorie mayonnaise.

Snacks of dried fruit.

Carrot cake, carrot muffins or raisin flapjacks.

Home-made soups – carrot and orange, tomato, chicken or parsnip soups are popular with children.

Grapes, strawberries and other berry fruits.

Crackers topped with faces made from cheese and vegetable shapes.

Home-made pizzas with sweetcorn, ham or tuna toppings.

Jacket potatoes served with a bean salad or baked beans.

Give grandchildren a role

One of the joys for many people once they have retired is that they have more time to spend with their grandchildren. If you are fortunate enough to see yours regularly, then use the opportunity to share some of your interests and enthusiasms with them. You are in an ideal position to set children on the right path to enjoying food and eating healthily all their lives.

If you grow your own food, let your grandchildren help out. You can sow seeds or plant seedlings together, and share the watering and weeding. Then, in summer and autumn you can enjoy eating your

Children enjoy picking peas, popping the pods and eating the peas raw, when their B$_1$ and C vitamins content is richest. Try to involve children in growing and harvesting your garden crop.

fresh salads and vegetables together. Your grandchildren will learn many valuable lessons from the experience of hands-on gardening. Even the most reluctant vegetable-eaters can become more enthusiastic about food they have helped to grow themselves.

Lessons in living Being around their grandparents can give children a broader perspective in life. They can learn an enormous amount from you, especially if you automatically involve them in your activities.

Children can help you to set the table for meals, for example, or if they are old enough, they can help you with the cooking, even if it is just scrubbing vegetables or mixing some pastry. If you have an old family recipe, perhaps you could introduce it to them, and make it together when they visit.

Many children are fascinated to hear older people talk about their early days. You can tell them about the kinds of food you ate as a child, how it was produced, where it was

bought, what the shops were like, how the food was wrapped and packaged, and whether you experienced food rationing.

If you enjoyed foraging for wild foods such as blackberries, elderberries and other hedgerow harvest when you were young, why not pass on your knowledge to the next generation? Take your grandchildren for walks in the countryside and show them how to find and gather these fruits (and, of course, which ones to avoid).

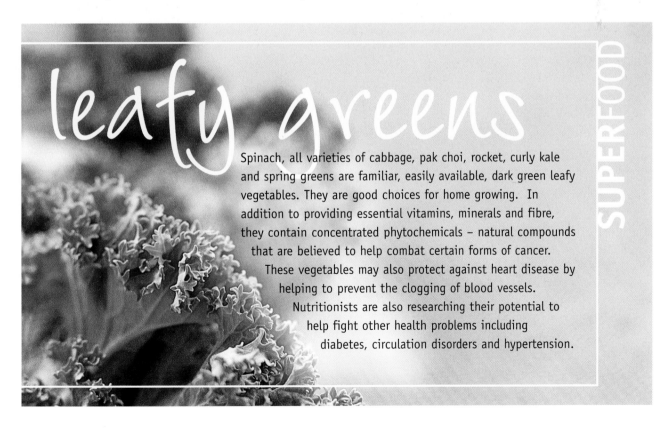

leafy greens

Spinach, all varieties of cabbage, pak choi, rocket, curly kale and spring greens are familiar, easily available, dark green leafy vegetables. They are good choices for home growing. In addition to providing essential vitamins, minerals and fibre, they contain concentrated phytochemicals – natural compounds that are believed to help combat certain forms of cancer. These vegetables may also protect against heart disease by helping to prevent the clogging of blood vessels. Nutritionists are also researching their potential to help fight other health problems including diabetes, circulation disorders and hypertension.

warm **asparagus** salad

This easily prepared salad makes a tasty lunch. For a more substantial meal, add one or two hard-boiled eggs, cut into wedges, or some cubes of your favourite cheese.

preparation time: **5 minutes**

cooking time: **5 minutes**

serves **4**

NUTRIENTS PER SERVING	
calories	110
carbohydrate	3 g
(sugars)	3 g
protein	4 g
fat	9 g
(saturated)	1 g
fibre	2 g

500 g (1 lb 2 oz) asparagus, trimmed
1 tablespoon olive oil
50 g (1¾ oz) rocket or mixed salad leaves
Few strips of lemon zest, to garnish
FOR THE DRESSING
Grated zest of ½ lemon
2 tablespoons tarragon vinegar
1 tablespoon lemon juice
2 tablespoons olive oil
½ teaspoon sugar
½ teaspoon Dijon mustard
1 clove garlic, crushed
Black pepper

1 Heat the grill to high. Line the grill tray with kitchen foil and lay the trimmed asparagus on top. Brush with olive oil.

2 Grill for 4–5 minutes or until the asparagus is just tender when pierced with a knife. Transfer to a dish and leave to cool.

3 Whisk all the dressing ingredients together in a small bowl or jug.

4 Arrange the salad leaves on individual plates, pile on the asparagus and pour over the dressing. Garnish with the strips of lemon zest.

pea and **lettuce** soup

For a comforting and filling lunch on a cold day, or for a light supper try this warming soup, packed with peas and a powerhouse of valuable nutrients. Use fresh or frozen peas, as both provide a wonderfully rich colour and good flavour.

preparation time: **10 minutes**

cooking time: **20 minutes**

serves **4**

NUTRIENTS PER SERVING	
calories	179
carbohydrate	16 g
(sugars)	7 g
protein	8 g
fat	9.5 g
(saturated)	6 g
fibre	7 g

40 g (1½ oz) butter
1 large onion, finely chopped
450 g (1 lb) shelled or frozen peas
2 Little Gem lettuces, shredded
1 litre (1¾ pints) vegetable or chicken stock
Salt and black pepper
Soured cream and croûtons, to serve

1 Heat the butter in a large saucepan over a moderate heat until it has melted. Add the onion and cook for 5 minutes or until it is just beginning to soften.

2 Add the peas, lettuce, stock and seasoning. Bring to the boil, reduce the heat, cover and simmer for 15 minutes, or until the peas are cooked.

3 Allow to cool slightly, then transfer to a food processor or blender and purée until smooth. Return the soup to the pan, adjust the seasoning and heat until warm. Garnish with a swirl of soured cream and a few croûtons. Serve with warm, crusty bread.

ginger-marinated chicken with fresh figs

This low-fat dish has delicious, spiced juices, guaranteed to give the accompanying vegetables a wonderful flavour. The longer the chicken is marinated, the better it tastes, but make sure it is tightly covered in the refrigerator.

preparation time: **5 minutes, plus at least 1 hour or up to 24 hours marinating**

cooking time: **35–40 minutes**

serves **4**

8 chicken thighs, skinned
3 cm (1¼ in) piece fresh ginger, grated
3 cloves garlic, crushed
4 fresh figs, quartered
1 tablespoon olive oil
Black pepper

1 Place the chicken pieces in an ovenproof casserole dish.

2 Mix together the ginger and garlic and spread over each chicken piece. Cover and chill in the refrigerator for at least 1 hour or up to 24 hours.

3 Heat the oven to 190°C (375°F, gas mark 5). Take the casserole out of the refrigerator and lay the fig pieces on top of the chicken. Drizzle over the oil, and season with black pepper.

4 Cover the casserole and cook in the oven for 35–40 minutes, or until the juices run clear when the chicken is pricked with a skewer.

5 Serve with new potatoes and fresh green beans.

NUTRIENTS PER SERVING	
calories	230
carbohydrate	4 g
(sugars)	4 g
protein	29 g
fat	11 g
(saturated)	3 g
fibre	0.5 g

adapting to circumstances

LIVING WITH ARTHRITIS

Pain, stiffness and swelling in the joints are all symptoms of arthritis, a common condition that can vary in intensity from a mild ache to severe pain. Arthritis affects three times as many women as men. The incidence increases with age – although it is by no means confined to the elderly. It is not a single disorder: there are about 200 kinds of arthritis, of which osteoarthritis, rheumatoid arthritis and gout are among the most common.

The nature of the problem

The majority of arthritis sufferers have osteoarthritis – in fact, almost everyone over 60 years is thought to have it to some degree.

Osteoarthritis has various causes – it may be hereditary, or arise from an injury to the joint. It occurs when the protective layer of cartilage covering the surface of the joints deteriorates. Cartilage is normally tough and well-lubricated, allowing joints to move smoothly, but when it is damaged the underlying bone is exposed, leading to spasms and stiffness. The lining of the joint also becomes inflamed and causes swelling as the joint fills with fluid.

Rheumatoid arthritis has a different cause: it is a disorder in which the immune system attacks its own body tissues (see page 116). Although this may be triggered by a severe injury such as a broken bone, the underlying causes are unknown. It affects three per cent of people in the United Kingdom, and is the most severe type of arthritis.

The symptoms are painful, swollen joints which often become distorted – this is most obvious in the fingers, feet, wrists, knees and

Eating to combat pain *The omega-3 fatty acids naturally present in oily fish such as these oatmeal-coated baked herrings are effective anti-inflammatory agents and may help to ease the pain of arthritis.*

hips. The early signs are stiffness in the hands and feet in the morning. Rheumatoid arthritis can affect anyone, including babies and young children, but it is most common in middle-aged women.

Gout is a metabolic disorder in which uric acid crystals accumulate in joints, resulting in inflammation and extreme tenderness. Far more common in men than in women, it tends to affect just one joint at a time, typically the base of the big toe, although knees, ankles and wrists can also be affected.

It is commonly believed that drinking too much port causes gout. In fact alcohol is not thought to be the direct cause, but it may trigger attacks. If you think this could apply

to you, you might consider cutting out alcohol altogether.

Gout sufferers should also avoid offal, shellfish, poultry, game and pulses. These foods are high in a substance called purine, which can raise the level of uric acid in the blood. Instead, concentrate on foods that are rich in potassium, such as bananas, oranges and green leafy vegetables. These all help your body to excrete uric acid.

Strategies to cope

If you have one of these kinds of arthritis, a mix of specialised drugs, exercise and a judicious use of alternative treatments such as acupuncture and osteopathy can be very helpful. It is best to adopt a positive but realistic attitude, accepting that there is no magic cure. At the same time, keep an open mind and try out some alternative remedies: you may find one that brings noticeable relief.

Food and diet can help to alleviate some symptoms, especially in rheumatoid arthritis, but there is no known cure for any form of arthritis.

How your diet can help

Foods that help to boost the immune system are very useful, and will help to maintain your overall health.
Eat fruit and vegetables for their antioxidant vitamins: spinach, watercress, carrots, sweet potatoes and mangoes are excellent sources of beta carotene, while citrus fruit, kiwi fruit, raspberries and strawberries are rich in vitamin C.

You can improve your diet by cutting down on processed foods, saturated animal fats, sugar and salt. You should also try to eat more wholegrain and white bread, pasta

and rice, lean meat, poultry (unless you suffer from gout), fish (especially oily varieties) and reduced-fat dairy products. And remember to drink plenty of fluids, especially water – aim for at least eight glasses a day.
The benefits of oily fish The anti-inflammatory effects of omega-3 fish oils are immensely helpful to people who have arthritis. These oils are found in the flesh of fish such as herring, mackerel, salmon, trout, tuna (fresh rather than canned), sardines and pilchards, as well as in the liver of cod and halibut. They encourage the body to produce prostoglandins, natural chemicals that help to control inflammation.

The effect of eating regular amounts of omega-3 oils, either as food or supplements, is so helpful that you may be able to reduce any anti-inflammatory medication by one third. You should always ask your doctor first, however.

Excluding problem foods Some people believe that food allergies and intolerances (see pages 124-125) contribute to inflammation of the joints. They therefore avoid entire food groups such as dairy foods, or meat and poultry, or exclude certain foods such as citrus fruit, or even eat only raw foods (see also the box above right). You should be aware, however, that without the supervision of a doctor or dietitian, eliminating several foods from your diet at once can make you deficient in vitamins and minerals.

If you suspect that a particular food may be causing a joint problem and want to investigate this possibility, seek advice from your doctor or a qualified dietitian, who may recommend a properly supervised exclusion diet.

foods to avoid

US arthritis specialist Dr Robert Bingham has claimed that a third of his rheumatoid arthritis patients reacted unfavourably to foods from plants of the Solanaceae or nightshade family.

• Potatoes, tomatoes, peppers, avocados and aubergines may contain substances which cause inflammation.

• There is no conclusive proof based on widespread trials, but you could test this yourself.

• Under medical supervision, try leaving these foods out of your diet for a week. If your pain diminishes, then you can adapt your diet accordingly.

Working alternatives *Treatments such as acupuncture, osteopathy and massage can give relief to arthritis sufferers. Acupuncture reduces inflammation and stimulates the release of endorphins, the body's own pain-killing chemicals.*

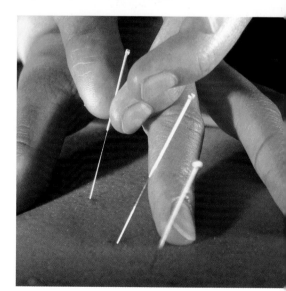

Drugs and your food

If you are using non-steroidal anti-inflammatory drugs such as ibuprofen to control your arthritis, always eat something before taking them. Otherwise, you may develop stomach ulcers, and in severe cases, these ulcers can bleed. As anaemia is very common in people who have rheumatoid arthritis, this makes matters worse. If you are anaemic, eat lean red meat, iron-fortified breakfast cereals, and canned sardines to offset the iron deficiency.

Another commonly prescribed drug, prednisolone, may lead to an increased risk of osteoporosis (see pages 45-49), so it is important to eat foods that are high in calcium. Choose low-fat sources such as semi-skimmed or skimmed milk, low-fat yoghurt and cheese, pulses, leafy green vegetables and canned fish.

Activity helps arthritis Low-impact exercises such as walking, swimming or the water aerobics these women are enjoying, helps to prevent joint stiffness. Exercising in water increases muscle strength without hurting arthritis-affected joints.

HEALTH OR HYPE?

alternative arthritis treatments

Cherries Eating 225 g (8 oz) of cherries per day – fresh or canned – lowers levels of uric acid in the blood and may help to prevent gout.

Green-lipped mussel Extracts from this New Zealand shellfish contain a unique group of eicosatetraenoic acids that are even more powerful than those in fish oils; if you are allergic to oysters or mussels, however, you should avoid taking these.

A vegan diet excludes food from animal sources: some research indicates that this may improve rheumatoid arthritis symptoms.

Turmeric Curcumin, the active ingredient in turmeric, has been found to be a highly effective anti-inflammatory.

Copper bracelets Trials using copper bracelets in rheumatoid arthritis have reported some good results; copper activates an enzyme that protects joints from inflammation. It has been found to be more consistently effective when combined with aspirin.

Keep the weight off

Maintaining a desirable weight is especially important if you have arthritis, as each extra pound puts more strain on your joints. Weight-bearing joints such as hips and knees can be particularly affected, as they bear the brunt of additional weight. If you need to lose weight follow a healthy eating plan and avoid crash diets (see pages 96-99).

Keep moving The more physical activity you do, the better for your arthritis: exercise stops your joints from becoming stiff and increases your muscle strength. Try to exercise as often as possible, and choose low-impact activities – high-impact movement may hurt inflamed joints. Swimming is ideal – it lets you move your muscles without straining your joints. Gentle weight-bearing exercises, such as walking, are also

very helpful. If any exercise causes extreme pain, however, or makes your joints hot and swollen, then you should stop. Discuss alternatives with your doctor or physiotherapist.

Can supplements help?

Fish oil capsules are a real help in rheumatoid arthritis. Cod or halibut liver oils contain omega-3 fatty acids and are often combined with vitamin D to help your body absorb calcium from food, and vitamin A. People with rheumatoid arthritis may also find it helpful to take a multivitamin and mineral supplement.

There is some evidence that evening primrose oil and starflower (borage) oil are effective. Their active ingredient is gamma linoleic acid or GLA, which helps to reduce inflammation. Both rheumatoid arthritis and osteoarthritis sufferers may benefit from these supplements.

Glucosamine sulphate helps to relieve tenderness and reduce the pain of osteoarthritis. It is uncertain whether it can reverse damage to the joints, but it helps to slow down joint deterioration by providing some of the ingredients needed to form bone. Several studies have found chondroitin to be effective for osteoarthritis of the knee and hip.

Other strategies Many people with arthritis find acupuncture, massage and osteopathy helpful. You can also make home-made cold or hot packs. Use a bag of frozen peas for cooling relief. Never apply it directly to your skin – wrap it in a cloth and place it over an inflamed joint for no more than five minutes at a time. For a hot compress, dip a hand towel in hot water, wring it out and fold into a flat pad. Place it over the affected joint for no more than five minutes.

MENUPLAN
for arthritis

Eating oily fish helps combat the effects of arthritis, particularly rheumatoid arthritis. Eat it two or three times a week – choosing different fish for variety.

BREAKFAST Have a high-fibre fortified breakfast cereal with semi-skimmed milk and fresh or dried fruit, accompanied by fresh orange juice. At weekends enjoy a kedgeree made with naturally smoked haddock or eat Scandinavian rollmops.

AT LUNCHTIME Try Smoked Trout and Oyster Mushroom Pâté (recipe overleaf); fresh sardines with lime juice; mashed sardines in tomato sauce on granary toast; or rollmops with wholemeal bread and green salad.

IN THE EVENING Enjoy Tarragon-crusted Tuna with Horseradish and Lime sauce (recipe overleaf); baked mackerel or herring with new potatoes; baked oatmeal-coated herring with gooseberry sauce; baked mackerel in cider; salmon and chive cream-cheese parcels wrapped in filo pastry (available ready-made); or avocado-stuffed trout.

DESSERTS Milk-based desserts such as Cinnamon Rice Pudding (recipe page 202) or Cardamom-scented Brulées with Blueberry Sauce (recipe overleaf) supply valuable calcium.

QUICK MEALS AND SNACKS Enjoy a bowl of vegetable soup with added cheese for calcium, or liver pâté on wholemeal bread with watercress and cherry tomatoes. Pasta Shells with Olives and Basil (recipe page 107) is quickly made; and a grilled lean lamb chop provides essential iron.

Enjoy a crisp apple by itself or sliced into breakfast cereal.

tarragon-crusted tuna **with** horseradish **and** lime sauce

A tangy horseradish sauce provides the ideal foil to the rich flesh of the tuna, and the wholemeal crust flavoured with tarragon adds a satisfying crunchy texture. Salmon works equally well.

preparation time: **15 minutes**

cooking time: **20 minutes**

serves **4**

NUTRIENTS PER SERVING	
calories	280
carbohydrate	17 g
(sugars)	4 g
protein	38 g
fat	10 g
(saturated)	2 g
fibre	2 g

100 g (3½ oz) fresh wholemeal breadcrumbs
10 g (¼ oz) fresh tarragon, finely chopped
1 egg, beaten
Black pepper
4 tuna fillets, each about 115 g (4 oz)
100 g (3½ oz) horseradish sauce
200 g (7 oz) low-fat Greek yoghurt
Grated zest of 1 lime

1 Heat the oven to 180°C (350°F, gas mark 4). Mix the breadcrumbs with the tarragon and spread on a plate.

2 Pour the beaten egg into a shallow dish and season it with pepper.

3 Dip each tuna fillet in the egg, then in the breadcrumbs, coating it on both sides. Place on a greased baking sheet and bake in the oven for 20 minutes, until brown and crisp.

4 Meanwhile, mix the horseradish and yoghurt together and stir in the lime zest. Serve with the tuna fillets.

smoked trout **and oyster mushroom** pâté

Oyster mushrooms, available in most large supermarkets, make a sophisticated pâté with superb flavour and texture. Enjoy it for lunch with oat cakes, crackers or wholemeal toast, or in the evening with a salad as a starter.

preparation time: **15 minutes**

cooking time: **7 minutes**

serves **3** as a starter

1 tablespoon olive oil
2 shallots, finely chopped
50 g (1¾ oz) oyster mushrooms, chopped
100 g (3½ oz) smoked trout fillets
100 g (3½ oz) reduced fat cream cheese
1 tablespoon lime juice
Grated zest of one lime
Black pepper

1 Heat the olive oil in a heavy-based frying pan. Add the shallots and fry gently for 2 minutes. Add the oyster mushrooms. Cover and sweat for 5 minutes, stirring occasionally. Transfer to a plate to cool.

2 Place the trout fillets, cream cheese, lime juice and zest in a food processor and blend until well chopped but not too smooth.

3 Add the cooled mushrooms and onions, season with black pepper and process for a few seconds to mix together.

4 Spoon the mixture into a lidded container. If you are not serving the pâté immediately, keep it in the refrigerator until required.

NUTRIENTS PER SERVING	
calories	150
carbohydrate	1 g
(sugars)	1 g
protein	11 g
fat	9 g
(saturated)	4 g
fibre	0

cardamom-scented brulées with blueberry sauce

Enjoy the subtle flavours of this elegant dessert. The sauce is hidden beneath the yoghurt and the contrast of flavours is sheer delight. It is much lower in fat than conventional crème brulée and the blueberries have a clean, refreshing taste.

preparation time: **10 minutes**

cooking time: **10 minutes**

serves **4**

150 g (5½ oz) blueberries, thawed if frozen
2 teaspoons caster sugar
Grated zest of 1 lemon
3 cardamom pods
500 g (1 lb 2 oz) low-fat Greek yoghurt
4 heaped teaspoons granulated sugar

1 Put the blueberries and sugar in a heavy-based pan and heat gently until they are lightly cooked. Add the lemon zest and leave to cool.

2 Remove the seeds from the cardamom pods and grind them to a fine powder in a pestle and mortar.

3 Stir the cardamom powder into the yoghurt.

4 Heat the grill to high.

5 Spoon the cooled blueberry mixture into 4 ramekins, and top with the yoghurt.

6 Sprinkle one teaspoon of sugar on top of each ramekin. Place under the grill and cook for 5–6 minutes, or until the sugar is bubbling and brown.

7 Keep the cooled brulées in the refrigerator until you are ready to serve them.

NUTRIENTS PER SERVING	
calories	50
carbohydrate	13 g
(sugars)	8 g
protein	113
fat	0
(saturated)	0
fibre	1 g

adapting to circumstances

BASIC RECIPES

The recipes in this section are essential to many of the recipes in the rest of the book. They are also invaluable as foundations on which to create dishes of your own.

Chicken stock

This recipe makes a light, clear, well-flavoured stock.

preparation time: **5–10 minutes**
Cooking time: **2½–3 hours**
Makes **1 litre (1¾ pints)**

1 cooked chicken carcass, and any
   trimmings
Uncooked chicken giblets
1 onion, roughly chopped
2 large carrots, roughly chopped
1 stick celery, roughly chopped
1 bay leaf
Few sprigs parsley
1 sprig thyme
3–4 black peppercorns
1.7 litres (3 pints) cold water

1 Chop the chicken carcass into 3 or 4 pieces. Place it in a large saucepan with the trimmings and giblets. Add the vegetables, herbs and peppercorns. Pour the water into the pan.

2 Leaving the pan uncovered, bring the water to the boil, skimming any froth from the surface. Cover the pan, reduce the heat and simmer for 2½–2¾ hours, skimming the surface occasionally.

3 Strain the stock through a muslin-lined sieve and leave to cool completely before refrigerating. Store in the refrigerator for up to 2 days or freeze for up to 3 months.

Vegetable stock

You can make this all year round using vegetables that are in season at the time.

Preparation time: **10 minutes**
Cooking time: **about 45 minutes**
Makes **1 litre (1¾ pints)**

450 g (1 lb) vegetables, such as
   equal quantities of carrots, leeks,
   celery, onion and mushrooms,
   chopped
1 garlic clove
6 peppercorns
2 sprigs parsley
2 sprigs thyme
1 bay leaf
1.2 litres (2 pints) water

1 Put all the ingredients in a saucepan, pouring in the water last. Bring to the boil, uncovered, skimming any froth off the surface.

2 Cover the pan, reduce the heat and simmer gently for 30 minutes, skimming the surface when necessary.

3 Strain the stock through a muslin-lined sieve and cool it completely before refrigerating. Store the stock in the refrigerator for up to 4 days, or freeze for up to 3 months.

Fish stock

Do not simmer this stock for longer than the recipe time: too long cooking makes it bitter.

Preparation time: **15 minutes**
Cooking time: **35 minutes**
Makes **1 litre (1¾ pints)**

1 kg (2 lb 4 oz) white fish bones and
    trimmings
85 g (3 oz) carrots, chopped
2 sticks celery, chopped
300 g (10½ oz) leeks, white parts
    only, chopped
1 bay leaf
2 sprigs parsley
250 ml (9 fl oz) dry white wine
1 litre (1¾ pints) cold water
3 black peppercorns

1 Rinse any blood off the fish bones and put them into a stockpot, flameproof casserole or heavy-based saucepan. Check the trimmings, removing gills from the head and any black skin. Rinse the trimmings, then add them to the stock pan.

2 Add the vegetables, herbs, wine and water and bring to the boil, skimming off any froth. When the liquid boils, reduce the heat, add the peppercorns and partially cover the pan. Simmer for 30 minutes, skimming the surface occasionally.

3 Strain the stock through a muslin-lined sieve or colander. Set aside for 1 hour, then strain again to make a really clear stock.

4 Store the cooled stock in the refrigerator for up to 2 days, or freeze for up to 2 months.

Pizza base

These pizza bases may be frozen, uncooked. Cook them from frozen with your chosen topping.

Preparation time: **30 minutes,**
    plus 1 hour rising
Makes **two 25 cm (10 in) pizza**
    bases

2 teaspoons dried yeast with ¾
    teaspoon sugar, or 1 sachet easy-
    blend yeast
350 g (12 oz) plain flour, wholemeal
    flour, or a mixture of the two
1 teaspoon salt
Warm water, to mix (see method)
2 tablespoons olive oil

1 If using dried yeast, dissolve the sugar in 75 ml (2½ fl oz) warm water, sprinkle in the yeast and set aside for 10–15 minutes, or until frothy. Sift the flour and salt into a mixing bowl, make a well in the centre and pour in the frothy yeast mixture, 125 ml (4 fl oz) warm water and the olive oil. Mix with a wooden spoon to a smooth dough.

2 If using easy-blend yeast, put it in a mixing bowl with the flour and salt and mix well together. Make a well in the centre and pour in 200 ml (7 fl oz) warm water and the olive oil. Mix with a wooden spoon to a smooth dough.

3 Turn the dough out on to a lightly floured surface and knead for 5 minutes. Cover and leave for 5 minutes. Knead again for 5 minutes, until the dough is smooth and elastic. Add a little flour if the dough seems sticky, or more water – just a tablespoon at a time –if it seems too dry.

4 Divide the dough into two portions. Place in lightly oiled bowls and cover with cling film. Leave in a warm place for 55 minutes, until the dough is doubled in size.

5 Knead each portion lightly then roll it out on a lightly floured surface to a 25 cm (10 in) round about 1 cm (½ inch) thick. Place on a lightly oiled baking sheet and push up the edges to form a shallow rim. The pizza bases are now ready for the topping to be added just before baking in a very hot oven.

Low-calorie mayonnaise

Preparation time: **7–10 minutes,**
    plus standing
Makes **about 100 ml (3½ fl oz)**

2 hard-boiled egg yolks
1 tablespoon white wine vinegar
1 tablespoon lemon or lime juice
Pinch of dried mustard powder
Salt and pepper
2 tablespoons low-fat natural yoghurt

1 Mash the egg yolks with the vinegar, lemon or lime juice, mustard powder and salt and pepper, to taste. Mix well.

2 Beat the yoghurt into the egg mixture to blend. Cover and leave to stand for 5–10 minutes to allow the flavours to develop.

common food chart

FOOD	QUANTITY G/OZ	CALORIES KCAL	PROTEIN G	CARB G	FAT G
BREAD, POTATOES AND OTHER CEREALS					
potatos (boiled)	115/4	86	1.7	20	0.3
potatoes, chipped	115/4	268	3.2	31.2	14.3
brown rice, cooked	225/8	232	4.9	49.7	1.2
kidney beans, cooked	55/2	62	5	11	0.3
chickpeas, cooked	55/2	73	5	20.5	1.3
wholemeal bread	2 slices	180	6.2	34	2.4
cornflakes (no milk)	25/1	102	1.8	24	0.1
wholemeal flour	115/4	357	14.6	73	1.5
plain flour	115/4	392	10.2	87	1.54
FRUIT AND VEGETABLES					
apple	1 medium	54	0.4	14	0
banana	1 medium	123	1.5	30	0.3
orange	1 medium	37	1.1	18.1	0.1
peach	1 medium	31	0.6	9.7	0.1
fresh peas	115/4	95	8	11.5	1.7
frozen peas	115/4	80	6.9	11	1
cabbage(boiled)	100/3½	14	1	2	0
spinach, blanched	225/8	41	5.4	6.5	0.5
carrots, raw	50/1¾	18	0.3	3.9	trace
broccoli (boiled)	100/3½	24	3	1	trace
MEAT, FISH AND ALTERNATIVES					
chicken, roasted with skin	115/4	248	26	0	16.1
without skin	115/4	170	29	0	6.2
2 grilled lamb chops	175/6	207	26	0	11.5
sirloin steak, grilled	85/3	176	27.4	0	6.0
calf's liver, fried	85/3	222	25.1	3.4	11.2
prawns, fried	85/3	192	17.4	8.4	9.3
salmon, poached	115/4	227	23	0	15
salmon, canned	85/3	179	16.7	0	7.4
DAIRY FOODS					
whole milk	100/3½	66	4.6	3.2	3.9
Cheddar cheese	25/1	113	7.1	0.6	8.3
egg, raw	1 large	75	6.3	0.6	5.1
yoghurt, low-fat, natural	115/4	65	6	9	1
FATS					
olive oil	1 tbsp	119	0	0	12.7
butter	1 tbsp	102	0.1	0.1	10.4

UK REFERENCE DAILY VITAMIN INTAKES

AGE	VIT B$_1$ MG	VIT B$_2$ MG	NIACIN MG	VIT B$_6$ MG	VIT B$_{12}$ MCG	FOLATE MCG	VIT C MG	VIT A MCG	VIT D MCG
0-3m	0.2	0.4	3	0.2	0.3	50	25	350	8.5
4-m	0.2	0.4	3	0.2	0.3	50	25	350	8.5
7-9m	0.2	0.4	4	0.3	0.4	50	25	350	7
10-12m	0.3	0.4	5	0.4	0.4	50	25	350	7
1-3y	0.5	0.6	8	0.7	0.5	70	30	400	7
4-6y	0.7	0.8	11	0.9	0.8	100	30	500	-
7-10y	0.7	1.0	12	1.0	1.0	150	30	500	-
MALES									
11-14y	0.9	1.2	15	1.2	1.2	200	35	600	-
15-18y	1.1	1.3	18	1.5	1.5	200	40	700	-
19-50	1.0	1.3	17	1.4	1.5	200	40	700	-
50y+	0.9	1.3	16	1.4	1.5	200	40	700	10
FEMALES									
11-14y	0.7	1.1	12	1.0	1.2	200	35	600	-
15-18y	0.8	1.1	14	1.2	1.5	200	40	600	-
19-50y	0.8	1.1	13	1.2	1.5	200	40	600	-
50y+	0.8	1.1	12	1.2	1.5	200	40	600	10
pregnant	+0.1	+0.3	-	-	-	+100	+10	+100	10
lactating	+0.1	+0.5	+2	-	+0.5	+60	+30	+350	10

UK REFERENCE DAILY MINERAL INTAKES

AGE	CALCIUM MG	PHOS MG	MAGN MG	SODIUM MG	IRON MG	ZINC MG	COPPER MG	SELENIUM MCG	IODINE MCG
0-3m	525	400	55	210	1.7	4.0	0.2	10	50
4-m	525	400	60	280	4.3	4.3	0.3	13	60
7-9m	525	400	75	320	7.8	5.0	0.3	10	60
10-12m	525	400	80	350	7.8	5.0	0.3	10	60
1-3y	350	270	85	500	6.9	5.0	0.4	15	70
4-6y	450	350	120	700	6.1	6.5	0.6	20	100
7-10y	550	450	200	1200	8.7	7.0	0.7	30	110
MALES									
11-14y	1000	775	280	1600	11.3	9.0	0.8	45	130
15-18y	1000	775	300	1600	11.3	9.5	1.0	70	140
19-50y	700	550	300	1600	8.7	9.5	1.2	75	140
50y+	700	550	300	1600	8.7	9.5	1.2	75	140
FEMALES									
11-14y	800	625	280	1600	14.8	9.0	0.8	45	130
15-18y	800	6254	300	1600	14.8	7.0	1.0	60	140
19-50y	700	550	270	1600	14.8	7.0	1.2	60	140
50y+	700	550	270	1600	8.7	7.0	1.2	60	140
lactating	+500	+400	+50	-	-	+6.0	+0.3	+15	-

RECIPE INDEX

recipe index

Index
PLEASE NOTE THAT THERE IS A SEPARATE INDEX FOR THE RECIPES IN THIS BOOK ON PAGES 342-343

studying 302–5
sugar 291, 314
travel 306–9
tryptophan 296, 308
vitamins 291, 292, 306

USEFUL ADDRESSES

THESE ORGANISATIONS PROVIDE INFORMATION ON DIET AND HEALTH,
OR ON FOODS AND DIET FOR SPECIFIC CONDITIONS.

Age Concern
Astral House
1268 London Road
London SW16
tel: 020 8679 8000
Information Line: Linkline 0800
009966
e-mail: ace@ace.org.uk
web site: www.ace.org.uk

Alcohol Concern
Waterbridge House
32-36 Loman Street
London SW1 0EE
tel: 020 7928 7377
fax: 020 7928 4644
e-mail: AC@alccon.dircon.co.uk
web site:
www.alcoholconcern.org.uk

Alzheimer's Disease Society
Gordon House
10 Greencoat Place
London SW1P 1PH
tel: 020 7306 0606
Helpline: 0845 300 0336 (Mon-Fri,
8.30am-6.30pm)
fax: 020 7306 0808
e-mail: info@alzheimers.org.uk
web site: www.alzheimers.org.uk

Arthritic Association
First Floor Suite
2 Hyde Gardens
Eastbourne
East Sussex BN21 4PN
tel: 01323 416550

fax:01323 639793
e-mail: info@arthriticassocia-
tion.org.uk
web site:
www.arthriticassociation.org.uk

**Association for Spina Bifida and
Hydrocephalus**
ASBAH House
42 Park Road
Peterborough PE1 2UQ
tel: 01733 555988
fax: 01733 555985

British Allergy Foundation
Deepdene House
30 Bellegrove Road
Welling
Kent DA16 3PY
Helpline: 020 8303 8583 (Mon-Fri,
9am-5pm)
e-mail:
allergybaf@compuserve.com
web site:
www.allergyfoundation.com

**British Association of
Dermatologists**
19 Fitzroy Square
London W1P 5HQ
tel: 020 7383 0266
fax: 020 7388 5263
e-mail: admin@bad.org.uk
web site: www.skinhealth.co.uk

useful addresses

British Dietetic Association
Paediatric Group
c/o 5th Floor Elizabeth House
22 Suffolk Street
Queensway
Birmingham B1 1LS
tel: 0121 6164900
fax: 0121 6164901

British Epilepsy Association
New Anstey House
Gate Way Drive,
Yeadon,
Leeds LS19 7XY
tel: 0113 210 8800
fax: 0113 391 0300
e-mail: epilepsy@bea.org.uk
web site: www.epilepsy.org.uk

British Heart Foundation
14 Fitzhardinge Street
London W1H 4DH
tel: 020 7935 0185
fax: 020 7486 5820
web site: www.bhf.org.uk

British Nutrition Foundation
High Holborn House
52-54 High Holborn
London WC1V 6RQ
tel: 020 7404 6504
fax: 020 7404 6747
e-mail: postbox@nutrition.org.uk
web site: www.nutrition.org.uk

Cancer Research Campaign
10 Cambridge Terrace
London NW1 4JL
tel: 020 7224 1333
General Enquiries: 0800 226237
web site: www.crc.org.uk

Coeliac Society
P.O. Box 220
High Wycombe
Bucks HP11 2HY
web site: www.coeliac.co.uk

Cystic Fibrosis Trust
11 London Road
Bromley
Kent BR1 1BY
tel: 020 8464 7211
fax: 020 8313 0472
e-mail: enquiries@cftrust.org.uk
web site: www.cftrust.org.uk

Diabetes UK
10 Queen Anne Street
London W1M 0BD
tel: 020 7323 1531
Careline: 020 7636 6112 (Mon-Fri,
9am-5pm)
e-mail: info@diabetes.org.uk
web site: www.diabetes.org.uk

Eating Disorders Association
First Floor, Wensum House
103 Prince of Wales Road
Norwich NR1 1DW

tel: 01603 619090
Helpline: 01603 621 414 (Mon-Fri,
9am-6.30pm)
Youthline (up to age 18): 01603
765050 (Mon-Fri, 4-6pm)
fax: 01603 664915
e-mail: info@edauk.com
web site: www.edauk.com

Hyperactive Children's Support Group
71 Whyke Lane
Chichester
West Sussex PO19 2LD
tel: 01903 725182 (Mon-Fri,
10am-1pm)
fax: 01903 734726
e-mail: web@hacsg.org.uk
web site: http://www.hacsg.org.uk

Imperial Cancer Research Fund
44 Lincoln's Inn Fields
London WC2A 3PX
tel: 020 7242 0200
fax: 020 7269 3100
web site: www.icnet.uk

Multiple Sclerosis Society
MS National Centre
372 Edgeware Road
London NW2 6ND
tel: 020 8438 0700
Helpline: (Freephone) 0808 800
8000
fax: 020 8438 0701
e-mail: info@mssociety.org.uk
web site: www.mssociety.org.uk

ME (Myalgic Encephalomyelitis) Association
4 Corringham Road
Stanford-le-Hope
Essex SS17 0AH
tel: 01375 642466
fax: 01375 360256
e-mail:
enquiries@meassociation.org.uk
web site:
www.meassociation.org.uk

Muscular Dystrophy Groupy
7-11 Prescott PlaceEdgeware Road
London SW4 6BS
tel: 020 7720 8055
tel: 020 7720 8055
Helpline: (Freephone) 0808 800
8000
fax: 020 8438 0701
e-mail:
info@musculardystrophy.org

National Association for Colitis and Crohn's Disease
4 Beaumont House
Sutton Road
St Albans
Herts AL1 5HH
tel: 01727 830038

fax: 01727 862550
Information line: 01727 844296
(Mon, Wed-Fri, 10am-1pm)
e-mail: www.nacc.org.uk
web site: www.nacc.org.uk

National Asthma Campaign
Providence House
Providence Place
London N1 0NT
tel: 020 7226 2260
Helpline: 0845 701 0203 (Mon-Fri,
9am-7pm)
fax: 020 7704 0740
web site: www.asthma.org.uk

National Childbirth Trust
Alexandra House
Oldham Terrace
London W3 6NH
tel: 020 8992 8637
fax: 020 8992 5929
web site: www.net-online.org

Vegetarian Society
Parkdale
Dunham Road
Altrincham
Cheshire WA14 4QG
tel: 0161 928 0793
fax: 0161 926 9182
e-mail: info@vegsoc.org
web site: www.vegsoc.org

ACKNOWLEDGMENTS

Carroll & Brown would also like to thank:

Editorial Assistant	Charlotte Beech
Picture Researcher	Richard Soar
Production Manager	Karol Davies
Production Controller	Nigel Reed
Computer Management	Elisa Merino, Paul Stradling
Illustrator	Ian Whadcock
Indexer	Laura Hicks

8 Pictor, **21** Gettyone Stone, **26** (right) Gettyone Stone, **33** The Stock Market, **46-47** Telegraph Colour Library, **47** Images Colour Library, **48** (right) Gettyone Stone, **49** (right) Image Bank, **55** Images Colour Library, **70** (left) Image Bank, **80** (bottom) Gettyone Stone, **82-83** Gettyone Stone, **85** (bottom) Pictor, **95** (left) Images Colour Library, **99** Image Bank, **109** (top) Gettyone Stone, **118** Telegraph Colour Library, **134** (right) Telegraph Colour Library, **138** (left) Telegraph Colour Library, **139** (left) The Stock Market, **139** (right) Telegraph Colour Library, **143** Gettyone Stone, **147** Gettyone Stone, **154-5** Telegraph Colour Library, **164** Telegraph Colour Library, **166** Gettyone Stone, **170** (bottom) Images Colour Library, **175** Images Colour Library, **180** (left) Gettyone Stone, **182** (left) Telegraph Colour Library, **199** The Stock Market, **206**, **206-7** Courtesy of Yo! Sushi Soho Ltd, **216-7** Gettyone Stone, **220** (left) The Stock Market, **221** (left) Image Bank, **221** (right) Images Colour Library, **223** Image Bank, **230** Image Bank, **233** Telegraph Colour Library, **236** Gettyone Stone, **237** Telegraph Colour Library, **243** (right) The Stock Market, **259** Gettyone Stone, **271** Telegraph Colour Library, **280-1** The Stock Market, **286** Images Colour Library, **290** (bottom) Telegraph Colour Library, **291** Image Bank, **292** Image Bank, **294** (bottom) Pictor, **299** Telegraph Colour Library, **303** Pictor, **304** Gettyone Stone, **307** (right) Gettyone Stone, **308** Courtesy of Virgin Atlantic, **311** Gettyone Stone, **312** Image Bank, **318** Gettyone Stone, **323** Gettyone Stone, **328** Image Bank, **333** Gettyone Stone, **334** Gettyone Stone.

Reader's Digest production credits:

Book Production Manager	Fiona McIntosh
Pre-Press Manager	Howard Reynolds
Pre-Press Technical Analyst	Martin Hendrick
Origination	Colourscan, Singapore
Printing and Binding	Brepols Graphic Industries NV, Turnhout, Belgium

040-903-01